# The Spirit-Baptized Church

T&T Clark Systematic Pentecostal and Charismatic Theology

**Series editors**
Daniela C. Augustine
Wolfgang Vondey

# The Spirit-Baptized Church

*A Dogmatic Inquiry*

Frank D. Macchia

t&tclark

LONDON • NEW YORK • OXFORD • NEW DELHI • SYDNEY

T&T CLARK
Bloomsbury Publishing Plc
50 Bedford Square, London, WC1B 3DP, UK
1385 Broadway, New York, NY 10018, USA
29 Earlsfort Terrace, Dublin 2, Ireland

BLOOMSBURY, T&T CLARK and the T&T Clark logo are trademarks of
Bloomsbury Publishing Plc

First published in Great Britain 2020
This paperback edition published in 2021

Copyright © Frank D. Macchia, 2020

Frank D. Macchia has asserted his right under the Copyright, Designs and
Patents Act, 1988, to be identified as Author of this work.

Cover design by Anna Berzovan
Cover image © naqiewei / GettyImages

For legal purposes the Acknowledgments on p. viii constitute an extension
of this copyright page.

All rights reserved. No part of this publication may be reproduced or transmitted
in any form or by any means, electronic or mechanical, including photocopying,
recording, or any information storage or retrieval system, without prior
permission in writing from the publishers.

Bloomsbury Publishing Plc does not have any control over, or responsibility for, any
third-party websites referred to or in this book. All internet addresses given in this
book were correct at the time of going to press. The author and publisher regret
any inconvenience caused if addresses have changed or sites have ceased to
exist, but can accept no responsibility for any such changes.

A catalogue record for this book is available from the British Library.

Library of Congress Control Number: 2019955015

ISBN: HB: 978-0-5676-8066-2
PB: 978-0-5676-9900-8
ePDF: 978-0-5676-8067-9
ePUB: 978-0-5676-8068-6

Typeset by Deanta Global Publishing Services, Chennai, India

To find out more about our authors and books visit www.bloomsbury.com and
sign up for our newsletters.

*For Murray W. Dempster, Cecil M. Robeck Jr., and Gerald T. Sheppard*

*Three Pentecostal teachers who showed confidence in me when I needed it most*

# Contents

| | |
|---|---|
| Acknowledgments | viii |
| Preface | ix |
| List of Abbreviations | x |
| Introduction | 1 |
|     Beyond Machines of Salvation | 2 |
|     Spirit Baptism: A Point of Integration | 5 |
| 1  The Spirit-Baptized Church | 11 |
|     Spirit Baptism as the Point of Departure | 11 |
|     Toward a Theology of Spirit Baptism | 13 |
|     Spirit Baptism: Old Testament | 16 |
|     Spirit Baptism: New Testament | 20 |
|     Spirit Baptism and Trinitarian Communion | 35 |
|     Toward an Ecclesial Personality | 48 |
|     Conclusion | 56 |
| 2  The Elect Church | 59 |
|     A Timeless Decree or an Anointing in Time? | 60 |
|     Election: New Testament Voices | 67 |
|     Election in Christ and by the Spirit: Final Reflections | 96 |
| 3  The Pilgrim Church | 105 |
|     Models of the Church | 108 |
|     Marks of the Church | 125 |
|     Conclusion | 158 |
| 4  The Witnessing Church | 161 |
|     The Church and Ecclesial Mediation | 161 |
|     The Church and the Example of Cornelius | 169 |
|     The Church and the Word | 172 |
|     The Church and the Sacraments | 185 |
|     Vocation: Spiritual Gifts and Mission | 200 |
|     Conclusion | 210 |
| Author Index | 213 |
| Subject Index | 215 |
| Scripture Index | 217 |

# Acknowledgments

I am filled with gratitude as I put the finishing touches on this book. Without hesitation, I must offer heartfelt gratitude to my wife, Verena, who has graced my life in ways too deep for words. Thank you for your patience and support as I labored through these chapters. I am also grateful to colleagues at Vanguard University whose partnership means a lot to me, and to Mandagie Brooke, who helped me with indexing. Moreover, my past journey as a Pentecostal scholar includes many who have supported my scholarship over the years. The dedication shows gratitude to three former teachers who have especially mentored me in the formative years of my vocation as a theologian. Lastly, my church, Grace Bible Church, has nourished and upheld me and my family in so many ways. I've had occasion to think of them all more than once while writing this book.

# Preface

This ecclesiology has been in the making for fifteen years now. When in 2005 I wrote *Baptized in the Spirit: A Global Pentecostal Theology*, I included preliminary reflections on the church in one of its chapters. My purpose for the book was to sketch in broad strokes how Spirit baptism should function as the point of integration for Pentecostal theology. Since then, I wrote books on justification by faith (*Justified in the Spirit: Creation, Redemption, and the Triune God*) and Christology (*Jesus the Spirit Baptizer: Christology in Light of Pentecost*). In both of these books, I attempted to follow through on my original vision by thinking through both soteriology and Christology within the framework of the gift of the Spirit given at Pentecost. It seemed fitting for me to complete my work by writing a full-blown ecclesiology with Pentecost at the center. This idea may not seem so very novel. After all, Pentecost as the birthplace of the church is a widespread notion among theologians. It is in this light that I still marvel at how many ecclesiologies still manage to be written without much appeal to this event or what it means for our understanding of the essence, vocation, or destiny of the church. I do not mean to imply that my effort here is all that novel. But I do hope that the way in which I focus the lens of Pentecost on the church will offer the reader a fresh look. I sit here on Pentecost Sunday deeply grateful for what happened on that first Pentecost. And, of course, I do not believe any of us working in the area of ecclesiology will ever be able to come close to exhausting the significance of that event for how we understand the doctrine of the church. I offer my own attempt at bearing witness in the pages that follow.

Pentecost Sunday, 2019

# Abbreviations

| | |
|---|---|
| AB | The Anchor Bible |
| AF | *Apostolic Faith* (Los Angeles) |
| CCT | *Challenges in Contemporary Theology* |
| CD | *Church Dogmatics* |
| DEM | Dictionary of the Ecumenical Movement |
| EM | *The Ecumenical Movement: An Anthology of Key Texts and Voices*, ed. Michael Kinnamon and Brian E. Cope (Grand Rapids, MI: Eerdmans; Geneva: World Council of Churches, 1997). |
| ER | *Ecumenical Review* |
| ERT | *Evangelical Review of Theology* |
| GPCS | Global Pentecostal and Charismatic Studies |
| GW I | *Growth in Agreement: Reports and Agreed Statements of Ecumenical Conversations on a World Level*, ed. Harding Meyer and Lukas Vischer (New York: Paulist Press; Geneva: World Council of Churches, 1984). |
| GW II | *Growth in Agreement II, Reports and Agreed Statements of Ecumenical Conversations on a World Level, 1982-1998*, ed. Jeffrey Gros, Harding Meyer, William G. Rusch (Geneva: WCC Pub., 2000). |
| HTR | *Harvard Theological Review* |
| IBCTP | Interpretation: A Bible Commentary for Teaching and Preaching |
| JBL | *Journal of Biblical Literature* |
| JES | *Journal of Ecumenical Studies* |
| JPT | *Journal of Pentecostal Theology* |
| JPTS | Journal of Pentecostal Theology Supplement Series |
| JTI | *Journal of Theological Interpretation* |
| LG | *Lumen Gentium* |
| NIDNTTE | New International Dictionary of New Testament Theology and Exegesis |
| NT | *Novum Testamentum* |
| PE | *Pentecostal Evangel* |
| Pneuma | *Pneuma: The Journal of the Society for Pentecostal Studies* |

| | |
|---|---|
| SBT | Studies in Biblical Theology |
| SD | *Studies in Dogmatics* |
| SDCTPA | Sacra Doctrina: Christian Theology for a Postmodern Age |
| SPCI | Studies in Pentecostal and Charismatic Issues |
| TDNT | *Theological Dictionary of the New Testament* |
| TI | *Theological Investigations* |
| TS | *Theological Studies* |
| TT | *Theology Today* |
| VT | *Vetus Testamentum* |
| WBC | *Word Biblical Commentary* |
| WCJ | *Works of Saint Cyril of Jerusalem*, tr. Leo P. McCauley and Anthony A. Stephenson, The Fathers of the Church: A New Translation (Washington DC: Catholic University of American Press, 1970). |
| WJW | *The Works of John Wesley*, Third Edition (Grand Rapids, MI: Baker Book House. 1979). |
| WTJ | *Westminster Theological Journal* |
| WUNT | Wissenschaftliche Untersuchungen zum Neuen Testament |
| ZAW | *Zeitschrift für die altestamentliche Wissenschaft* |

# Introduction

Cecil M. Robeck has provocatively remarked that Pentecostal ecclesiologies, when they are written, "will be compatible with the prophetic promise of Joel."[1] He meant by this, Joel 2 as quoted in the context of Acts 2:17-21:

> In the last days, God says,
>   I will pour out my Spirit on all people.
> Your sons and daughters will prophesy,
>   your young men will see visions,
>   your old men will dream dreams.
> [18] Even on my servants, both men and women,
>   I will pour out my Spirit in those days,
>   and they will prophesy.
> [19] I will show wonders in the heavens above
>   and signs on the earth below,
>   blood and fire and billows of smoke.
> [20] The sun will be turned to darkness
>   and the moon to blood
>   before the coming of the great and glorious day of the Lord.
> [21] And everyone who calls
>   on the name of the Lord will be saved.

Peter quotes this text in his Pentecost sermon. His audience consisted of Diaspora Jews who had gathered in Jerusalem to celebrate Pentecost but were suddenly drawn in by a theophany of sound (of a rushing wind and speaking in tongues) and of vision (tongues of fire). Peter quotes from Joel 2 in the new context of the beginning of its fulfillment. Something remarkable had happened that seemed too good to be true, something otherworldly and, yet, felt down at the core of creaturely reality. God had arrived through a mighty outpouring of the Holy Spirit. *God* had arrived as a mighty flood of life poured forth through the Lord and Messiah, Jesus Christ. Christ had entered into the depths of bondage to sin and death so that rising again he could open up his life to us. This gift of life is the promise that Joel proclaimed: life abundant, the communion of love enjoyed between the Father and the Son and now opened up to the world in the arrival of the Spirit. The *Spirit* as promise? Whoever heard of a promise

---

[1] Cecil M. Robeck Jr., "Pentecostal Ecclesiology," in *T & T Clark Companion to Ecclesiology*, ed. Kimlyn J. Bender and D. Stephen Long (London: Bloomsbury T & T Clark, forthcoming), *passim*.

that is not a thing that can be given in exchange for something else? Isn't this the way promises work in the world? I promise you *this* in exchange for *that*! But *this* promise of the Spirit is not a thing, and it cannot be exchanged for any other thing of comparable worth, because there *is* nothing of comparable worth. This gift is offered entirely by grace and opens one to an infinite depth of divine love. This gift of communion with God is also a communion in God with all others. One cannot accept this communion of life and stay the same, for it expands the soul and makes one's life hospitable toward others. All that we can do is receive this promise in faith and live from it in gratitude. The Spirit, from Pentecost to Christ's return, is thus an undeserved gift that keeps on giving. This gift, this promise, is at the core of what we call "the church." So, when we speak of the "church," we speak of something extraordinary, a mystery that cannot be grasped by human understanding or contained by humanly built institutions. It overflows and drives us toward its eschatological fulfillment, the kingdom of God.

## Beyond Machines of Salvation

Nothing like the church exists anywhere else, nothing parallel in any other promise, gift, or community of persons. We are on sacred ground here, at the nexus of divine-human encounter, the beginnings of the kingdom of God on earth. The term "ecclesiology" comes from the Greek word ἐκκλησία (*ecclesia*), which literally means a calling together of a gathering or an assembly. In the ancient world, people typically gathered for any number of reasons, either political or cultural. In the Christian context, the *ecclesia* is a gathering too but one that cannot be adequately defined or understood through political or cultural categories. The church is not a mere assembly of those who gather because of a common political structure or purpose, or a shared cultural heritage or set of values. Churches as institutions are indeed political and cultural realities. Like all human organizations, they function in these ways. We currently hold the glory of the Lord in vessels of clay (2 Cor. 4:7), though one day in vessels of glory. Until then, we "are being transformed in his image from glory to glory" (2 Cor. 3:18). As weak vessels of clay, churches are always vulnerable to cultural and political influences that are contrary to the image of Christ. Those who view the church only through a political or cultural lens, however, have not yet penetrated the mystery of the church at its core. The church in faithfulness to its inner mystery in the communion of love in and through God should exercise the politics of Jesus, which is the politics of self-giving love and liberating justice. That is our call, namely, to live according to that inner reality by grace so as to be a sign of that grace in the world. This mystery of communion in and through God is dynamic; we are called to grow ever deeper into Christ and the love of the Father and ever more expansive in the reach of our witness outward to the ends of the earth.

The church is an ongoing event in the Spirit's work, though there are enduring practices (like proclamation, sacraments, and spiritual gifts) that serve the unity and continuity of the church over the expanse of time and place and allow it to mediate Christ to others (or be the means by which Christ self-imparts by the Spirit). Make no mistake about it, though, these practices are tools in the hands of the Spirit. Without the Spirit, there is no unity or continuity. Therefore, we must always be on our guard against attempting an "institutionalization" of the Spirit, which is an effort to reduce grace to a commodity, and humanity to a one-dimensional consumer. The natural human drive to reduce the church to an effective service provider for religious consumers is deeper than we think. We have been conditioned by cultural and economic contexts to think and to speak this way of the church. Sensitive to this problem, Jan Milíč Lochman wrote provocatively against the notion of the church as a "salvation machine," an assembly line that imparts salvation with impeccable precision.[2] Grace is commodified as a "thing" and marketed, "sold on the market like cheapjack's wares" (to quote Dietrich Bonhoeffer).[3] Lochman notes that we live in a world that is also shaped by "salvation" machines, offering false claims of salvation like health, wealth, or social influence. These are graceless promises of "salvation" offered to people who have been reduced to the level of one-dimensional consumers and producers. The promise is as empty as the image of the human being to which the appeal is made. All salvation machines have this tendency toward one-dimensionality. "A one-dimensional view of salvation enables them to operate more smoothly, 'interference free,'" and the "unidimensional person" becomes easier to stereotype, manipulate, and control; "the machines stand for a world that is geared for productive efficiency."[4] Lochman finds some version of "salvation technology" both within and outside the church, in both capitalist and socialist economies, and in all cultures. It is ubiquitous. Salvation is not found in a system or its efficiency but rather in "real life" from God that shatters or bursts open human systems, using them in ways that transcend them.[5] Similarly, James K. A. Smith writes of secular "liturgies" and habits that shape our longings in ways that are contrary to the kingdom of God. The liturgies of the church are intended by God as vessels of the Spirit to shape our desires according to the way of Christ in the world.[6]

The start of salvation given in the abundant outpouring of divine love at Pentecost in Acts 2 shatters our manipulative and dehumanizing salvation machines. This love that broke through the barriers of sin and death on the cross is offered abundantly to humanity at Pentecost by grace alone. Those who receive are helpless to earn it, but they must yield to its life-changing influence to receive it. It costs nothing, but it will change everything. This salvation smashes through the salvation machines of society and exposes them as blasphemous. It comes to us as an abundant outpouring that exposes the empty promises of salvation machines (secular and religious) and puts these machines and their enablers on notice. They are part of this dying world; they will be ground to a halt and shattered once the kingdom of God arrives in fullness.

The opening of Luke's Gospel features the key point of entry of this divine love into human flesh. The Spirit of God, "the power of the most high," hovers on a weak and humble maiden Mary, who yields her body by the grace of God to the incubation and birth of something radically new, the very beginnings of the kingdom of God on earth. This hidden mystery interrupts the smooth efficiency of worldly kingdoms with the

---

2  Jan Milíč Lochman, *Reconciliation and Liberation* (Philadelphia, MN: Fortress Press, 1977), 10–11.
3  Dietrich Bonhoeffer, *The Cost of Discipleship* (New York: Touchstone, 1995), 43.
4  Lochman, *Reconciliation and Liberation*, 13–14.
5  Ibid., 10–17.
6  James K. A. Smith, *You Are What You Love: The Spiritual Power of Habit* (Grand Rapids, MI: Brazos Press, 2016).

breaking in of a new possibility for the future, which can only be called the Word of the Father in flesh. The powerful and creative wind of the Spirit conceives in Mary's womb a sanctified body that will be the vessel of the faithful Son in his overcoming of sin and death and mediation to the world of the Spirit of life and communion, something that cannot be commodified, distributed, or announced with empty promises. The Father raises him from the dead by the Spirit and exalts him to his lordship. The Spirit overflows that astounding event so as to open its victory to all. Our baptism in water signifies the death of the old self caught in the throes of sin and the rising up of the new self united to the risen Christ. We are taken up into the infinite depth of divine communion and given the promise of life in the kingdom of God, life in the Spirit in conformity to Christ. Through the work of the Spirit, the church mediates this incorporation into Christ's body. The Pentecostals have always rightly interpreted Acts 2 with the razor edge of criticism against any institutionalization of the Spirit. They were right in this. But they only needed to appreciate more than they sometimes did that enduring practices emerge from the outpouring of the Spirit which function in the mode of faith as instruments of the Spirit, and they must always be renewed as such. Practices of the Spirit such as proclamation and sacraments are always dependent on a grace that cannot be commodified and are always open to "interruptions" through inspired utterances and other acts of grace, expressions of groaning in travail for the fullness of liberty to come, and bursts of joy. We partake together in a foretaste of liberty in the Spirit that is increasingly evident among us.

The birth and destiny of the church as a vocational communion of love is to be understood according to three movements. The first is *outpouring*. It begins at Pentecost with the outpouring of the Holy Spirit from the Father and through the Son (Acts 2:32-36). The outpouring of the Spirit has its source in the Father's love for the world. It has its ongoing mediation through the Son in his faithful devotion to the Father and the Father's cause in the world. And the outpouring is present in creative power and freedom, having cosmic breadth and eschatological reach in the Spirit. The second movement is that of *incorporation*. Through faith, people are allowed to receive the gift of life and even to enter and participate in it. They are taken up in the reality of the Spirit by faith and incorporated into Christ's body, which allows for communion with Christ and, through Christ, with his heavenly Father. This communion is not enjoyed by disconnected individuals; it is shared horizontally among believers in and through God as it is shared with God. It is a dynamic communion that encourages an ever deeper journey into its depths that will culminate when we are "swallowed up" in life at the resurrection (2 Cor. 5:4). The third movement is vocational or *charismatic and missional*. The communion of love shared with and in God is not a closed circle. The sending forth of the Son and the Spirit reveal that divine communion is an open and ever-expanding circle, one that is hospitable, inviting, and constantly offered to others. Incorporation into divine communion thus turns participants not only inward (toward a journey into Christ and the heart of the Father) but also outward, because the loving Father and the faithful Christ are turned outward too. God gives by self-imparting and overflowing. The inward journey of incorporation is thus simultaneously the outward journey of charismatic ministry and mission. The faith of the church takes on objective significance; the church becomes by grace a sign and instrument for the divine self-impartation in the world. In the dependent and receptive mode of faith, the sanctified and empowered fellowship of the church mediates the divine self-giving to others. Through its proclamation (spoken and embodied), baptism, the breaking of bread, spiritual gifts, and mission, the church becomes the ongoing means of God's work toward establishing the divine kingdom on earth. God will make the earth the divine dwelling place. The church as the temple of divine dwelling, of divine communion, becomes the destiny of creation. In the Spirit, the church prefigures the future world in its witness to Christ, the pioneer and perfecter of our faith.

## Spirit Baptism: A Point of Integration

The church is a vocational fellowship that exists in these three movements of outpouring, incorporation, and vocation. I will describe these movements according to the overarching metaphor of the baptism in the Holy Spirit, which is ideally suited for this purpose. The baptism in the Spirit in all of its dimensions and its eschatological fulfillment involves all three of these movements. There is also adequate space within this expansive metaphor for the distinctive emphases of Pentecostal pneumatology: sanctified embodiment, empowered witness, speaking in tongues, multiple gifts of the Spirit, spiritual warfare, divine healing, missionary zeal, and eschatological passion for the coming of Christ and his kingdom on earth. A pneumatological ecclesiology within the wide-open expanse of the baptism in the Holy Spirit is hospitable to all of the accents that Pentecostals hold dear. Cecil Robeck was right, Pentecostal ecclesiology has to start at the promise of the divine outpouring given in Joel and initiated at Pentecost. Our ecclesiology will even end there as well, for Spirit baptism finds its personal fulfillment at the resurrection of the dead, the swallowing up of mortal life into immortality (2 Cor. 5:4), and globally in the final gathering of the people of God in the embrace of the Triune God. This eschatological fulfillment of Spirit baptism is the fullness of life that the church is born to taste and to signify in the here and now. If we think we've been filled with the Spirit now, just wait until we are freed by the Spirit-body of the resurrection (1 Cor. 15:44). We haven't seen anything yet.

One could tell by now that my use of the term "Spirit baptism" is more expansive than that which is common among Pentecostals. Of course, there is more than one understanding of Spirit baptism among Pentecostals. One could argue (as I have) that all of the different understandings of Spirit baptism among Pentecostals share the central passion of locating the church at the place where the Spirit is received in fullness. We will speak of this issue more fully in terms of its biblical foundations and theological meaning in our next chapter. I only wish to sketch here how my view fits with the others. The Oneness (apostolic) Pentecostals (representing about a quarter of the global Pentecostal Movement) tend to view Spirit baptism as the culminating point of conversion to Christ and incorporation into his body.[7] Conversion is a complex

---

[7] They are called "Oneness," because they hold that God in essence is only one. This one God is incarnated in Christ and present now through him. Their version of the Trinity is thus economic or manifested in time. It is not internal to God. They advocate a kind of Christocentric modalism.

event for them, consisting of repentance, faith, water baptism (in Jesus's name), and the reception of the Holy Spirit, with the evidence of speaking in tongues. Their key text is Acts 2:38: "Repent and be baptized, every one of you, in the name of Jesus Christ for the forgiveness of your sins. And you will receive the gift of the Holy Spirit." Except for the expectation of tongues, this view of Spirit baptism would have broad ecumenical appeal. The Oneness Pentecostal view of Spirit baptism thus has both soteriological and vocational meaning, which is a significant advantage theologically. They do not have to deal with the bifurcation of sanctification and empowerment for gifted service that handicaps other forms of Pentecostal soteriology and ecclesiology. Oneness Pentecostals share with all Pentecostals a strong Christocentrism, which orientates the Oneness branch of the Movement toward believing that all elements of life in the Spirit are granted through incorporation into Christ's body by faith. Theological historian, David William Faupel, has even called the Oneness Pentecostal view of Spirit baptism the "quintessential" view among Pentecostals, the one most consistent with the typical Pentecostal Christological focus.[8] In this light, those who suspect that Pentecostals intend to detach pneumatology from Christology fundamentally misunderstand the ethos of the movement.

Outside of the Oneness Pentecostal Movement, Pentecostals are most known for their doctrine of "subsequence" or "separability" when it comes to Spirit baptism. This view separates Spirit baptism from salvation or incorporation into the body of Christ and identifies it instead as empowered witness or a general deepening of life in the Spirit, especially through participation in supernatural gifts of the Spirit. That is, even though the filling or empowerment of the Spirit may occur at the moment of the Spirit's initial possession of us at our conversion to Christ, it is theologically separable from this and thus could happen later. These Pentecostals don't deny that the Spirit indwells believers at their conversion to Christ; they view Spirit baptism as a deeper experience of the Spirit in life. To complicate matters, there is a debate among these Pentecostals as to whether or not Spirit baptism needs to be preceded by a crisis experience of entire sanctification (completely yielding one's intentions to the way of Christ). Early Pentecostals from the Wesleyan Holiness Movement insisted on entire sanctification as a necessary preparation for Spirit baptism. They thus held to three separable moments in the reception of the Spirit: conversion to Christ, entire sanctification, and empowerment for witness (the deeper life of the Spirit). Pentecostals from outside of the Wesleyan Pentecostal wing of non-Oneness Pentecostals held only to a twofold reception of the Spirit (conversion and Spirit baptism). In both camps, the theological polemics accented this aspect of separability to the point of confusion. One could ask, If I have the Spirit already, why do I need to receive the Spirit again? As clarification, the charismatic movement popularized Kilian McDonnell's idea that the Spirit received at Christian initiation is "released" later in life through dramatic moments of Christian awakening or empowerment. This view became popular in classical Pentecostal circles as well. A prominent metaphor used to explain this release of the Spirit was taken from Jn 7:38, the Spirit received at conversion to Christ later

---

[8] David William Faupel, *The Everlasting Gospel: The Significance of Eschatology in the Development of Pentecostal Thought*, JPT Series 10 (Sheffield: Sheffield Academic Press, 1996), 44–46.

overflows one or is released in life as a source of blessing to others. One could still speak metaphorically of the Spirit "coming upon" believers so as to enable human yielding to such a release or overflowing of the Spirit from within. But one would still say that the Spirit is given once at Christian initiation and remains for those who are in Christ. Though the Spirit is imparted only once (at initiation to Christ by faith under the sign of baptism), the Spirit is thought to be released (experienced) in phases (perhaps as breakthrough experiences in deeper sanctification and empowered witness). Baptized in the Spirit, we continue to drink of the Spirit (1 Cor. 12:13). The idea of "one Spirit baptism many fillings," however, sounds too disconnected and static. We speak here of one Spirit baptism that is granted at incorporation into Christ's body by faith but is also eschatological in fulfillment, drawing us ever deeper in, toward a swallowing up in life (2 Cor. 5:4), or welling up from within, toward overflowing as the soul expands and our capacity to receive opens up into new areas of life (Jn 4:14). The awakening to our empowered vocational (charismatic, missional) life can be so transformative as to represent a new beginning in our receptivity to the Spirit, one that opens us to the Spirit in greater fullness. And so it is. Is it so hard to imagine that the Spirit would be experienced in greater fullness at the point of one's discovery of their gifting or vocation in bearing witness? The point is that one cannot divide up the gift of the Spirit but one can distinguish different phases in one's receptivity or experience of the Spirit in life.

In this light, one may speak of Spirit baptism as anchored in the gift of the Spirit granted at initiation to Christ and incorporation by faith into his body but then released or received experientially in greater fullness at subsequent moments toward the final fulfillment of the Spirit's fullness eschatologically. In fact, I will argue that the ultimate reception of the Spirit occurs at the resurrection of the dead. Then, mortality will be "swallowed up by life" (2 Cor. 5:4). Put differently, the ultimate release of the Spirit is the welling up of the water of life "unto eternal life" (Jn. 4:14). This and this alone is the ultimate baptism in the Spirit. The fullness for which Pentecostals seek occurs with the "Spirit body" of the resurrection. Christ is the "life giving spirit" to impart this ultimate fullness of his risen life to us (1 Cor. 15:44-45). Thus, the gift of the Spirit and its release in life both belong to Spirit baptism. In a way, we have been Spirit baptized but its ultimate end or fullness is still ahead. Its point of ultimate fulfillment is before us and not behind us. It is for this reason that water baptism signifies our union through resurrection with the risen Christ: "For if we have been united with him in a death like his, we will certainly also be united with him in a resurrection like his" (Rom. 6:5). Given the fact that water baptism signifies the conformity to the risen Christ that occurs at our resurrection, is it so far-fetched to see the Spirit baptism signified at this water rite as fulfilled in resurrection too? The entire Christian life is one large journey into deeper union with Christ that attains to the Spirit's fullness only at its conclusion. The phrase "filled with the Spirit" used in the New Testament (Acts 2:4) is proleptic, part of a now and not yet. We *are* and we *are not yet* filled. Thus, Paul can say we *are* children of God by the Spirit (Rom. 8:15-16) "as we await eagerly our adoption to sonship," which he defines as the resurrection, "the redemption of our bodies" (v. 23).

Understood eschatologically, Spirit baptism becomes suitable for a pneumatological ecclesiology that brings together those various themes popular among Pentecostals and Charismatics but within a more encompassing theological framework. We are in the Spirit's outpouring incorporated into communion in a way that changes us into agents of communion, which is commensurate with conformity to the image of Christ. As Robert Webber wrote, the spiritual life of the church occurs within "the union of God dwelling in us and we in him," and "the way to experience this mystery is to live in it, to embody it."[9] Our life incorporated into communion is thus turned toward the hospitable and inviting reach of God's self-impartation to the world. Impartation involves incorporation, and incorporation involves vocational embodiment and mediation. We as the church unite around being a vocationally oriented fellowship of the Spirit. Jesus prayed for his followers "that all of them may be one, Father, just as you are in me and I am in you. May they also be in us so that the world may believe that you have sent me" (Jn. 17:21).

Initial Pentecostal efforts at ecclesiology are also implicitly attempting to connect the sanctifying and the empowering work of the Spirit. But most are using the classically Pentecostal "fivefold gospel" of Jesus as Savior, sanctifier, Spirit Baptizer, Healer, and Coming King.[10] They are following Donald Dayton's groundbreaking treatment of the theological roots of Pentecostalism as their guide.[11] Lacking is the integrating force of what is arguably the key emphasis of Pentecostals, namely, the gift of the Spirit granted at Pentecost. This is not to exclude Christology from the founding of the church, since Pentecost both fulfills the messianic mission and launches the Spirit's.[12] Without clarifying how the five points of the fivefold schema relate or form an integrative whole, one's ecclesiology can appear fragmented, leaving unaddressed problems such as the bifurcation between sanctification and vocation (purity and power) that has accompanied most forms of Pentecostal pneumatology.

I appreciate in this light Dale Coulter's provocative attempt at integrating the fivefold gospel under the umbrella of Jesus's new humanity and the vocation it implies. For Coulter, the fivefold gospel was simply "the early Pentecostal way to identify and articulate Jesus's praxis and the vocation it implied." Actualized in the Spirit, "this vocation remains the church's vocation and the church remains faithful to her head insofar as she embodies it."[13] Coulter thus writes of a "twin vocation" that belonged to Christ and was picked up analogously by the church in Christ's outpouring of the Spirit from his faithful life, namely, to be the "new human being (*modus vivendi*) and to call others to embrace this new humanity through the proclamation of the kingdom of God (*missio dei*)."[14] Salvation and sanctification indicate the former, and Spirit baptism and healing are grouped under the latter. However, questions remain. Can one justify

---

[9] Robert Webber, *The Divine Embrace: Recovering the Passionate Spiritual Life* (Grand Rapids, MI: Baker Books, 2008), 20.

[10] John Christopher Thomas, ed., *Towards a Pentecostal Ecclesiology: The Church of the Fivefold Gospel* (Cleveland, TN: CPT Press, 2010).

[11] Donald W. Dayton, *Theological Roots of Pentecostalism* (Grand Rapids, MI: Zondervan, 1988).

[12] See my development of this point in my *Jesus the Spirit Baptizer: Christology in Light of Pentecost* (Grand Rapids, MI: Eerdmans, 2019).

[13] Dale Coulter, "Christ, the Spirit, and Vocation: Initial Reflections on a Pentecostal Ecclesiology," *Pro Ecclesia* XIX, no. 3 (2010): 318 (318–39).

[14] Ibid., 319.

exegetically and theologically making Spirit baptism and healing merely the means of calling others to Christ's new humanity?

What helps is the fact that Coulter still has sanctified vocation as his overall point of integration. He could help Pentecostals who take a missional approach to ecclesiology to conceptually integrate sanctification with missional empowerment. The advantage of a missional approach to Pentecostal ecclesiology is that there is already a body of literature advocating such ecclesiologies from which they can draw. The disadvantage of this missional approach in my view is that it lacks to a degree the resources necessary for adequately accounting for the mystery at the heart of the church's union with Christ. The bride does not marry her groom merely to serve him or his cause in the world. There is an intimate sharing of life and ecstatic enjoyment at the heart of that union that is not reducible to vocational or missional categories, though it can't be understand without them. This is the great advantage of *communio* (or communion) ecclesiologies, such as the one promoted by Miroslav Volf.[15] I hold that a more expansive understanding of Spirit baptism offers us rich resources for appreciating that inner mystery of communion as both a depth to penetrate and an embodied witness through which to mediate that life to others.

In constructing an ecclesiology with an eschatological view of Spirit baptism as the all-encompassing framework, the ensuing discussion will proceed as follows. In the first chapter, I will lay the dogmatic foundation for the Spirit-baptized church in the self-giving of the Triune God. In the following chapter, I will discuss the elect church. Election is not a prominent theme for Pentecostal theology, or for any strongly pneumatological ecclesiology for that matter. But this is precisely why the discussion is needed. I intend to particularize election as focused on Christ but actualized ecclesially through Spirit baptism. The third chapter will explore the pilgrim church, with an emphasis on models and marks of the church. The church on a journey in the Spirit from the "now" to the "not yet" will be my overarching emphasis. The final chapter will feature the witnessing church, which describes the church's practices. The church's participation in the self-mediation of the Triune God, which climaxes with human life in the fullness of the Spirit, will be my point of emphasis. The entire vision will find its point of integration in my expansive vision of the baptism in the Holy Spirit. Peer into the promise of Joel through the lens of the Spirit's arrival at Pentecost and one sees the exalted Christ as the mediator of the Father's love. One sees our incorporation into that embrace and our commitment to mediate its reach to the ends of the earth, to the fullness of life in the Spirit. That's our destiny as the church. Intimate communion with God and dedication to the victory of that communion in the world is the nature and purpose of the church.

---

[15] Miroslav Volf, *After Our Likeness: The Church as the Image of the Trinity* (Grand Rapids, MI: Eerdmans, 1997).

# 1

# The Spirit-Baptized Church

The church is the Spirit-baptized people of God. In saying this, I agree with Simon Chan: "To call the church Pentecostal is to recognize the definitiveness of the Pentecostal event, i.e., of the baptism in the Holy Spirit in shaping the church's identity."[1] This means that the church is at its core the people united to Christ and incorporated by the Spirit into communion for a vocational purpose. Incorporation is the point of emphasis here. Incorporation is the meeting place between the divine outpouring and human communal and individual participation by grace in its embrace. This communion is not a closed circle, nor is it enjoyed only for our own benefit. This divine communion extended to us is extended to those beyond us. It is extended through Christ and the outpoured Spirit. So participation in the embrace of divine communion conforms us more and more into the image of the Christ who gave himself for the sake of mediating divine love to the world. This accent on Spirit-baptismal incorporation means that the church is *both* the central environment in and through which the Triune God self-imparts in the world *and* the central locus of the response of faith. The ultimate goal of Spirit baptism is described well by William Seymore's paper, *The Apostolic Faith*: "We shall be living in the new heavens and the new Jerusalem and Jesus will return the kingdom into his Father's hand and sit down among the brethren, and we shall have the same glory that Jesus had before the foundation of the world. God will be all in all and we shall be swallowed up in immortality."[2]

## Spirit Baptism as the Point of Departure

The conviction expressed in highlighting Spirit baptism as God's overflow and incorporation of others is that theologies of the church often focus on communion or mission without adequate appreciation for how each necessarily involves the other. Pneumatology is the key to this link, but this emphasis on a pneumatological ecclesiology requires Trinitarian breadth and specificity. I wish to suggest here that the grace of incorporation into the communion and mission of the Triune God through

---

[1] In part, Chan writes this in response to my earlier work which makes the same point, *Baptized in the Spirit: A Global Pentecostal Theology* (Grand Rapids, MI: Zondervan, 2006). Simon Chan, *Pentecostal Ecclesiology: An Essay in the Development of Doctrine*, JPT series 38 (Dorset: Deo Publication, 2011), 74.

[2] No author, *AF* 1, no. 1 (1906): 3.

*Spirit baptism* can provide us with this kind of specificity. As I noted in my Introduction, I define Spirit baptism more broadly than what happens at Christian "initiation" through faith (the typical evangelical view) or the rites of initiation, principally water baptism (the typical sacramental view). I also interpret Spirit baptism more broadly than a post-conversion empowerment for service (the majority Pentecostal view). Spirit baptism as developed here involves all of these things but is ultimately eschatological in its realization, encompassing all of these insights. It is descriptive of the very nature of the church itself as the ever-more deeply incorporated and ever-more expansively incorporating people. Spirit baptism has its decisive moment at one's initiation by faith into Christ and his body, but it is confirmed and deepened under the signs of water baptism and the sacred meal and it is experientially realized in one's opening up to deeper dimensions of the sanctified embodiment of the gospel and to both charismatic and missional empowerment. Spirit baptism reaches for eschatological fulfillment, which will occur when mortality is "swallowed up by life" in the coming fullness of the kingdom of God (2 Cor. 5:4). I thus follow Donald Gelpi in saying that it is not Spirit baptism that occurs in faith or water baptism; rather, it is faith and water baptism that occur in Spirit baptism, which is the more encompassing reality.[3]

This chapter will seek to expand on the idea that the baptism in the Holy Spirit could be explored fruitfully as the core idea of our understanding of the church. A pneumatological ecclesiology depends on it. More specifically, the church is birthed and flourishes in the baptism in the Holy Spirit. In making this argument, I will attempt to highlight as foundational the divine action at the base of the church's origin and ongoing life. It is possible to focus on a favored core practice that constitutes the church and then make it the center from which the other practices are understood (such as proclamation, eucharist, charismatic ministry, and mission) without adequately appreciating first the outpouring and incorporating work of the Triune God abundantly at work throughout all of these practices. It is also possible to play a communion ecclesiology over against a vocational or missional ecclesiology and vice versa. The two meet in the Triune God, who is an open communion of persons that overflows longing to take others into the divine embrace.

Communion and vocation occur within Spirit baptism understood as the act of divine outpouring and the consequent incorporation of the other as other. Spirit baptism grants both communion and vocation their substance and direction, and vice versa. As an abundant outpouring (Rom. 5:5) Spirit baptism opens a journey into the depths of divine love that exceeds one's comprehension, to grasp together "how wide and long and high and deep is the love of Christ" (Eph. 3:19). That will be an ocean of love into which we will be swallowed up in eternity (2 Cor. 5:4). Spirit baptism as overflowing love is also directed by God to embrace the other. The outward movement of this outpouring prevents communion from institutional confinement. Driven by the freedom of the Spirit and informed by the faithfulness of the Son, Spirit-baptized communion cannot be self-enclosed or self-serving institutionally. It is thus vocational, meaning charismatic and missional. Spirit-baptized communion creates space for the

---

[3] See Koo Dong Yun's discussion of Gelpi's view in his *Baptism in the Holy Spirit: An Ecumenical Theology of Spirit Baptism* (Lanham, MD: University Press of America, 2003), 44–48.

other, and their God-given otherness is not just tolerated; it's welcomed and cherished. Indeed, "church" is not fundamentally our project; it's God's. God alone is the Spirit Baptizer, the One who overflows and embraces the other, as other. We live from the overflowing and incorporating life of the Triune God and seek in our corporate life to embody and further it.

The gift of the Spirit is individually received, but it also may be said to be that which accounts for the inception of the church. My assumption throughout my discussion will be that the church does not administer Spirit baptism (Spirit outpouring and incorporation); Spirit baptism administers the church and all of its practices. The church merely celebrates, embodies, and extends it to others. As Moltmann wrote:

> It is not the church that administers the Spirit as the Spirit of preaching, the Spirit of sacraments, the Spirit of ministry or the Spirit of tradition. The Spirit "administers" the church with the events of word and faith, sacrament and grace, offices and tradition.[4]

It is time to drill deeper. We turn to a biblical and theological description of the baptism in the Holy Spirit as a fruitful point of departure for a theology of the church.

## Toward a Theology of Spirit Baptism

In focusing on this theme of Spirit baptism as the key to understanding the doctrine of the church, I am taking my point of departure from my Pentecostal setting. Spirit baptism is the crown jewel of Pentecostal spirituality. It may be said that the Pentecostals have put this theme on the table of ecumenical discussion. It is our chief distinctive. But as the reader knows by now, I am using the term more broadly than is the case among the majority of voices within the history of classical Pentecostalism.

Briefly put, the term "baptizing in the Holy Spirit" (only the verb is used in the New Testament) is taken from John the Baptist's announcement that the coming Messiah will "baptize" others in the Holy Spirit. All four Gospels and the book of Acts, the narrative foundation of the New Testament, make this announcement of the coming Spirit Baptizer programmatic for understanding Jesus's messianic mission (Mt. 3:11; Mk 1:8; Lk. 3:16; Jn 1:33; Acts 1:5). John will baptize those who repent in water, but the Messiah will baptize them in the Spirit by way of fulfillment. The Messiah will occasion a "river" of the Spirit into which he will "baptize" those who repent and believe. Those who reject will be "baptized" in the fire of judgment (cf., Lk. 3:17). Shortly after this announcement, all four Gospels report that Jesus comes as the awaited figure. John's Gospel records that John the Baptist knew Jesus was the awaited Messiah, because John saw the Spirit descend on him (Jn 1:33). Jesus is publicly revealed as the favored and beloved Son of the Father (e.g., Lk. 3:22). This is a turning point in God's dealings with

---

[4] Jürgen Moltmann, *The Church in the Power of the Spirit* (Philadelphia, MN: Fortress Press, 1993), 64.

humanity. The Son is shown to be the Chosen One (Jn 3:33-34) to fulfill the messianic mission for all of humanity, indeed, for all of creation.

As we will note, little did John the Baptist know that Jesus would fulfill his messianic mission by suffering the dreaded baptism in fire in order to open a path for humanity to the baptism in the Spirit. In Acts, Jesus quotes from John's announcement of the coming baptism in the Spirit (Acts 1:5), which conspicuously excludes Luke's earlier reference to the baptism in fire. Jesus bore that for humanity on the cross, the baptism of his death (Lk. 12:49-50). His announcement concerning the coming Spirit baptism caused his disciples to ask the question about the eschatological restoration of Israel (1:6), implying a link between the two. Spirit baptism was understood to have an eschatological fulfillment. John the Baptist spoke of it in the context of his preaching concerning the coming kingdom (Mt. 3:2), and Jesus told the disciples about it in the context of his discourse on the coming kingdom as well (1:1-5). The fact that they were to wait in Jerusalem for it had eschatological significance, since this is the city thought to be the key location of end-time salvation. After the Spirit falls, Peter's quote from Joel 2 makes a connection with end-time salvation (Acts 2:17-18). Spirit baptism leads not only to the birth but also to the eschatological fulfillment of the people of God. Jesus notes that Israel's restoration is in the Father's timing but then adds that their Spirit-baptized witness will reach "to the ends of the earth" (1:8). Only then can the ends of the earth become the possession of God's anointed (Ps. 2:8), when the witnessing church by his grace makes it so. The Spirit-baptized communion of God's people finds its *telos* in the ultimate fulfillment of this mission, for it brings about the final gathering (incorporation) of all of the saints in God. The eschatological fulfillment of the baptism in the Spirit for Luke occurs when the communion of saints reaches its diversely global expanse in a way that includes "the ends of the earth."

Paul mentions Christ's baptizing others in the Spirit and also connects it to the incorporation of an ever-expanding diversity of believers into Christ's body. "For we were all baptized in one Spirit so as to form one body—whether Jews or Gentiles, slave or free—and we were all given the one Spirit to drink" (1 Cor. 12:13). Spirit baptism has an eschatological reach in this ever deeper, ever-more expansive drinking together of the Spirit. Only when the church is exalted by the Spirit and attains final communion in Christ can we say that mortality is "swallowed up by life" (2 Cor. 5:4). Such implicitly is the baptism in the Holy Spirit ultimately fulfilled. Does this mean that Spirit baptism is not our initiation to Christ? It is initiatory, but initiation is to be eschatologically defined, both as a "now" and as a "not yet" reality. We are initiated to Christ and incorporated into his body by faith under the sign of water baptism, but that initiation has an eschatological point of reference, pointing to a spiritual fulfillment that is not yet. Paul's writes of baptism: "For if we have been united with him in a death like his, we will certainly also be united with him in a resurrection like his" (Rom. 6:5). Our current drinking of the Spirit is a foretaste, a journey into deeper union with Christ that is fulfilled at the point of resurrection.

We will be exploring all of this more thoroughly under the sections on Spirit baptism in the Old and New Testaments. Suffice it to say here that theologians from different church families have interpreted the biblical doctrine of Spirit baptism differently depending on their ecclesiology. Those from a primarily evangelical word ecclesiology (in which the church is the people of the Word of God) will tend to view Spirit baptism as regeneration by faith in the gospel. The church then focuses on the ongoing hearing and obedience together of the Word of God. Those of a more sacramental ecclesiology will view Spirit baptism as the gift of the Spirit given in the rites of initiation, especially water baptism. The church then becomes the place where initiated (water-baptized) Christians commune together with the Lord at the Lord's table. Those who hold to a Pentecostal ecclesiology will be prone to view Spirit baptism as that which empowers the witness and expands the charismatic life of the church. The church is then the place where the people of the Spirit minister through various spiritual gifts, overcome together the powers of darkness, and missionize in Christ's name.

Among them all, the baptism in the Holy Spirit as a doctrine rightly highlights the gift of the Spirit. How this gift is received and actualized is the key point of difference. In each Christian family, Spirit baptism becomes functionally supportive of that communion's particular understanding of Christian initiation, and this understanding then serves to describe the core of its entire ecclesiology. But what if one defines the gift of the Spirit eschatologically or in a way that fulfills and transcends the church? Spirit baptism would be viewed as belonging first to the kingdom of God or to the Triune God's self-giving in service to the final communion of saints in conformity to the risen Christ. And what if one then locates the nature and purpose of the church within that project? It would not be the church or its practices of initiation that determine the nature of Spirit baptism. Spirit baptism would be too expansive and all determining to function as that which legitimates a confessional family's understanding of Christian initiation and its concomitant ecclesiological accent. As an eschatological concept, Spirit baptism would accommodate all biblically responsive understandings of Christian initiation and ongoing life. Spirit baptism does not occur in the birth of faith in Christ and the rites of initiation; all of these occur in Spirit baptism. Though anchored in the event of a believer's initiation, Spirit baptism reaches for eschatological fulfillment in the ongoing communion and vocation of the church, finding its fulfillment in the fullness of the Spirit that is manifested in the conversion of the nations, the restoration of Israel, and the final new creation in the fulfillment of God's reign. All of the ecclesial families would be in some legitimate sense regarded as faithful in their particular accent to the larger reality of Spirit baptism but urged to more fully appreciate in practice the equally important accents of the other confessions. I am not pretending to offer readers an all-expansive vision of Spirit baptism that harbors no shortcomings. Of course, I have a perspective too. Others who may differ with me on my specific proposals can bless me if they offer their own vision of the Spirit-baptized church. This book is meant to invite that kind of conversation.

In expanding on my earlier work,[5] I propose that the church is birthed from (and determined by) the baptism in the Holy Spirit eschatologically understood. Spirit baptism functions for me to grant greater specificity to the larger project of a pneumatological ecclesiology. Toward this end, I will maintain that Spirit baptism is

---

[5] Macchia, *Baptized in the Spirit*; *Justified in the Spirit: Creation, Redemption, and the Triune God* (Grand Rapids, MI: Eerdmans, 2010); *Jesus the Spirit Baptizer: Christology in Light of Pentecost* (Grand Rapids, MI: Eerdmans, 2018).

indeed initiatory in significance not only (and restrictively) as a one-time event but also as an ongoing event that leaves its imprint on the church, the imprint of the Spirit- and fire-baptized Christ. The Spirit-baptized church itself becomes initiatory in nature, used of the Spirit in its shared life to bear witness in all of its practices in a way that continuously facilitates the incorporation of all flesh into the body of Christ, to the very ends of the earth. Only when the ends of the earth become the possession of God's anointed (Ps. 2:8; Acts 1:8) will the Messiah's baptizing in the Spirit and the nature of the church as the Spirit-baptized people find ultimate fulfillment. Only then will the communion of saints embody Christ and be in the fullest sense the temple of the Spirit's dwelling. Only then will mortality be "swallowed up in life," which I take to be the ultimate experience of Spirit "baptism" (2 Cor. 5:4). The remainder of this chapter will be devoted to elaborating on what I mean by the baptism in the Holy Spirit and justify its use as the central theme of my pneumatological ecclesiology.

## Spirit Baptism: Old Testament

The Spirit-baptized church has deep Old Testament roots. At the creation, God speaks and the Spirit hovers (Gen. 1:1f). The Spirit is the divine agent who enables creation to receive the divine word, making it possible for communion between God and humanity to exist. Lloyd Neve has made the case that the *ruach* of the Old Testament is best translated in many cases as "Spirit," with the image of divine "breath" in mind rather than the less personal "wind," since, when God is the acting subject, the wind comes forth bringing a personal divine presence or action to bear on the need depicted in the text.[6] Even when "wind" is in the background of the text, the term *ruach* is often used specifically to depict certain aspects of how God applies the divine life to creation. God thus creates in creaturely life a capacity for the divine life. "God has life and when he bestows this life on his creation the life itself can be called *ruach* (Isa. 32:15)."[7] Power, life, and wrath were themes often highlighted when the divine life as *ruach* was applied to creation.[8] In creation, the breath of God rests as a mighty presence upon the emptiness and darkness of the waters of the deep as the power by which the Word of God creates the cosmos (Gen. 1:1-2). Robert Alter's translation appropriately refers to "God's breath hovering over the waters."[9] The poem pictures this divine breath as "a line of defense against the pressing chaos."[10] Yet, the verb for hovering also calls up a nesting image, implying a mixture of powerful defense (overcoming) and personal nurturing.[11] Creation by the breath of God becomes more personal when God breathes life into Adam, transforming lifeless dust into a living being who breathes and can commune with God (2:7). The motif of humanity's total dependence on God's Spirit for their

---

[6] Lloyd R. Neve, *The Spirit of God in the Old Testament* (Cleveland, TN: CPT Press, 2011), 1–13.
[7] Ibid., 2.
[8] Ibid.
[9] Robert Alter, *The Hebrew Bible, Translation and Commentary,* Vol. 1 (New York: W. W. Norton & Co., 2019), 11.
[10] Walter Brueggemann, *Genesis*, IBCTP (Atlanta: John Knox Press, 1982), 30.
[11] Robert Alter, *The Hebrew Bible*, 11.

existence and thriving is clear.[12] Humanity was created to be the dwelling place of the Spirit in conformity to the Word of God. "The Spirit of God has made me; the breath of the Almighty gives me life" (Job 33:4). God spread the cosmos out like a tabernacle in which to dwell (Isa. 40:22) but this is even more so the case with the tabernacle of the human body, especially human bodies in shared communion.

Humanity's original disobedience brings hardship to life. Thorns and thistles replace the lush vegetation of the Garden, a symbol of banishment from divine blessing. The harshest of all consequences is undoubtedly the death sentence of Gen. 3:19: "For dust you are and to dust you will return." Humanity is banished from the Garden that contains the tree of life (3:22). Though created from dust with the capacity for mortality, the implication is that humanity was made for more than this. Humanity was made for the Spirit of life and eternal communion. Sin is thus not just transgressing a moral or legal principle; it's a denial of life in communion. It alienates and leaves a deep and sorrowful loss in its wake. Divine grace, however, is present throughout the story of humanity's fall. Humanity is still allowed to live and experience a degree of blessing despite their disobedience, for God clothes them in their shame—a sign of continued life being applied to them (3:21).[13] And the foreshadowing of Eve's seed crushing the serpent's head is rich with Christological implications (3:15). Yet, throughout the Old Testament, death continues to be the barrier that limits the flourishing of life in God's Spirit. There are hints that God's faithfulness and blessing will remain, even in death (Ps. 139:9). There are even a few references to resurrection: "Let those who dwell in the dust wake up and shout for joy!" (Isa. 26:19; cf. Dan. 12:2; Job 19:26). All of this anticipates the ultimate power of the Spirit that will one day overflow the boundary of death and provide passage for humanity to eternal communion with God. This is what the New Testament will call the baptism in the Holy Spirit.

Since humanity disobeys God, the divine *ruach* is not only a promise but also a threat. As Neve shows, the *ruach* of God could also be a force of judgment, of banishment from God's favor. Isaiah 30:28 contains a dire warning: "His breath is like a rushing torrent, rising up to the neck. He shakes the nations in the sieve of destruction." Indeed, the wrath of God in the Old Testament is pictured as a mighty destructive wind. Judgment also took on the image of drowning within a watery grave in the story of Jonah:

> You hurled me into the depths,
>   into the very heart of the seas,
>   and the currents swirled about me;
> all your waves and breakers
>   swept over me.
> I said, "I have been banished
>   from your sight;
> yet I will look again
>   toward your holy temple."
> The engulfing waters threatened me,

---

[12] Brueggamann, *Genesis*, 45.
[13] Ibid., 49–50.

> the deep surrounded me;
>   seaweed was wrapped around my head.
> To the roots of the mountains I sank down;
>   the earth beneath barred me in forever.
> But you, LORD my God,
>   brought my life up from the pit. (2:3-6)

Though the waters in the quote are not pictured as the Spirit of God, the image is still a potent reminder that the wrath of God can swallow one whole. Such was the image of *sheol* or the realm of death:

> For the grave cannot praise you,
>   death cannot sing your praise;
> those who go down to the pit
>   cannot hope for your faithfulness. (Isa. 38:18)

The deliverance and restoration of Israel by the Word and Spirit of God is not primarily individual but corporate. It is in our language ecclesial. Israel is claimed by God at the Exodus as the covenant people. The freedom story of the Exodus is the preface of the law given through Moses (Exod. 20:1-3), implying that the law was a "signpost to freedom."[14] The grace of election and freedom comes first; the law follows as witness ("I am the LORD your God, who brought you out of Egypt, out of the land of slavery. You shall have no other gods before me"). The law preserved absolute love for God and ongoing faith expressed as trust and loyalty (Deut. 6:4). The practice of the law would be a reminder that everything Israel has comes from the hand of God (Deuteronomy 8). The law was thus spiritual (Rom. 7:14), an object of meditation and delight in giving glory to God (Psalm 119). There are key moments when Israel as the people of God is called as an assembly (Sinai, the dedication of the Temple, the republishing of the law by Ezra), which "emphasizes the truth that the people of Israel are constituted by the word of Yahweh as the bearers of the divine covenant and promise."[15] God's presence with Israel is assured through the proclamation of the divine name, which recounted God's mighty deeds of deliverance (Exodus 33). The revelation of the name disclosed God as transcendent, while the glory manifested revealed God's nearness.[16] With the Assyrian threat near at hand, Israel is already pictured as straying from their covenant vows and the presence of God. God called Israel "son" at the Exodus, but the more Israel was called in this way the further from God they drifted (Hos. 11:1-2).

Later, in the process of Babylonian exile, Israel felt that it had failed beyond recovery. They were devastated by hopelessness to the degree that life had been totally drained from them: "Our bones are dried up and our hope is gone; we are cut off" (Ezek. 37:11).

---

[14] Jan Milič Lochman, *Signposts to Freedom: The Ten Commands and Christian Ethics* (Philadelphia, MN: Augsburg Fortress, 1982).

[15] R. H. Fuller, "Church, Assembly," in *A Theological Word Book of the Bible*, ed. Alan Richardson (New York: Collier Books, 1950), 46 (46–49).

[16] See Samuel Terrien, *The Elusive Presence: Toward a New Biblical Theology* (New York: Harper Collins, 1983).

Israel is pictured as a vast valley of dry bones turning to dust. God's question to the prophet in 37:3 is thus key: "Can these bones live?" If not, Israel had indeed reached the end of their story, of their elect purpose. God sovereignly decides that these bones will indeed live again. In a way reminiscent of Adam's creation from the dust by the breath of God, Ezekiel's prophecy is made effectual when the breath symbolic of God's Spirit sweeps into the valley to raise Israel up from the dust of despair. Imparting new life through the Spirit and the word of prophecy is the unique domain of the Lord of creation: "I will put breath in you, and you will come to life. Then you will know that I am the Lord" (37:6). Israel as a covenant people is rich with an institutionalized cult that guides their worship and life, but at their core they live from the Spirit mediated by the word of prophecy. The Spirit received through the word will be key to their restoration as a people.

Ezekiel connects this restoration to Israel's return from exile, making this return more than a mere physical relocation (37:14). Ezekiel analyzes the problem in the previous chapter (ch. 36) in which God faults Israel for profaning his name before the nations. But involved in their return, God will put the divine Spirit in them and they will have their hearts turned from stone to flesh. They will obey the law in devotion to God and by implication honor God before the nations (36:22-27, cf. 39:7). Prophecies of the restoration of Israel in Ezekiel "all share the common themes of Israel's ingathering, the sanctification of the divine name in the eyes of the nations, Israel's return to its land, and the people's recognition that 'I am God.'"[17] This restoration for Ezekiel is obviously profoundly spiritual and viewed as the fulfillment of humanity's creation from the dust by the breath of God. The Spirit gives life for communion with God and divine vocation. Humanity is enabled to receive God's revelation and to bear witness to God's holy name in speech and action.[18] N. T. Wright notes that in the Israelite mind at the time of Jesus there was a sense in which the return from exile was still incomplete as a spiritual reality. A spiritual restoration was yet to come.[19]

Joel foretells of a latter-day outpouring of the Holy Spirit that will cause God's people to prophesy and all who call upon the name of the Lord will be saved (2:28). There will be deliverance "even among the survivors," implying that the coming outpouring of the Spirit will occasion either judgment or restoration, depending on the response (2:32). The coming of the Spirit is implicitly tied to the coming of an anointed one who will bear the Spirit of Torah piety: wisdom, understanding, counsel, might, knowledge, and fear of the Lord (Isa. 11:1-3). He will set the captives free and proclaim the day of the Lord's favor (61:1-3). There were kings who dotted the landscape of Israel's history but none of their reigns involved such an outpouring of the Spirit and the nation's final restoration; none of them credibly took as their possession the ends of the earth: "And I will make the nations your inheritance, the ends of the earth your possession" (Ps. 2:8). The Messiah will ascend to the throne of God to reign over the nations (Dan. 7:13-14).

---

[17] Tova Ganzel, "The Descriptions of the Restoration of Israel in Ezekiel," *VT* 60 (2010): 200 (197–211).
[18] Th. C. Vriezen, *An Outline of Old Testament Theology* (Newton, MA: Charles T. Branford, 1970), 212.
[19] N. T. Wright, "Yet the Sun Will Rise Again: Reflections on the Exile and Restoration in Second Temple Judaism, Jesus, Paul, and the Church Today," *Exile: A Conversation with N. T. Wright*, ed. James M. Scott (Downers Grove, IL: IVP Academic), 19–82.

Gerhard Von Rad remarked that with each king Israel was implicitly asking, "Are you he who is to come, or shall we look for another?"[20] The question was urgent for the deliverance and restoration of the nation and the salvation of the nations were at stake. The atonement offered to Isaiah (Isa. 6:6-7) will need to be extended to all before they can prophesy and attain final restoration as God's people.

Who will make atonement for their sin and all of humanity to whom Israel was called to bear witness? As we will see, before the Messiah ascends to reign he will pass through the fire of humanity's condemnation and death on their behalf but he will not thereby be consumed:

> After he has suffered,
>   he will see the light of life and be satisfied;
> by his knowledge my righteous servant will justify many,
>   and he will bear their iniquities. (Isa. 53:11)

After providing atonement and overcoming the forces of sin and death, he will reign as the Spirit bearer and occasion a mighty outpouring of the Spirit on the earth. The burning hope with which the Old Testament closes is directed to the one who will come bearing the Spirit so as to redeem God's people and restore them to their witness, with the eschatological purpose of claiming the very ends of the earth for the kingdom of God. We will see that "Pentecost is the celebration of Jesus' enthronement as Israel's Messiah and of the Spirit as his 'executive power' in Israel's restoration."[21]

## Spirit Baptism: New Testament

"Jesus will never be without a church."[22] This is because he is the Spirit Baptizer, who unites others to himself to form one body over which he is the Head, forever. Whether Jesus anticipated the birth of a church after his death is a controversial issue in the scholarship.[23] It is true that Jesus only uses the term for church two times in the Gospels; both are in Matthew (16:18; 18:17). And his mission during his sojourn on earth was directed to the household of Israel (Mt. 15:24) and the fulfillment of the kingdom of God (12:28). Yet, there are strong clues that his mission will take him beyond Israel. Luke connects the declaration of Christ's sonship at his baptism in the Spirit with Adam's designation as the "son of God," which opens the benefits of Christ's sonship to Adam's seed (Lk. 3:38). Such is Israel's mission, to bless all peoples. Jesus thus hints that his mission will take him to those who live outside of the bounds of Israel (4:24-27; 23:47). Acts will note that Israel will be restored when the disciples as the beginnings of

---

[20] Gerhard Von Rad, *Old Testament Theology, Vol. II: The Theology of Israel's Prophetic Traditions* (New York: Harper & Row, 1965), 374–75.
[21] George Montague in reviewing Max Turner's book, *Power from on High: The Spirit in Israel's Restoration and Witness in Luke-Acts* (JPTS 9; Sheffield: Sheffield Academic Press, 1996), *The Catholic Biblical Quarterly* 60, no. 1 (1998): 177 (177–78).
[22] Eduard Schweizer, *Church Order in the New Testament*, SBT, No. 32 (London: SCM Press, 1961), 23.
[23] Ibid., 20–33.

eschatological Israel (twelve disciples in the place of twelve tribes) bring their witness to the ends of the earth. Indeed, the ends of the earth are to be made the possession of God's anointed (Ps. 2:8). Toward that end, God's people will revere God's name before the nations when they receive the Spirit (Ezek. 36:23-27), the horizon toward which Christ the faithful Son led his disciples to pray (Lk. 11:2). Thus, Christ's choosing his disciples has ecclesiological significance; it points to Pentecost and the formation of eschatological Israel for its fulfillment. In the Gospels, Jesus prefers the Son of Man title for himself, which points to Dan. 7:13 and to a global and eschatological fulfillment. As eschatological Israel, the disciples and the larger circle of Christ followers will be the basis of a people who will fulfill Israel's calling by transcending it as it was typically understood within a more restricted, nationalist framework.

The disciples and those who follow in their way will baptize all nations in the name of the Father, Son, and Holy Spirit to signify their common baptism in the Holy Spirit (Mt. 28:19). This does not mean that ethnic Israel is "replaced" or forgotten. As we will explore in our next chapter, in Romans 9–11 Paul still hopes that his kinsmen will return to their calling and participate in the messianic and eschatological future now opened up to them in the outpouring of the Spirit. The riches of the Spirit in communion with Christ belong to them too, especially to them. Their loss was the Gentiles' gain so to speak, but their inclusion will bless the church and its witness. Indeed, if "their loss means riches for the Gentiles, how much greater riches will their full inclusion bring!" (Rom. 11:12). Such a return of the natural branches to the tree of life, which was most likely both a missionary hope and an apocalyptic mystery for Paul, would understandably expand Israel and deepen the church's appreciation of its Jewish roots. Such is only possible on the basis of the church's biblical and historic confession of Christ as Messiah and Lord, the one and only Baptizer in the Spirit (Acts 2:33-36). He is the tree or vine into which Gentiles are grafted and from which natural branches are pruned or cut off (Rom. 11:22-24; Jn 15:1-8). The Spirit Baptizer will cause the birth and eschatological flourishing of a Spirit-baptized church but the fire baptism that he bore so as to open us all to the Spirit is still a danger to those who reject him. The branches that are removed are burned up in the fire (Jn 15:6).

Jesus was conceived as the holy Son of God by the Holy Spirit to reveal and impart God through the medium of human flesh in a way that involves new life: the birth of a new community in him. His conception was miraculous as a sign of the eschatological or final significance of what he came to accomplish. The Spirit rested on Mary's womb in a way analogous to the Spirit's resting on the deep at the creation (Lk. 1:35). John the Baptist was filled with the Spirit in his mother's womb but only Jesus was *conceived by the Spirit* (1:15; 35). Only he was conceived as the favored Son, the one who will bear the Spirit in his body in order to extend God's mercy from generation to generation to many potential sons and daughters (1:50). Adam became a living soul by the Spirit to produce seed in his physical image but Christ was earmarked to become the life-giving spirit that produced a family bearing the Spirit in his exalted image (1 Cor. 15:45). John adds that Christ is the eternal Word or self-expression of the Father. Sharing the divine nature (Jn 1:1), the Son alone is the means by which God is seen. He comes forth from the Father to reveal him (1:18). He becomes flesh so that the glory of the Father can be seen and received, for the Son as the Word of the Father is now embodied in flesh. God was revealed in various ways among the prophets of old but only the Son will reveal in flesh the "radiance of God's glory" and the exact image of the divine being or nature (Heb. 1:3).

As God among us, Christ's revelation is life-giving and an open invitation to communion in him: "For as the Father has life in himself, so he has granted the Son also to have life in himself" (Jn 5:26). We are asked to abide in him as he abides in the Father, a communion of life in the love shared between the Father and the Son in the Spirit. We are asked to love each other as we dwell together in the love of the Triune God (15:1-17). Christ is the Word through whom all things were created (1:1-5), and he will also be the mediator of the Spirit of eternal life for all those who believe on him (4:13-14). He becomes the Word or Sacrament of the Spirit for all time. He will bear the Spirit in his flesh for this purpose, to defeat sin and death so as to impart the Spirit of life and communion to all flesh. He came that we might have life, and that to the full (10:10). He will conquer sin and death and reign as Messiah so as to give eternal life to those given to him by the Father (17:2).

As noted earlier, the key announcement that prepared the way for Jesus's messianic mission is given by John the Baptist. The Jordan where John the Baptist baptized the repentant was not ideal due to its shallow depth, especially in the winter months. But the river had historical significance, since the Israelites crossed the Jordan on their way into the Promised Land. The repentant led by John the Baptist implicitly left their sins behind in the Jordan and reentered the land with a burning hope for a new era of salvation. And John provided them with a dramatic image of how that era would come. Using his baptismal rite as the root metaphor, he pictured the Messiah as occasioning a river of the Spirit in the world into which the Messiah will "baptize" the repentant unto restoration. The non-repentant would face judgment. Note Luke's account:

> John answered them all, "I baptize you with water. But one who is more powerful than I will come, the straps of whose sandals I am not worthy to untie. He will baptize you with the Holy Spirit and fire. His winnowing fork is in his hand to clear his threshing floor and to gather the wheat into his barn, but he will burn up the chaff with unquenchable fire." (3:16-17)

There is a mixture of images here. The messianic baptizing in the Spirit is obviously restorative. The restored are the ones who represent the wheat to be stored into barns. But the imagery turns to fire and wind once the judgment is described. The baptism in fire consumes the unrighteous or they as the chaff are blown away by the strong wind leaving the wheat to be stored for a useful purpose. It would be appropriate to assume that the coming of the Spirit is doing the work of both restoration and judgment. The baptism in both Spirit and fire (restoration and judgment) are accomplished by the end-time Spirit that will sweep across the earth at the coming of the Messiah. The Spirit is explicitly connected to the restoration of the repentant and only implied in the fire of judgment. Dunn helps us through this complexity by referring to a messianic baptism of "Spirit and fire" in which the Spirit is the agent of the fire too, though the Spirit is properly and fundamentally described as restoring repentant Israel.[24]

---

[24] James D. G. Dunn, "Spirit-and-Fire Baptism," *NT* 14, no. 2 (April 1972): 81–92.

The idea that John the Baptist may with the entire Spirit-and-fire baptism have been referring to the sanctification of the repentant (with the fire burning away the sin from their lives) individualizes John's metaphor too much and fails to account for the dividing of the ways between the repentant and the non-repentant that is part of John's larger message. Likewise, the idea that John's entire metaphor is a destruction of judgment, with the baptism in the Spirit and fire representing judgment only, also misses the same dividing-of-the-ways motif. The separating of the wheat from the chaff and the storing of wheat into barns implies a restoration motif. Plus, John the Baptist is speaking at least in part to hopeful repentants who were looking for the time of redemption and restoration. To refer to judgment only would hardly have spoken to their situation. John was proclaiming the arrival of the kingdom of God as the overall context of his message (cf., Mt. 3:2). In that context, the Baptist looks forward to a messianic arrival in the power of the Spirit. He will bring the Spirit with him as a mighty force that ushers in the kingdom of God on earth (Mt. 12:28). The result will be the redemption and restoration of the repentant and the judgment of the non-repentant.

John's Gospel informs us that John the Baptist knew that Jesus was the chosen Spirit Baptizer, because John beheld the Spirit rest upon him (Jn 1:33-34). John's Gospel does not mention Jesus's baptism in water, making the arrival of the Spirit the decisive factor in Jesus's identity as the Spirit Baptizer. Matthew, Mark, and Luke connect this arrival more closely to Jesus's water baptism (Mt. 3:13-17; Mk 1:4-11; Lk. 3:21-22). Luke mentions that Jesus was praying to the Father at the time of the Spirit's arrival, implying a personal connection between Jesus's submission to the Father's will and the Father's response in sending the Spirit upon him. Beholding the event of the Spirit's resting upon Jesus, John the Baptist could only stand in awe. He does not stand within this fulfillment but before it. He is a forerunner—a witness to its coming arrival. Only Jesus conceived by the Spirit has eschatological transcendence. Only he will usher in the kingdom of God that both he and John proclaimed. Hence Jesus, and not John, is essential to the message that they proclaimed, for in accepting Jesus's message, the repentant will end up accepting *him* as essential to that gospel (Jn 1:12). His arrival as the divine Logos in flesh is at core the promise of reconciliation of God with all flesh. His bearing the Spirit is the promise of Spirit bearing for all flesh. This cannot be said of John the Baptist. He is in no sense an equal partner, for he is not the light that has come to conquer the darkness; all that he can do is bear witness to that light which is Christ (1:6-8).

As noted earlier, when the Spirit arrives to rest on Jesus, the heavens open and the Father declares: "You are my Son, whom I love; with you I am well pleased" (Lk. 3:22). Both the heaven rending open and the voice of God imply an apocalyptic event that is to be recognized as pivotal for the coming of the kingdom of God.[25] Dunn is right: "The decisive change in the ages was effected by the Spirit coming down upon Jesus."[26] The resting of the Spirit in the form of a dove (Lk. 1:22) implies a new creation motif, perhaps harking back to the brooding of the Spirit upon the deep at creation, or the

---

[25] John Nolland, *Luke 1–9:20*, WBC 35A (Dallas: Word, 1989), 162.
[26] Dunn, *The Baptism in the Holy Spirit*, 26.

sign of new creation at the time of Noah.[27] As noted earlier, Luke traces Jesus's lineage all the way back to "Adam the son of God" (3:38). Jesus is baptized in the Spirit not only to redeem and restore Israel but also to bring the blessings of salvation in the Spirit to all nations, to all of Adam's seed. Christ as the eschatological Adam is hailed the eschatological Son of God by his heavenly Father at the waters of the Jordan to fulfill the mission to Adam and Eve's seed. Jesus's reception of the Spirit may be called Jesus's own baptism in the Spirit, for he must bear the Spirit before he can impart the Spirit through the medium of his faithful life upon others. His conception by the Spirit already foreshadows and sets him apart for his reception of the Spirit at the Jordan, and both foreshadow Jesus's resurrection in the fullness of the Spirit (cf., Rom. 1:4).

In the light of the eschatological significance of Jesus's baptism in the Spirit, I wish to stress two features of Jesus's Spirit baptism: The first is that the Spirit rests upon Jesus and remains (Jn 1:33). God had promised Israel that the Spirit will not depart from them (Isa. 59:21). Jesus represents the fulfillment of that promise. As the eternal Son of the Father, Jesus has access to an enduring supply of the Spirit and as the sinless man he bears the Spirit without possibility of separation or blasphemy. Moreover, the Spirit is committed to remain with Jesus all the way to the cross and beyond so that Jesus as the Spirit Baptizer can bear the Spirit so as to impart the Spirit upon all flesh as his first act when taking his throne as Messiah and Lord (Acts 2:32-36). His Spirit baptism is both an event and a journey that will find fulfillment in his resurrection. And so is our Spirit baptism an event with a vast eschatological fulfillment. Christ rises in the fullness of the Spirit; his exaltation is the culmination of his Spirit baptism, for his risen body is a "spiritual body" (better, "Spirit body"), becoming a "life-giving spirit" (1 Cor. 15:42-45).

Pentecost is the pivotal point between Jesus's Spirit baptism and his baptizing others in the Spirit, and the former is paradigmatic of the latter. Christ mediates the Spirit through the Word or Sacrament of his faithful, Spirit-baptized life. So, Christ's work throughout his sojourn on earth ends up being revelatory of the Spirit's work, and the Spirit's work is after Pentecost revelatory of Christ's. So in imparting the Spirit, Christ ends up imparting his crucified and risen life to us. In the Spirit, we walk in the path of his cruciform life, in fellowship with his sufferings and the power of his overcoming life (Gal. 2:20; Phil. 3:10). Pentecost is the pivot point from the Christ of the Spirit (Christ following the leading of the Spirit) to the Spirit of Christ (the Spirit revealing and imparting Christ to others) as Moltmann has helpfully stated.[28] The pivot point is Christ as the Imparter of the Spirit to all flesh. That the Spirit remained with the Son all the way to the cross means that the event of the cross contained within it a hidden passage through the fire of condemnation and death—a passage that is fulfilled at the resurrection. Rising in the fullness of the Spirit, he is vindicated as the faithful Son (1 Tim. 3:15) and sanctified as the one who justifies and sanctifies others (Jn 17:19). He imparts the Spirit to us out of that abundance. The resurrection and Pentecost mean

---

[27] Donald Hagner, *Matthew 1–13*, WBC 33A (Dallas: Word, 1993), 58.
[28] Jürgen Moltmann, *The Spirit of Life: A Universal Affirmation* (Minneapolis: Fortress Press, 1992), 60–70.

that "crosses" endured today can also have that same potential (that groaning) for a new beginning in God, because God is with us even in the depths of despair.

Second, as implied earlier, Christ received the Spirit at the Jordan without measure (Jn 3:34). As the eternal Son of the Father he has an unimaginably abundant access to the life of the Spirit: "For as the Father has life in himself, so he has granted the Son also to have life in himself" (5:26). Christ will realize the full effects of this abundance in his fleshly sojourn to the cross and the resurrection. As Clark Pinnock notes, Christ is ontologically the Son at his incarnation but he becomes the Christ in his flesh by way of the Spirit from his incarnation all the way to his exaltation.[29] He does this so that all flesh might receive the benefits of his Spirit-anointed life, which includes the privilege of participation in his mission. The Son prays that he will attain in his flesh the glory that he had as the Son from before the foundation of the world (Jn 17:5). From his abundance of the Spirit will flow rivers of living water (7:38).[30] He thus becomes the Word or Sacrament of the Spirit to all flesh. The church's kerygmatic and sacramental life depends on his mediation of the Spirit as the Word or Sacrament of the Spirit for all time. It pleased God to have the fullness of deity dwell in his embodied existence so that in his exalted state he would be the never-ending resource of spiritual fullness for us: "For in Christ all the fullness of the Deity lives in bodily form, and in Christ you have been brought to fullness. He is the head over every power and authority" (Col. 1:19-20). Paul's reference to all the fullness of deity living in bodily form was fully revealed at Christ's resurrection. Our commonly shared access to the Spirit is of course dependent on him, for by him we are baptized into the one Spirit "and we were all given the one Spirit to drink" (1 Cor. 12:13). And the revelation of the fullness of the Spirit in us (the revelation of the children of God, Rom. 8:19) will occur at *our* resurrection.

At Jesus's resurrection, the Father declares with eschatological finality by way of the "Spirit of holiness" that Jesus is the Son who will impart the benefits of his sonship to us (Rom. 1:4). He does this by granting us the Spirit of sonship by which we cry Abba as he did, as we await the culmination of our own baptism in the Spirit in his image (Rom. 8:15-23). Jesus rose from Mary's womb conceived of the Spirit as the Son set apart for this eschatological purpose. He then rises from the Jordan baptized in the Spirit and commissioned for his redemptive and restorative journey. He finally rises from the dead in the fullness of the Spirit installed at the right hand of the Father as Lord and Messiah to impart the Spirit and with the Spirit his own life to all flesh (Acts 2:33-36).[31] Only at Pentecost when the Spirit Baptized becomes the Spirit Baptizer is Jesus's mission as Messiah (who bears the Spirit) and as Lord (who imparts the Spirit) complete. Jesus came to give life to the full (Jn 10:10), for Christ was granted authority

---

[29] Clark Pinnock, *Flame of Love: A Theology of the Holy Spirit* (Downers Grove, IL: InterVarsity Press, 1999), 91-92.
[30] In part, I favor the reading of Jn 7:38 that states "out of him" (Christ) will flow rivers of living water that will well up within believers unto eternal life (4:14). See Joel Marcus, "Rivers of Living Water from Jesus' Belly (John 7:38)," *JBL* 117, no. 2 (1998): 328-30.
[31] I have found helpful here Kilian McDonnell, *The Baptism of Jesus in the Jordan: The Trinitarian and Cosmic Order of Salvation* (Collegeville, MN: Liturgical Press, 1996), 168-69.

to reign so as to give life to others (17:2). He rises as the "life-giving spirit" (1 Cor. 15:45).[32]

Jesus's Spirit baptism also occurred in the midst of his baptism in fire on our behalf. His life of being led by the Spirit leads not only to his victory and exaltation (the fulfillment of his baptism in the Spirit) but also to his humiliation and death on our behalf (his baptism in fire). He takes on flesh for this purpose. Note this text in Hebrews 2, where Christ thanks God for giving him his family of brothers and sisters. He is not ashamed to wed himself to sinners as his brothers and sisters so as to save them from the devil's slavery to sin and death. For this purpose he takes on flesh. Note the whole passage:

> [12] He says,
> "I will declare your name to my brothers and sisters;
>   in the assembly I will sing your praises."
> [13] And again,
> "I will put my trust in him."
> And again he says,
> "Here am I, and the children God has given me."
> [14] Since the children have flesh and blood, he too shared in their humanity so that
>   by his death he might break the power of him who holds the power of death—
>   that is, the devil—[15] and free those who all their lives were held in slavery by
>   their fear of death. (2:12-15)

The Son who is the "radiance of the God's glory" and the "exact representation of his being" (1:3) is not ashamed to bind himself to sinners, take on their mortal flesh, and journey before them to their captivity to the devil, to condemnation and death, so as to save them. The faithful Son who is the eternal word of the Father's love condescends in the power of that love to take on mortal flesh in the Virgin's womb (Jn 1:1-18), not considering equality with God as "something to be used to his own advantage" (Phil. 2:6).[33] Following the Christological hymn of Phil. 2:6-11 further,[34] he "made himself

---

[32] See my development of this approach to Christology in *Jesus the Spirit Baptizer: Christ in Light of Pentecost*.

[33] The literal wording of the text here points to Christ's refusal to "grasp after" or "steal" divine glory through mighty deeds as Greek heroes such as Hercules were famed to have done. Rather than Christ's life representing an upward climb toward divine status for his own aggrandizement, Jesus's path was the exact opposite. He came from a divine glory that was his by nature and by sovereign right but freely out of love identified with lowly humanity and took on their suffering and rejection so as to deliver them and bring them to glory. So the translation of the NIV here, that Christ did not use his divine identity "to his own advantage" is a good one. Though not literal, it captures well the spirit of the text.

[34] Ernst Lohmeyer made the argument nearly a century ago that most of Philippians 2:6-11 was a hymn sung in the ancient church because the original language seemed lyrical. Especially since the Greek is not typically Pauline, it seems quoted from a hymnic source. Also, Lohmeyer argued that the Greek is awkward in places where it appears to imply an Aramaic original. If this song were a Greek translation of an Aramaic original, it would arguably go back to the original Jerusalem church and be among the most ancient texts in the New Testament. Note Ernst Lohmeyer, *Kyrios Jesus; eine Versuchung zu Phil. 2, 5-11* (Heidelberg: C. Winter, 1928). For an excellent summary of his argument in English, note Colin Brown, "Ernst Lohmeyer's Kyrios Jesus," in *Where Christology*

nothing by taking the very nature of a servant"[35] and "being made in human likeness" "humbled himself by becoming obedient to death—even death on a cross!"

Jesus's journey to the cross is his baptism in fire on our behalf. John the Baptist foresaw that Christ would baptize others in the "Spirit and fire," and John witnessed him being baptized in the Spirit for this purpose at the Jordan. As noted earlier, John did not know that Christ would first himself experience the baptism in fire to provide humanity with deliverance from condemnation and to grant them entry into the baptism in the Spirit. Jesus speaks of this baptism in fire in Lk. 12:49-50: "I have come to bring fire on the earth, and how I wish it were already kindled! But I have a baptism to undergo, and what constraint I am under until it is completed!" The baptism that Jesus feels constrained to take is the baptism of his death. Significantly, he speaks of his own fire baptism in the context of the fiery judgment that he will ignite upon the earth at the end time in bringing the kingdom of God (as John the Baptist foretold). Jesus wishes that the fire were already ignited and the kingdom already come. But he knows that he has a baptism in this fire to endure first, the baptism of his death. As Joseph Fitzmyer notes, the fire baptism of Christ's death in Lk. 12:49-50 "is not one that he merely administers to others but that he must undergo; he who baptizes with fire must himself face the testing and *krisis* that the figure connotes."[36]

Elsewhere, Jesus describes his coming death as analogous to Jonah's sinking beneath the waves of banishment from God, but not one that will ultimately lead to his permanent demise. As we saw earlier from Jon. 2:3-6, Jonah's plunge beneath the waves was more threateningly spiritual than physical, "I have been banished from your sight" (2:4). It was a plunge into a realm of divine judgment. But Jonah maintained hope and

---

*Began: Essays on Philippians 2*, ed. Ralph P. Martin and Brian J. Dodd (Louisville, KY: Westminster John Knox, 1998), 6–42.

[35] The original language behind the phrase, "made himself nothing," indicates literally being "emptied" (he poured himself out). The term for this (transliterated *ekenosen*) probably refers in this hymn to Christ's pouring out his life as a sacrificial offering for us. But the word "kenotic" (connected to *ekenosen* as used in Phil. 2:7) has a lengthy history in Christology, sparking a debate over what exactly the divine Son had to empty himself of in taking on mortal flesh. Though this is not the point of Phil. 2:7, the debate over whether or not the Son emptied himself of any divine attributes in becoming flesh raged on. The idea that he laid aside certain divine attributes such as omniscience or omnipresence in becoming flesh seems difficult to comprehend, since God cannot give up attributes that are essential to his nature and still be divine. The idea that he didn't give up any attributes but simply did not exercise them during his sojourn from the womb to the cross seems more promising. But this idea makes one wonder whether or not the divine Son was still transcendent while he was also fully present in flesh. In other words, did the eternal Son of the Father continue sustaining all things in creation (Heb. 1:3) while he journeyed in flesh? It would seem so. Thomas V. Morris has argued that the Son had a higher consciousness and more expansive presence and work that exercised all divine attributes (omniscience, omnipresence, etc.) and a lower consciousness that fully experienced the limitations of human flesh, entirely dependent as any flesh would be on revelations given from the Father and in the Spirit for what he knew and did. His dual consciousness would have functioned in a way that is analogous to our own conscious and subconscious mind. We have one mind that exists on two levels, a conscious one that is more limited in scope and a subconscious mind that is more expansive. Using that as an analogy, we can understand how Jesus as the Son of the Father in flesh could have one mind that has two functions—a more expansive (transcendent) and a more limited (in flesh) at the same time. Though the higher consciousness would experience all that the lower consciousness does, the reverse would not be true for Jesus's human consciousness until the exaltation. See Morris's *The Logic of God Incarnate* (Ithica, NY: Cornell University Press, 1986).

[36] Joseph A. Fitzmyer, *The Gospel according to Luke I-IX*, AB, Vol. 28 (New York: Doubleday, 1970), 995.

rose up from this plight to preach to Nineveh. So also will the Son of Man descend into a fire baptism that will plunge him into the depths of banishment from God. But, as with Jonah, he will rise on the third day to fulfill God's mission on the earth. Here is Jesus making this connection with Jonah in Mt. 12:38-41:

> Then some of the Pharisees and teachers of the law said to him, "Teacher, we want to see a sign from you."
>
> He answered, "A wicked and adulterous generation asks for a sign! But none will be given it except the sign of the prophet Jonah. For as Jonah was three days and three nights in the belly of a huge fish, so the Son of Man will be three days and three nights in the heart of the earth. The men of Nineveh will stand up at the judgment with this generation and condemn it; for they repented at the preaching of Jonah, and now something greater than Jonah is here."

When the Jewish leaders who clashed with Jesus requested a visible sign to authenticate his claims, Jesus directed them to the "sign of Jonah," which bitingly identified them with Nineveh! The sign they would receive is the sign of Jonah as fulfilled in Jesus's death for our sins and resurrection so as to offer us new life. The horizon of this statement from Jesus is thus the mission of the Spirit-baptized church at Pentecost.

That one greater than Jonah will bring about such a sign involves the fact that Jonah was a disobedient prophet who had to be plunged into despair in order to bring him to his mission in spite of the offense that he took at the thought of God showing grace to the wicked enemies of Israel (Jon. 4:1-3). By contrast, Jesus gives his life for Israel and the nations as the embodiment of God's love for them. Not only this, but Jonah proclaimed a message in which he himself played no essential role, while Jesus as the divine Son in flesh was himself the center of the good news that the world will receive through his work: "Yet to all who did receive him, to those who believed in his name, he gave the right to become children of God" (Jn 1:12). Jesus will suffer condemnation for the whole world and will rise in the fullness of the Spirit to bring others into his fullness. No mere human prophet, even a remarkably obedient one, can accomplish this!

Jesus's baptism in fire actually has its roots in the incarnation, for Jesus was conceived as flesh by the Spirit for such a baptism as this: "Since the children have flesh and blood, he too shared in their humanity so that by his death he might break the power of him who holds the power of death—that is, the devil" (Heb. 2:14). At the Jordan, at the moment of his Spirit baptism and installation as Messiah, he took his first public steps in the direction of his baptism in fire. Recall what was said earlier about how John the Baptist's water rite dramatized repentant Israel's leaving its sins behind in the Jordan and reentering the Promised Land with hope for the coming Messiah and the restoration in the latter-day outpouring of the Spirit that he will bring. Jesus did not need to be baptized by John. He did not need to repent or leave his sins behind. But he joins himself to the sinners in order to lead them from condemnation and death to justification and life. He joins the sinners in the waters of repentance to "fulfill all righteousness" (Mt. 3:15), which he will do in his journey to the cross. He will fulfill righteousness for the entire world. Jesus emerges from his reception of the Spirit at the Jordan mightily filled with the Spirit and proclaiming himself as the Messiah who will bring to the earth the coming restoration:

> The Spirit of the Lord is on me,
>   because he has anointed me
>   to proclaim good news to the poor.
> He has sent me to proclaim freedom for the prisoners
>   and recovery of sight for the blind,
>   to set the oppressed free,
>   to proclaim the year of the Lord's favor. (Lk. 4:18-19)

In Christ, God turns with mercy to sinners and begins a new latter-day time of redemption, restoration, and social liberation.

Then the Spirit leads him to his temptation in the desert, where he faces testing not only as Israel did in their desert wandering but also as Adam and Eve did from the dark and crafty tempter in the Garden. But throughout, Christ is faithful to the Father's will. As the faithful Son, he opens up his prayer life to others and indicates that only in him is new covenant access to the Father possible (Mt. 6:9; 11:27; cf., Jn 14:6; Acts 4:12). As the faithful Son and man of the Spirit, he fulfills Israel's mandate to revere the Father's name on all the earth as it is revered in heaven (Mt. 6:9; recall what was said earlier from Ezek. 36:22-27). He breaks bread with sinners, forgives them when they repent, and heals the sick and outcasts. In healing them, he shows God's favor to them (cf., Lk 15:1; Mk 2:10-12). He proclaims judgment on the Temple and implies that he is now the center of God's presence and favor on earth, of access to the Father. They will cling to a temple that God will take down and the temple of his body that they will seek to take down God will raise up (Mt. 24:2; Jn 2:19).

He journeys to the Garden, where he faces his supreme moment of trial prior to the cross. As he nears the cross, he becomes the man of sorrows: "My soul is overwhelmed with sorrow to the point of death" (Mk 14:34). Asking the disciples to pray that they not fall into temptation, he informs them that the Spirit is willing but the flesh is weak (14:38). The Spirit here is the willing Holy Spirit, who is leading Jesus to the fulfillment of the Father's will, the same Spirit that led him to his trial in the desert at the start of his ministry (1:12).[37] The flesh is weak but the Spirit is willing. Jesus feels the weakness of flesh too but finds the strength to follow the willing Spirit, which is his own desire as well. Jesus tests his discernment of the Father's will one last time in the Garden, praying for the passing of this cup of suffering, but only if the Father wills it: "Yet not what I will, but what you will" (14:36). There is no masochistic desire for suffering here. Jesus walks this path because it is the Father's will; it is unavoidable. The willing Spirit directs Christ to his destiny as the Father has willed it and accompanies him there.

So what is the role of the atonement in Christ identity and work as the Baptizer in the Holy Spirit? To begin with, let us discuss the importance of this question. Relevant

---

[37] D. Lyle Dabney, "Naming the Spirit: Towards a Pneumatology of the Cross," in *Starting with the Spirit*, Task of Theology 2, ed. Stephen Pickard and Gordon Preece (Hindmarsh, AU: Australian Theological Forum, 2001), 51–52.

here is Jürgen Moltmann's observation that one cannot be so dazzled by the glory of the resurrection that one neglects Jesus's experience of alienation on the cross.[38] Plus, the incarnation-atonement link forged by the West (especially Anselm) helped to secure the fact that Christ is in himself the event of reconciliation for all time. Atonement is the event that brings to fulfillment the implications of the wedding of God and flesh that are found in the incarnation. Karl Barth may be viewed as a representative of the weight granted to the incarnation-atonement connection in the West. For Barth, Jesus's salvific work indicated by the incarnation is completed at the cross. At the cross, the Son of Man not only goes out to the "far country" of human alienation but also returns from the far country to the household of the Father. The resurrection then "reveals" the victory of the cross over sin and death so as to open access to this victory to humanity, and Pentecost then tends to be reduced to the subjective possibility of responding to the revelation of the resurrection in faith.[39] As helpful as it is, the possible shortcoming of this incarnation-atonement link is that the role of the Spirit in Christ's messianic mission can be neglected, as it has. The significance of his reception of the Spirit at the Jordan (highlighted in the Gospels) is then eclipsed. The promise that he will baptize in the Spirit then plays no role in how we understand the climax of his mission at his death and resurrection. What role the Spirit plays in his atonement is unclear. What does Anselm have to say about this in his classic tome on the atonement? Almost nothing. The cosmic significance of the atonement for Anselm implies it, but the explicit connection between atonement and pneumatology is not made.

I have suggested a way forward with my idea of Christ's death and resurrection as the climax of Jesus's baptism in the Spirit and fire on our behalf. This climactic event makes Christ the objective event of reconciliation between God and humanity *and* it makes Jesus the one who mediates the Spirit to us. That Christ is baptized in the fiery pneuma at the cross only to emerge vindicated and sanctified by that very same Spirit can be a step forward in bringing clarity. At the cross and through the resurrection, Christ opens passage for sinners through the fire of condemnation and death to the "Promised Land" of the Spirit and the new creation, which he ushers in at Pentecost by baptizing in the Spirit. We speak of a new exodus. The cross in this light occurs as Christ offers himself up "by the eternal Spirit" on our behalf (Heb. 9:14) and concludes when this Spirit is offered to us so that we could as a community of prophets and priests benefit from, and join ourselves to, his self-offering to God.

This idea can also help us to see the soteriological significance of Christ's resurrection by the Spirit. The resurrection becomes the fulfillment of Christ baptism in the Spirit—a point that is needed to grant the resurrection its full significance in our understanding of Christ's messianic mission. Clark Pinnock rightly complains, "It is incredible how in systematic theologies hundreds of pages are given to theories of atonement (meaning the death of Christ) and hardly any to the soteriological significance of the resurrection."[40] The resurrection is more than the revelation of the

---

[38] Moltmann, *The Church in the Power of the Spirit*, 36–37.
[39] See Karl Barth's lengthy discussion of the homecoming of the Son of Man, *CD*, Vol. IV, pt. 2, *The Doctrine of Reconciliation*, ed. G. W. Bromiley and T. F. Torrance (Edinburgh: T & T Clark, 1978), 20–154.
[40] Pinnock, *Flame of Love*, 99.

victory of the cross. Yes, the victory of the resurrection is present already at the cross but only as its *telos*. The resurrection is the fulfillment of the cross in that the Spirit of life is involved in Jesus's self-offering as he makes passage through the baptism in fire for us. But the resurrection as the fulfillment of that passage, the complete realization in his flesh of his baptism in the Spirit, makes the resurrection a fulfillment in its own right. As the Reconciler, Jesus also becomes the sacrament or word of the Spirit to all flesh. Pinnock rightly notes that sin and death requires both reconciliation and life as the solution. I have argued elsewhere in this light that even the resurrection is incomplete without Pentecost, for as Paul tells us, Jesus rose from the dead the life-giving spirit (1 Cor. 15:45). That he came to give life and that more abundant (Jn 10:10) is part of the gospel.

To be a little more specific, the faithful Son had our iniquity laid on him (Isa. 53:6) and bore our sins for us (1 Pet. 2:24). His crucifiers considered him stricken of God but he was pierced for *our* transgressions (Isa. 53:4-5). He is condemned at the cross so that in his rising in the Spirit he may justify us (Rom. 4:25) and sanctify us (Jn 17:19; Rom. 1:4). He was wounded at the cross so that rising in the Spirit he could heal us (Isa. 53:5). He enters our captivity to sin and death on the cross so that rising in the Spirit we may be freed from their hold (Heb. 2:14-15). He partook of our mortality so that rising in the Spirit he could grant us a share in his immortality (2 Cor. 5:4). He was baptized in the fire of God's judgment so that rising in the Spirit his own Spirit-filled life could overflow onto others who receive him and his gospel by faith. In passing through the fire of judgment as the faithful Son and man of the Spirit, he replaces the fire with a sanctifying journey into God. The Spirit joins with him and the Father in this divine overcoming of wrath so as to extend love to undeserving sinners. The Triune God overcomes God's own wrath at the cross so as to extend mercy to sinners. In passing through the fire in this way, Jesus opens space in himself for sinners, all sinners, in all of their diversity. He is already at the cross joining with the Spirit in creating space for his church.[41] He passes through the fire of condemnation representing them all and passes through it to the communion and life in the Spirit, the communion of his own sonship in relation to the Father. In the Spirit we cry Abba (Rom. 8:15-16). He is exalted to the throne to reign at the right hand of his Father, who is the source of the Spirit of life. Christ's first act is to fulfill the Father's promise of restoration by imparting the Spirit from the Father to all flesh out of his own fullness (Acts 2:33-36). "Son though he was, he learned obedience from what he suffered and, once made perfect, he became the source of eternal salvation for all who obey him" (Heb. 5:8-9). This makes him the Spirit Baptizer and the people of God the Spirit-baptized church.

In faith under the sign of water baptism, we join Christ in his passage from death to life. We are "baptized into his death" through baptism meaning that we join our death to his and pass through it with him. In so doing we allow our baptism in fire to be transformed into his sanctifying journey, in which we leave our sins and our condemned selves behind and embrace a new identity as baptized in the Spirit in union with Christ, which eschatologically is the risen church (Rom. 6:5). As a foretaste, we drink together of the Spirit in communion toward deeper union with Christ toward

---

[41] Wolfhart Pannenberg, *Systematic Theology*, Vol. 2 (Grand Rapids, MI: Eerdmans, 1994), 432.

deeper and more expansive eschatological fulfillment (1 Cor. 12:13). The center of our loyalty shifts from the former self who lived in sin and condemnation to the new self earmarked for resurrection who is even now centered on Christ, in communion with him, and in service for him. We move from being slaves to sin and death to being sons and daughters of God, brothers and sisters of Christ. We await our adoption to sonship and daughtership which occurs at the resurrection ("the redemption of our bodies," Rom. 8:23), but even now we can cry "Abba" by the Spirit and be assured by the Spirit that we are already God's family of children (8:15-16). We hallow God's name before the nations and through our Spirit-empowered witness to the risen Christ become the central means by which the ends of the earth become the possession of God's Messiah (Ps. 2:8). Paul captures this new exodus idea of the atonement well in Rom. 8:15: "The Spirit you received does not make you slaves, so that you live in fear again; rather, the Spirit you received brought about your adoption to sonship. And by him we cry, '*Abba*, Father.'" We do not fear a return to bondage for the exodus to life has already been taken, even of it is not yet eschatologically possessed (8:23). Out of Egypt God called Israel as "son" (Hos. 11:1). Out of *sheol* God declared Jesus as the Son with eschatological finality by the Spirit (Rom. 1:4). Christ is the Son for all time; Israel was called to foreshadow him. Christ's exodus is the exodus for all time; Israel's is but a type. So now we by faith in Christ receive the Spirit of sonship from him and are incorporated into his body and into his communion with the Father. It is this exodus with Christ from sin and death to the life of the Spirit that we confirm and signify in water baptism. We die with him and rise with him (Rom. 6:1-6). We share in the baptism of his death so that the fire that would otherwise consume us is now the means of our sanctification.

So also the eucharist plays a role in enhancing and furthering the communion enjoyed in the church's baptism in the Spirit. Spirit baptism encompasses both water baptism and the life of the eucharist. We should bear in mind that Jesus spoke of his death as a ransom—an offering that would secure our freedom from captivity, but he later enriched the meaning further by speaking of his death as a sacrificial offering in which his broken body and spilled blood, his life poured out without condition, opens up the possibility of a new covenant life shared together in communion. As Jesus noted at the Last Supper, his death is covenant making, or opens a path to the new covenant of the Spirit celebrated at baptism and eucharist. His blood is the cup of the new covenant (1 Cor. 11:25). Pentecost is the horizon of the cross. The Spirit-baptized church that hears the word, is baptized, and gathers at the Lord's table has passed with Christ from death to life, or is passing from death to life, baptized ever-more deeply into Christ, toward fulfillment at resurrection, our ultimate vindication (justification) and sanctification.

There is indeed a major place for a doctrine of atonement within the fulfillment of John the Baptist's announcement that Jesus will baptize in the Holy Spirit and fire. In being the mediator of the Spirit, Christ is in his very person and work the reconciliation between God and humanity. But this reconciliation is not static or shallow theologically. It's more substantively and pneumatologically a dynamic communion of life in the Holy Spirit. The reconciliation between God and humanity representatively made possible in Jesus's death on the cross and resurrection replaces alienation with communion. As the victory of that communion, the resurrection does not just reveal the cross; the resurrection fulfills it. In opening up that communion to humanity, Pentecost completes the journey, for the cross was never meant to be a drama enclosed within the Son's relationship to the Father. Jesus experienced the cross *for us*. He journeys through that fire bearing the Spirit as an exodus, overcoming the destructive barriers of condemnation and death so as to open a path for humanity to communion and life. The resurrection completes that journey representatively; Pentecost opens up that journey as an actuality for all flesh. It is for this reason Christ died, for this reason he took on anointed flesh. Baptized in the Spirit, we make that journey with him from death to life, from alienation to communion. The entirety of the church's life as an effective sign of grace celebrates and mediates this passage from death to life offered to us all at Pentecost. But Spirit-baptized communion is not merely spiritual; it is to be physical, swallowing up mortality into immortal life (2 Cor. 5:4). It is not merely individual; it is ecclesial. The church's baptism in the Spirit thus finds its ultimate fulfillment in the final communion of saints at the eschatological gathering of the church as a restored people—a church that makes the very ends of the earth the possession of God's anointed.

Spirit baptism is an eschatological reality that takes the church and all of its members from their inception in Jerusalem to the conclusion of their mission at the ends of the earth, from their initiation to communion to the final eschatological gathering of all saints in God, from the down payment of the Spirit to being swallowed up in life (2 Cor. 5:4). Since Christ is in his person the Word or Sacrament of the Spirit for all time, the church's kerygmatic and sacramental life centrally celebrates *him* as present in the Spirit. There is no kerygma or sacrament in the church without his embodied life now exalted as mediator of the Spirit to us so that we could be conformed to his image and share both in his communion and in his vocation. It cannot be stressed enough that in mediating the Spirit Christ mediates his own faithful life to us as well as the love of the Father that lies behind it as its eternal impetus. Christ imparts the Spirit, but the Spirit also looks for Christ when transforming us. This transformation is essential to our becoming the church.

There are two issues yet to discuss concerning Spirit baptism and the founding of the church: first, we should note that among the four Gospels Luke and John grant us the most explicit presentation of the actual link between Jesus's role as Baptized and Baptizer in the Spirit. Mark and Matthew do not conclude their Gospels with a clear fulfillment of Jesus's role as Spirit Baptizer. Matthew implies it by closing his Gospel with Jesus's instructing his disciples to baptize the nations in the name of the "Father, and of the Son, and of the Holy Spirit" (28:18). Surely this formula implies incorporation into Christ and the love of his Father by way of the Holy Spirit. One can only assume that the Spirit is to be present from the Father and through the Son. Luke's and John's Gospels explicitly describe how Christ fulfills his role as the Spirit Baptizer, but John's account ties it more closely to the post-resurrection appearances than Luke's.[42] There are also commonalities that both accounts share.

---

[42] For an excellent discussion of how these two texts compare see Dunn, *Baptism in the Holy Spirit*, 75–77.

Both John and Luke agree that the Spirit is to be imparted after Jesus ascends to the Father (Jn 14:16, 26; 15:26; and 16:7). Both agree that Jesus mediates the Spirit. Despite the implication of a difference in timing, both events seem descriptive of what the church regards as the event of Pentecost. Raymond Brown thus concludes: "We may hold that functionally each is describing the same event."[43] It may be that the Johannine breathing forth of the Spirit is symbolic of what will happen at Pentecost (Jesus engaging in prophetic drama of what will occur when the Spirit is received). No actual impartation of the Spirit would then have occurred there, for one does not have any response by the disciples to indicate an actual reception of the Spirit as one has at Pentecost in Acts 2. We may include Paul in this functional equivalence as well, since he too describes an impartation of the Spirit after Christ's ascension that brings into being the gifted ministries of the church. Christ, for Paul, ascended "higher than all the heavens" to "fill the whole universe" and give "gifts to his people" (Eph. 4:7-10). There is indeed only one reception of the Spirit (at our incorporation by faith into Christ) though we certainly continue to drink from the Spirit and experience decisive moments of overflowing (self-transcendence) in ways that carry different experiential accents.

Second, the above comparison of John and Luke causes us to ask whether Luke's locating the outpouring of the Spirit at the Day of Pentecost is historically justifiable. Dunn makes a good case for the basic historicity of Luke's Pentecost account. Though in Galatians 1–2 Paul defends his kerygma due to its having come directly from the risen Christ, he also assumes that the Jerusalem church has primacy. He met "with those esteemed leaders" to be sure that he was not running his race in vain (Gal. 2:2). All indications from Acts and Paul are that the Jerusalem church exercised wide authority over the spreading Christian mission. Dunn concludes therefore, "The Jerusalem Pentecost must have been *the* 'Pentecost' for most of the young church."[44] Moreover, why were there so many of Jesus's original Galilean followers in leadership and attendance in Jerusalem if they were not convinced that the Jerusalem church was to be the place where the church and its mission were to be launched?[45] That Jesus sent them there to wait on the Spirit for the onset of the church's life and mission does match events as we know them.

The Spirit-baptized church as a reality played out in history raises questions about the eternal source of the church in the immanent communion and mission of the Triune God. We'll touch on this issue again in our next chapter on the elect church. But some discussion of the Trinitarian act that founds the church is required here. Indeed, the church is born in the communion of the Triune God as well as in the mission that its overflowing presence in the world opens up for all of humanity.

---

[43] Raymond Brown, *The Gospel according to John, XII–XXI*, AB, Vol. 30 (New York: Doubleday, 1970), 1038.
[44] James D. G. Dunn, *Jesus and the Spirit: A Study of the Religious and Charismatic Experience of Jesus and the First Christians as Reflected in the New Testament* (Philadelphia, MN: Westminster, 1975), 138.
[45] Ibid., 139.

## Spirit Baptism and Trinitarian Communion

Simon Chan notes that the pneumatological emphasis of Pentecostal ecclesiology "provides the key to unlocking a fuller understanding of the church since it is through the coming of the Spirit that the full Trinitarian nature of God is revealed."[46] The Spirit-baptized church lives from communion in the life of the Triune God and from the mission of this God who overflows to open this communion to others and incorporate them into it. As Daniela Augustine wrote, "Where the Spirit is, there is the *koinonia* of the Trinity, extending its loving embrace in invitation to humanity to partake of the divine communal life and be transfigured into its likeness."[47] The Triune God opens the divine life to the world through the Son and in the outpouring of the Spirit and then incorporates those who by grace faithfully yield to that life. This is what we term the baptism in the Holy Spirit as an ongoing and ever-deepening reality, both corporately as the church flourishes in history and individually as believers grow together toward deeper union with Christ. The relationship of the church to the Trinity thus becomes a topic of interest for a pneumatological ecclesiology focused on Spirit baptism. This topic of the Trinity in relation to the church has indeed become an important issue in ecumenical theologies of the church. The church is sometimes challenged with the call to become an icon of Trinitarian communion. Some understandably warn that the utter uniqueness of Triune communion should cause us to recognize the significant limitations involved in calling the church its icon. The point here is that the circle of communion that constantly self-transcends and overflows by reaching out to the other and creating space for them implies a communion of the many that is inviting and self-transcending. It is this image that the church is to take on and be shaped into.

There is no question that the Triune life is important to the rediscovery of communion as essential to the church. The Greek term *koinonia* (communion, fellowship, mutual participation) is key to understanding the nature of communion as a theological concept: "In the Christian understanding, trinitarian koinonia is the foundation of all *koinonia*."[48] Lorelie Fuchs develops this insight in her masterful treatment of *koinonia* as the key to an ecumenical ecclesiology ("ecumenical" referring to the quest for the visible unity of the church). She notes that this concept of *koinonia* has become enormously important to ecclesiology in ecumenical discussions, especially in helping churches view the Trinitarian life of God as key to their shared life on a local, confessional, and interchurch basis. *Koinonia* has functioned methodologically to help churches discover their concrete or visible path toward unity as a process, since communion occurs on different levels. On this path, *koinonia* becomes a gift and a call, with the possibility of attaining degrees of visible communion on the way toward a more significant sharing of life together.[49] Pentecostals accepted this call early in their ecumenical participation. The 1989 Final Report of the Third Quinquennium of the

---

[46] Chan, *Pentecostal Ecclesiology*, 8.
[47] Daniela C. Augustine, *Pentecost, Hospitality, and Transfiguration: Toward a Spirit-Inspired Vision of Social Transformation* (Cleveland, TN: CPT Press, 2012), 20.
[48] Lorelie F. Fuchs, *Koinonia and the Quest for Ecumenical Ecclesiology: From Foundations through Dialogue to Symbolic Competence Communionality* (Grand Rapids, MI: Eerdmans, 2008), 26.
[49] Ibid.

international Catholic-Pentecostal dialogue accepted *koinonia* as its key theme. Note the foundation granted to the life of the Triune God:

> Both Pentecostals and Roman Catholics believe that the *koinonia* between Christians is rooted in the life of Father, Son and Holy Spirit. Furthermore, they believe that this trinitarian life is the highest expression of the unity to which we together aspire: "that which we have seen and heard we proclaim also to you, so that you may have fellowship with us; and our fellowship is with the Father and with his Son Jesus Christ." (1 Jn 1 :3)
>
> Both Roman Catholics and Pentecostals agree that the Holy Spirit is the source of *koinonia* or communion. The Church has been gathered in the Holy Spirit. (cf. 2 Cor. 13:13)[50]

Pentecostals, like other free church traditions, tend to neglect *koinonia* as a rich ecclesiological reality worth exploring theologically, which is needed to overcome a view of the church as merely serving to edify individual piety and witness.

Incorporation into Trinitarian *koinonia* or communion through the gift of the Spirit is suggested by the New Testament itself as key to the life of the church. In John, Jesus prays to the Father that his followers be united in divine love, and then describes this unity as a dynamic sharing of life: "That all of them may be one, Father; just as you are in me and I am in you. May they also be in us so that the world may believe that you have sent me" (Jn 17:21). Jesus describes his relation to the Father as a shared love that is from all eternity and that the Father wishes to extend to humanity. Jesus prays, "I in them and you in me—so that they may be brought to complete unity. Then the world will know that you sent me and have loved them even as you have loved me" (17:23). The Spirit is the bond of communion for John: "This is how we know that we live in him and he in us: He has given us of his Spirit" (1 Jn 4:13). By the Spirit we are united to Christ and Christ to us and incorporated into his communion with the Father in the bond of the Spirit. *Koinonia* is also to be described as the communion shared horizontally among believers in God that arises as a result. Communion in the Spirit is not just something we do; it is something we *are* as love transforms us and is made complete in us, in our shared life together. We are being shaped in the likeness of self-giving, self-incorporating love, which is the image of the Triune God revealed in Christ the Spirit Baptizer. "No one has ever seen God; but if we love one another, God lives in us and his love is made complete in us" (4:12). This is the love that God showed us by sending Christ to death on the cross in order to bring us to life ("This is how God showed his love among us: He sent his one and only Son into the world that we might live through him," 4:9).

Paul also discusses Spirit baptism as a participation in Christ by the Spirit (which water baptism and the Lord's Supper signify, Rom. 6:3-5; 1 Cor. 10:16) and through this a participation in the benefits of his communion with the Father. It is in the Spirit

---

[50] "Perspectives on Koinonia," the report from the third quinquennium of the dialogue between the Pontifical Council for Promoting Christian Unity of the Roman Catholic Church and some classical Pentecostal Churches and Leaders 1985-1989, # 29-30, *GW II*, 739.

that the love of the Father toward the Son is poured out in our hearts (Rom. 5:5). By this love we pray *Abba* to the Father and partake of the riches of sonship in Christ (8:15-16). According to Paul, Christ has given his life in devotion to the Father and the Father's cause in the world. In the Spirit, we now share in Christ's self-giving love as it is poured out for the world: "I have been crucified with Christ and I no longer live, but Christ lives in me. The life I now live in the body, I live by faith in the Son of God, who loved me and gave himself for me" (Gal. 2:20). Though initiatory in significance as an event, our baptism in the Spirit for Paul is not static, *merely* a one-time event that one moves beyond in their spiritual journey into Christ. The deeper one participates in Christ, the deeper one is "baptized" in the Spirit of communion. Paul prays that believers "may have power, together with all the Lord's holy people, to grasp how wide and long and high and deep is the love of Christ, and to know this love that surpasses knowledge—that you may be filled to the measure of all the fullness of God" (Eph. 3:18-19). There are various dimensions to this fullness (existential, communal, charismatic, missional) and growing toward it in a shared life with others is soul-expanding.

Luke as well tells us that the outpouring of the Spirit from the Father through the Son leads to a sharing in apostolic faith (the teaching of the apostles), the breaking of bread, communion in the Spirit (Acts 2:42), and a shared mission (1:8). The Father pours forth the Spirit through the Son so as to bring into being this communion that springs forth as the consequence of the Pentecost event (2:33-36). Acts bears witness to an ever-expanding communion in the midst (and through the instrumentality) of core practices that embraces an increasingly diverse communion of saints. The church mimics the expansively self-giving, self-incorporating love of the Triune God, the Spirit-baptizing God. Through core practices like proclamation, water baptism, the breaking of bread (2:38-42), spiritual gifts, and shared mission (1:8), the church not only is ever-more deeply the Spirit-baptized people but also becomes ever-more instrumental in the work of the Spirit-baptizing God.

The significance of Trinitarian *koinonia* for ecclesiology follows on the heels of a revival of Trinitarian theology in the twentieth century. We may echo Geoffrey Wainwright here: "The signs of our times are that, as in the fourth century, the doctrine of the Trinity occupies a pivotal position."[51] In the nineteenth century, Friedrich Schleiermacher concluded his monumental *The Christian Faith* with a brief description of the doctrine of the Trinity along the lines of a modalistic interpretation of the Triune life.[52] One could attempt to make the case that placing the life of the Triune God at the conclusion of his system was granting this doctrine a place of honor. But the more convincing implication is that he was actually treating the doctrine of the Trinity as more of an addendum than as his crowning statement. After all, he describes the doctrine of the Trinity as so questionable that "the main pivots of the ecclesiastical

---

[51] Geoffrey Wainwright, "The Doctrine of the Trinity: Where the Church Stands or Falls," *Interpretation* 45, no 2 (1991): 117 (117–32).

[52] Modalism is the view that the Father, Son, and Spirit are to be viewed functionally as modes of God's self-revelation rather than as personal relations internal to God. Oneness Pentecostals hold this view of God.

doctrine—the being of God in Christ and in the Christian church have their own integrity in the faith of the church apart from it."[53]

Karl Barth famously *began* his massive *Church Dogmatics* with a view of God as Trinitarian in nature or, more exactly, with a view of revelation as Triune in structure. He used the Trinity to secure an understanding of divine revelation as given entirely by grace. God is the Subject, Object, and Predicate of revelation, and humanity is drawn into this divine self-communication as divinely intended participants. If God is Father (Subject), revelation has its source in the infinite depth of God's loving purposes. If God is Son (Object), revelation (of God and of humanity in God) is visibly embodied for all time by Christ and mediated to others through him and his obedience. Revelation is once and for all time visibly given to the world as a gift of reconciliation in the Son. If God is Holy Spirit (Predicate), the human capacity to responsibly and obediently appropriate this revelation from Christ by faith is viewed as a gift as well. Humanity cannot act favorably toward God from an imagined position of autonomy or self-made initiatives aimed at self-fulfillment. In the Triune God, revelation is given as a gift by the sovereign act of God as Revealer, Revealed, and Revealedness. God is shown to be Lord of salvation in every sense in which this term can be described, from its infinite depth to its expansive appropriation in faith. Humanity cannot take the initiative in any aspect of salvation within the divine self-giving. God as Father, Son, and Spirit is the Lord of salvation in a "threefold" way, in every aspect of revelation and its transformative goal.[54] The church for Barth is born and lives from this sovereign and free act of divine self-giving, one that comes to us and is received by grace alone. Our kerygmatic life in the Spirit merely bears witness to the proclamation implicit in Christ's resurrection; our sacramental life in the Spirit being a mere extension of this sacramental mediation of Spirit and truth given in the person of the risen Christ as well. The vocation (charismatic service and mission) of the church partakes of the service and mission of the Triune God. For God the Father through the Lord Jesus and the Spirit is "over all, through all, and in all" (Eph. 4:6). As Moltmann puts it, the history of the church is to be viewed "in the trinitarian history of God's dealings with the world."[55] The result is that the life and mission of the church occur within the "wide-open space" of communion in the life of the Triune God.[56]

Barth allows the uniqueness and interrelationality of the three persons to play a significant role in God's life and self-giving. In volume 1, part 1 of the *Dogmatics*, he develops the relationality of the three persons according to the twin doctrines of appropriation and *perichoresis*. Appropriation has to do with the unique role of each of the divine persons in God's self-revelation, and *perichoresis* is the shared life of the three persons within the one God.[57] Later, Barth developed the idea that the communion of love shared in the Triune God is the source and sustenance of human fellowship in

---

[53] Friedrich Schleiermacher, *The Christian Faith*, #179 (Philadelphia, MN: Fortress Press, 1979), 741.
[54] Karl Barth, *CD*, Vol. 1, pt. 1, 332.
[55] Moltmann, *The Church in the Power of the Spirit*, 4.
[56] Ibid., 62–63.
[57] Karl Barth, *CD*, Vol. 1, pt. 1, 370–75.

God. There is implied in Barth's Trinitarian theology an analogy of love between the Triune life of God and the love we experience in God.[58]

Problematically for some, Barth showed dissatisfaction with the use of the word "persons" to designate the agents of the Father, Son, and Spirit in the divine life and self-disclosure. Given the modern tendency to define "person" as a separate ego, the application of this term to the Father, Son, and Holy Spirit seemed to Barth as potentially tritheistic (three gods rather than one God in the eternal communion of the three). Barth suggested instead the term *Seinsweise* (ways or modes of being) to describe the three. He did not intend by this term a modalistic understanding of God. He criticized modalism for seeking to transcend the concrete communion of Father, Son, and Spirit so as to arrive at an abstract view of God as hidden beyond the revelation of the three.[59]

Moltmann does not find Barth's Trinitarian theology robustly relational enough. He finds in Barth a Hegelian influence that caused Barth to picture God as a single subject in threefold self-relation. Moltmann finds in this conception an inadequate appreciation for the rich relationality between the Father, the Son, and the Spirit implied in the story of Jesus. He notes, "The new Trinitarian thinking, in contrast, starts from the history of Jesus Christ and develops the doctrine of the Trinity from Jesus' relation as Son to the Father."[60] In this, he is actually following Barth. But the results of this method are somewhat different in Moltmann. Using this story as his point of departure, he develops a "social" understanding of the Triune God that highlights the interaction of three subjects, who share one divine life (rather than one subject in threefold self-relation as in Barth).[61] The oneness of God as Lord is to be understood through the primary lens of Jesus's interaction with his Father under the anointing and leading of the Spirit as revealed in the actual story of Jesus. The oneness of God is to be understood in the light of the relationality revealed in this communion of life rather than the other way around.

Yet, Moltmann also holds to the perichoretic unity of God. The three persons in communion are completely and inseparably in one another. When one sees Jesus in the narrative of the Gospels, according to Moltmann, one sees the Father who sent him and the Spirit poured forth from the Father resting on him and acting through him. It is thus impossible to comprehend each of the other two persons apart from the others. "The three actors in our salvation history are so present in one another that they cannot be separated without destroying the salvation."[62] Moltmann thus understands the three divine persons from the lens of the redemptive story as in mutual interpenetration and indwelling (Jn 17:21) engaging as one God together in self-giving love for the world. In doing so, God becomes inextricably involved in the world and its suffering. In sending the Son into flesh, the Father attaches the Son to the destiny of creation. The Father's longing for the creation is shown to be rooted in the Father's longing for the Son. Through the Son, the reciprocal love between the Father and the Son is extended

---

[58] Karl Barth, *CD*, Vol. IV, pt. 2, 757.
[59] Karl Barth, *CD*, Vol. 1, pt. 1, 351–53.
[60] Moltmann, *The Living God and the Fullness of Life* (Westminster John Knox, 2015), 65, see 64–65.
[61] Ibid.
[62] Ibid., 62.

to creation. The Spirit is the Spirit of divine empathy and suffering love for the other, the similar other of the Son (like with like) and the radically other of mortal and sinful creation. At the cross, the Son identifies with the God forsaken, the result being that the Father "experiences in the forsakenness of the beloved Son the eclipse of God in the world."[63] But the Son overcomes this eclipse by uniting his will to the Father's cause of saving humanity. The Son offers himself up to the Father and the Father raises the Son by the Spirit to be the Savior for all of creation. The unity of divine love overcomes the alienation of the cross for the sake of the world. By the Spirit, the world is taken up into this divine unity, this single communion of love. The Spirit mediated through the Son becomes the means by which the Son gathers the others into the circle of love that constitutes God's united Triune life. The divine self-reconciliation holds within it the salvation of the world. The gathering in of others in Christ fulfills the divine longing for the other, the ecstasy of love reciprocated.[64] This narrative is the context for Moltmann's statement quoted earlier that the life of the church occurs in the wide-open space of Triune communion. In Moltmann's theological vision, the church is part of this grand love story of all of creation being taken up into reconciliation with God, the victory of God's own suffering love for the world.

Wolfhart Pannenberg also has in common with Moltmann the conviction that reflection on the Trinity must have as its point of departure the revelation of God in Jesus Christ.[65] Focusing from the start on the story of Jesus causes one to conclude that Jesus as the Son "differs from the Father and is related to him" and also the Spirit "is distinct from the Father and the Son and yet closely related in fellowship with them."[66] This unity in distinction makes the communion of the divine persons essential to the very nature of God as one. In other words, the unity of God is mediated through the distinct interaction of the three. Trinitarian theology has classically focused on how the Son and the Spirit came eternally forth from the Father in order to distinguish the persons from each other. The Son has a filial relation to the Father because the Son came eternally forth from the Father by generation. The Spirit is not the Son, since the Spirit came forth eternally from the Father by procession or breathing rather than generation or begetting (the West spoke only of the two processions). The Father is the eternal fount of all deity. Pannenberg notes that in this focus on the eternal coming forth of the Son and the Spirit from the Father, the tendency was to imply that the Son and the Spirit are ontologically dependent on the Father, while the Father (being "unoriginiate") is viewed as not dependent on the other two persons. This one-sided dependence of the Son and the Spirit on the Father caused Arius and others to question the full deity of the Son and the Spirit.[67] It is vital to add here the metaphysical problem of divine suffering. Since Arius could not imagine true deity as suffering (for suffering seemed to involve divine lack), he felt compelled to separate the crucified Christ from the Father as consisting of two different essences (the Father alone as "true God" and the Son as a created being representing something less than God). We could also add

---

[63] Ibid., 66.
[64] Ibid., 67.
[65] Pannenberg, *Systematic Theology*, Vol. 1, 300.
[66] Ibid., 305.
[67] Ibid., 308–19.

that the Arian severing of the essential link between the Father and the Son (the latter viewed as less than truly divine) also severs the link between God and the life of the church. The church is no longer the Spirit-baptized people, who participate in the self-giving of the true God in the world.

Pannenberg attempts to avoid Arian implications in a couple of ways. First, he describes the Triune work of salvation in a way that resists a one-sided dependence on the Father by the Son (and by implication the Spirit). Indeed, it is possible to talk about the eternal coming forth of the Son and the Spirit from the Father in a way that depicts God as a flowing stream of divine love in which the Father as the source is just as dependent on the Son and the Spirit as the flowing forth from it as they are on the Father as the source, a point that Athanasius was fond of making. Conceiving of God as an eternal fountain of life, Athanasius criticized Arius's idea that the Son was created out of nothing (that "there was once when the Son was not") as being tantamount to saying "there was once when the fountain was dry, without life and wisdom. But this would not be a fountain."[68] Second, without denying the significance of eternal generation and procession, Pannenberg shifts the emphasis from the eternal origins to the ends of the relations within God so as to make the point that these relations are fully revealed only in the light of the goal toward which they are directed, as shown, for example, in texts like 1 Cor. 15:24-28. Efforts to define the relations without this eschatological horizon are vulnerable to metaphysical considerations imported from the outside, which have tended to result in either subordinationism (the Son and the Spirit are less than God) or modalism (a lack of eternal relations in God). More elaborately, the deity of Father, Son, and Spirit for Pannenberg has primarily to do with the unique nature of the interactions of the three as revealed in history in the light of the goal toward which they are directed, namely, the establishment of God's lordship over the creation. "The Father does not merely beget the Son. He also hands over his kingdom to him and receives it back from him."[69] The redemption of the world takes place within this exchange between the Father and the Son in the Spirit. The relations of the divine persons reach for the eschatological fulfillment of the divine reign in creation, for it is here that the lordship that constitutes God's very being reaches its goal and full self-disclosure. It is here that the divine "unity in difference" reflected in the communion of the divine persons takes on concrete meaning. So the Son is distinct from the Father by being eternally earmarked for revelation, the Word of the Father to be the embodiment of the Father's reign over the new creation, an embodiment distinct from the Father. The Spirit is distinct from both the Father and the Son by being the One who anoints the new creation (starting with the body of the Son) as a reality that reflects the Son to the Father's glory but is still distinct from the Son (not absorbed by him). Yet, all three are united in one divine reign over all.

In short, Pannenberg highlights the distinction of the persons "in relation" in order to explain the divine potential and desire to take in others in a way that preserves their otherness. Space for the otherness of creation does not take place outside of God

---

[68] Athanasius, "Orations against the Arians," Book 1, no. 19, in *Trinitarian Controversy*, ed. William G. Rusch (Minneapolis: Fortress Press, 1980), 69.
[69] Pannenberg, *Systematic Theology*, Vol. 1, 320.

(there is no such "outside") but rather within the divine communion in the relation between the Father and both the Son and the Spirit. Creation occurs from the Father but also distinct from the Father because it occurs in the Son. It occurs in the Son but also distinct from the Son because it occurs by the Spirit.[70] The Spirit does not rob the creation of its otherness and diversity because the Spirit brings the divine lordship to the many. The Spirit anoints, which preserves the unique personhood and callings of creatures within the life of the Son.

Pneumatology thus preserves the distinction between Christ and his church. All that the Son does to give rise to the church the Son does by the Spirit, which causes the Son to create space in himself as the Head of his body for this communion with others. For example, following Dorothea Soelle, Pannenberg resists a "totalitarian" understanding of atonement, which reduces humanity to a generic mass that is Christologically defined in ways that wipe out differences. At the cross, Christ already creates space within his life for the countless others he represents there.[71] Simon Chan helps us further here by taking note of the fact that the Spirit as "third person" is the principle person of the Godhead that freely opens the communion of the Son with the Father to the multitude of others in all of their otherness.[72] The many tongues of Pentecost become the lens through which to interpret Christ's representation of all flesh at the cross. The Spirit is the principle of diverse incorporation and witness. The role of the Spirit at the cross already opens space in Christ for both. In this light, it is because the Son offers himself representatively on behalf of others on the cross "by the eternal Spirit" (Heb. 9:14) that this representation preserves the God-given uniqueness of the others being represented. God's offer of solidarity and embrace at the cross respects the others as others but seeks also to transform them into Christlikeness in a colorful variety of ways.

Also, Pannenberg notes that the divine lordship is essential to God. Sovereign lordship is not merely something that God exercises; it's descriptive of God's very essence as Lord of all. Thus, the establishment of God's reign constitutes God's deity in relation to creation. God's lordship is established through the Son's willful glorification of the Father and the Father's glorification of the Son, and the Spirit's glorification of the Father and the Son. This mutual glory shows a mutual dependence of the three that undercuts both subordinationist and modalist abstractions. Since God's essential lordship is established through the interactive communion of the three persons, the deity of all three depends on the self-distinction and self-giving of the three in relation to each other. Each divine person is that person only in relation to the others and God is God only in the communion of the three. By such interaction as played out through the incarnate Son and the outpouring of the Spirit upon all flesh, God's deity is manifested throughout creation, being fully established and revealed in the new creation which fulfills God's reign in the world, a reign in which the church is both the sign and the instrument. In the fulfillment of God's kingdom in and through the church, communion cherishes both unity and otherness (in a way that is analogous to

---

[70] Ibid., 308–19.
[71] Pannenberg, *Systematic Theology*, Vol. 2, 432.
[72] Chan, *Pentecostal Ecclesiology*, 66.

the Triune life). As the Triune God creates space for the others, so also does ecclesial communion. This communion is thus both just and vocational, or vocational in a way that fosters a just regard for the unique presence and participation of others in all of their God-given otherness.

My own focus on Jesus the Spirit Baptizer has been inspired in some respects by Moltmann and Pannenberg. The difference is that I have elaborated more than they on the Spirit's role at the cross by focusing on John the Baptist's announcement concerning Jesus as the One who will baptize in the Holy Spirit and fire. *Jesus himself must bear this baptism in fire in order to baptize others in the Spirit.* What Moltmann calls the Son's sinking into forsakenness should thus be understood pneumatologically as the Son's baptism in fire so as to provide passage through it unto the restoration of the Spirit and life. He enters into our alienation from the Spirit (from the communion of the Triune God) but does so as the Son of the Father and the man of the Spirit. By taking our alienation and suffering into himself, the Son becomes the means by which the Triune God overcomes God's own wrath so as to provide passage for humanity to divine mercy. Christ thus replaces that eclipsing of God in the world with the possibility of a God-filled world. I thus also focus on Pentecost as the culminating point of Jesus's messianic mission. It is not the resurrection that is this point, for Jesus's baptism in the Spirit is not fulfilled until he imparts that baptism to others. He came that we might have life and that more abundantly (Jn 10:10). He rises to the Father in the fullness of the Spirit, in the fullness of sanctifying grace, so as to pour forth this Spirit onto all flesh. Another way of putting this is to say that the Spirit overflows the Son so as to include the many in him.

There are a few additional remarks I would like to make about Trinitarian *koinonia* as a framework for viewing the church as the Spirit-baptized people. As is obvious from what God has revealed about the nature of Triune communion, the unity of the Godhead is mediated by the fellowship of the three, which means that, theologically, diversity is cherished as being indispensable to unity. So it must also be *analogously* in the church. Unity is not uniformity but rather a unity within an expanding diversity of persons and gifts. The church is not just tolerant of God-given diversity; the church invites and celebrates it, creates space for it. The church is willing to change (expand and diversify) do so, so as to extend an embrace that is liberating and just. But in changing, the church remains unchanging in its faithfulness to Christ who did the same. The difference is that sometimes the church must do this with repentance and conversion in response to its history of idolatrous conformity to the dominant culture. This conformity allowed the churches to live at peace with the dominant culture but only by silencing the voices of its prophets. Change will only occur when those who oversee the house of God listen with fresh ears to what the Spirit is saying on behalf of Christ to the churches once more.

Additionally, communion is a valid substantive emphasis for our understanding of the Spirit-baptized church, but only as illuminated by Spirit baptism. For in the light of Spirit baptism we can see most clearly the inseparable relationship between communion and vocation (ministry and mission). Communion in the context of an emphasis on Spirit baptism is ever seeking and inviting, self-imparting, overflowing, and ultimately incorporating. It serves an overflowing incorporation that embraces and cherishes God-given otherness. This communion is thus also inviting and longing for the other and the other's embrace and healing. The church is consequently willing to adjust and change in its unchanging faithfulness to Christ so as to open space for the unique witness and gifting of those who come, for Christ's openness in the freedom of the Spirit to the diversity of others requires no less of us. This needed link between communion and vocation is one reason why a eucharistic ecclesiology must be rooted more deeply and explicitly in what water baptism signifies within the larger Spirit-baptismal work of the Triune God. The church overflows and incorporates; its communion is open ended, longing and reaching for the other, profoundly charismatic and missional in direction. Among the reasons that baptism is practiced only once while the Lord's Supper many times is that baptism signifies the all-encompassing baptism in the Spirit in which all else takes place.

Communion links the church to Christ in a way that preserves distinction. Pannenberg especially helps us to see that the Son is one with the Father through self-distinction from the Father, so also is the Spirit one with the Son in self-distinction from him. The church birthed in the Spirit is thus a church birthed not only in union but also in distinction from the Son. It is not possible to view the church as the "prolongation of Christ" (*Christus prolongatus*) without significant qualifications and a proper emphasis on the covenantal relationality between the church and Christ. The Spirit in freedom enables and transforms the church so as to actualize its witness to Christ in history. Thus, an ecclesiology that does not adequately distinguish the church from Christ may indeed reveal a concomitant inadequacy to emphasize the Spirit enough as constitutive of the church. Rather than speaking of the church as the prolongation of the incarnation, it is better to speak as Pinnock does of the church as the prolongation of Christ's anointing by the Spirit,[73] though even here we must be clear that his baptism in the Spirit is the source of ours, for he alone bore the Spirit permanently and without measure as the divine Son in flesh so as to be once and for all the medium of the Spirit for all flesh. We are no adoptionists, who merely envision Christ sharing his prophetic inspiration with us as Moses did with the seventy elders in Numbers 11.[74] The Spirit as constitutive of the church's vocational communion does indeed unite the church intimately to Christ and draw the church ever-more deeply into Christ.

It hardly needs to be said that the church communes and bears witness in weakness. The church bears witness to the kingdom but is not identifiable with it. As Gregory of Nyssa tells us concerning the kingdom or reign of the Father, Christ is the King and the Spirit is the kingdom.[75] As the substance of the kingdom willed by the Father, the Spirit speaks the words of Christ to the church in a way that both challenges and heals the church. In response, the church is to strive for more of the Spirit by striving for deeper participation in the kingdom, or in Christ. So the kingdom-church relation is the

---

[73] Pinnock, *Flame of Love*, 116.

[74] I don't deny that the Numbers 11 text plays a role in our interpretation of Acts 2 but only in the light of the deeper meaning of Christ's impartation of the Spirit that the incarnation in the light of the entire Christ event provides.

[75] Gregory of Nyssa, *On the Lord's Prayer*, no. 3. See my discussion of this in Macchia, *Baptized in the Spirit*, 89.

Christ-church relation, which grants sovereignty to God and God's word alone. We as ordained ministers serve as guides and not as ruling agents. It is a good thing that our reign is reserved for the eschatological future only after we've already been glorified and perfectly conformed to Christ's servanthood and to his liberating purposes. The kingdom-church relation is the Spirit-church relation, which is experienced in the dialectic of strength revealed in weakness, of a witness that falls short of Christ but is still used by the Spirit to speak to others on behalf of Christ.

Yet, our union with Christ by the Spirit is intimate and mutually conditioning, though not in the same way, since Christ alone is the sovereign Head and source in this union. Christ's incorporation of the church into himself by the Spirit conditions Christ's existence, by Christ's own will and action. In faithfulness to the Father and in the freedom of the Spirit, the Christ is forever the Christ for others. He is forever purposed to be the God-man, the mediator of the covenant God, the Head of his body, our Lord of life, and elder brother. This intimacy of union reflects the perichoretic nature of divine love (as Christ said to the Father, "Father, just as you are in me and I am in you. May they also be in us," Jn 17:21). We speak analogously of course. But this intimacy of communion means that we seek to mimic Christ in the power of the Spirit to suffer with those who suffer and rejoice with those who rejoice (1 Cor. 12:26). We bear one another's burdens because we've allowed those who are burdened to penetrate our defenses. We allowed them to come close enough to touch us deep within. We come to mimic a divine communion that is driven by suffering love for the other. As Miroslav Volf has shown, we must exclude the other if they seek to dominate or otherwise exploit us. Christ had to exclude and resist in his faithful journey to the cross. But, like Christ, the will to embrace for all remains. For those who reach out in need and are open for mutually enriching embrace, we cast aside the distancing from this other in order embrace.[76] This is our participation in Spirit-baptismal incorporation. We are shaped in the image of Christ, and, in this shaping, we allow ourselves to be conditioned by one another in a way analogous to how Christ allowed himself to be conditioned by us. As he became our Lord and elder brother, so we in loyalty and witness to him become servants and brothers and sisters to one another. Our last section will sketch the rudiments of a Spirit-baptized and, hence, ecclesial anthropology. There's one more Trinitarian issue that I wish to explore first.

Instrumentalism, treating the Spirit as the mere instrument of the Son or the Son as the instrument of the Spirit, is a threat to a pneumatological ecclesiology. It is a threat at two levels. First, viewing the Spirit as the mere instrument of the Son subordinates pneumatology to Christology, which can also lead to a Christomonistic ecclesiology that regards the Spirit as a mere aid to the church's prolongation of Christ, especially through the ordained ministry's presumption of Christological authority. The Eastern churches understandably trace this subordination of the Spirit to the West's defense of the *filioque* (which literally means, "and the Son"). To bolster resistance to Arianism (which denied the full deity of Christ) the churches in the West (especially from the

---

[76] His chapter on exclusion is truly illuminating; see Miroslav Volf, *Exclusion and Embrace: A Theological Exploration of Identity, Otherness, and Reconciliation* (Nashville: Abingdon, 1996), 57–98.

seventh century onward) added to the Nicene Creed the confession that the Spirit proceeds from the Father *and the Son* (*filioque*). The *filioque* was thought to highlight the Son's sameness of essence with the Father (the Spirit's procession from both the Father and the Son was thought to bolster the confession of the Son's sameness of essence with the Father). But does this move not potentially exclude the church's confession of the Father *alone* as the eternal fount of deity? Also, the *filioque* arguably resulted in the tendency to regard the Spirit as subordinate to the Son and as merely instrumental in the church's unqualified identification with Christ. The idea that the Spirit proceeds from the Father alone *through* the Son is a promising step in the right direction, but even this needs to achieve balance.

As noted earlier, the West also blamed the East of an instrumentalization of the Son. If the Son came to merely mediate the Spirit to all flesh so as to grant to mortal flesh immortal communion, is not Christology now subordinated to pneumatology? How then is Christ in himself the event of reconciliation between God and humanity? How is he then the eternal foundation upon which the church is built? As noted earlier, the churches of the West answered such questions with its towering doctrine of atonement. But, arguably, they did so in a way that neglected the Spirit. Anselm's monumental elaboration on the Chalcedonian Definition by showing how it provides the atonement with its necessary theological framework solidified the towering dogmas of incarnation and atonement as the means by which Christology would never be subordinated to the Spirit as the mere instrument of the Spirit's work. Christ is in himself the event of reconciliation between God and humanity. But this Christological solution eclipsed the necessary role of the Spirit in the messianic mission, including the atonement. My solution was to use Jesus's baptism in the Spirit and fire as a lens through which to view his death and resurrection as a pneumatological event, but one which, in and of itself, is *the* reconciling event for all time. In his death, the Son is baptized into the fire of condemnation and death so as to make passage for humanity to the Spirit and the new creation. Christ is that passage, in his very person as well as his work, and that passage is the reconciling event for all time. Christ's very person is defined by his self-giving in revelation of the Father's love and in following the Spirit's lead. This is what the story of Jesus tells us about him as the place of reconciliation or communion between God and humanity, the place in which the church is born and has its life.

Trinitarian balance occurs in a mutual dependence of the persons in the one life of the Triune God. Helpfully, Thomas Weinandy depicts the Son's eternal generation from the Father as through the Spirit's eternal anointing *and* of the eternal procession of the Spirit from the Father as through the mediation of the only-begotten Son. The eternal Son was thus always the anointed Christ and the eternal Spirit was always the Spirit of the Son.[77] The Father as eternal source or fount of all deity depends on the Son and the Spirit for the fullness of deity, since the Son and the Spirit fulfill the Father's self-giving and reign. The end result is a God who incorporates others by indwelling them in a way analogous to the intimate communion of the divine persons: "Father, just as you are in me and I am in you. May they also be in us so that the world may believe that you have

---

[77] Thomas Weinandy, *The Father's Spirit of Sonship: Reconceiving the Trinity* (Eugene, OR: Wipf & Stock, 2011).

sent me" (Jn 17:21). The vocational communion that seeks to incorporate the others into the liberating love of God occurs within the divine communion and is shaped by it. We are the Spirit-baptized people who seek through the instrument of our witness to bring others into this same baptism and the ever-deepening vocational communion that belongs to it. The life of the church into which all come is a rich and interactive sharing of life. In his attempt at developing the promise of Pentecostal ecclesiology, Clark Pinnock focused on the divine dance as a source of inspiration for the interactive and unified worship of the church in the power of the Spirit:

> The divine dance (*perichoresis*) supplies the basis for personal dynamics of the community. The church needs to order its life in this manner so as to echo the community of Father, Son and Spirit. Let the open fellowship of God be mirrored in the open fellowship of the church as it was in Jesus' own open friendships.[78]

The Spirit-baptizing God is not only the God of communion and celebration; this God is overflowing and self-imparting. This God seeks to overflow all boundaries so as to incorporate all who would come, to take them within the divine embrace. It is for this liberating embrace that God created humanity, so that we may be taken up in this embrace in such a way as to experience it together with others in communion. God is precisely this God of overflowing and embrace by nature and self-determination. This is who God is in freedom and commitment. The Father generates the Son and breathes forth the Spirit so as to be the eternal source of self-giving and self-incorporating love in time. The Son was eternally generated from the Father via the Spirit so as in divine freedom to be the one sent forth of the Father and by the Spirit in the economy (in history). The Son is the one who becomes flesh by way of the Spirit, his messianic vocation being a journey in the Spirit. The Spirit proceeds eternally from the Father via the Son to be the one sent of the Father through the Son so as to gather all others into him and into the communion of life with the Father. The persons of the Triune God fill one another in a way that overflows in openness and yearning for the other as other. A redemptive story springs forth from and within the divine outpouring that is characterized as self-sacrificial love, a love that bears the image of a cross. This divine overflowing seeks to fill the others with cruciform love so that they bear this cross too but in a way that is taken up and ultimately fulfilled in the communion of saints, in the richness and victory of the resurrection. The unity of the Triune God is a gift to be fulfilled in the uniting of all within the divine communion. As Moltmann wrote, "God does not desire to be united with himself without the uniting of all things with him."[79] And we could add to the phrase "with him" also "in him." For this unity of love, we were created. As Pinnock observed, "The Trinity is an open, inviting fellowship, and the Spirit wants the church to be the same."[80]

---

[78] Clark Pinnock, "Church in the Power of the Spirit: The Promise of Pentecostal Ecclesiology," *Journal of Pentecostal Theology* 14, no. 2 (2006): 154 (147–65).
[79] Moltmann, *The Church in the Power of the Spirit*, 63.
[80] Pinnock, *Flame of Love*, 117.

## Toward an Ecclesial Personality

Our journey into Christ and toward spiritual fullness is soul-expanding. To live in isolation or perhaps confined to our closest circle of family and friends restricts our soul expansion to narrow limits. The church places us into a charismatic sharing of life and a missional outreach that expands the soul in its capacity for God. God reveals the limitless divine openness for all of creation in the redemptive drama and wills to locate us as participants in this drama so as to expand us, make us more like God. What we learn about the self-impartation of the Triune God through revelation illuminates who we are to be as respondents within the community of faith. The more we understand God in his self-giving, the more we understand what God intends for us, created in the divine image and destined for the image of Christ. The more we understand Christ, the more we understand our true selves. For "the Word's potentiality for being understood coincides with man's potentiality for understanding himself."[81] The Word reveals a self that is made for communion, with God and others in God. "To experience faith is to become an ecclesial being" (Volf).[82] If we flee the church, we are to that degree fleeing God's perfect will for us and fleeing ourselves as created and regenerated by God to be in communion with others. I do not mean to say that there can be no relation with Christ apart from the church, only that such a relation would lack something vital to our very being. Spirit baptism and incorporation within the life of the church transforms us in a way that fulfills what we were created to be, people of communion by the Spirit and in the image of Christ.

Our creation in the image of the Triune God implies that we were made for communion in God. The fact that anthropology is to be conceived as relational and social is an insight that has gained strength in our time, which has the potential of making the church increasingly relevant to people's spiritual quest. As Karl Rahner pointed out, the modern tendency to appropriate religion "in a private kind of interiority" to escape the rigors "of their concrete historical and social nature" is no longer credible today. "We are aware today in a quite new and inescapable way that man is a social being."[83] It is not the idea of faith within community per se that turn many off today but rather the institutional forms that this community takes on that are always in need of renewal, often in dire need. We will take up this issue in our final chapter.

At any rate, the relationality at the base of the church starts with the Triune God who self-imparts from within the divine communion that is opened up to the world. Divine freedom in relation to the church is preserved by the insight that the fundamental relation is the Triune God and not the divine-human relation that occurs in Christ and in the life of the church. God self-imparts not out of any need to find personal fulfillment but out of the freedom and limitless fullness of God's own overflowing love. "And he is not served by human hands, as if he needed anything. Rather, he himself

---

[81] Moltmann, *The Church in the Power of the Spirit*, 211.
[82] Volf, *After Our Likeness*, 174.
[83] Karl Rahner, *Foundations of Christian Faith: An Introduction to the Idea of Christianity* (New York: Seabury Press, 1978), 322.

gives everyone life and breath and everything else" (Acts 17:25). Faith means that we depend on God and not God on us. The faith that comes to birth depends primarily on divine grace bestowed from Christ and in the presence of the Spirit. But the faith that occurs in our union with Christ in the Spirit is also a willful act that fulfills the human quest. This faith is deeply personal and individually unique. Yet, it is also even more profoundly a shared reality. The church in various ways and on various levels shapes our faith and we experience it together with others. As Eric Jay notes, "'Church' does not mean the sum of individuals who have a private relationship with Christ and a private inspiration of the Holy Spirit. It is a community of believers incorporated into Christ's filial relationship with God."[84] To exist in communion is to exist from and in a sharing of life. This shared nature of faith means that faith needs communion. Its quest cannot be fulfilled in isolation (though there is a place for solitude) but also as a journey taken with others, for this is the nature of the divine reality opened to us in the Spirit. Thus, in discussing the dogmatic foundations of the church through Christ and in the gift of the Spirit, we not only have to look at how the Triune God self-imparts; we also have to consider the relational anthropological dynamic involved in our incorporation and ongoing response in faith. How does the church in Christ and by the Spirit participate in and bear witness to fulfilled humanity that we find in Christ? What is ecclesial personhood?

Humanity is created as the vessel of the Spirit of communion. Their very being is created for the way of the Spirit in the world. Genesis 2:7 shows that humanity was created to be taken up into God by becoming a bearer of the divine Spirit: "Then the LORD God formed a man from the dust of the ground and breathed into his nostrils the breath of life, and the man became a living being." But humanity is no island. The Spirit is after all the Spirit of communion: "It is not good for the man to be alone" (2:18). The Spirit of communion reaches implicitly for shared and corporate participation and covenant faithfulness—a point that is implied in the divine image shared between male and female in 1:27. But shared participation and covenant faithfulness are by no means limited to the first couple, but extends outward to leave its mark on what the entire Old Testament says about the people of God. Israel's relationship with God is mediated by the covenant people and is experienced as a reality that is shared in corporate liturgy, celebration, and responsibility. Individual faith is still valued, especially when the people as a whole stray from God. Key individuals bear the torch of faithfulness for the people and call them back to it. Yet, the people are still the locus of the divine calling and promises. These things are still ecclesially mediated. This calling and these promises find fulfillment in Israel's Messiah. It becomes clear in the light of Pentecost that humanity was created to participate in God and God's cause in the world by bearing the Spirit *in the image of the faithful Son*. The faithful Son breaks open a path to communion, opens his communion with the Father to others in the Spirit, and conditions his own existence by becoming the Lord of the covenant. Christ's incarnate and anointed personhood is covenantal and communal, and, analogously, so is ours in

---

[84] Eric G. Jay, *The Church: Its Changing Image through Twenty Centuries* (Atlanta: John Knox Press, 1980), 26.

him. As Barth argued, Jesus does not just fulfill the original human pair. Rather, they prefigure Christ, for Christ is the true humanity for all time.[85]

So what does the quintessentially Spirit-baptized man tell us about ideal humanity? In short, his taking on flesh all the way to the cross implies that personhood in the fullness of the Spirit of life will be oriented toward self-giving love, even suffering love. This love was directed by the Son to the Father with such passion that the Father's cause in the world comes to function as Christ's very sustenance, the very bread that his soul needs to flourish (Lk. 4:4). He communes with the Father with such intimacy that the Father is in him and he in the Father, an intimacy that Christ opens up as the source of salvation to humanity (Jn 17:21). This love is directed to humanity, promoting mercy and justice, especially toward the abused and the neglected, as shown in Jesus healing ministry and table fellowship. Personhood has its anchor in communion with God but extends outward in hospitality toward others. It seeks to embrace the other as other. Ultimately, personhood in the baptism in the Spirit is cruciform in nature. As Cornel West is fond of saying, one must "die" to love adequately: "Love is a form of death. And you have to learn how to die in order to learn how to love."[86] There is no fruitful sharing of life with others unless the penchant of the self to exploit others as objects of self-promotion or self-gratification is given over to death. "I am crucified with Christ" (Gal. 2:20a). Only then can a new self emerge that is fit for communion, or is "decentered," yielded to Christ and to the generous self-giving of the Spirit as revealed in him.[87] "The life I now live in the body, I live by faith in the Son of God, who loved me and gave himself for me" (2:20b). Cruciform love does not yield to the efforts of others to exploit one as an object of self-serving manipulation. That would be a twisted caricature of the cruciform love of which we speak. Christ gave his life for humanity, but he resisted their efforts to exploit him for their own purposes all along the way. He was devoted supremely only to the Father's call on his life. In cruciform love, rather, one gives of oneself for the sake of the other's repentance and redemption, for the sake of their realization of God's will for *their* lives. Only as people in relation enter into mutual service for the sake of God's cause in the world can personhood find its true fulfillment.

Personhood through self-giving love has its anchor in God and its thriving in communion with others. This interplay of individual and corporate dimensions requires unpacking. There is no question but that humans are inherently relational. This point is obvious from the scriptures noted earlier. But it is also obvious from nature itself. We come into this world nourished in a womb, which already binds us to another in intimate dependence. Our first memories are commonly of faces, especially of caregivers, who reflect acceptance to us. They nurture us in ways that become fundamental to our being in the world. As we mature, our network of relations expands and we take on different roles that are important to who we are. We are a father or mother, a son or daughter, perhaps a sibling. We are a friend, a neighbor, a

---

[85] This is the central point of Barth's disagreement with Bultmann's interpretation of Romans 5 in Barth's little classic, *Christ and Adam: Man and Humanity in Romans 5* (London: Forgotten Books, 2018).

[86] Cornel West, "Love is a Form of Death," The Table Video, The Center for Christian Thought, Biola University, https://cct.biola.edu/love-form-death/

[87] Volf, *Exclusion and Embrace*, 70.

coworker, and a fellow church member in communion. All of these roles identify us; they shape our sharing of life and purpose with others. They extend our embodied presence in the world. We speak languages that bind us to people through levels of interdependent communication. Our race and cultural influences deeply connect us to others as well and shape our embodied presence. Martin Buber rightly penned, "In the beginning was the relation."[88] Relationship is not external to us; it's ontological or integral to who we are. And relation as ontological does not change over time. It only becomes increasingly complex, deep, ever-more important to who we are in the world. We realize through it all that we receive far more than we give and that this grace should provoke in us gratitude and generous self-giving.

Yet, relationality requires individuality as well. The individual is not to be absorbed into a corporate whole. As Dietrich Bonhoeffer noted, "One could . . . say that by recognizing a You, a being of alien consciousness, as separate and distinct from myself, I recognize myself as an 'I,' and so my self-consciousness awakens."[89] Such is true not only one-to-one within the confines of an I-Thou relation; it is also true of a community fellowship in which I am awakened to my unique identity and gifting in contributing to the common good of a fellowship of many. Indeed, relationships require a sense of self that is distinct from others. Otherwise one is dissolved into a dominant corporate mind or will and true relationality succumbs to tyranny. Carl Jung's *Undiscovered Self* is a compelling reminder of the destruction of the self that can occur if an individual loses their distinct sense of self by being absorbed into a mass movement as an indistinct part of the whole.[90] Individuality is required for healthy participation in relationships or communities. Individuality is as basic to our development as relationality; in fact, it is essential to relationality itself. Anthony Storr's *Solitude: A Return to the Self* notes that a young child gains the capacity for trusting relationships in the ability to be *alone*. The child's early capacity to trust others develops when periods of being alone do not result in utter abandonment. The child learns to trust others more profoundly and to develop at the same time a sense of their own self-worth and reliance. The caregiver's absence thus becomes just as important to a child's healthy development as their presence. Storr notes that solitude continues to be just as important to one's healthy development as time shared with others.[91]

An individual's solitude (not isolation, but solitude) in God provides the anchor that protects us from unjust assimilation or manipulation by others. If individuals can seek to turn each of us into an object of their self-serving goals, a fellowship or a society can do so all the more forcefully and stealthily. The society can do so with language, media, institutional structures, and cultural mores. Solitude before God is the center from which one can gain the sense of personal dignity, calling, and gifting that helps one resist manipulation, serving others precisely through that very resistance. Jung writes, "Have I any religious experience and immediate relation to God, and hence

---

[88] Martin Buber, *I and Thou* (New York: Charles Scribner's Sons, 1970), 78.
[89] Dietrich Bohoeffer, *Sanctorum Communio: A Theological Study of the Sociology of the Church* (Minneapolis: Fortress Press, 1998), 71.
[90] Carl Jung, *Undiscovered Self: The Dilemma of the Individual in Modern Society* (New York: Signet, 1957).
[91] Anthony Storr, *Solitude: A Return to the Self* (New York: Free Press, 2005), 16–28.

that certainty that will keep me, as an individual, from dissolving in the crowd?"[92] This is indeed the crucial question. Jesus's relationship with his Father in the power of the Spirit was the center from which he resisted the attempted manipulations of the leadership of Israel, the crowds of Israelites, Pontius Pilate, and even his own disciples. In solitude he was able to renew himself in that center time and again. The church should be the place where one's anchor in God is learned and shared in communion with others. But even the people of God can sometimes fail you. When one comes into fellowship with others, one must be true to the self that God has liberated by the power of the Spirit for communion and Christ's service. As Volf noted, the liberated self must both exclude and embrace according to the cause of Christ's self-giving love that shapes and guides us. But the will to embrace must always be there.[93] One should remain open to form common cause with others especially in the church who will come alongside so as to bring about larger renewal among the people of God. In the meantime, we must sometimes be *for* others by being *against* them. Sometimes, secular voices will be used by God to speak to the church. No matter what, the church's scriptures and sacraments will have the capacity to transcend the weak vessels that handle them to point the people of God to the horizon of God's kingdom. The Spirit will draw the church toward that horizon and grant them the capacity to pray with their Lord to his heavenly Father, "Your kingdom come, your will be done, on earth as it is in heaven" (Mt. 6:10).

Paul's discourse about the spiritually gifted church in 1 Corinthians 12–14 allows space for private self-edification as well as for participation in the fellowship of the saints in which members shift in their emphasis to edifying others (14:4). Personal calling and empowerment allow individuals to have something important to contribute to the larger *koinonia* of life. The individual's prophetic voice once tested by the measure of the gospel is to be encouraged to make its mark in the life of the church. If guided by the Spirit, each individual will indeed make an impact on the life of the church. Indeed, as Daniela Augustine notes, "only the Spirit can sustain the significance of the individual voice in the communal symphony empowering each voice across all demographic boundaries."[94]

Yet, if the corporate can dissolve the individual, individualism can also fracture the communion of the many doing harm to human fulfillment as well. Community is not merely made up of an aggregate of individuals who come together with competing self-interests. Nor is a common cause, a common interest, or a common value enough to bring about real communion. Communion requires a deep mystery at the heart of the church, something that can only be called grace or gracious communion. Recognition of this mystery will produce a deep sense of gratitude for a community's common life together that no one can construct and no one can take away. In theological terms, I refer to the presence of the Holy Spirit by whom Christ shares his life and mission as our Head with us on behalf of the heavenly Father. The love of the Father poured out by the Spirit through Christ brings us together into communion with the Triune

---

[92] Jung, *Undiscovered Self*, 33.
[93] Volf, *Exclusion and Embrace*, 66.
[94] Augustine, *Pentecost, Hospitality, and Transfiguration*, 29.

God. Together in communion with God we discover a communion with each other that is a substantive part of the life of faith. Our individual relationship with God does not lose its significance within the communion of saints, nor is the communion we share together understandable from the vantage point of any one person or even the aggregate of the many individuals. The whole in communion is greater than the sum of its individual parts.

The individual receives much more from the church than the church receives from the individual. The church is born with the core practices (word, sacraments, gifts, mission, etc.) that are instrumental in the Spirit's work among and through the saints. Though personal solitude and spiritual disciplines are vital to one's spiritual journey, the church is still the social base through and in which that journey occurs. Indeed, the church depends on the unique faith of every individual for its diversity and vibrancy, and there are moments when key individuals could be the sparks by which congregations catch fire in their faithfulness to the cause of Christ in the world. But even here, such individuals have been shaped by the very church they now serve in such important ways. They are giving back that which they've received in ways more profound than they will ever know. They've left their unique imprint through that which they give back, but they are still channeling a grace back to the fellowship that God had earlier used to shape them.

To be clear, the church does not save us; Christ alone does that. But the church is the sign and instrument that Christ uses by way of the Spirit to save us. Each individual must approach Christ for saving grace. The church cannot do this on our behalf. But, as Bonhoeffer maintained, the church is still the fellowship that brings Christ to us and brings us to Christ.[95] The church's witness is the instrument and ecclesial context for our immediate encounter and relationship with Christ. This is the universal prophethood or priesthood of believers. We must make the journey into Christ for ourselves, in part from the solitude of our personal time with God. But the church is still the indispensable means through which Christ encounters us and from which we respond. Our encounter with Christ may be described as a mediated immediacy—a concept we will explore in our final chapter. We will also have the opportunity to do the same for others. In doing the same for others, our souls expand and are shaped more and more profoundly into Christ's image, for Christ is the one for others.

Indeed, if it were up to me, I would remain confined to the inner circle of my beloved family and closest friends. But, though the witness of the church may come to me most profoundly through close friends or relatives, the church includes many others important to my spiritual journey as well, some perhaps far different from me, maybe even undesirable to me in the natural realm. But the church requires that I serve them and open myself to their gifted service. In so doing, I expand in my ability to take on Christ. The church guides me in this process of serving in Christ's image. As Geoffrey Wainwright has shown, the liturgy and life of the church is the social context in which Christian identity is shaped. The scripture is to be the standard by which this shaping is judged, but this standard is not read and lived in a vacuum. The church

---

[95] Dietrich Bonhoeffer, *Spiritual Care* (Minneapolis, MN: Fortress, 1985), 30–32, see also 60–65.

provides the interpretive framework, though one that must always be tested against the text and the doctrinal milestones proved to be faithful to it.

So, which is primary, the corporate fellowship or the individual? Friedrich Schleiermacher has posed the issue this way: Protestantism "makes the individual's relation to the church dependent on his relation to Christ," while Catholicism "makes the individual's relation to Christ dependent on his relation to the church."[96] Does everything depend on the individual's relationship to Christ? If so, then the church would be viewed as a service agency to aid in the individual spiritual journey. By implication, the individual's relationship to the church would typically be viewed as secondary and nonessential, replaceable with other avenues of spiritual help. Does everything depend on one's relationship to the church? There is no question but that it does. This does not mean that our private life of solitude is not important; it just means that we are implicitly cradled by the faith and life of the church in such moments. Those who have initially witnessed of Christ to us did so from the life of the church. And we always receive more from the communion of saints than we know, even where we think we've been largely on our own in our spiritual journey. As John Calvin wrote of "mother church," "There is no other way to enter into life unless this mother conceive us in her womb, give us birth, nourish us at her breast, and, lastly, unless she keep us under her care and guidance until, putting off mortal flesh, we become like the angels."[97] But one must exercise caution, since the legitimate principle of the priority of the church can be abused. Individuals can be made to feel like passive receptors of clerical and liturgical actions. Individual faith can end up being described as having no direct relationship to Jesus Christ and no significant contribution to make to the faith of the church. Those charged with oversight in presuming to represent Christ can abuse their position and exclude those whom Christ has embraced.

Yet, we cannot seek to remedy such abuses by basing ecclesiology on the individual's spiritual journey. The resulting individualism has caused evangelicalism and the larger free church tradition to succumb to an individualistic and even market-driven ecclesiology (the church as a "salvation machine" or as a service agency for individual needs, which markets itself aggressively to the community on that basis). Speaking of the free church tradition, Volf rightly warns that in standing with the "everything depends on the relationship with Christ" option, "the charge of naked ecclesial individualism looms before us."[98] To grant the church priority while safeguarding against its abuses, Volf proposes that the faith of the individual is mediated through the corporate faith of the church as confessed, preached, sung, prayed, and so on, even if the link be through a single messenger. To avoid the church's abuse of its priority in the individual's life of faith, Volf maintains that the ecclesial mediation of grace to the individual is not merely at the hands of the clergy; all believers participate in mediating Christ to others. So the so-called laity is still actively involved in the church's mediating

---

[96] Schleiermacher, *The Christian Faith* #24, 103.
[97] John Calvin, *Institutes of the Christian Religion*, IV. 1. 4 (Virginia Beach, VA: CreateSpace Publishing, 2017), 359. I am grateful to Hendrikus Berkhof for this quote, *The Doctrine of the Holy Spirit* (Philadelphia, MN: Westminster John Knox, 1976), 48. He convincingly argues for the priority of the church to the individual. See 48–64.
[98] Volf, *After Our Likeness*, 160.

action. Though there are moments when the clergy may stand over against the church when proclaiming the Word of God, that experience is set within a church in which all speak the word of Christ in a similar way (Eph. 4:15). And all in the church are active together in being for the world by sometimes speaking over against it. Volf qualifies the mediation of the church further by adding that Christ is still the subject acting on the individual through the mediation of the church. The church is not a second subject of salvation alongside Christ. Christ alone saves through the instrumentality of the church. There is still a sense in which the encounter with Christ through the church is immediate to the individual. (We will elaborate on this "mediated immediacy" in our final chapter.) So the faith of the individual is vital to the church's witness and mediation. The church and the individual are "mutually determinative," though the church has the priority.[99]

The faith of the church is indeed rooted in repentance in preparation for its role in mediating Christ. Both faith and repentance are mutually dependent. The repentance of the church is a turning away from sin and faith is a turning toward God. This movement of repentance and faith is one turning—a *metanoia* (conversion) brought about by the seed of the word and the regenerative power of the Spirit. Without faith, repentance loses direction and can sink into the quicksand of self-loathing and self-destruction. Recall Luther's agonizing search for a gracious God or the lengthy *Busskampf* (repentance struggle) of some forms of pietism, which, in some cases, went on for long periods of time in search of comfort. Faith is indeed a battle at times, but the fight should find sustenance by the assurance of the Spirit (Rom. 8:15) who sides with us in our groaning in weakness for God (v. 26). Yet, faith without repentance is cheap grace, as Dietrich Bonhoeffer reminded us, which is an affirmation of forgiveness without a genuine turning from sin so as to embrace Christ alone as Lord. From a church that advocates faith without repentance, as Bonhoeffer wrote, "the world finds a cheap covering for its sins; no contrition is required, still less any real desire to be delivered from sin."[100] Grace is "sold on the market like cheapjacks' wares. The sacraments, the forgiveness of sin, and the consolation of religion are thrown away at cut prices."[101] Repentance that leads to faith cannot be a mere church practice without genuine contrition of heart that becomes in reality a living posture sustained by the comfort of grace and the joy of self-giving. As Luther wrote as the very first of his 95 Theses, "When our Lord and Master Jesus Christ said, 'Repent' (Mt. 4:17), he willed the entire life of believers to be one of repentance." And faith is not just mental assent to abstract truths but rather a turning with heart, mind, and action to God and God's purposes for the world. With heart, faith is trust in Christ and a participation in him as our only hope; with mind, it is a submission to the word of the gospel and the church's ongoing inquiry into its meaning; and with action, it is a path by which the word may increasingly be embodied among us for the sake of the world, guided and inspired by love.

---

[99] Ibid.
[100] Bonhoeffer, *The Cost of Discipleship*, 43.
[101] Ibid.

The Spirit of God in witness to the gospel grants the human soul eschatological transcendence, the capacity to give oneself over to God as an offering to the Father in the image of Jesus (Rom. 12:1). All that opposes this transformation is given over to death so that the self may be refashioned by the power of Christ's resurrection (Gal. 2:20). This process is not only personal but also communal, for the church seeks to inspire all to do this in unity while speaking the truth of Christ to one another in love (Eph. 4:15) and by partaking of the Lord's Supper together (1 Cor. 11:23-28). So the soul, granted eschatological transcendence, is expanded to make room for others in all of their God-given diversity, to help bear their burdens (Gal. 6:2), sharing with them the comfort of the gospel in the midst of repentance (2 Cor. 1:6). The human soul that inherently strives for its own unique purpose in communion with others finds fulfillment in the church as the sign of the new humanity in Christ.

## Conclusion

The church is the Spirit-baptized people of God. The dogmatic foundations of this understanding of the church is a vision of the Triune God as a communion of love that is open to the world and involved in self-giving, abundantly so, to the point of being described as overflowing love, the love revealed from the incarnation to Pentecost. This overflowing love may then be described as an intersubjective communion of faith and witness, because it has its origin in the self-giving life of the Triune God: The Father loves the Son and the Son loves the Father, and both love within the Spirit that overflows to incorporate the many. The life of the church occurs in the wide-open space of the Triune God, in that the divine communion of love opens up to us in the story of redemption. The Spirit is the one who encircles, celebrates, and opens that love to an ever-increasing diversity of others who share in the celebration and the vocation of that love. Divine outpouring and incorporation thus respect the others in all of their divinely created uniqueness.

The baptism in the Spirit is the means by which the Triune God self-imparts and incorporates others into the divine life. This process is enacted in Christ's baptism in Spirit and fire on our behalf. He passes through the fire and rises in the fullness of the Spirit so as to impart the Spirit, and with the Spirit, his own faithful life, to all flesh. The resulting incorporation into God may be described as a Spirit "baptism" because it represents a being taken into a limitless ocean of love that swallows us up entirely. The eschatological fulfillment of this Spirit baptism is both substantively deep, mortality being "swallowed up" in life (2 Cor. 5:4), and corporately expansive and diverse, to the ends of the earth (Acts 1:8).

In the church, there is no abstract corporate emphasis in which individual faith is dissolved away as insignificant, nor is there an abstract individualism in which the church's corporate life as mediator of grace is reduced to insignificance. Christ comes to individuals in the mediation of the church, but all faithful individuals play a vital role in this mediation. And it is Christ who acts by the Spirit through the church to save using the participation of all in word, sacrament, gifted ministries, and mission.

Spirit baptism is mediated by the church and is fulfilled in the quality and expanse of its corporate life, but it is also a profoundly individual experience. Though the church has priority over the individual, the individual life of faith is still cherished as essential to the church, in terms of its goal of mediating Christ to people for the sake of their salvation and incorporation by faith. Spirit baptism transforms us all into the very embodiment of this self-giving, overflowing love, or, into the image of Christ and into the freedom and communion of the Spirit. This embodiment is what we will call the church.

# 2

# The Elect Church

The Pentecostal team in the 1977–82 Roman Catholic-Pentecostal dialogue noted that they "stress that the church itself was created by the calling (election) of Christ."[1] Christ is both the elect of God and the one who opens his election to others through the ever-more-expansive outpouring of the Spirit. Christ's own election was actualized in time and visibly attested at his baptism in the Spirit according to Jn 1:33-34: "And I myself did not know him, but the one who sent me to baptize with water told me, 'The man on whom you see the Spirit come down and remain is the one who will baptize with the Holy Spirit.'34 I have seen and I testify that this is God's Chosen One." He opens his election to us by imparting the Spirit to us. That election is being chosen to a holy purpose to commune with God but also to share in the vocation that this new life opens to us.

Election is not a strong topic among most Pentecostals, though it should be. It should be not only because it's biblical but also because election occurs in the New Testament centrally under the anointing of the Holy Spirit, first and all-inclusively in Jesus but also in and through the mediation of a people who are elect in him. This election thus occurs not only in history but also, in a sense, in eternity. It occurs in history, because it occurs decisively at the anointing of the Son by the Father and, by extension, through the Son's impartation of the Spirit to others. It occurred prior to Christ among the Israelites and their forebearers—but even this foreshadowed Christ. It occurs in eternity, because the anointed Son and the Spirit are eternal, integral to the self-election of the Triune God for the sake of humanity. As we will see, it's principally the revelation that the anointed Christ is the elect One that causes the New Testament to regard election as eternal.

There are indeed questions to explore in unpacking these ideas. If election is both eternal and a divine decision enacted in time, how do they relate? If Christ is the elect One for all time, how do we describe that election in relation to us? Is election primarily corporate or individual? Is it soteriological (oriented to communion) or vocational (oriented to ministry)? Is election open to all, and if so, how do we account for the particularity assumed in some election texts (the elect as distinguishable from the rest of humanity)? I am not able to pursue the myriad of questions that can be asked about the complex topic of election with any thoroughness in the context of this chapter.

---

[1] "Final Report of the Dialogue between the Secretariat for Promoting Christian Unity and Some Classical Pentecostals," 1977–82, #51, *GW II*, 727.

But I do hope with broad strokes to connect election not only to Christ but also to the expanding work of the Spirit in the world. I will attempt to show that election is rooted in a love for humanity that is eternal because it is rooted in the love shared between the Father and the Son in the overflowing reach of the Spirit. It is a historical reality for the same reason. There is much to unpack in the pages that follow.

## A Timeless Decree or an Anointing in Time?

Election immediately calls to mind, for most people acquainted with the doctrine, anything but a reality to be experienced in the baptism in the Spirit. Rather, election is viewed more often than not as an eternally fixed or timeless decree. Ardent defenders of it are prone to see such a decree behind every election text in the Bible. The major question was whether or not the eternal decree of election was based on God's foreknowledge of human faith. Best known through John Calvin and especially his followers, this side of the debate typically insists that God's election is not based on foreknowledge of human actions but rather on God's sovereign good pleasure alone. God decides from all eternity who should be saved and who should be damned (or, perhaps, "passed over" or allowed to sink into the condemnation that they deserve). Those who choose this option will usually seek to defend the justice of such a divine decision, noting that God is not obligated to save sinners who are worthy of condemnation. In my view, this argument places divine self-regard above mercy toward others, which arguably dislodges divine justice from its foundation and *telos* in divine love. Apart from the discussion of whether the demands of justice do not mandate a universal opportunity for salvation, what about the demands of divine love? A love that is selective falls short of the infinite and limitless love assumed of God in the scriptures. How can an infinitely loving God take pleasure from passing over millions who are destined for eternal disaster? As we will see, texts like Jn 3:16 ("for God so loved the world...") and 2 Pet. 3:9 ("not wishing that any should perish...") are compelling as descriptors of the limitless love of God for humanity. So are the texts that depict the love we are to have for others in mimicking God. For example, Paul said that he agonized so deeply over the unfaithfulness of his kinsmen that he would be willing to suffer banishment from Christ for their salvation (Rom. 9:1-4). Paul agonized for all of his kinsmen, not just a select group of them. Are we to assume that God's love agonizes any less, and for any fewer? If God did not choose to save many of those over whom Paul agonized, Paul's love would be superior in its breadth and depth to God's! To merely reply that one has no right to protest against God (9:19-21) begs the question, since the object of protest here is not God but an interpretation of God. And so the debate goes on. But one thing I do hold that the Calvinist side of the debate has right is the idea that election is indeed rooted fundamentally in God's sovereign will and not in the direction that human decision-making might want to take history. It all depends on how one frames this divine will theologically.

Even those who are more or less opposed to Calvinism will agree that election is essentially an eternal decree. Rooted in the thought of Origen and inspired by the thoughts of Jacob Arminius (and later, John Wesley), their difference from Calvinism had mainly to do with whether or not election as a timeless decree is based on God's foreknowledge of human faith. If so, God is understood as electing those whom God foresees will believe. Human faith then becomes the crucial dividing line between the elect and the non-elect. Calvinist opponents of this option accuse it of stripping God of divine sovereignty, as though election is merely God's rubber-stamping what humans have decided for themselves. Of course, those who base election on foreknowledge may very well view faith as willed and enabled by God, so that faith hardly represents merely what "humans decide for themselves." Moreover, rather than "rubber-stamping" human decisions, God would be eternally delighting in the divine handy work among those who yield to grace in history, which was sovereignly willed for all of humanity from time eternal. Yet, even given these important qualifications, one could still question whether the Bible places the crucial point of emphasis on human faith when it comes to election. I will argue that human faith is crucial but only within a limited aspect of the doctrine (individual participation in corporate election). I trust it will become clear as we proceed that election as a larger doctrine is based even more fundamentally on the sovereign grace of God. But the sovereignty of election does not mean that God sovereignly chooses from all eternity some to be saved and some to be damned. Rather, God from all eternity sovereignly elects Christ, a divine self-determination that involves a self-imparting God opened up to all of humanity through Christ and in the overflowing and abundant reach of the Spirit. It is only within this sovereign choice that the human response of faith has significance and purpose.

I will begin to unpack this idea with a crucial point. Though the idea that election is an eternal decree has become the central feature of election in classical debates over the doctrine, it is important to note that in the Old Testament election is a divine decision that occurs *in history*. As we will see, election is also eternal, but if we leap to that idea from the beginning, we end up with an abstraction that is unrelated to historical choices that occur between God and humanity. We must thus begin with history, the only place that the Old Testament allows us to begin. A divine plan is indeed implied in the patriarchal narratives of Genesis. God gives a promise to Abraham that will have far-reaching significance in history (and even beyond) for the salvation of humanity (Gen. 22:17) and the rise of Joseph to power fulfills a divine intention: "You intended to harm me, but God intended it for good to accomplish what is now being done, the saving of many lives" (50:20). Yet, there is no explicit indication within this larger narrative of a decision that is timeless or that predates creation. God chooses Abraham to receive the promise of salvation (15:4-6) and reaffirms the promise in response to his faith and loyalty ("because you have done this and have not withheld your son, your only son, I will surely bless you," 22:16-17a). And Joseph's life seems to follow a divine intention but one that is worked out during his lifetime. Similarly, God chooses Israel out of loyalty to the covenant established with the patriarchs and out of compassion for Israel's weakness and suffering: "I have heard the groaning of the Israelites, whom the Egyptians are enslaving, and I have remembered my covenant" (Exod. 6:5). God then calls them out of Egypt to be the favored Son (Hos. 11:1). The election and concomitant calling of Israel are not described in these texts as a decree from eternity past. The election of Israel is always portrayed as "a concrete historical act on God's part that forms the starting point and basis of the salvation history of God and his people."[2] In a thorough discussion of this issue, Sigurd Grindheim notes as well that in the Old Testament, "election is never explicitly associated with a time before or at creation."[3] Election is a historical event located in the time frame of the patriarchs (Isa. 41:8; 51:1-3; Ps. 105:6; 135:4; Neh. 9:7) or the Exodus/wilderness wanderings (Deut. 4:37; 7:6-7; 10:15; Ezek. 20:5; Hos. 11:1; 13:4-5).[4]

In Deut. 7:7-9 God chose Israel as the "fewest of all peoples" (v. 7). God delivered them from slavery because God loved them and kept the oath made to their ancestors. There is no reference to a timeless decree in this text. This commitment is made in history, and the immediate setting of God's choice of Israel is an affection that God formed for the nation due to the fact that they were weak and oppressed ("the fewest of all peoples"). God chose those who were least likely to be chosen, but for the much larger purpose of occasioning repentance among the nations. The use of this weak vessel to occasion the redemption of the world will show forth not only the compassion and justice of God but also the power and glory of God's grace in the face of the arrogance of dominant human powers on earth. God's election is sovereign and directed to God's goals for history, but human faithfulness still plays a role in the plan: "He is the faithful God, keeping his covenant of love to a thousand generations of those who love him and keep his commandments" (Deut. 7:9). But the goal as we will see is the offer of mercy to all.

Those who reject God's offer of grace will suffer judgment. This includes those within the covenant of the elect who are being used to bear witness to God's glory and grace. The metaphor that is implied here (and is used in the prophetic books as an illustration) is that of a betrothal. Israel was chosen out of Egypt as betrothed to God and will eventually be wedded to God after a time of judgment. Note Hosea:

> "In that day," declares the LORD,
> "you will call me 'my husband';
> you will no longer call me 'my master.'" (Hos. 2:16)

Israel's journey with God spans the time frame from their past betrothal to their future wedding. Hosea also uses a child-parent metaphor. God calls Israel as the favored son out of Egypt, the Exodus itself functioning here as the event of God's calling (11:1). Israel is now a wayward child who is called to return to the father's household (11:2). God's choice of Israel remains firm but has a history that includes unexpected turns, including judgment. But there is always a faithful remnant that carries the torch of election for the covenant people until they can be restored. Election begins in time and shifts from grace to judgment only to reach for grace once more as its consummation in the eschatological fulfillment of God's reign.

The prophetic tradition responded to Israel's failures by urging them to look with hope to the era of the Spirit for future restoration. According to Isaiah, Israel's prophetic

---

[2] Kurt Koch, "Zur Geschichte der Erwälungsvorstellung in Israel," *ZAW* 67 (1955): 212 (205–26); quoted in Pannenberg, *Systematic Theology*, Vol. 3 (Grand Rapids, MI: Eerdmans, 1998), 442.
[3] Sigurd Grindheim, *The Crux of Election* (WUNT 2. Reihe 202; Tübingen: Mohr Siebeck, 2005), 8. See also Pannenberg, *Systematic Theology*, Vol. 3, 442–43.
[4] Grindhein, *The Crux of Election*, 8.

calling ("in the womb") and their election will find fulfillment when the Spirit comes upon them:

> This is what the Lord says—
>   he who made you, who formed you in the womb,
>   and who will help you:
> Do not be afraid, Jacob, my servant,
>   Jeshurun, whom I have chosen.
> ³ For I will pour water on the thirsty land,
>   and streams on the dry ground;
> I will pour out my Spirit on your offspring,
>   and my blessing on your descendants. (Isa. 44:2-3)

The Lord will come "like a pent-up flood that the breath of the Lord drives along" to those who revere the divine glory (59:19). The Spirit will not leave the chosen people:

> "The Redeemer will come to Zion,
>   to those in Jacob who repent of their sins," declares the Lord.
> "As for me, this is my covenant with them," says the Lord. "My Spirit, who is on
>   you, will not depart from you, and my words that I have put in your mouth
>   will always be on your lips, on the lips of your children and on the lips of their
>   descendants—from this time on and forever," says the Lord. (vv. 20-21)

Isaiah then recalls that God called Israel and remained close to them. "In all their distress, he too was distressed" (63:9). But then Israel rebelled "and grieved his Holy Spirit" (v. 10). God opposed them in their sin but did not abandon them. They will not grieve the Spirit forever.

Of crucial importance is the fact that the Spirit of God's presence with Israel during the Exodus sets the Exodus apart as the event of election. This same divine presence that went with and before them will open up the possibility of Israel's reclaiming their election as the people of the Exodus by yielding once again to the Spirit:

> Then his people recalled the days of old,
>   the days of Moses and his people—
> where is he who brought them through the sea,
>   with the shepherd of his flock?
> Where is he who set
>   his Holy Spirit among them,
> ¹² who sent his glorious arm of power
>   to be at Moses' right hand,
> who divided the waters before them,
>   to gain for himself everlasting renown. (vv. 11-12)

This theme of election by the Spirit of God is found in Ezekiel as well. The fact that election can include judgment shows that Israel was not chosen merely for its own sake. The Creator is no tribal deity who can be reduced to functioning as the guarantor of the elect people's success. To the contrary, God chose Israel to serve divine purposes within a much larger global context so as to show mercy on all. God will fulfill these purposes through the elect people by any means necessary, including their judgment. And their devastating failures will show that they will fulfill their election only by the mighty Spirit of God. To begin with, note Ezek. 36:22-23:

> [22] Therefore say to the Israelites, "This is what the Sovereign LORD says: It is not for your sake, people of Israel, that I am going to do these things, but for the sake of my holy name, which you have profaned among the nations where you have gone. [23] I will show the holiness of my great name, which has been profaned among the nations, the name you have profaned among them. Then the nations will know that I am the LORD," declares the Sovereign LORD, "when I am proved holy through you before their eyes."

It is God's purposes and not Israel's that determine the purpose of election. Reading further, God ends with a promise that Israel will reclaim their calling when they are filled with the Holy Spirit and follow God's law: "I will give you a new heart and put a new spirit in you; I will remove from your heart of stone and give you a heart of flesh. And I will put my Spirit in you and move you to follow my decrees and be careful to keep my laws" (vv. 26-27). Israel will not be abandoned but will be raised up as from the dead by the Spirit of God when they are allowed to return to their land from captivity: "I will put breath in you, and you will come to life. Then you will know that I am the Lord" (37:6). Indeed, God affirms, "I will no longer hide my face from them, for I will pour out my Spirit on the people of Israel, declares the Sovereign LORD" (39:29).

Most importantly, the anointed One of Israel becomes the eschatological focal point of Israel's election by the Spirit. He will lead the people to their chosen destiny. Note especially Isa. 42:1:

> Here is my servant, whom I uphold,
>   my chosen one in whom I delight;
> I will put my Spirit on him,
>   and he will bring justice to the nations.

The Chosen One of Israel will lead the nation to the fulfillment of its elect destiny:

> [7] I will proclaim the LORD's decree:
> He said to me, "You are my son; today I have become your father.
> [8] Ask me,
>   and I will make the nations your inheritance,
>   the ends of the earth your possession." (Ps. 2:7-8)

None of the anointed kings of Israel were able to fulfill this destiny. As Von Rad noted, with each king Israel asked implicitly, "Are you he who is to come, or shall we look for another?"⁵ The Spirit will rest on the Chosen One, granting him wisdom and understanding, counsel and might, knowledge and fear of the Lord (Isa. 11:2). The Spirit will rest on him, and he will proclaim good news to the poor, bind up the broken hearted, proclaim release to the captives, and release from darkness to the prisoners, announcing the year of the Lord's favor (61:1-2). There will be a mighty outpouring of the Spirit to bring end-time salvation and usher in the new age (Joel 2:18-32). The Old Testament does not explicitly make the Messiah, who bears the Spirit, the Lord who will pour forth the Spirit. That revelation will be John the Baptist's signature teaching. It will become clear through this insight that the Messiah who bears the Spirit is in himself the wellspring of the Spirit who seals election for all peoples of the earth.

The upshot of these texts is that even though in the Old Testament election occurs in history under the call of God as attested by the anointing of the Spirit, the chosen people can grieve the Spirit and disregard the call to love and serve God above all else (Isa. 63:8-10; Hos. 11:1-2). Election is thus based on the faithfulness of the anointed Messiah, Jesus of Nazareth. Karl Barth helps us to see that election is disclosed and accomplished once and for all time in the story of Jesus, in his sojourn from the womb to the cross and the resurrection, all the way, I would add, to Pentecost and beyond. In Barth's explanation of election, Jesus is in his very person the fulfillment of Israel's election; Israel's election foreshadows his. He alone is the beloved and faithful Son (the one and only). He is not only the elect Son; he is also the electing God or the means by which others are elect in him. The union of divine and human natures in Christ thus means for Barth the wedding of elect humanity and the electing God in permanent covenant relation. Barth explains:

> The doctrine of election is the sum of the Gospel because of all the words that can be said or heard it is the best: that God elects man; that God is for man too the One who loves in freedom. It is grounded in the knowledge of Jesus Christ because He is both the electing God and elected man in one.⁶

Election cannot be conceived of in abstraction for Barth but only concretely in Jesus Christ as the revelation of both elect humanity and the electing God in time, in the event of Jesus Christ.⁷ God's election is thus "a divine activity in the form of the history, encounter and decision between God and man" that plays out in Jesus Christ.⁸ We will explore Barth's Christocentric understanding of election further in my Final Reflections.

Of importance here is Otto Weber's additional insight that Christ's anointing (the descent of the Spirit upon Jesus) is the public attestation of Christ's election.⁹ This event of messianic anointing is not typically granted such a central focus when it comes to the doctrine of election. And, yet, the Gospel of John tells us that John the Baptist

---

5   Von Rad, *Old Testament Theology, Vol. II*, 374–75.
6   Karl Barth, *CD*, Vol. 2, Pt. 2, *The Doctrine of God*, ed. G. W. Bromiley and T. F. Torrance (Edinburgh: T & T Clark, 1957), 3.
7   Ibid., 76.
8   Ibid., 175.
9   Otto Weber, *Foundations of Dogmatics*, Vol. 2 (Grand Rapids, MI: Eerdmans, 1983), 498.

recognized at the descent of the Spirit upon Jesus that Jesus is indeed the "Chosen One" "who will baptize with the Holy Spirit":

> Then John gave this testimony: "I saw the Spirit come down from heaven as a dove and remain on him. And I myself did not know him, but the one who sent me to baptize with water told me, 'The man on whom you see the Spirit come down and remain is the one who will baptize with the Holy Spirit.' I have seen and I testify that *this is God's Chosen One.*" (1:32-34)

God promised the elect people that they will be known as those with whom the Spirit will remain ("My Spirit, who is on you, will not depart from you," Isa. 59:20). This promise is fulfilled with Israel's Messiah, in whom their election is fulfilled.

Matthew rarely uses explicit election language, but he implies that Jesus's reception of the Spirit at his baptism is the key event of Christ's election in time. When describing Jesus's being brought out of Egypt as a young boy, Matthew quotes Hos. 11:1, "Out of Egypt I have called my son," a text that indicated in its original context God's calling Israel as the elect "son" of God through the Exodus. Though Israel departed from their elect sonship (11:2), Matthew presents Israel's Messiah as faithful. In fulfillment of Israel's election through the Exodus, when the Spirit went with and before the people, Jesus passes through the waters of the Jordan at his baptism only to have the Spirit descend upon him and the Father declares from heaven, "This is my Son whom I love; with him I am well pleased" (Mt. 3:17). The Spirit then goes before Jesus, leading him into the desert where he is tested for forty days as Israel was tested for forty years, and, again, where Israel failed, Christ proves to be the faithful Son. Later, it is said in Matthew of the anointed Christ, "Here is my servant *whom I have chosen*, the one I love, in whom I delight; I will put my Spirit on him, and he will proclaim justice to the nations" (12:18). Christ's election under the anointing of the Spirit thus fulfills Isa. 42:1:

> Here is my servant, whom I uphold,
>   my chosen one in whom I delight;
> I will put my Spirit on him,
>   and he will bring justice to the nations.

Luke also indicates that the Spirit Baptizer who receives the Spirit after his baptism is the elect One. At the transfiguration, Jesus is declared by the Father as the Chosen One in language that recalls his reception of the Spirit at the Jordan: "A voice came from the cloud, saying, 'This is my Son, *whom I have chosen*; listen to him'" (Lk. 9:35).

The Jordan as the location of Christ's election under the anointing of the Spirit is significant, since, as noted in our previous chapter, he takes his place with sinners at his baptism. He does this not only for wayward Israel but also for all of humanity for whom Israel was called to be a witness. Luke implicitly draws the boundaries of the anointed Christ's election this wide by referring to Adam as "the son of God" in the lineage that is given just after Christ's anointing as the Son of the Father (Lk. 3:38; cf., 3:22). As noted earlier, Christ stands with those who are abandoned ("passed over");

he takes on our baptism of fire (our judgment). As the faithful Son and bearer of the Spirit he enters into humanity's judgment of fire on the cross (12:49-50). He suffers their fate of abandonment and judgment.[10] "But He was merciful in that he took the author of evil to His bosom, and willed that the rejection and condemnation and death should be His own."[11] He rises again as the Son vindicated and sanctified in the Spirit in order to open passage for all flesh to God's gift of life, which is at the core of God's final purposes for history. This is the final Exodus by the anointed Messiah for all people, and he will impart the Spirit to all flesh so as to open his Exodus, his election, his sonship to all flesh. He was set apart by the Spirit as the holy Son of God in the womb for such a purpose as this (1:35). None can compare to him. He is not just one chosen among others. He is the Chosen One in (and from whom) all others receive their election.

He is the revelation not only of the elect One but also of the electing God. When he chooses his disciples, he establishes an inner circle that shares in his election: "You did not choose me, but I chose you and appointed you so that you might go and bear fruit" (Jn 15:16). The foundation of their elect life was the calling that came from Christ and not their own self-determination. Indeed, their election shares in his, for he is the vine; they are but the branches of it (vv. 1-2). At Christ's return, the angels will "gather his elect from the four winds, from the ends of the earth to the ends of the heavens" (Mk 13:27). His elect! The Messiah will take as his possession (his treasured possession; note the election language here) the very ends of the earth (Ps. 2:8). At Christ's return, he will gather his elect from these ends. As Acts 1:8 notes, the elect people will take their witness to the ends of the earth so that all may be incorporated into the Messiah as his elect through the baptism in the Spirit. All are anointed for this reason. Let us explore specific New Testament voices with these general thoughts in mind. We will see that election is both historical and timeless because it's Christological and pneumatological, or, more expansively, focused on the timeless will and self-giving in history of the Triune God.

# Election: New Testament Voices

## Ephesians 1: Spirit Baptism as the Seal of Election

Ephesians 1 is sometimes referred to as the *textus classicus* of election. More than any other text, it highlights the Christological center and boundless pneumatological circumference of election. Paul stresses in this chapter that election is derived from

---

[10] As noted in Chapter 1, Jesus's wish in Lk. 12:49-50 that the fire of judgment foretold by John the Baptist (with his announcement that the Messiah will baptize in fire) were already kindled at the advent of the kingdom. But he knew that he must first endure this fire himself for the sake of others: for the sake of their escape and baptism in the restorative Spirit. See Macchia, *Jesus the Spirit Baptizer: Christology in Light of Pentecost*, 229–42.

[11] Karl Barth, *CD*, Vol. 2, Pt. 2, 167, see 166–67.

Christ and shared among the many in the Spirit. It starts with our being blessed with all "spiritual blessing" in Christ from eternity past (1:3-4):

> ³ Praise be to the God and Father of our Lord Jesus Christ, who has blessed us in the heavenly realms with every spiritual blessing in Christ. ⁴ For he chose us in him before the creation of the world to be holy and blameless in his sight.

This horizon of the eternal past then points to the eschatological unity of communion "under Christ" in the ultimate horizon of the eternal future (v. 10): ". . . to be put into effect when the times reach their fulfillment—to bring unity to all things in heaven and on earth under Christ." This larger election text then lands at the current historical nexus between the two "eternities" under the sealing of the Holy Spirit, which is the eschatological reality of inclusion in Christ and the elect people through faith and water baptism. This is the central historical reality of election (its actualization and expanding boundary) in which the readers then lived (vv. 13-14):

> ¹³ And you also were included in Christ when you heard the message of truth, the gospel of your salvation. When you believed, you were marked in him with a seal, the promised Holy Spirit, ¹⁴ who is a deposit guaranteeing our inheritance until the redemption of those who are God's possession—to the praise of his glory.

There are four points to notice here: first, the language of being God's "possession" is election language ("You will be my treasured possession," Ex. 19:5). Second, being elect is actualized in time by being "included in Christ" and "marked in him with a seal." Sealing was used in the ancient world of slaves to indicate possession, a dehumanizing act which this text turns into a liberating and humanizing one. Third, this seal that includes us in Christ and seals us in him as God's possession occurs through the reception of the Spirit. This is what marks us as belonging to the anointed Messiah, the elect man of all time. And, fourth, this reception of the Spirit guarantees future redemption through resurrection, the fulfillment of our baptism in the Holy Spirit. The implication is that the risen Christ opens his election to us through the mark of the Spirit, which guarantees ultimate entry into the blessings of the Spirit in resurrection, the spiritual blessings in heavenly places earmarked for the elect in Christ from all eternity (1:3). Union with Christ through Spirit baptism is thus the cutting edge of the realization of election in time, in between the spiritual blessing granted to Christ's body from eternity past and the horizon of being "under him" in the eschatological unity that is still future. The seal of the Spirit in union with Christ by faith is the moment in time that actualizes the blessing granted in Christ in eternity past and guarantees the future fulfillment of ultimate union with Christ that will come in the future.

The verses immediately prior to the above text (vv. 11-12) repeat that we were chosen "in him" and then follows with, "having been predestined according to the plan of him who works out everything in conformity with the purpose of his will" (v. 11). The purpose of this predestination is "in order that we, who were the first to put our hope in Christ, might be for the praise of his glory," a reference to the original Jewish believers (v. 12). And then follows the beginning of v. 13: "And you also were included in Christ when you heard the message of truth," most likely a reference to Gentiles. The term "predestine" is also used earlier in the chapter (v. 5): "He predestined us to adoption through Jesus Christ according to the good pleasure of his will." The term "having been predestined" (προορισθέντες) simply refers to something that is foreordained.[12] I would like to make a few observations as to its meaning in this context. First, the predestination seems eternal in this text, since it is connected to a choosing or election that occurs "before the foundation of the world" (v. 4). Second, predestining occurs "in Christ," tied to his election and its purposes. It is his election that is being opened up to others; his sonship was predestined to be shared with others through adoption. Third, predestining seems connected to the plan to open eschatological Israel to Gentiles so that at the end there can be a grand unity under Christ: "He made known to us the mystery of his will according to his good pleasure, which he purposed in Christ, to be put into effect when the times reach their fulfillment—to bring unity to all things in heaven and on earth under Christ" (vv. 9-10). There is no indication in the larger text that individuals are predestined to believe while others are being passed over. The confidence with which some apply this grid over the text seems unwarranted to me. Rather, Paul appears to be saying that the opening up of Christ's election beyond Jews so as to include Gentiles was part of a larger ordained plan that will find fulfillment in the eschatological unity for which Jew and Gentile are sealed by the gift of the Spirit. Paul is standing on the edge of the gentile mission which is Spirit driven, and he sees unfolding before him an eternal plan that Christ open his sonship to others (by way of adoption) in precisely this way.

There is every reason to believe that this foreordained plan enacted in Christ and by the Spirit is potentially opened to all. In the eschatological reach of the Spirit, should we expect anything less? The gift of the Spirit received by faith is the place where inclusion in Christ is actualized, attested, and sealed for eschatological fulfillment. As we saw earlier, Isaiah looks to the Spirit as having brought the Israelites through the Exodus and as the ultimate power of future fulfillment (63:9-14). The Holy Spirit in the church in Ephesians 1 is "a deposit guaranteeing our inheritance until the redemption of those who are God's possession—to the praise of his glory" (1:14). Though Israel as the elect people grieved the Spirit in Isaiah 63:10, the church of Ephesus sealed by the Spirit as God's possession are asked to avoid such a fate: "And do not grieve the Holy Spirit of God, with whom you were sealed for the day of redemption" (4:30). They are to yield to being filled with the Spirit, giving glory to God in unity (5:18; cf., 4:3). The Spirit is the deposit of every spiritual blessing earmarked for us in 1:3 and by implication eschatologically realized in the grand unity in Christ in 1:10.

Ephesians 1 and Isaiah (and other Old Testament texts) are strikingly different in that in Isaiah the election occurs in history at the Exodus and is rooted in the covenant made with Israel's patriarchs. In Ephesians 1, the election occurs in history also, but this history is Christologically and pneumatologically defined, which pushes election into the eternal designation of Christ as the elect One and source of spiritual blessing for all time. Christ was always determined to be the Spirit Baptizer. The larger text describes

---

[12] K. L. Schmidt, "προορίζω," in *TDNT*, Vol. V, ed. Gerhard Kittle and Gerhard Friedrich (Grand Rapids, MI: Eerdmans, 1967), 456.

every aspect of union with Christ by the Spirit as accessible "in him" (or some variant of that phrase) eleven times, enough to be stylistically awkward. Election in Ephesians is thus based on the substance of that ancient patriarchal promise highlighted in the Old Testament, but defines this substance Christologically. Jesus Christ is God's eternal Son anointed for his reign as possessor and imparter of the promised Spirit. For the blessing of Jacob is indeed to be found in the outpouring of the Spirit (Isa. 44:1-3). Rooted in Christ rather than merely the promise given to the patriarchs, election gets pushed back into the eternal mystery of the Son as the Beloved of the Father (we may add) in the circle of the Spirit. The curtain covering the inner source of election hidden to the Israelites is now pulled back. The eternal Christ is the elect One in whom all others for all time are set aside for the glory of communion in the Triune God.

What in particular does it mean to say that we have been spiritually blessed and chosen before the foundation of the world "in him" (Eph. 1:4)? First, election occurs under spiritual blessing. And so it was with Jacob's seed (Isa. 44:1-3), and so it was with the eternal Son. Being elect "in him" means that we share in his eternal anointing, communion, and Spirit-empowered mission as revealed in time. Second, "chosen in him" means that election is a gift. Eternal election is *his* first and foremost; it is defined by *him* and thus only available *in him and with him*. It is his anointing properly; it is ours as a gift. It is his sonship, the benefits of which are opened to us through adoption according to God's predestined will. In other words, Christ's eternal sonship was always meant to be a gift. With the gift of the Son comes the gift of his election. As a gift, election is not to be taken for granted. Election is possible only because from all eternity Christ was the anointed Christ for others, the Christ who gives himself in the power of the Spirit for the sake of others, who offers himself, his favored, blessed, and called status, as a gift to others. Election in Christ by grace means that only *his* election is direct; ours is *indirect*. *In electing him*, God was electing all of us too. But we are not a mere byproduct of his election, since he was elect *for us*. The outward movement of the Triune God is eternal, integral to the act of election as its purpose. We are chosen in him or in God's logically prior decision in the anointed Christ to be the God for us as Creator and Redeemer, the God who includes us in the Father's embrace of the beloved Son, who counts us along with the incarnate and anointed Christ as God's possession. By being eternally Christ for us, the one and only object of the Father's election becomes this divine good favor in action extended to us on God's behalf. His election becomes a gift of grace. He is the Spirit Baptizer, who seals us by his Spirit to actualize in time the spiritual blessing set aside for us (1:3) and to grant us a foretaste of the eschatological unity of all things under Christ the Head (1:10).[13]

Before proceeding to our third point, let us linger with this issue of election by grace a bit longer. If we overlook this point of election in the Son, we miss the true reason why our election is based on grace alone, why it is not based primarily on foreknown human faithfulness. We see why election by grace alone does not mean that God capriciously for some reason unknown to us decided to choose only us and leave everyone else in the lurch. Such a decision would not be grace, for grace as the turning of a loving God to sinners cannot by definition fail to reach for all who

---

[13] Ibid, 104.

are lost. The Christ through whom all things were created is also the Christ through whom all things are set aside in God's redemptive purpose. The Christ was always the anointed Christ for *all* others. Election is based on grace alone because Christ's eternal favor with the Father has been opened up to humanity, because Christ determined in harmony with the love of the Father and the limitless freedom of the Spirit to be the Christ for us all, from all of eternity. In choosing and loving him, the Father was at the same time choosing and loving us all. Barth put the matter concerning all of humanity this way, "In that He (as God) wills Himself (as man), He also wills them. And so they are elect, 'in Him,' in and with his own election."[14] Barth thus interprets Eph. 1:4 (that we are chosen in Christ before the foundation of the world) to mean that from all eternity, God "sees us in His Son as sinners to whom He is gracious."[15] Eternal election in the Son is potentially extended as a gift to all; but it is only received in history by faith and in the Spirit.[16]

Third, as mentioned earlier, election in the Son has as its predestined goal our adoption in Christ (Eph. 1:5) and, more expansively, the bringing of "unity to all things in heaven and on earth under Christ" (v. 10). Election is limitless in reach. Christ is the Son by nature. We are chosen sons and daughters only by adoption. But this adoption is purposed for all. The open-ended "all things" of v. 10 is not to be overlooked, for the implication here is that those chosen in Christ before the creation are not confined by fixed and narrow limits. Rather, the "chosen" in Christ reaches at least potentially for all of humanity and all of creation. All of humanity is called to realize their humanity beneath Christ as their Head. The full attainment of all that has been "legally" laid aside for them as their inheritance is by the Spirit's sealing actualized. This sealing is granted under the outward sign of water baptism. With this spiritual benefit comes a call to serve. Those who accept the call discover that they are on the cutting edge of an election opened from all eternity in Christ to all of humanity. This realization drives the mission of the church.

Paul thus states that we were predestined "according to the plan" that has this unity of all things under Christ as its outcome (Eph. 1:11-12), the final communion of saints. We were ordained by Christ to play a role in this vast and boundless eschatological goal. Of course, the unity of the church as the new humanity under Christ as their Head is key to the larger cosmic unity implied in v.10. In fact, the renewal of creation is the setting for the vast renewal of humanity through the church; indeed, all things will be renewed for the sake of Christ, for the church will display Christ's fullness in a way that is clearer than that which the rest of creation can disclose: "And God placed all things under his feet and appointed him to be head over everything for the church, which is his body, the fullness of him who fills everything in every way" (vv. 22-23). So it seems that the fellowship of those being chosen in Christ before creation is not meant to be restricted to a limited number but has as its purpose a potentially limitless unity under Christ.

---

[14] Ibid., 117.
[15] Ibid., 124–25.
[16] See Robert Shank, *Elect in the Son: A Study of the Doctrine of Election* (reprint; Grand Rapids, MI: Bethany, 1989), 121, 152–53.

The flow of Paul's argument that God will reconcile all things in Christ and through the Spirit-anointed church is also echoed in Col. 1:15-20. Allow me to include that text here for the sake of comparison:

> [15] The Son is the image of the invisible God, the firstborn over all creation. [16] For in him all things were created: things in heaven and on earth, visible and invisible, whether thrones or powers or rulers or authorities; all things have been created through him and for him. [17] He is before all things, and in him all things hold together. [18] And he is the head of the body, the church; he is the beginning and the firstborn from among the dead, so that in everything he might have the supremacy. [19] For God was pleased to have all his fullness dwell in him, [20] and through him to reconcile to himself all things, whether things on earth or things in heaven, by making peace through his blood, shed on the cross.

God is not willing to allow the creation to sink back into the dark void from which it was delivered at the time it was made. Rather, in making Christ the key to the eschatological *telos* of creation, another destiny is foreordained, the eschatological unity of all things in Christ ("in him all things hold together"). God has chosen to reconcile all things in Christ and by the Spirit. God has elected Godself for all of humanity, for the sake of all of creation. God doesn't simply pass over that which God has made. The Creator is also the Redeemer.

Fourth, this being chosen from eternity in Christ and for spiritual blessing in him implies a storing up of inheritance in Christ for all of creation. As noted earlier, the difference between the blessing already granted to humanity in Christ (Eph. 1:3-4) and the blessing claimed and realized by faith through the seal of the Spirit (1:13-14) is the difference between an inheritance "legally" set aside and an inheritance officially actualized by faith and sealed for future fulfillment. The sons and daughters in the far country must return to the household of the Father to reclaim the squandered inheritance foreordained for them. In all of their fallenness, humanity is already seen as meant for Christ, in him earmarked as heirs of every spiritual blessing (1:3). It would be a colossal mistake to think that the recipients of this inheritance are a select group only. The "all things" called to unity under Christ described in verse 10 has the ring of a universal reach and an open invitation. Humanity outside of faith in Christ is like the outcast brother in the far country. They were created to be God's offspring (cf., Acts 17:28) to have their inheritance in the eternal Son as the one and only Beloved of the Father. The Son is eternally the Son for them, so they are loved in him too, in him called to be God's offspring and to have every spiritual blessing that is bestowed on the Son. Though sinners, God sees them through the lens of Christ as recipients of every spiritual blessing. In bestowing these blessings on the Son, the Father already stores them up for all of humanity. The Son goes to the far country on the cross to bring them back as his brothers and sisters to the household of the Father. There they can claim the spiritual benefits already stored up for them in the Son. If they remain in the far country, they lose something already meant for them, already vital to who they are as creatures created for God. The good news is that God's call knows no boundaries. And God remains committed to bring the lost sons and daughters home.

## Romans 8: Election through a New Exodus

What secures our future glorification as a firm hope? Paul answers in Romans 8 that the Spirit bears witness to our spirits that we are children of God, but this witness, as valuable as it is, speaks from what Christ has done to prove and make available the love of God for all. Most relevant here is the way in which Paul describes the elect people in language that recalls the Exodus but recasts the narrative within the realm of Christ as securing the liberating path to the life of the Spirit, which is ultimately the path to glory. Note 8:14-17:

> [14] For those who are led by the Spirit of God are the children of God. [15] The Spirit you received does not make you slaves, so that you live in fear again; rather, the Spirit you received brought about your adoption to sonship. And by him we cry, "*Abba*, Father." [16] The Spirit himself testifies with our spirit that we are God's children. [17] Now if we are children, then we are heirs—heirs of God and co-heirs with Christ, if indeed we share in his sufferings in order that we may also share in his glory.

As the Spirit took Israel through the Exodus (Isa. 63:11-12), so now in Christ the Spirit takes the church through their journey to the "promised land" of glory, the new creation in Christ. This journey from bondage to sin and death to the liberty of life in the Spirit is signified in baptism (6:1-5). On this anointed journey, we are assured of our belonging in Christ to his Father as our Father too. In Christ and by the Spirit we pray "Abba," which comforts us in the midst of life's many trials, assuring us that our suffering will not be in vain. As with Christ, our suffering will lead to glory.

The challenges and uncertainties of life are indeed great. We groan for glorification under the burdens of mortal flesh (8:23). The hoped-for goal is the "freedom and glory of the children of God" (v. 21), the redemption of our bodies (v. 23), which seems so close (in the Spirit's down payment) and yet so far (as we groan within mortal flesh and current suffering). The saints, however, are not to be overwhelmed by the agony of groaning for such glory or the negative conditions under which we groan, for Paul is convinced that "our present sufferings are not worth comparing with the glory that will be revealed in us" (v. 18). It's the confidence that glory is ordained for those who are in Christ and who love God that occasions Romans 8.

Notice the enduring purpose that all who are in Christ have been foreordained to fulfill:

> And we know that in all things God works for the good of those who love him, who have been called according to his purpose. [29] For those God foreknew he also predestined to be conformed to the image of his Son, that he might be the firstborn among many brothers and sisters. [30] And those he predestined, he also called; those he called, he also justified; those he justified, he also glorified. (8:28-30)

All things are used of God to bring us further into Christ and toward the final victory of his glorification! Hardships are to be endured with this comfort in mind. After all,

Christ's sufferings led to glory, so shall ours in him! Earlier in Romans, Paul brings to expression his key idea that "all have sinned and fallen short of the glory of God, being justified freely by his grace" (Rom. 3:23). Those who have answered the call of the gospel in faith and have been united to Christ by the Spirit can know that God has foreordained their restoration to glory. Nothing can eliminate that purpose; all things will lead us deeper into it.

The eschatological horizon of election in the earlier text ("also glorified," v. 30) highlights the future transformation and restoration of the church. Christ's body has been foreordained to share in the destiny of its Head, Christ Jesus. The referent here is primarily corporate. The church is indefectible and will endure the vicissitudes and snares of fallen historical existence. To echo Alan Richardson: "Paul of course does not think of the church as a collection of individuals, but as a body: it is the *body* which is foreknown, foreordained, called, justified, and is to be glorified. There is no suggestion here or elsewhere in the NT that some individuals are predestined to a mechanical salvation."[17] The promise of glory belongs to individuals too, but it is one that they must actualize and continue to claim for themselves in faith. For the promise is given to those "who do not live according to the flesh but according to the Spirit" (8:4). We are predestined or foreordained by God to attain the ultimate victory over sin and death but only as members of Christ's body. So the crucial question shifts to whether or not one lives by faith as a member of that body. God provides the enablement, but God won't persevere for us! In other words, we are not in Christ's body because we've been predestined to glory; rather, we are predestined to glory because we are in Christ's body. It's a promise that we continue to claim in enduring faith. We do not yet possess this foreordained glory, but Paul wants to assure us that this is the purpose foreordained for us as the body of Christ. We as members of Christ's body are part of God's foreordained plan that the body conform to its Head, not only in our journey into him now but finally also in eschatological glory. In being baptized into his body, we were thus baptized into glory (6:5). We've been sealed or marked for this destiny. Let us continue to live consistently with that marking.

Paul talks about those God fore-loves, or foreknows in a loving way, for the sake of the victory of divine love in the world. Then Paul mentions the call, justification, and glorification, which is altogether a predestined conformity to Christ. These elements of salvation are "not chronologically different moments, but logically distinguishable aspects of salvation that lay, as it were, 'within' one another."[18] Moreover, the precise meaning of the terms "foreknow" and "predestine" here are ambiguous and determined by their contexts. Foreknowing (or in this context, fore-loving) belonged first to Israel according to Rom. 11:2. The fore-loving of Israel is eternal because it has as its ultimate reason the preexistent Christ, the one anointed of the Father for Israel and the nations. Furthermore, predestining ($\pi\rho oo\rho i\zeta\omega$) in the Greek literature outside of the New Testament does not refer to a timeless decision, though the term in Christian

---

[17] Emphasis is original. Alan Richardson, *An Introduction to the Theology of the New Testament* (New York: Harper & Row, 1958), 279.

[18] Summarizing Bo Reicke's view, Robert Sloan, "'To Predestine' ($\Pi\rho oo\rho i\zeta\omega$): The Use of a Pauline Term in Extrabiblical Tradition," in *Good News in History: Essays in Honor of Bo Reicke*, ed. L. Miller (Atlanta: Scholars Press, 1993), 128 (127–35).

literature was qualified in a minority of cases to have an eternal meaning.[19] Again, if it is qualified as eternal in significance it is because of a Christological connection. What seems clear is that Paul is describing with all of these elements a journey that all believers would have recognized as true to their life together. Their journey together is ecclesial and historical, a process of incorporation into Christ's body (a baptism in the Spirit) that defines their joint "Exodus" in Christ and in the Spirit. All of the categories recall in summary fashion the historical purpose for Israel, which only foreshadowed the eternal purpose of Christ and his body. Now, the body united to Christ its Head by the Spirit of God is the intended referent of this text (those who love *him* make up the body God foreknew, predestined, justified, and glorified). But this blessing is not for them alone but for all who attach themselves to Christ by the Spirit. Distinct *from* the outside world, they are set apart to mediate election *to* the world.

The driving force of this "glorious chain" (fore-loving, predestining, calling, justifying, glorifying) is the assurance of glorification for those who suffer. They do not suffer alone but as members of a body earmarked for glory. The setting for this chain goes back to the groaning for adoption experienced among those who have the first fruits of the Spirit, an adoption that is yet to be had in the redemption of their bodies or their future glorification (the resurrection is the full harvest of the Spirit's work, Rom. 8:23). We can only hope for this glorified state, because this reality is not yet seen. To those who feel discouraged by this absence of sight, Paul grants the reminder that such is the nature of hope. "Who hopes for what they already have?" (8:24). So, one learns to wait patiently for it (8:25). Paul recognizes that such patience is difficult and must often be hammered out in the midst of confusion, not knowing what the will of God is in a context of threat and suffering. We are not even sure how to pray; words fail when no physical deliverance from hardship seems at hand. Paul assures them that the Spirit will take their sighs and groans (perhaps most audibly heard in glossolalic utterances) and turn them into yearning for God's hidden work through such situations to conform the church to the image of the Son (8:26).

Such comfort leads at the end of Paul's discussion to a resounding assurance that no danger or threat, no type of hardship, not even death itself, can sever us from God's loving purpose for the church that is revealed in Christ crucified and raised (8:31-39). This is election in the Son appropriated by faith. God has us well on the path to the full victory of this appropriation and will never abandon us along the way. We are indeed more than conquerors for we lean on one far greater than ourselves. The church is ordained to complete its mission of witness to the Son (in life and proclamation) all the way to the ends of the earth.

Sandwiched in between the assurance that the Spirit speaks through our sighing and the ultimate assurance that nothing can rip us from our destiny in Christ is the chain of fore-loving, calling, justification, and glorification (8:30). In describing this chain, Paul's purpose is *not* to pull back the curtain to some hidden eternal decree so as to expose his audience to a privilege that a large part of the world can never have. He is rather showing them that all those who freely come to Christ were made part of a body that from eternity is ordained by God to go the distance and that God is committed

---

[19] Ibid., 127–35.

to make that happen for everyone who participate by faith. The journey is to go all the way to the ultimate glory from which humanity had fallen and to which Christ has come and the Spirit bestowed to restore us. Paul describes how all of creation awaits the revelation of God's children raised to reflect the glory of God that radiates from Christ, because that will lead to the liberation of all of creation (8:19-20).

Paul brings Romans 8 to a resounding conclusion, which surrounds our spiritual senses like the crescendo of a grand symphony. There is nothing that can separate us from God's loving purposes in Christ and in the Spirit. All those who turn to him can be assured of this. Christ has taken our side in the struggle against the powers of death and darkness. He justified us and intercedes for us. In him we are more than conquerors, for he carries us by his victory and by his Spirit. No trouble or hardship can drive a wedge between us:

> For I am convinced that neither death nor life, neither angels nor demons,
>   neither the present nor the future, nor any powers, [39] neither height nor depth,
>   nor anything else in all creation, will be able to separate us from the love of
>   God that is in Christ Jesus our Lord. (vv. 38-39)

As in Eph. 1:10, election aims at a vastly inclusive vision of redemption in Christ as its intended point of fulfillment. Don't lose heart, Paul seems to be saying to believers, Christ through his faithful church will carry you throughout your journey from baptism to glorification, until the baptism in the Holy Spirit is eschatologically fulfilled. *The church body that mediated election to its members will accompany them toward the full realization of that election in time.* Paul's purpose is both to assure and to rouse his audience to deeper loyalty, including the mission to open the life of the Son chosen for humanity to the entire world. As the chosen people, they have come through the waters of baptism bearing the Spirit and looking to the new creation. God has guaranteed to be with them and to bring them all the way to this "promised land."

## Romans 9-11: Election as a Grafting

As Paul moves from the end of chapter 8 to the beginning of chapter 9, he confronts a difficult question. If God is committed to the endurance of his chosen people, whatever happened to Israel? Why didn't *they* endure? Why have these natural branches been cut away from the tree of God's people so that life may surge toward the branches of the Gentiles that have been grafted in? Tragically, Christ came to that which was his own but his own did not receive him (c.f., Jn 1:11). Was the word of promise fulfilled in Christ ineffective or inadequate to the task of preserving *Israel* (9:6)? Is there any hope that they may yet be grafted back in?

The answer in Romans 9-11 is complex, but it revolves around Paul's defense of the adequacy of God's word to mediate God's intention in history which is to open up the divine life to all flesh: "It is not as though God's word has failed" (9:6). The hard truth is that on an individual level disbelief is the only cause of failure: "Consider therefore the kindness and sternness of God: sternness to those who fell, but kindness to you, provided that you continue in his kindness. Otherwise, you also will be cut off"

(11:22). Faith is upheld by God's word (10:17), but God will not believe for us. Human faith still involves willful human participation. But God remains faithful and continues to pursue the fallen (the divine goal is to show mercy to all, 11:32). Moreover, Paul implies that God in a sense *did* preserve Israel, in the form of a faithful remnant that embraced Jesus as Messiah: "For not all who are descended from Israel are Israel" (9:6; cf., 11:7). But is this remnant idea (borrowed from the Old Testament) sufficient as an answer, given the fact that the chosen people as a whole still failed?

Here is where other elements of Paul's discussion need to be taken into consideration. We should first recognize that the two issues (the adequacy of God's word and the perseverance of Israel in the form of a faithful remnant) are mutually defining. They both have their anchor in the Old Testament, for there was always a faithful remnant to carry the torch for the rest of the elect people by bearing witness to the strength of God's word to carry Israel through prolonged times of testing and failure. Recall Ezekiel's vision of a devastated people who will come to life again by the Spirit as they respond to the prophetic word that comes from God: "Then he said to me, 'Prophesy to these bones and say to them, "Dry bones, hear the word of the LORD!"' 'This is what the Sovereign LORD says to these bones: I will make breath enter you, and you will come to life'" (37:3-4). Notice that the faithful remnant in the Old Testament does not replace hope for the larger nation. The remnant is viewed as temporary, as a bridge in between national failure and a future restoration on a much larger scale that will bring the nation as a whole back to their larger calling as a people. Likewise, Paul believes that Israel as a nation will indeed rejoin the mission: "Did they stumble so as to fall beyond recovery? Not at all!" (11:11). Until then, the corporate election of the nation remains more or less an unfulfilled potential.

Those who restrict Israel's election to the faithful remnant miss the fact that in Romans 9–11 Paul clearly applies election in a corporate sense to all of the physical descendants of Abraham: "*Theirs* is the adoption to sonship; *theirs* the divine glory, the covenants, the receiving of the law, the temple worship and the promises. *Theirs* are the patriarchs, and from them is traced the human ancestry of the Messiah, who is God over all, forever praised" (9:1-4). Paul refers with all of these statements to "those of my own race, the people of Israel" (9:3-4). He does not refer only to fellow Jews who have not been hardened and received Christ. In chapter 11 he says that those who have stumbled and are hardened among his kinsmen have *not* permanently fallen (11:11). This is because God's election of Israel as a nation, "on account of the patriarchs," is "irrevocable" (11:29). The subject here is clearly ethnic Israel for they are the ones who are enemies for the sake of the Gentiles and are loved because of the patriarchs (v. 28).[20] Though election is only realized by faith in the Word of God and incorporation into Christ by the Spirit, there is still a divine call that remains irrevocable extended to larger people groups (actually, to all of humanity). Paul is convinced that this call will be answered on a broad scale before history comes to an end. Israel as a nation will be restored.

---

[20] Scott Hafemann, "The Salvation of Israel in Romans 11:25-32: A Response to Krister Stendahl," *ExAud4* (1988), 53.

Let me be clear. Physical descent is not adequate for the actualization Israel's election, for not all who are called to be the elect people end up actualizing that election by faith; not all Israel will prove to be "Israel" by faith in the gospel and incorporation into God's people by the Spirit (9:6). But neither is the lineage of Abraham insignificant. Christ himself came from this lineage, and those of this lineage play a role in God's elect plan. Israel was chosen and called to play a maternal and mediating function in preparing the way for the Messiah and in participating in the fulfillment of the messianic mission. But individual and salvific participation in this calling depends on faith. If the falling away is massive enough, a faithful remnant must carry the torch for the nation. That is the situation as Paul saw it in Romans 9–11. Israel as a nation failed right at a crucial turning point, where the nation was meant to partake of the eschatological outpouring of the Spirit for the latter-day mission. The Israelite remnant exists as part of the church, eschatological Israel, and Paul's hope is that the nation as a whole will join them.

There is thus a difference in Romans 9–11 between a corporate election that is irrevocable and filled with unrealized potential (and intended by God to achieve vast fulfillment in time through those who believe) and individual actualization of this election that is contingent on willful participation in Christ and which the corporate whole is called to serve. All of Israel is corporately elect in Christ in the sense that they are earmarked for a vocational purpose that ends in the salvation of many. Israel as a nation will be restored to its calling and its obedience as an apocalyptic mystery, but not without loss. Indeed, throughout time, only the remnant truly participates in the life of the mission. So, one could say without fear of contradiction at any given moment that not all among the elect people have actualized their election in the Spirit by faith.

So, key to election is the word of promise that witnesses of Christ and is to be grasped by grace through faith alone: "It is not as though God's word had failed" (9:6). In explaining this statement, Paul maintains two great truths. First, to argue that election is solely by grace does not imply divine caprice. Paul is more specific: "It does not, therefore, depend on human desire or effort, but on God's mercy" (9:16). More elaborately, election takes place in and for the mission of the word of the gospel, which is at its core Christ himself, the goal of which is to show mercy to all (9:6; 11:32). Jacob, and not Esau, is chosen for the mission of the word of promise in the world. The focus with these two is not on individuals but on peoples (as it always was: "two nations are in your womb," Gen. 25:23). Israel is uniquely chosen for the mission of this word; Israel is, for Paul, chosen in and for it, for the sake of the world and for the glory of God. Israel's election, however, is meant to exceed Israel, for the mission is directed to the nations, *and that includes the people of Esau*. "Jacob I loved, Esau I hated" (9:13) makes for stinging rhetoric and has a point to make in its original context (Mal. 1:2-3), but quoted in Romans 9 it is significantly qualified by the larger truth that *God elects Jacob for Esau's sake* (Israel is elected for the sake of all people, 11:32). God is no tribal or national deity but the God of a gospel that has no boundaries and is offered in mercy to all (11:32).

Second, sometimes the merciful gospel encounters rejection and a hardening occurs. But even this is meant to bring the unrepentant nation through the time of trial necessary to occasion mass conversion down the road. Thus, Paul speaks of those that are hardened as not having stumbled beyond recovery (11:11). The belief that mercy and hardening are opposites fixed by an absolute and unchanging decree makes it difficult to understand the flow of Paul's argument in Romans 9–11, especially the breadth of its conclusion in 11:32. There is a hardening that both Gentiles and Jews experience that has as its purpose the showing of mercy to all and the establishment of grace as the overarching basis for election. In Romans 9–11 Paul grants us the narrative underpinning for his programmatic statement in 3:23 that all have sinned and fallen short of the glory of God being justified freely by grace. The goal of election is to grant failing humanity, including the people who stand in the lineage of Abraham, the repentance that leads to life (cf., Acts 11:18). The hardening of Pharaoh rehearsed in 9:17 was well known to Israel. It was always a part of Israel's narrative; God brought down the high and the mighty in order to exalt the lowly, all for God's glory on the earth. Raising Pharaoh up to bring him low was his judgment by God. This hardening does not mean that he was a puppet, and God simply pulled the strings. There is nothing in the narrative that forbids us from thinking that Pharaoh willfully participated in his rise and fall in a way that accounts also for what happened. After all, the narrative does say that Pharaoh hardened his own heart as well: "When Pharaoh saw that the rain and hail and thunder had stopped, he sinned again: He and his officials hardened their hearts" (Ex. 9:34). It could have been otherwise. Hardening is what God does through what we do: "So I gave them over to their stubborn hearts to follow their own devices" (Ps. 81:12). Actually, Paul anchors Pharaoh's hardening to a larger one experienced among all of the gentile peoples who rejected the witness to God given through nature (1:28). "God gave them over in the sinful desires of their hearts" (1:24). But Pharaoh did not need to be hardened for God's glory over Egypt to be revealed. God can use any circumstance to accomplish the divine goals for history.

It cannot be stressed enough, however, that Pharaoh is not the only one who is hardened in Romans 9. Hardening is not reserved for pagan dictators alone in Romans. Even Israel through whom the blessings of election were meant to flow (9:1-4) is hardened too! But Paul's narrative makes the larger point that this hardening is due to unbelief, not as the origin of that unbelief, but rather allowing it to proceed in a way that will end up serving the purposes of divine mercy. Toward this end, the hardening of Israel was not meant to be the final word. Through their hardening, the faithful remnant of Israel that comes to believe during this time will be reborn on the other side of the Messiah's resurrection and will provide the link between the old and the new people. The Gentiles will come to see the glory of the risen Christ whom his own people betrayed. The hardening of the Israelites will, for Paul, hopefully provide the means necessary for them as a nation to let go of their own expectations so as to yield to their God as revealed in the story of Jesus. The idea that Israel must be hardened for the sake of its future repentance and rebirth as a people is an old prophetic theme. Their stupor is generally intended as a temporal time of judgment for the rebellious to bear up under until true repentance occurs. No easy repentance is allowed. No shallow commitments encouraged.

Sometimes, spiritual knowledge is withheld in the history of Israel until the recipients have come to the place where they are truly ready for it. This point shows that hardening is ironically meant to prepare a people for future softening. Thus, when

Isaiah is told that God will dull Israel's seeing and hearing and confirm them in their callousness (6:9-10), Isaiah asks, "For how long, Lord?" (6:11). And God responds, "Until the cities lie ruined." Only then will their seeing, hearing, and open hearts be allowed, for in that particular context only at the end of a time of trial will such an awakening lead to lasting repentance. But even then there is no guarantee that they will repent any time soon. Indeed, Isaiah 1 has God imploring Israel to repent after the time of judgment had passed:

> Why should you be beaten anymore?
>   Why do you persist in rebellion?
> Your whole head is injured,
>   your whole heart afflicted. (1:5)

Then comes the climactic appeal:

> "Come now, let us settle the matter," says the Lord.
> "Though your sins are like scarlet,
>   they shall be as white as snow;
> though they are red as crimson,
>   they shall be like wool. (1:18)

I read Romans 11 in much the same way. Those who are in a state of rejection are not eternally predestined and unalterably fixed to forever be this way. The time of rejection on behalf of a people may last much longer than God intends. But God does not intend that time to be permanent. In fact, 11:11 is clear. The hardened have not stumbled beyond recovery. In this light, one should not overlook Paul's statement in 9:2 that God foreknew (or better, fore-loved) Israel as a people, by which Paul surely meant the covenant people as descendants of Abraham, which is why he laments that so many of his kinsmen have unnecessarily denied this divine love by denying Christ. As noted earlier, he is even willing to suffer condemnation and banishment from Christ for the sake of their salvation (9:3)! He is surely referring to all of his kinsmen here. Is anyone prepared to say that God's passion for all of the lost of Israel (and for the entire world) is any less expansive or deep? Indeed, God's love is even more expansive and deep; infinitely more. Paul is in fact hopeful that the elect people will involve a much larger inclusion of those who were currently in a spiritual stupor and not part of the remnant (11:11-12). The angry wish carried over from Psalm 69 in 11:10 (may their "backs be bent forever") brings to expression the prophetic frustration with the stubborn rejection of so many, who should belong to the covenant. But Paul follows this immediately with an important corrective: "Did they stumble to fall beyond recovery? Not at all!" (11:11). Surely, the ones who have stumbled is a reference to those currently placed in a stupor because of their rejection. In 11:28-29, Paul claims that "the gifts and the call" granted to ethnic Israel "on account of the patriarchs" referred to in 9:1-4 are "irrevocable." The corporate calling of Israel is irrevocable though the individual participation in it is conditioned by faith. Paul's missionary and eschatological hope is for a vast revival of faith among his kinsmen over whom he weeps at the start of his discussion in the opening verses of chapter 9, hoping that the nation as a whole returns to God. When does Paul envision this restoration as to occur? This restoration appears as a missionary goal, but even more than this, as an apocalyptic mystery. Perhaps Paul points implicitly to Christ's return (those who pierced him will mourn, Rev. 1:7).

In short, Pharaoh's hardening was used by God to bear witness of God's glory before Israel. The Pharaoh that pursued Israel for the sake of their demise ended up placing them inadvertently into the hands of their God, which ended in the triumph of divine mercy that brought spiritual riches to Israel (even to Pharaoh's own people, Exod. 14:18). So also was Israel's hardening for the sake of providing a witness to the Gentiles. The nation that handed their Messiah over to Rome to be crucified also inadvertently handed him over to the triumph of mercy over human rejection, which became the gospel to be proclaimed to the nations (of Israel it is said, "their transgression means riches for the world, and their loss means riches for the Gentiles," Rom. 11:12). As the Egyptians themselves were blessed by Pharaoh's hardening, so also the faithful remnant from Israel could witness the glory of God's power and mercy on display by what their nation had done. What a reversal. God always does the unexpected, but the end result is the same. God uses even human rejection to show mercy, indeed, to show that all have sinned, Gentile and Jew, and have been granted mercy by grace alone (Rom. 3:23; 11:32).

That God uses human rejection to show mercy does not mean those who reject did so as determined by God. The notion that those who rebel against God do so primarily as a result of divine determination would have been new to Paul. In fact, he stresses throughout Romans that those who rebel against the divine will do so contrary to that will and are therefore fully to blame for it. God shows God's divinity and power through nature so that those who turn to idolatry instead "are without excuse" (Rom. 1:20). God gave them over to a depraved mind but only as a consequence of their decision to "not think it worthwhile to retain the knowledge of God" (1:28). As noted earlier, Pharaoh's hardening was part of a much larger gentile problem! In fact, God gave the divine Son over to condemnation *as well* so that those who have rebelled may yet be justified (4:25; cf., 8:32). The pagans too have not fallen beyond recovery! One should not despise God's merciful forbearance with sinners, because the divine patience is meant in fact to lead to their repentance (2:4). God bears with vessels of wrath here not only to show mercy to others through their rejection but also to include *them* in that mercy as well. Paul considers the idea that our evil is willed by God for the sake of the greater good to be a slanderous notion (3:8; 6:1). God will indeed use human rejection to accomplish the divine purposes but not because God predestines or wills such rejection! One is not destined to sin so that grace may increase (6:1-2)! Indeed, Paul highlights in Romans our responsibility for our actions: "For if you live according to the flesh, you will die; but if by the Spirit you put to death the misdeeds of the body, you will live" (8:13). One is cut off from the tree of life in Romans 11 because of unbelief.

So also the discourse of Romans 9–11 contains the strong statements about human disobedience as itself responsible for the judgment that sinners endure. Notice how Paul responds to the argument that Jews were removed from the tree of life so that life may flow to the many Gentiles that were grafted in. In significantly qualifying his interlocutor here, Paul stresses willful rejection as the primary cause of the removal of unbelieving Jews and faith the occasion (secondary cause) of their engraftment. God is not pulling the strings. People are included or not due to unbelief or faith:

> You will say then, "Branches were broken off so that I could be grafted in." Granted. But they were broken off because of unbelief, and you stand by faith. Do not be arrogant, but tremble. For if God did not spare the natural branches, he will not spare you either. Consider therefore the kindness and sternness of God: sternness to those who fell, but kindness to you, provided that you continue in his kindness. Otherwise, you also will be cut off. And if they do not persist in unbelief, they will be grafted in, for God is able to graft them in again. (11:19-23)

Of course, God is the one who opens the door of election in and through the Son and the Spirit and enables those who choose the path of faith. But one cannot read the above texts in support of the idea that faith or lack thereof is merely the result of a divine determination. The stern warning to choose rightly or suffer the consequences would not make any moral sense (any sense at all) if God's decision already determined the outcome in advance.

In Old Testament election texts, there is no inconsistency between the sovereignty of grace in election and the necessary condition of a faithful response, which may or may not be present depending on the person's choice in the matter ("keeping his covenant of love to a thousand generations of those who love him," Deut. 7:9). There is a focus to maintain in Paul's discussion on both God's ability to fulfill the divine purpose in the world despite human failure, even using it, and the dire consequences that come from human refusal to participate in that mercy. This focus on one should not be maintained at the cost of another. When Paul states that God is sovereign and free to form clay pots toward the end that God chooses (Rom. 9:21), he makes no secret about what that end is, namely, mercy ("It does not, therefore, depend on human desire or effort, but on God's mercy," 9:16), more specifically, mercy on all (11:32). Election is not the result of humans seizing the day and successfully pushing through their own agenda (like the effort at the Tower of Babel) but rather God's using even human rebellion to open mercy to all. Thus, Paul obviously does not mean to say that humans could not have possibly chosen to be anything other than the pots that they've become. And what kind of pot one becomes is not fixed for all time in Romans 11. The "Jacob" (or Israel) that was elected in Romans 9 (esp. vv. 1-5) is as a people living apart from the tree of life and even those currently grafted in are warned that they can be lopped off if they stop believing (11:17-24). When Paul notes that election is not based on human desire or works, he obviously did not intend to say that faith was never really an option for those who are hardened.

In fact, all of the texts that Paul reads and quotes with regard to the potter-clay metaphor accent human agency and responsibility. Paul in Rom. 9:20 quotes Isa. 29:16, "Shall what is formed say to the one who formed it, 'You did not make me'?" The whole point of this text in Isaiah is not that God is sovereign and can do whatever God chooses with someone. It is rather that a people cannot make self-serving plans and act as though God is in the dark. To think such a thing is as absurd as thinking that the potter knows nothing of the clay with which he works: "Can the pot say to the potter, you know nothing?" (29:16b). Though God forms the clay, the point is not God's predetermination of the "clay's" behavior, rather, God faults *them* for it. The point is that God is intimately involved in Israel's journey, is molding them into a people, and is thus fully aware of their deceptive ways. Wrongful ways will have real life consequences, and God knows them all. But there is not a hint in this text from Isaiah that the pot does not bear full responsibility for being such a pot and could indeed have been other than this.

As for the divine action involved in what the pottery becomes, note what is stated in a similar text from Jeremiah 18:

> Then the word of the Lord came to me. He said, "Can I not do with you, Israel, as this potter does?" declares the Lord. "Like clay in the hand of the potter, so are you in my hand, Israel. If at any time I announce that a nation or kingdom is to be uprooted, torn down and destroyed, and if that nation I warned repents of its evil, then I will relent and not inflict on it the disaster I had planned. And if at another time I announce that a nation or kingdom is to be built up and planted, and if it does evil in my sight and does not obey me, then I will reconsider the good I had intended to do for it." (Jer. 18:5-10)

Again the potter-clay metaphor means that election is not a privileged status to take for granted. God is free to judge or not to judge elect Israel depending on their responses to the mercy that is shown. As with any use of an Old Testament text within the New Testament, new or more expansive readings do occur. Arguably, a New Testament author typically quotes an Old Testament text to invite a reader to read it with the new and more expansive eyes provided by its fulfillment. But one should at least think twice if a proposed interpretation of the New Testament use of an Old Testament text seems completely *contrary* to the original meaning of that text.

The protest, "For why does God still blame us? For who can resist God's will?" (Rom. 9:19) requires unpacking as well. As noted earlier, Paul's overarching point is that God has used human rejection to show mercy to receptive hearts. The imagined interlocutor protests the idea that God would harden hearts and then use them to accomplish divine purposes. Why would the transgressors be blamed for wrongdoing if God used them in this way so that grace may abound? How can they be expected to take a path other than rejection if such were part of God's mission of mercy?

If Paul had agreed with the presumptions of his imaginary interlocutor, it would have been the only time he did so among the times he used this rhetorical device. Paul's response that one cannot talk back to God rejects the presumption that God must morally justify divine actions to us, and rightly so. Nor are Pharaoh's and Israel's rejection of grace simply predetermined in a way that excludes willful human participation. In response, Paul nuances his description of God's use of human transgression to multiply grace. Paul does so by describing the use of transgression as forbearance. In God's patience with the transgressor, God will use that transgression to offer grace to those who are open to receive. Notice 2:4: "Or do you show contempt for the riches of his kindness, forbearance and patience, not realizing that God's kindness is intended to lead you to repentance?" Similarly, Paul notes in 9:22-23 that God "bore with great patience with objects of wrath prepared for destruction" to "make the riches of his glory known" to objects of mercy "whom he prepared in advance for glory." Notice the asymmetry between the objects of wrath and those receiving mercy. Whereas God "bears with" objects of wrath as they resist God's plan of mercy, God actively makes glory known to objects of mercy that are receptive. Whereas the objects of wrath are "prepared for destruction" (passive voice), objects of mercy are prepared actively and directly by God ("whom he prepared in advance for glory"). God seems to be one step removed from the actions of the objects of wrath. God is not the author of evil.

This insight is not unknown to the Reformed tradition. But it is important to add here that the objects of wrath are not determined by an absolute or immutable decree, even if this is recognized as indirectly willed through noninclusion within those elected to salvation. By way of response, I would maintain that there is no indication in Romans 9–11 that the objects of wrath being prepared "in advance" for judgment are anything else than the effects of their history of resisting grace. And God bears with these vessels of wrath not only to use their rebellion to show mercy to others but also with the larger goal of possibly making them into vessels of mercy. Note again 2:4: "Or do you show contempt for the riches of his kindness, forbearance and patience, not realizing that God's kindness is intended to lead you to repentance?" Paul is convinced that God purposes such a turn for the nation of Israel that is currently under judgment but will in God's future be grafted back into the tree of life. Indeed, they have not fallen beyond recovery (11:11).

If God chose Jacob and not Esau and, in choosing Jacob, hardened Pharaoh in Pharaoh's attempt to destroy Jacob's seed, God can now harden "Jacob" to open salvation to the pagans. It's divine purpose of offering grace to all that drives the narrative and not self-serving interests or considerations of merit. Thus, the choosing of Israel (Jacob) was dependent on God's purposes and not Israel's, and the hardening of the wicked Pharaoh in Israel's liberation used to fulfill God's purposes rather than Pharaoh's plans. In both cases, God's purposes are paramount and succeed, while human purposes (both Israel's and Pharaoh's) are not determinative. One need only read the story of Israel's liberation (especially the first six chapters of Exodus) to discover how dependent faltering Israel (including a faltering Moses) was on God's elect will and enduring power. Left to their own devices, the story would have taken a disastrous turn. Similarly, Pharaoh had his own ideas about how the story of Israel was to end, but God had other plans. The pursuance of his plan led to his hardening by God. But his hardening did not derail God's plans; God used it to accomplish them. When it comes to God's elect will (providing a witness of the divine mercy and glory throughout the world) human resistance is indeed futile! For God will use even that resistance to accomplish it! Such is the story of the cross! Human rejection is turned into a means of grace.

The church's stance today toward Israel is well expressed by this statement of the World Council of Churches at Amsterdam shortly after the Second World War (1948) with the Holocaust in the background: "To the Jews our God has bound us in a special solidarity linking our destinies together in his design."[21] Yet, this design supports mercy

---

[21] Quoted in Paul Van Buren, "Israel and the Church," DEM, ed. Nicholas Lossky, et al. (Grand Rapids, MI: Eerdmans, 1991), 536.

and justice for all people, including the Palestinians. In anticipation of this hoped-for future we can only bow a knee and join Paul in leaving such things up to God's design,

> Oh, the depth of the riches of the wisdom and knowledge of God!
> How unsearchable his judgments,
> and his paths beyond tracing out!
> [34] "Who has known the mind of the Lord?
> Or who has been his counselor?"
> [35] "Who has ever given to God,
> that God should repay them?"
> [36] For from him and through him and for him are all things.
> To him be the glory forever! Amen. (Rom. 11:33-36)

## Luke-Acts: The Election of the Nations

For Luke, Jesus is conceived in Mary's womb by the Spirit as the Son of God (Lk. 1:35). Christ is then declared the beloved Son of God and receives the Spirit abundantly from the Father at the Jordan (3:22), for he will baptize all flesh in the Holy Spirit (3:16). At the end of Luke 3, Adam is called a the "son of God" (2:38), implying that Christ is the last Adam, the one who will fulfill Israel's election by solving the problem of Adam and recapitulating the entire human race to form one people, consisting of Jew and Gentile. When Jesus is transfigured before Peter, James, and John, God affirms Christ's sonship in language that recalls his anointing at the Jordan, but now the election language is explicit: "A voice came from the cloud, saying, 'This is my Son, whom I have chosen; listen to him'" (9:35). Jesus's election is mocked at the cross by rulers of Israel, "He saved others; let him save himself if he is God's Messiah, the Chosen One." But the Centurion's confession at the cross that Jesus was indeed "righteous" signals the coming of the Gentiles to faith in Luke's narrative (23:47).

When Christ poured forth the Spirit from his own faithful life, Peter proclaims that the Jewish leaders condemned him by handing him over to death. But he was also handed over "by God's deliberate plan and foreknowledge" (Acts 2:23). God vindicated him by raising him from the dead as Messiah and Lord (vv. 24-36). Though Jesus's crucifiers meant it for evil, God meant it for good. It is not the evil of the crucifiers that God was behind; God willed instead the redemption that Jesus's submission to death would accomplish. We are threading a needle here, but it's one that requires threading. Luke highlights the evil of crucifixion as an unjust murder that God foreknew (meaning here, knew in advance) and factored into a larger plan in which this injustice would be used to offer mercy, even to the crucifiers. Notice this climax to Stephen's indictment of Israel's leadership in Acts 7:51-52:

> "You stiff-necked people! Your hearts and ears are still uncircumcised. You are just like your ancestors: You always resist the Holy Spirit! [52] Was there ever a prophet your ancestors did not persecute? They even killed those who predicted the coming of the Righteous One. And now you have betrayed and murdered him.

Acts calls Jesus's death an unjust and evil act that God always intended to use to bring about a redemptive justice offered to all who repent.

Through resurrection and Spirit outpouring, the anointed and elect One of the Father for all time shared his election with all of Israel; he opened it in fact to all flesh through the impartation of the Spirit without regard for age, race, social class, or sex (Acts 2:1-36). All are now called to participate in the beloved Son's communion with his Father. All are anointed in power to join in Christ's mission as the Chosen One of God, thereby being instrumental in his making the ends of the earth his cherished possession: "But you will receive power when the Holy Spirit comes on you; and you will be my witnesses in Jerusalem, and in all Judea and Samaria, and to the ends of the earth" (1:8; cf., Ps. 2:8). That election is opened to all through the witness of the church in the power of the Spirit.

Luke carefully crafts his description of Pentecost so as to highlight its parallel to Jesus's own anointing as the elect One at the Jordan. As Christ's election was attested under the anointing of the Spirit, so they now receive this same Spirit from him so as to partake of his election. The Spirit descends on Jesus who is found praying and waiting, and the Spirit comes accompanied by a visible theophany from heaven (alighting as a dove) (Lk. 3:21-22). Jesus then proclaims the meaning of the event (4:16-20). Both miracles and persecution follow, and persecution ends in crucifixion and resurrection. Similarly, the disciples are prayerfully waiting on the Spirit, and, when the Spirit descends from heaven, there is also a theophany (sound of a wind and tongues of fire) (2:1-4). Peter proclaims the meaning of the event (2:14-41), and both miracles and persecution follow which lead to the martyrdom of Stephen, whose final prayer for God not to count this sin against them (7:60) is similar to Jesus's final prayer from the cross (23:34). The disciples live a cruciform life in anticipation of resurrection. The election of Jesus revealed and declared at his reception of the Spirit at the Jordan is now extended to include the chosen apostles and the entire communion of saints. Acts tells the story of how that election continues to expand and diversify through the ongoing baptism in the Holy Spirit. The Lord through this was adding to their number (Acts 2:47).

The election of the disciples is historically actualized when Christ chooses them. When Christ appears to them and teaches them before his ascension, the disciples ask if the restoration of God's chosen people, Israel, was then to occur (Acts 1:5). Jesus's answer is telling, because it points them to a broader understanding of election than they had previously understood. Jesus tells them that it is not for them to know "the times or epochs which the Father has fixed in his own authority" (NASB) (Acts 1:7). Then he points them to the part that they are to play in the fulfillment of these times and epochs. Their baptism in the Holy Spirit will empower them to take their witness to the ends of the earth (1:8). This empowered calling is their rite of passage to Israel's elect purpose in history, which is at its core the elect purpose of Israel's Messiah. The bottom line is this: Israel will be restored only after the Gentiles are reached with the gospel, for God had promised to Abraham that the nations will be blessed through his seed. That promise had to be fulfilled before the people descended from Abraham could find the fulfillment of their own election in history. That God will reach the nations by the power of the Spirit while Israel looks on, using at first only a small band of disciples, will be a testimony to the power of God.

What are these "times and epochs" that the Father has ordained for all peoples according to Acts 1:7, and what do they have to do with election? As background, there is every indication that Luke has in mind the Tower of Babel rebellion and the confusion of tongues that occurred there. As we noted earlier, God confused the tongues of the people at Babel in order to break up their quest for power and scatter them throughout the earth as God had mandated of them in Gen. 1:28. For centuries it was noted that Pentecost "reversed" the dispersion of tongues at Babel. St. Augustine penned, for example, "Through proud men, divided were the tongues; through humble Apostles, united were the tongues."[22] There is considerable support for this idea in Acts and exploring it will bring us into the heart of what Jesus means by the ordained times and epochs. However, only the judgment of the diversification of the tongues at Babel is reversed but not its promise. The Jews who gathered at Pentecost were "from every nation under heaven" (Acts 2:5). These Diaspora Jews were there to celebrate the Feast of Pentecost, which at that time recalled the covenant God made with Israel at Sinai. The glory of God's presence at Sinai ended up being overshadowed at the Pentecost event by the holy flames of God's presence. These Diaspora Jews from all nations ended up hearing the wondrous deeds of God announced in languages that each understood from their gentile homeland (2:4-12). This is the beginning of eschatological Israel's witness to the nations of the wondrous deeds of God! The gentile mission had begun with those who gathered on that day, appropriately launched by a key part of the faithful remnant from among Israel. Of course, the linguistic divisions were not erased. There is after all no sin in cultural diversity. In fact, the mandate to fill the earth in Gen. 1:27 implies that God cherishes diversity. But what Pentecost did signal was the reversal of the misunderstandings and toxicity of division that accompanied humanity throughout its history. The judgment of Babel brought with it confusion and disunity, which were reversed at Pentecost. But the promise of Babel was the dispersion throughout the earth in fulfillment of God's elect will for humanity. The mission of the Spirit through the Spirit-baptized church in Acts will seek to bring that mission to fulfillment.

A careful examination of Acts 17 will reveal that Luke actually did have Babel in mind. In summarizing Paul's sermon on Mars Hill in Athens, Luke highlights the fact that God is not to be viewed as definable by human efforts at idolatry. The Tower of Babel was a temple of worship made to reach the heavens so as to make a name for its builders. Of relevance to the Babel story, Paul in Luke's narrative telling uses the shrines of Athens to make the point that God does not need the edifices of human religion, for God is not confined to human temples and is not served by human hands "as if he needed anything" (17:24-25). Rather, God is the gracious source of all good things in creation, an abundant favor that is not part of a system of exchange ("You do this for me and I'll do that for you"). No, God cannot be placed in our debt. As a gracious Creator, God freely "gives life, breath, and everything else" (v. 25). Our basic existence is a gift, for we ourselves were created to function as a temple of the divine presence created by grace for the benefit of others and for the glory of a merciful Creator. God's plan to bring us all to that place of fulfillment has no room for our self-serving agendas.

---

[22] St. Augustine, *Psalm LV*. 10 (1976), http://www.ccel.org/ccel/schaff/npnf108.ii.LV.html

Interestingly, the Babel event is granted an interpretation that is more sympathetic than judgmental. Luke relegates the idolatry of Babel and beyond not so much to human rebellion (which was, of course, basic to it) but rather human ignorance ("In the past God overlooked such ignorance, but now he commands all people everywhere to repent," v. 30). For this reason, the shrine to the "unknown God" was so significant to Paul as the provocation for his message (v. 23).

Most clearly relevant to Babel is the fact that Paul's sermon in Acts 17 focuses specifically on the human journey from Adam to Babel, and beyond. This verse is key: "From one man he made all the nations, that they should inhabit the whole earth; and he marked out their appointed times in history and the boundaries of their lands" (v. 26). This is humanity, created by God and mandated to fill the earth. This is also humanity resisting this mandate but then dispersed for their own good to fulfill the divine mandate and be saved from themselves. But notice in the previous verse that God does not abandon these human communities dispersed throughout the earth. God remains with them throughout their diverse journeys as various people groups, marking out their "appointed times" and the changing geographical boundaries of their pilgrimages. These "appointed times" in v. 26 links us to the beginning of the Acts narrative, where Jesus in the context of the question about Israel's restoration refers to "times or epochs which the Father has fixed in his own authority" (1:7). Acts 1:7 uses the terms *kairos* (καιρός, or times) and *chronos* (Χρόνος, or epochs). Among the ancient Greeks, *chronos* can simply mean the flow of time but *kairos* often meant more than this: "Kairos was often used with ref. to those opportunities that present themselves, often unexpectedly, and that require decisive response."[23] In the Old Testament, these times were characterized not only by the natural flow of events but also by God's special dealings with people.[24] Especially in times of distress, the Israelites hoped for a "καιρός of compassion" (Ps. 102:13). For the ungodly surrounding Israel, *kairos* could be an opportune time for repentance.[25] Luke uses *kairos* in Acts 17:26 of God's providential actions among the nations, directly linking this verse to the times known only by the Father in 1:7.

*Kairos* is an oft-used term in Acts. Of the eighty-five times the term appears in the New Testament, Luke-Acts accounts for more than a fourth. In Acts 1:7 *kairos* refers to divinely willed moments in a larger epoch of time that will lead to the final restoration of Israel. In 17:26, the appointed *kairous* refer similarly to the providential care of gentile peoples during their journeys, specifically when this care functions as a sign of divine grace in the world meant to inspire a thirst for God. The following verse makes this meaning clear: "God did this so that they would seek him and perhaps reach out for him and find him" (17:27). Luke tells us that Paul in his sermon founds this Gentile seeking for God not only on signs of grace in the histories of different peoples but also more deeply in human nature itself. Quoting Greek poets, Paul says that gentile peoples will be prone to seek for God, because "'in him we live and move and have our being.'

---

[23] "Καιρός," NIDNTTE, Vol. 2, E—A, ed. Moses Silva (Grand Rapids, MI: Zondervan, 2014), 587 (586–92).
[24] Ibid., 588.
[25] Ibid., 589.

As some of your own poets have said, 'We are his offspring'" (17:28). Ironically, the God after whom the Gentiles seek is already closer to them than they are to themselves, essential to their very life and being in the world. Though ignorant and easily led astray to idols, these gentile peoples will be drawn to grope after the God who is already closer to them than they are to their own heartbeats. God is intimately involved in the lives of gentile peoples. God has the home court advantage in the gentile mission, and Christ is active through the Spirit to make full use of it.

Acts highlights the astounding fact that every effort made to oppose the divinely ordained mission is used by God to move the mission forward. Threats and beatings only cause the Jerusalem assembly to be endowed with greater power by the Spirit to speak boldly of Christ (Acts 4:31). "With great power the apostles continued to testify to the resurrection of the Lord Jesus. And God's grace was so powerfully at work in them all" (v. 33). After the apostles are jailed, an angel let them out. Upon their release, they're found defiantly teaching in the temple courts (5:17-21)! When discussing the matter, the wise Pharisee, Gamaliel, gives sage advice that if God is in this there is no way of stopping it! One ends up on the losing side of history: "But if it is from God, you will not be able to stop these men; you will only find yourselves fighting against God" (v. 39). When Christians flee Jerusalem because of persecution, God uses this to spread the mission (7:54-8:8). When the chief persecutor, Paul, seeks to follow them to Syria, Christ blocks his path and converts him, rather dramatically it seems (9:1-19). This single conversion then leads to missionary journeys throughout the gentile world that yielded much fruit, for Paul is especially chosen to suffer much and accomplish even more for Christ. "This man is my chosen instrument to proclaim my name to the Gentiles and their kings and to the people of Israel. I will show him how much he must suffer for my name" (9:15-16). God turns the tables on the church's chief persecutor by making him the chief among the persecuted for the sake of the mission. In times of persecution and peace the disciples of Jesus increase in number (2:47; 6:7; 9:31). Nothing can ultimately stop what God has ordained. The mission will move forward toward its eschatological *telos*, the ends of the earth, for the ends of the earth must become the treasured possession of God's anointed (Ps. 2:8; Acts 1:8). Though God drives the mission, the church is called to participate with all that they have. As Gerhard Lohfink said of election: "Being chosen is not a privilege or a preference *over others*; but existence *for others*, and hence the heaviest burden in history."[26]

God not only moves the larger flow of the mission forward in Acts. It seems that there are *kairos* moments involving key individuals that dot the landscape of the narrative and that function like appointments prearranged by God. These individuals open doorways to larger groups (Samaritans, Gentiles among the God fearers, a larger circle of Gentiles). Notice how God works on the heart of the Ethiopian eunuch in Acts 8 and then sends Philip to meet him in the desert at just the opportune moment to guide him across the finish line of his conversion. In chapter 10, God works on both Cornelius and Peter to arrange a meeting at just the right moment as well. In fact, Cornelius is so ripe for conversion by the time Peter gets to his home that he

---

[26] Emphasis is original. Gerhard Lohfink, *Does God Need the Church?* (Collegeville, MN: Michael Glazier Books, 1999), 37.

and his household convert while Peter is still preaching! The Jews who have rejected Paul's message are told that their rejection led to the word going forth among the Gentiles. When Paul proclaims the good news to them, "all who were appointed for eternal life believed" (13:48). The term used for "appointed" here is interesting. There is nothing in the text that identifies this appointment as a timeless decree. This participle, *tetagmenoi*, is in the middle voice and hence carries the sense of their being prepared in their walk with God for just that moment in time to hear and accept the gospel.[27] God worked among them "that they would seek him and perhaps reach out for him and find him" (17:27). As with the Eunuch and Cornelius, this is a divine appointment in which they participated in their search for God. Such is a consistent theme in Acts. There is no indication here that this is an eternal decree and that other Gentiles in the crowd were eternally damned. In fact, 13:48 indicates that all of the Gentiles present at the event converted: "When the Gentiles heard this, they were glad and honored the word of the Lord."

Selecting such dramatic incidences to reveal the power of God at decisive points to drive the mission forward was typical for Luke. The emphasis here would simply be that not only the Jews but also the Gentiles could be viewed as appointed to salvation in Christ and in the mission of the Spirit. As I read the book of Acts, I am struck by the degree to which God prepares people in advance and then pushes the mission forward toward its intended conclusion at the ends of the earth. God does the heavy lifting. The church functions as the chief sign and instrument, but God does the work. Yet, people are not mere puppets, moving according to a divine predetermination. Bear in mind that the sermon in Acts that is most optimistic about the inherent search for God among the Gentiles is preached to an Athenian audience with mixed results (17:32-34).

## The Gospel of John: Whoever Believes

According to John's Gospel, Christ is revealed as the Chosen One at his anointing by the Spirit at the Jordan (1:33-34). His choosing his disciples opens his election under the abundant life of the Spirit to them. "Have I not chosen you, the Twelve?" (6:70). Even Judas is chosen, though he will ultimately fail; in fact, John indicates he never properly responded (6:70). Their mission will open this anointing and this election to the world, for all who drink of the Son will experience the welling up of the Spirit to eternal life. They will be kept by the Son to be sure, but they will also be carried on a never-ending force of the Spirit's work in their lives.

For John also, the election of the Son by the Spirit actualizes in history an eternal election, for the Son was always the divine Word that reveals the Father and will mediate the Spirit. He also brought all things into existence and is the light that gives all of humanity the essential truth of their existence and destiny (1:1-5). There is no truth that defines the divine purpose for their destiny than this one. This is the truth that comes forth from the Father, is revealed in the Son, and is mediated by the Spirit through the witness of the church to the world. The Word became flesh and tabernacled among us, and we beheld his glory (1:14-16). Humanity was created to become part

---

[27] See Shank, *Elect in the Son*, 87.

of this tabernacle and to invite all others to its communion of life. Christ bore mortal flesh so that in resurrection he could enter glory on humanity's behalf (17:5), for he sanctified himself that they all may be sanctified in him (17:19). The drama of his life, death, and resurrection as the source of life to all flesh is in itself the story of election played out for all to see. This is the drama that lay hidden in the heart of God from all eternity and that was revealed in flesh for the sake of the whole world (3:16). Christ came as the key to the meaning of our lives; yet, humanity did not know him. He came unto his own, and even they did not recognize him. But to as many as did believe on him, they were given the right to be his brothers and sisters, elect in him (1:10-12). But the door is never closed according to John, for he tells us that God sent the Son out of love for the world (3:16). God's judgment against them is not an abstract decree but has its cause in the fact that, though Christ was the light of their true existence and destiny, they preferred darkness instead (3:19).

Jesus prayed to his Father in Jn 17:23 that his church be one so that "the world will know that you sent me and have loved them even as you have loved me." In eternally loving the Son, the Father loved a people who will share in that love by sharing in the Son. John's Gospel thus views the Jewish faithful, who embraced Jesus as Messiah, as a gift from the Father to the Son. Though they freely responded to grace throughout their journey toward Christ, they were also drawn by the Father to the Son (6:44). They are thus referred to as a gift that the Son will cherish always and grant full share in his destiny in the fullness of immortal life:

> All those the Father gives me will come to me, and whoever comes to me I will never drive away. [38] For I have come down from heaven not to do my will but to do the will of him who sent me. [39] And this is the will of him who sent me, that I shall lose none of all those he has given me, but raise them up at the last day. (6:37-39)

In its immediate context, the gift of these followers to the Son is descriptive not of a timeless decree but rather of lives characterized by a yielding to the Father's drawing (6:44), journeys that led them to Christ. We often think of Christ as the gift of the Father granted in the Spirit to humanity. The thought here is that all things were created for Christ, as a gift to *him* (cf., Col. 1:16). He came to that which was his own (those who should belong to him) but his own did not receive him (Jn 1:11). But others who received him became the Father's gift to him. The church was always intended as the gift of the Father to the Son in accordance with the longing of the Triune God.

There is thus no contradiction in John between election and the offer of salvation to the whole world, for God so loved the *world* that "*whoever* believes in him shall not perish but have eternal life" (Jn 3:16). This "whoever" is open to all, directed to the whole world. There is a long string of "whoevers" in John that highlights the universal reach of God's overflowing grace: whoever lives by the truth comes to the light (3:21); whoever believes in the Son has eternal life (3:36); whoever drinks the water Christ gives them will never thirst (4:14); whoever hears Christ's word and believes on the one who sent him has eternal life (5:24); whoever comes to Christ will never grow hungry (6:35); whoever eats the bread of life will live forever (6:51); whoever believes will have living water flow out from them (7:38); whoever follows Christ will never walk in darkness

(8:12); whoever obeys Christ's word will never see death (8:51); whoever enters the gate which is Christ will be saved (10:9); and whoever lives by believing in Christ will never die (11:26). The open offer to the whole world to accept is not only mentioned by John but is also a strong point highlighted throughout that keeps hitting the reader like a hammer, calling them to glimpse the limitless expanse of divine grace. To assume that God did not intend this call to be genuinely offered to the whole world arguably contradicts all of the earlier texts (especially 3:16) and makes a sham of the offer. John's strong emphasis on this "whoever" must not be downplayed. Though God's drawing provides the enablement (6:44), what we do with that enablement is also determinative. This does not make grace a thing that we can take advantage of or reject, nor does it make grace an overwhelming power that forces compliance. Grace is the liberating force of love; but it can be resisted or even received "in vain" or without arriving at its divinely intended end (cf., 2 Cor. 6:1). There is no ambiguity here in my view. The universality of the call qualifies the divine choice as open-ended.

So, what does it mean for John to say that Jesus's followers were "chosen"? Interestingly, nowhere in John does it say that God from eternity decided who would follow Christ and *who would not*. In John, the Son is the one and only Chosen One (1:33-34). Others are chosen as an open invitation to be engrafted into *him* as the only true vine (15:1). He is the only begotten from eternity by the Father (1:18) to have life in himself as the Father does (5:26), sharing glory with the Father (17:5) as well as love (17:24). He was at the beginning with God the Father and came forth to make the Father known and be in himself the true fruit bearer of all fruit bearers, for he is the vine and his followers are but his branches (15:1-4). Only Christ is the Spirit Baptizer for John; only he is the mediator of the Spirit of life, the open door to election. Those who believe are drawn by the Father (6:44), for faith is indeed a gift. Yet, being drawn does not eliminate human responsibility for John. "I am the gate; whoever enters through me will be saved" (10:9). The giftedness of faith in John accents God's promise to keep Christ's followers safe and fruitful, so long as they remain in Christ their spiritual vine (15:4-5). The warning about the consequences of not remaining is given to living branches already in the vine and not to those who have never truly lived (15:6). This warning is no mere hypothetical. Those who receive the Spirit by faith have their rite of passage to join in the life and mission of the elect One: "As the Father has sent me, I am sending you. And with that he breathed on them and said, 'Receive the Holy Spirit'" (20:21). The baptism in the Holy Spirit is the means by which we officially join Christ's election, including being sent by the Father under the anointing of the Spirit.

In Revelation, the Lamb that is slain and exalted is the hermeneutical key for discerning God's elect will for creation and for the elect people in history. As Christ was wounded because of our transgression but was raised up, so was creation in him and in his image (God declares, "I am making everything new," 21:5), and so were the saints in him. What is said about the "book of Life" in Revelation should be included here as well. The list of "names" in the book of life is undoubtedly joined to the one name above all names by which we are saved, Jesus Christ. Christ will write on them his "new name" along with the name of God and the name of the city of God (3:12). The martyrs also have God's and Christ's names written on their foreheads, unlike those who have instead the name of the beast (13:17), the "antichrist." The names of the faithful are noteworthy primarily because Christ has named them as his own. Bear in mind that the book of life belongs to the Lamb (13:8; 21:27). It is *his* book and not theirs, and those listed are there because they bear *his* name. His name is the "Word of God" and "King of Kings and Lord of Lord's" (19:13, 16). Yet, they are also there because they have joined the faithful who bear his name and are faithful to it themselves. They have endured hardship for his name and not grown weary (2:3). They were true to his name (2:13), have kept his word during times of trial and not denied his name (3:8). The prophets lead the church in revering Christ's name (11:18). "Who will not fear you, Lord, and bring glory to your name?" (15:4). Yet, their own unique names or legacies are not lost. They will not have their names "blotted out" from the Lamb's book of life, for Christ will remember them, acknowledging them before his Father and the angels (3:5, cf. Exod. 32:32).

In the light of this acknowledgment, it would seem that the Lamb's "book" is perhaps symbolic of Christ's limitless and intimate knowledge of the faithful and the "recording" of their names symbolic of the Lamb's taking note of them. These names are noteworthy to Christ or, better, are allowed to have a share in the Lamb's own noteworthiness before God and the angels. The "names" here are more than personal titles; they represent the core commitment of these persons' lives, what we could perhaps call their spiritual legacy. They are those who have tried to live in a way that is glorifying of the Lamb. They could never be worthy in themselves, but they have nevertheless borne genuine witness. Here is where election becomes appropriately personal. God makes room in Godself for humanity in all of their particularity and diversity. Every unique journey and legacy is implied in the body of Christ as God envisioned it from all eternity. The goal of the new creation is God's dwelling on the earth with all those who have endured life's trials and overcome by the blood of Jesus and the power of the Spirit: "And I heard a loud voice from the throne saying, 'Look! God's dwelling place is now among the people, and he will dwell with them. They will be his people, and God himself will be with them and be their God'" (21:3).

## 1 and 2 Peter: Make Your Election Sure

Our last New Testament reflection takes us through 1 and 2 Peter, widely known as a mediating voice between Paul's strong accent on grace and James's equally strong emphasis on works (faith in action, what Paul refers to as faith working through love, Gal. 5:6). 1 Peter 1:1 addresses the letter to the "elect" throughout the provinces of Pontus, Galatia, Cappadocia, Asia, and Bithynia. Then comes a striking Trinitarian definition of election as involving those "who have been chosen according to the foreknowledge of God the Father, through the sanctifying work of the Spirit, to be obedient to Jesus Christ and sprinkled with his blood" (v. 2). The grammar of this verse is difficult. The idea that the obedience mentioned here is Christ's obedience on the cross is grammatically unlikely. I have found Sydney Page's arguments here to be convincing. Obedience to Jesus Christ "and sprinkling with his blood" is encouraged among the elect with Exod. 24:4-8 as background. In that text the leaders of Israel vow obedience to God and are then sprinkled with the blood of a sacrificed bull. Peter thus refers to an election that is due to the love of the Father and the sanctifying work of the Spirit and has as its goal the obedience of believers who have had the sprinkling of Christ's blood applied to them in faith.[28] More specifically, the election in 1 Pet. 1:2 is rooted in the foreknowledge (fore-loving) of the Father but is appropriated in history through being sanctified (set apart from sin) by the Holy Spirit so that we may be obedient to Jesus Christ with whose blood we have been "sprinkled."

For 1 Peter, the elect have been born anew through the resurrection of Jesus Christ unto an inheritance "that can never perish, spoil or fade" and is "kept in heaven" for them (1:4). They will be "shielded by God's power" until the final revelation of God that will come at the end (v. 5). Their inheritance is undoubtedly kept in heaven for them because this is where Christ is at the right hand of the Father yet to be revealed in power at the conclusion of all things. It is his risen life that contains the substance of their inheritance and their hope. Chapter 1:19-21 speaks of being redeemed by Christ then adds that he is the Chosen One for all time: "He was chosen before the creation of the world, but was revealed in these last times for your sake. Through him you believe in God, who raised him from the dead and glorified him, and so your faith and hope are in God" (vv. 20-21). That Christ is the Chosen One for all time is a theme that one finds in Paul, John, and Peter (Eph. 1:3-4; Jn 1:18; 1 Pet. 1:21-22), making it a widespread element of the faith of the church surrounding the writing of the New Testament. Christ is not the mere means by which we are elected. He is the elect One in whom we are elect by faith in him.

1 Peter confirms in the next chapter that Christ is "chosen by God and precious to him" (2:4), language used of Israel in the Old Testament ("you will be my treasured possession," Exod. 19:5). But here we see that it was always Christ who was God's treasured One; Israel merely partook of his favor with the Father and was called to bear witness to that divine favor in history. Their failure set the background for Christ to be embodied in flesh as the one who has this favor and lives obediently to it. But the living stone that the Father treasured was rejected and thrown aside by humanity for destruction (2:4). This living stone overcame human rejection and is now used of God as the foundation for the building of a temple of dedicated stones built up into a sacred dwelling place: "You also, like living stones, are being built into a spiritual house to be a holy priesthood, offering spiritual sacrifices acceptable to God through Jesus Christ" (v. 5). We also are living stones chosen and precious to God, a dwelling place for the Spirit of God to offer ourselves to God through Jesus. The foundation stone of the temple now becomes the offering in the temple through which we offer ourselves. The elect One invites us to be elect through him and in the gift of his Spirit for the sake of offering ourselves to God through him.

2 Peter 1 grants us deeper insight into the role of the obedient life in God's election and calling of believers. Most important is this text worth quoting in full:

> [5] For this very reason, make every effort to add to your faith goodness; and to goodness, knowledge; [6] and to knowledge, self-control; and to self-control,

---

[28] Sydney H. D. Page, "Obedience and Blood Sprinkling in 1 Peter 2," *WTJ* 72 (2010): 291–98.

perseverance; and to perseverance, godliness; ⁷ and to godliness, mutual affection; and to mutual affection, love. ⁸ For if you possess these qualities in increasing measure, they will keep you from being ineffective and unproductive in your knowledge of our Lord Jesus Christ. ⁹ But whoever does not have them is nearsighted and blind, forgetting that they have been cleansed from their past sins. ¹⁰ Therefore, my brothers and sisters, make every effort to confirm your calling and election. For if you do these things, you will never stumble, ¹¹ and you will receive a rich welcome into the eternal kingdom of our Lord and Savior Jesus Christ. (1:5-11)

This catalogue of virtues ("faith," "goodness," "knowledge," "self-control," etc.) arguably gets the reader to the heart of 2 Peter. The author is encouraging believers to resist the moral decadence of their society so as to persevere by "confirming" their calling and election within a sanctified people set apart to bear witness, implying that election is something one must appropriate in faith (v. 10). The term in Greek for "confirm" is βέβαιος, which has the sense of being firmly grounded, established, or made more sure. The proposal of some that the meaning here is confirmed as valid "before others" is possible linguistically but not contextually, for the larger context highlights perseverance rather than public witness.

One's appropriation of election occurs in baptism and, from there, as one by grace "ascends" a ladder of virtues with mutual affection and love as the ultimate goal. Of course, mutual affection and love are arguably the starting point and means toward the attainment of all other virtues, but they are also their aim. Without such intentional cultivation of virtuous affections and behavior, one can succumb to a kind of spiritual and moral blindness, a lack of discernment as to the true nature and purpose of one's unique calling and election. To use a modern idiom, one can slip into a form of "cheap grace" that assumes forgiveness without repentance, or grace without the cost of discipleship that comes with it.

2 Peter is not advocating legalism but rather a receptivity of grace that yields the entire life to its inner and outer workings. Of course, God's power is sufficient to keep us on the path to virtue ("his divine power has given us everything we need for a godly life," 1:3). The goal is perseverance ("if you do these things, you will never stumble," v. 10), which climaxes in a rich welcome to the kingdom of Christ (v. 11). That stumbling is potentially serious is implied by the fact that one could indeed fall short of inclusion into the kingdom of Christ if the encouragement of the passage is not heeded. That genuine believers who are elect and called of God could still stumble this seriously is shown by the reference to those who through moral laxity are made to forget that they were indeed cleansed from past sins (v. 9). Note the warning in the following chapter: "If they have escaped the corruption of the world by knowing our Lord and Savior Jesus Christ and are again entangled in it and are overcome, they are worse off at the end than they were at the beginning" (2:20). They become like a dog returning to its own vomit or a swine to its mud (v. 22). The references here are obviously offensive and they are meant to be, so as to draw attention to the ugliness of the moral laxity prevalent at that time and posing an ongoing danger to the elect. God's grace is sufficient to keep us, but we also need to yield to that grace (by that grace) to establish ourselves more firmly among the elect.

## Election in Christ and by the Spirit: Final Reflections

The Bible does not grant us a systematic theology of election. So there will remain room for genuine debate over the many things that are said about it through the various contexts of the biblical canon. I will attempt to briefly discuss several issues that arise from various texts discussed earlier. This discussion is only meant to suggest some major lines of thought. By way of definition, election is, throughout the scriptures, a divine act that arises out of grace and has as its overarching purpose mercy toward humanity to the glory to God. The two are inseparable, for God is glorified in showing mercy and making all things new. Election is a divine act of choosing out of an abundance of divine love and grace but there is also implied judgment for rejection. Inseparably connected to election is calling. God chooses all in choosing the Son and calls the chosen for the fulfillment of divine purposes through the witness of the Spirit. The two (election and calling) are thus inseparable. As Otto Weber maintained, the "calling" that is experienced in the gospel "is not the result but the form of the election of God."[29] Because of calling, election happens "'then and there,' 'thus and so,' 'at sundry times and places' in concrete human experiences, in the experience of the heard Word and the faith which results."[30] God's calling experienced in faith is the "actual realization" of election in time.[31]

The most interesting insight that comes from an investigation of the scriptural teaching on election is the vast difference that exists between the biblical presentation of election and the classical Christian debate over the issue. In the Old Testament God choses most basically from a divine purpose but also in response to human choices, first by the patriarchs of faith but also by Israel as a people. Election and calling are relational and dynamic. They follow a plan but also have a history and an unfolding that involves human choices. Indeed, they always have unexpected turns or results, following God's sovereign will rather than human expectations or desires. But humans are held accountable as though they had a real choice in how they responded to God. And their choices matter; they play a role in the outcome. Within the classical debate, however, both Calvinist and Arminian understandings of election assumed the idea from the beginning that election is an eternal or timeless decree directly related to the choosing of the elect people, except Calvinists base it on God's sovereign choice or good pleasure and Arminians on God's foreknowledge of human choices, a difference that then created the debate between divine sovereignty and human free will. Though election is eternal, ignoring it as a historical reality causes versions of eternal election to be abstract.

Following Barth, I have maintained that there is no timeless decree, only the self-giving God who has eternally self-determined to be the God for others. Election is thus free from the uncertainties and idolatry of human choice in that it is at its core God's gracious self-election as the Triune God. Especially important to the New Testament understanding of election is its Christocentric nature. Karl Barth has especially shown

---

[29] Weber, *Foundations of Dogmatics*, Vol. 2, 498.
[30] Ibid., 498–99.
[31] Ibid., 499.

that an "eternal decree" (*decretum absolutum*) is nowhere described in the New Testament. Besides being abstract, such a decree would problematically eclipse the fact that the eternal Word of the Father, Jesus Christ, is the only eternal "decree" there can ever be. Christ the Logos (Word) of the Father brought all things into existence on behalf of the Father and represents forever their purpose and destiny. For Barth, Christ cannot be reduced to functioning as the mere instrument for fulfilling a divine decree concerning who should and should not be saved. Barth thus rejects a notion of election "which is independent of Jesus Christ and is only executed by him."[32] Subordinating Christ to the absolute decree in this way causes the decree to transcend the will of God enacted in Christ for humanity. Who then is the God of this decree if it transcends the revelation of God and of divine purposes given in Christ? By disconnecting God from the revelation of Christ in this way, "What an abyss of uncertainty is opened up!"[33] Election, which is meant to be a reason for rejoicing, comfort, and commitment to the world, is suddenly at risk of leading to fatalism, anxiety, or a sense of entitlement. Rather than election causing us to peer into the depths of the Logos made flesh when attempting to fathom God's ordained will for humanity, we end up looking beyond toward something that transcends Christ, which for Barth can only be "nothingness, or rather the depth of Satan."[34] Indeed, as Thomas Torrance penned, "There is no God behind the back of Jesus Christ."[35]

Barth's Christological interpretation of election is thus uncompromising: Jesus Christ "is the decree of God, behind and above which there can be no earlier or higher decree, and beside which there can be no other, since all others serve only the fulfillment of this decree."[36] There is no election that does not serve bringing all things under Christ as the Head, *all things* (Eph. 1:10)! For all things were made through him and for him (Col. 1:16). Christ crucified and risen is what God decrees for all of history, for all of humanity, and for all of creation. Christ as God's election for creation is all encompassing, the purpose to be accomplished in the midst of all things. Barth is adamant, "Before Him and without Him, and beside Him, God does not, then, elect or will anything."[37] Apart from Christ, "there is no election, no beginning, no decree, no word of God."[38] He is the mystery to be grasped in all of history. Barth looks at the entry of Christ into flesh to redeem it and asks, "If this is not election, what else can it be? What choice can precede the choice by which God has of Himself chosen to have with Himself in the beginning of all things the word which is Jesus!"[39]

Christ is not merely the means by which the elect are called and saved; such an instrumentalist Christology will never do. He is the election and the electing. He is the elect human and the electing God in flesh revealed. The Gospel of Mark informs us that during the time of messianic woes on the earth, the time of trial will be shortened,

---

[32] Karl Barth, *CD*, Vol. 2, Pt. 2, 65.
[33] Ibid.
[34] Ibid., 25.
[35] Thomas F. Torrance, *The Christian Doctrine of God: One Being in Three Persons* (New York: T & T Clark, 2016), 243. I am grateful to Bobby Grow for bringing this quote to my attention.
[36] Karl Barth, *CD*, Vol. 2, Pt. 2, 94.
[37] Ibid., 94.
[38] Ibid., 95.
[39] Ibid., 100–1.

"for the sake of the elect, whom he has chosen" (13:20). Upon his return, the angels will gather "*his* elect" from the four winds, from the ends of the earth" (13:27). *The Spirit-baptized elect One elects others by opening his chosen life to them under the anointing of the Spirit.* The final gathering of the people of God from all over the earth (from its very ends) represents *his elect*, his treasured possession (Ps. 2:8). As the electing God, Christ reveals God's self-determination throughout eternity to be the God revealed in the Christ who boundlessly gives himself to all others so that they may all share in the divine life. But Christ also reveals the elect One, who shows us the destiny ordained for humanity as created and redeemed by God.

Not only is election in the New Testament Christocentric but it is also pneumatological in realization. Perhaps the most neglected aspect of election is the focus of the Bible on divine anointing by the Spirit as the key moment in time when the divine calling is actualized and the divine election appropriated as one's own. This anointing is foretold with regard to Israel but comes to focus on Israel's Messiah. *Christ is the elect One of God as the Spirit Bearer and is the electing One as the Imparter of the Spirit.* His anointing at the Jordan is his installment as the Messiah, the Chosen One of God. He then shares his election with his followers by imparting the Holy Spirit to them. Barth is generally not given credit for his inclusion of the pneumatological and ecclesiological role in election. Suzanne McDonald has a point when she maintains that this dimension of election needs development—a task that she undertakes throughout her helpful book on the subject, where she bases election on Christ and locates its expanding boundary at the priestly mission of the church in relation to the rest of humanity (representing God to them and them to God).[40] She notes that the "vocation of the elect is to proclaim to the rest of humanity that the election of Jesus Christ is their own election."[41] The presence of the Spirit is the sign of the community's election in Christ and the church's Spirit-empowered witness is the means by which others are incorporated into the community of the elect.[42] Election is thus geared toward service.[43] I have added greater specificity to her argument by focusing on Jesus's anointing (both in time and in eternity) and the church's anointing in him as the focal point of election. Christ fulfilled his anointed path by going to the cross on behalf of humanity. Thus, election under the anointing of the Spirit is to be cruciform. Sigurd Grindheim rightly notes that election in Judaism prior to the time of Christ tended to focus on peculiarities of visibly obeying the law. However, the New Testament points instead mainly to a cruciform life lived out in the power of the Spirit as the chief characteristic of those who are elect.[44] Though election in history has particularity, focused on a peculiar people sharing in the election of its Lord and Savior, it also has an expanding boundary and a limitless horizon, driven by the church's search for the

---

[40] Suzanne McDonald, *Re-imaging Election: Divine Election as Representing God to Others & Others to God* (Grand Rapids, MI: Eerdmans, 2010)..
[41] Ibid., 47.
[42] Ibid., 48.
[43] Ibid., 94–98.
[44] Grindheim, *The Crux of Election*, passim.

lost and the suffering as a force for healing. By the Spirit, the church will ultimately be conformed to Christ's elect humanity.[45]

Notably, Barth gave the election of the community in Christ priority over the election of individuals, as though saying that we as individuals are elect in Christ through the mediation of the church, by belonging to the church through union with Christ.[46] He stated of election, "Its direct and proper object is not individuals generally, but one individual—and only in Him the people called and united by Him, and only in that people individuals in general in their private relationships with God."[47] Through the witness of the church, Christ by the Spirit opens Christ's election to others. Jesus is not only the elect human for all humans; he is also the electing God who extends his own election to others by imparting the Spirit centrally through the witness of his body. Barth notes that, because Jesus is alive in his church through the power of the Spirit, election is mediated to others from Christ through the life of the community.[48] As Israel was once the chosen people in foreshadowing Christ's election, and mediating election to all who joined in worshipping Israel's God, so now the church becomes "the environment of the elected man, Jesus of Nazareth" for all others. The church is the place where others are incorporated into Christ's election through the Spirit and by faith.[49] We could say that the church is the place where others are elect in Christ by faith and through the baptism in the Holy Spirit.

We partake of Christ's election by partaking of the election of the church. Barth thus says of those who are united to Christ by being incorporated into the life of the church that they are "included in the election of the community—in the community, by the community."[50] By the call of God mediated through the community of faith, individuals "actualize" the election that is offered to all of humanity in Christ. Indeed, "for his part man can and actually does elect God, thus attesting and activating himself as elected man."[51] Of course, we do not intend to limit election to the boundaries of the visible church, for the Spirit of the Lord is like the wind that blows where it wills. Moreover, there are indeed tares among the wheat in the visible church that God will remove at the final harvest. This complexity must be fully admitted. But we are still justified in viewing the visible church as the central locus of election in Christ and its mission as the chief expanding boundary of the realization of election in time.

There is also further complexity to this discussion of corporate election. The election of Israel connects not only to the church as an analogous body but also to other peoples in the secular realm, for Israel was also a nation. Luke's Acts makes this connection, finding significance in the presence of Diaspora Jews at Pentecost from every nation and people (2:5) and referring to the times and seasons that God planned for all peoples in their journeys so as to lead them to the witness of the church to Christ (1:7; 17:26).

---

[45] McDonald, *Re-imaging Election*, 89.
[46] In the *CD*, Vol. 2, pt. 2, section 35, Barth discusses the election of the community in Christ first (section 34) before discussing the election of the individual in Christ through the church.
[47] Ibid., 43.
[48] Ibid., 410-11.
[49] Ibid., 260.
[50] Ibid., 197.
[51] Ibid., 177.

The election of Israel is irrevocable. Though they are going through a prolonged time of hardening due to their unbelief, they are according to Rom. 11:11 expected (perhaps at Christ's return) to be restored. The witness must reach the nations to the ends of the earth first (Acts 1:6-8). Along the way, individual participants in Israel's election may not endure. Similarly, all peoples have an irrevocable calling. The nations will be blessed through Abraham's seed, which is Christ (Gen. 22:18; Gal. 3:16). The church as a whole may also be described as indefectible (Mt. 28:20) though individuals within it may not endure.

The ecclesiological mediation of election is a theme that did not begin with Barth. It actually goes back to Friedrich Schleiermacher and especially Albrecht Ritschl.[52] Contemporary to Barth, Otto Weber took a similar approach to election, and his conclusions are worthy of note. Drawing also from Barth, Weber maintains that the election of humanity was accomplished once and for all in Jesus Christ's life, death, and resurrection. Without denying the significance of the incarnation (where God was wedded to human flesh), Weber locates the public event of election at Christ's anointing by the Spirit at his baptism.[53] As noted earlier, this is where the Father declares Christ as the beloved Son. And this is where John the Baptist knows that Christ is indeed the "Chosen One" (Jn 1:33-34). This focus on anointing then helps us to understand how Pentecost provides the bridge from Christ's election to the church, and to how the Christ opens his election to the world through the life and mission of the church. The "sociality" of election through the mediation of the Spirit-indwelt and empowered church is a helpful way of overcoming the abstract and individualistic nature of the classical debate over this subject. So through the church empowered by the Spirit, God not only elects from eternity but also "continues electing into the new creation to come."[54]

Since God's eternal self-election is for others, it necessarily involves a history, though it is not bound to history. It transforms history into eternal communion. So we can affirm Pannenberg's blunt statement, "We cannot simply abandon the idea of an eternal election."[55] Admittedly, explicit New Testament evidence for an election that is eternal is not abundant, the clearest being 1 Pet. 1:20, where Christ is said to be elect before the creation of the world, and Eph. 1:4, where the elect are said to be chosen "in Christ" from "before the creation of the world." Revelation also refers to a "book of life" written from before the creation of the world (Rev. 17:8), which is connected to the Christ who was crucified from before creation (13:8). Though explicit scriptural evidence for an eternal election is not plentiful, the theological reasons for it are compelling. The reason assumed in the New Testament is the eternal Christ anointed by the eternal Spirit. That Christ is the elect One of all times is the most important reason why the New Testament uniquely and explicitly makes election eternal. More expansively,

---

[52] Fr. Schleiermacher, *Christian Faith* (London: T & T Clark, 2016), 536–60; A. Ritschl, *The Christian Doctrine of Justification and Reconciliation*, Vol. 2 (Clifton, NJ: Reference Book Publication, 1966), 121–28. See Pannenberg, *Systematic Theology*, Vol. 3, 458–59.
[53] Weber, *Foundations of Dogmatics*, Vol. 2, 498.
[54] Steven D. Paulson and Jerome Klotz, "The Promise of Predestination," *Lutheran Quarterly* 16 (2016): 252 (249–75).
[55] Pannenberg, *Systematic Theology*, Vol. 3, 447.

election is willed in the eternal life of the Triune God (connected to Jesus as the Word of the Father who bears the Spirit). Significantly, Eph. 1:3 roots eternal election in Christ as a spiritual blessing earmarked for the elect, which is then appropriated in time through the sealing of the Spirit (1:3, 13-14). The eternally anointed Christ is the spiritual blessing opened to all of humanity and appropriated by faith through the ministry of the church. In addition, there are also secondary theological reasons to assume an eternal election. The eternal God who lives "from everlasting to everlasting" (Ps. 90:2) cannot be confined to time when it comes to election. God is not bound by time, forced to choose moment by moment what to do when it comes to the divine will for history. The eternal God has purposes that are realized in time and are responsive to human decisions, but election is nevertheless eternal because it is rooted in the changeless love and overarching purposes of the Triune God.

However, one should not start with the eternal when it comes to election. How can we! "For where can it ever be disclosed to us except where it is executed?"[56] I repeatedly urged readers when looking at election texts not to jump immediately to the assumption that what is being described is an eternal and timeless decision. Besides not wanting to read meanings into a text that are not there, my purpose was to help them see first and foremost the full historical nature of those divine decisions. My purpose was not to deny that there is an eternal decision involved in divine acts in history, only to prevent viewing those eternal choices as abstract or capricious. My purpose was to highlight the crucial role of human response in election and to understand the eternal election for humanity in Christ and by the Spirit as open, relational, responsive, and expanding. Interestingly, the Christological and pneumatological roots of election not only secured, for Barth, the importance of election as eternal but also secured election as a divine activity in time. "Because it is identical with the election of Jesus Christ the eternal will of God is a divine activity in the form of history, encounter and decision between God and man."[57]

All that we can know about God's eternal purposes is from what God has done in time, especially in the person of Christ and the impartation of the Spirit through the instrumentality of the church, and what the scriptures tell us about the eschatological future that will conform all things to Christ. Once the historical dimension of election is taken fully into consideration, the eternal nature of election can be properly included and explained, not as something that is antithetical to election in time but rather as encompassing it all for purposes that ultimately transcend history. For, as Pannenberg has shown, the eternal as rooted in the eternality of God encompasses what God does in time. Though there is a distinction to be made between time and eternity, there is not to be an unresolvable opposition. Following Hegel, Pannenberg rightly notes that a notion of the infinite that opposes it to the finite cancels its infinity, for the infinite in this case would be defined by this opposition and necessarily limited by it. So, for all of its distinction from finite time, eternity must embrace it and be positively related to it in order to be truly infinite or boundless (all encompassing). The eternal God embodies history so as to transform it into a bearer of the infinite, the eternal dwelling

---

[56] Ibid., 105.
[57] Ibid., 175.

place of God. In the process, creaturely historical existence and responsiveness to God are allowed to play a role in how God's eternal purposes unfold and are brought to eschatological fulfillment.[58]

The eternality of election raises the issue of divine foreknowledge. The scriptures assume that God has an ordained plan that is foreknown and that humans are held responsible for the roles that they play in the ensuing narrative. The scriptures also assume that God works out the plan in a way that is relational and responsive to humans. But the scriptures don't explain how all of these things can be so. As for foreknowledge, there are at least a couple of instances in the New Testament (Rom. 8:29; 1 Pet. 1:20) where God's foreknowing seems to refer to a fore-loving or a knowing that cherishes the ones who are known. Yet, foreknowledge is also referred to in a less personal way (Acts 2:23). There is currently a lively debate over the nature of divine foreknowledge and the role that it plays in election. The issues are complex. For example, even calling it "*fore*-knowledge" implies knowledge of a people or events *before* they exist as a historical reality. This assumption has been placed under critical scrutiny. In part, it raises the question as to the nature of time. If time is analogous to a frozen river and God transcends it in willing it, there may be no such thing as a "before" to speak of. However, if time is analogous to a rushing stream moving forward and not yet arriving at its destiny, the situation potentially changes, especially if the future is not yet objectively real. In this case, one may speak analogously of a "before," not in the sense that the future as a yet-to-be-fulfilled potential does not exist in God's "knowing," but rather in the sense that God's knowledge of that not-yet future would be different in nature from God's knowledge of past and present. Exactly how God's predetermined purposes will be realized are known by God in the sense that God in infinite wisdom can foretell how people and events will respond to divine actions.[59]

Moreover, God's knowing what will happen and how people will respond raises the question of human freedom. Are humans free to respond to God by divine enablement (in the sense that they may or may not decide to respond favorably) if God already knows what they will do? An argument can be made that freedom as enabled (not predetermined) by God would still be possible. The case would then not be that something must happen because God knows it. It would rather be that something will happen and, because God knows all things, God will know this "something" too. But God still appears too passive in this formulation. Thus the question would still need to be posed concerning how God factors in human responses within a foreordained plan. Here are my preliminary proposals in a nutshell. First, election does not fundamentally consist of God's simply electing those who freely come by grace; rather, God elects Godself to humanity and that election focused on the anointed Christ is an eternally sovereign choice that is not ultimately dependent on human will, desire, or plans. The victorious Christ as the Bearer and Imparter of the Spirit *is at its essence* that which God has ordained for creation. What this means is that God's ordained purposes would

---

[58] Wolfhart Pannenberg, *Systematic Theology*, Vol. 1 (Grand Rapids, MI: Eerdmans, 1991), 401–10.
[59] William Lane Craig has made a convincing argument for this view, *The Only Wise God: The Compatibility of Divine Foreknowledge and Human Freedom* (Eugene, OR: Wipf and Stock, 2000), 21–38.

not be simply identifiable with all that happens in history. These purposes must rather be discerned *within* all that happens as the redemptive potential that God wills to be realized through (and perhaps in spite of) the event in question ("in all things God works for the good," Rom. 8:28). Predestination has less to do with events and more to do with the redemptive purpose to be worked out through events. What has been predestined must be spiritually discerned. It is not always obvious to the naked eye.

If God wills all to be elect, does the victory of God's redemptive purposes mean that all will be saved? Barth notes that in being the elect One for salvation, Christ also descended into the damnation earmarked for those who reject. All of condemned humanity is thus no longer to be viewed apart from Christ.[60] The church serves a priestly function by interceding for them before God, so that they come to see how he has bound himself to them.

Does this insight imply that all will be saved? Not necessarily. I have all along referred to election and calling as intended by God to be universal though not everyone may answer the call and actualize it for themselves. Barth explained it this way: All are granted by God the promise of election through the witness of the church and are meant by God to accept that promise, though all may not respond in a way that actualizes its fulfillment.[61] Barth says of God's attitude toward all those who reject:

> He wills that he too should hear the Gospel and with it the promise of election. He wills, then, that this Gospel should be proclaimed to him. He wills that he should appropriate and live by the hope which is given him in the Gospel. He wills that the rejected should believe, and that as a believer he should become a rejected man elected.[62]

The risen Christ is the elect man fulfilled (indeed, as risen he bears the Spirit in fullness), and he takes others into himself by the Spirit, which allows them to actually share in his election and to look with hope to its ultimate fulfillment in him. An election that was earmarked for them from all eternity (in "heavenly places") is now actualized by them in time. Election has not yet reached its eschatological fulfillment in the unity of all under Christ (Eph. 1:10). Does this eschatological unity mean that all in the end will somehow be saved? In response to this question, Barth conceded that the Bible does indicate that not all will be included, although he could find no reason within Christ for exclusion. Concerning the elect, Barth writes, "We cannot consider their number as closed, for we can never find any reason for such a limitation in Jesus Christ."[63] Though not all may actualize their election by faith, they are all still ones to whom Christ is sent and "for whom His call is objectively valid."[64] Barth concludes, "We can say only that the election of Jesus Christ has taken place on behalf of the world.... And

---

[60] Ibid., 90.
[61] A very good treatment of Barth on election that accents the difference he makes between the promise of election (for all) and the actualization of election among those who believe is Michael O'Neil, "Karl Barth's Doctrine of Election," *Evangelical Quarterly* 76, no. 4 (2004): 311–26.
[62] Karl Barth, *CD*, Vol. 2, pt. 2, 506.
[63] Ibid., 422.
[64] Ibid., 423.

this, of course, we do have to say with the strongest possible emphasis and with no qualifications."⁶⁵ The elect community that actualizes their election in Christ by faith and in the Spirit must now serve the call of election by mediating it to all of humanity: "How can any elect man—for they are all elect in him—do otherwise?"⁶⁶

Does God foreknow who will come? Yes, but God's intention and mission objectively (and genuinely) reaches for all, not only because God has created them all as God's own and claimed them all at the cross but also because this is who God is. In Revelation 21, the lake of fire exists symbolically outside of the heavenly city; this eschatological gathering of the elect is bordered by loss. But for all of eternity, the doors of the heavenly city will remain open as symbolic of a divine longing, without fear of invasion from the dark powers, for they have been eliminated once and for all (Rev. 21:25), and all who wash their robes through Christ may enter in (Rev. 22:14). God has elected Godself for the entire world and human rejection does not change that. We are to be and to do the same. Even if it may seem clear that human rejection will in some cases be permanent, we will continue to love and reach out to them, not only because they were willed by God to be our brothers and sisters but because this unceasing love and welcome is who we are too.

---

[65] Ibid.
[66] Ibid.

# 3

# The Pilgrim Church

How may we describe the nature of the Spirit-baptized church? Baptized in the Spirit and united to Christ by faith, the church is the "effective sign and instrument" of the Father's liberating reign in the world.[1] United to Christ, the church lives from the outpouring and incorporating work of the Spirit for the sake of the kingdom. "The kingdom of God, therefore, is the church's constant orientation, abiding motivation, critical court of appeal and final goal."[2] We can point to a cluster of ways of describing the church that help explain its path as a people who live on the cutting edge of the Spirit's work in the world. In line with prior renewal movements of the church catholic, the Protestant Reformation appropriately heralded the idea of *semper reformanda*, the church always under reformation. Focused more on inward experience, Pentecostals have always viewed the church as in constant need of "revival." Such experience is for Pentecostals oriented toward sanctification, charismatic gifting, and empowered witness. The life source at the heart of the church's life is outward moving and shaped by the path of Jesus Christ in faithful fulfillment of the Father's will. Also, influenced by his Baptist roots, Harvey Cox fittingly highlighted the fact that the earliest Christians were called "the way," which points to the church's corporate faith as a path of discipleship or loyal witness to Christ in the world. What a difference from the church of the empire only a few centuries into the future![3] And, due in part to the influence of the Second Vatican Council, the idea of the "pilgrim church" has become popular in ecumenical circles. This view of the church fits well with the above-mentioned ecclesiological tendencies, which are kingdom oriented. This idea is that the church is *on the way* from what it is chosen and called to be to what it is challenged to *become* in its concrete life and witness. This way or path is a pilgrim journey, for the church's home is in the kingdom to come, which they hope will one day reclaim the earth for God's glory (Mt. 6:12). The pilgrim church "on the way" is dedicated to the salvation of humanity. The church is blessed with the presence of Christ, but is not yet fully conformed to Christ, so their journey in the Spirit is both sanctified and sanctifying, partaking of the fullness of life in Christ but still always groaning and reaching for its

---

[1] See the final report of the Anglican-Lutheran dialogue, "The Diaconate as Ecumenical Opportunity," Hanover, Germany, 1995, #13, *GW II*, 42.
[2] See the final report of the Lutheran-Roman Catholic dialogue, "Church and Justification," Wurzburg, Germany, September 11, 1993, #304, *GW II*, 556.
[3] Harvey Cox, *The Future of Faith* (New York: HarperCollins, 2009), 73–84.

ultimate fulfillment (Rom. 8:22). All of the above insights fit well with what I regard as the Spirit-baptized church on its way to greater fullness of life and witness.

The kingdom of God takes priority to the church, for the church is its central sign and instrument in the world. The kingdom is rooted theologically in God's lordship and comes to us as God's liberating reign imparted to us in the coming of Christ and the Spirit.[4] As Gregory of Nyssa taught, Christ is the King and the Spirit is the kingdom in realizing the Father's reign in creation.[5] Christ not only proclaimed the kingdom but also embodied and mediated it as the wellspring of the Spirit. As the mediator of the Spirit in the world even before Pentecost occurred, Christ stated that in his mighty deeds of deliverance in the power of the Spirit the kingdom was coming upon his audience (Mt. 12:28). They were set free and transformed by the liberating reign of God experienced in the Spirit being mediated by Jesus. Those set free live by the Spirit, which is the realm of God's liberating lordship. They dedicate themselves to the communion and justice of the kingdom of God. The life of the church in the power of the Spirit experiences the liberating presence of the kingdom and is devoted to its current purposes in the world and to its ultimate future in the new creation (Rom. 14:17; 2 Cor. 5:17). Hans Küng laments the church's abandonment of its "eschatological self-interpretation." As a consequence, "Christ becomes less and less the expected Lord; he is increasingly taken over by the church as its present possession." The church identifies itself with the kingdom.[6] The priority of the kingdom to the church forbids the church from its inception from taking on such a self-serving, self-justifying posture and sets it on a Christlike path of absolute devotion to the goals of the kingdom of God in the world. It will resist the lure of worldly wealth, recognition, and power, and will constantly give itself to the purposes of grace and justice. "Kingdom first" eliminates all delusions of realized eschatology, making it clear that the church is fallen and lives from a grace that is liberating and present but not yet fully realized. They will constantly be reminded that they will not find fulfillment until the kingdom comes in fullness. Within this eschatological "now" and "not yet," the people of God strive to comprehend their inner mystery, which is communion with God and participation in the divine self-giving, in relation to their historical form, which is fallen and incomplete, groaning for the fullness of liberty to come (Rom. 8:23).

On the one hand, we must resist a simple identification of Christ with the church. Christ's identification with his body is the identification of the one with the many in communion and not a merging of the two into one subject. Let us never forget the stinging warning of Karl Barth: "To a greater or lesser extent, the church is a vigorous and extensive attempt to humanize the divine, to bring it within the sphere of the world of time and things, and to make it a practical 'something,' for the benefit of those who cannot live with the Living God, and yet cannot live without God."[7] *God* humanizes the divine in the incarnation, and on divine rather than human terms and for divine

---

[4] See George Eldon Ladd's essay, *The Gospel of the Kingdom: Scriptural Studies in the Kingdom of God* (Grand Rapids, MI: Eerdmans, 1959), 13–23.
[5] Gregory of Nyssa, *On the Lord's Prayer*, no. 3. See my development of this idea in Macchia, *Baptized in the Spirit*, 89f.
[6] Hans Küng, *The Church* (New York: Sheed and Ward, 1967), 87.
[7] Karl Barth, *The Epistle to the Romans* (New York: Oxford University Press, 1977), 332.

rather than human purposes. We as the church hold his glory in weak vessels of clay that will not conform to its treasure until the resurrection (2 Cor. 4:6-7). In this light, I find it enormously difficult to imagine a context in which I would join with the Second Vatican Council in saying of the church that "by no weak analogy, it is compared to the mystery of the incarnate Word."[8] We must strenuously avoid any implication that the church's essence is divine, as Hans Küng reminds us. Küng elaborates: "The individual believer, after all, does not become a 'divine' reality because he is filled and governed by the Spirit."[9] Why should we speak of the church this way? Moreover, can the church as fallen in its historical sojourn ever be more than a "weak analogy" of the life of our Lord in flesh? Christ was sinless and bore the Spirit without measure. Yes, Paul describes the mystery of the gospel as "Christ in you, the hope of glory" (Col. 1:27). But, again, we hold this glory as vessels of clay (2 Cor. 4:7). And the church's inner essence consists of our participation in Christ by faith and not Christ himself. Until the time we are transformed through resurrection into his glory, the church is the "infirmary of the sick" striving for healing in Christ, as Luther once wrote.[10] Indeed, the "historical form of the church thus participates in the eschatological reality of Christ, but Christ does not become historicized as a piece of the world."[11]

On the other hand, we must resist a total separation of Christ and the church, without a real notion of incorporation and participation in the divine self-giving through the Spirit. This mystery of Christ in us, in communion with us, must be continuously celebrated as the hope for the world. As Chris Green has noted, Pentecostals have a tendency to view the church as "nothing more than 'the requisite delivery system' for ministry."[12] Indeed, the church "is not a mere training subject or training ground for the edification of pious individuals" (Volf).[13] As we noted earlier, the church is not a "salvation machine" for religious consumers. Surely the mystery at the heart of the church is deeper than this! We participate in the very life of God in communion, ministry, and mission.

With the mystery of Christ in us in mind, it becomes clear that the church can only be truly grasped in faith and cannot be adequately described according to functional, sociological, or pragmatic criteria alone. Of course, as a fallen and historical reality, it may be studied like any empirical reality and understood according to the dynamics of institutionalization common to all institutional realities. And such studies must be received not only with gratitude for signs of prophetic witness that show themselves but also with repentance for all that falls short of them. Yet, such signs point to a deeper mystery at the core of that church's faith that finds expression through the institutional realities (more or less), and which can only be meaningfully grasped in faith. This is why the church is at its essence a confession of faith ("We believe in one, holy, catholic

---

[8] LG, #8.
[9] Küng, *The Church*, 174.
[10] Martin Luther, *LW*, Vol. 25, 263.
[11] David W. Congdon, "The Nature of the Church in Theological Interpretation: Culture, Volk, and Mission," *JTI* 11, no. 1 (2017): 115–16 (101–17).
[12] Chris S. Green, "The Body of Christ, the Spirit of Communion: Re-Visioning Pentecostal Ecclesiology in Conversation with Robert Jenson," *JPT* 20 (2011): 15–16 (20–36).
[13] Miroslav Volf, *After Our Likeness: The Church in the Image of the Trinity* (Grand Rapids, MI: Eerdmans, 1998), 174.

and apostolic church"). We can only confess the church as a gift of God kept alive by the presence of Christ through the Spirit; we cannot as of yet adequately grasp or verify it empirically.

In short, the presence of Christ (and the kingdom to come) from which the church at its essence lives and the church's outward form as an empirical fellowship institutionally structured cannot be separated nor regarded as identical. Christ identifies himself with his body, but his body is not identical with him. I like how Moltmann preserves both the difference and the identity between the church and the present Christ: "Between difference and identity lies the sacramental idea of the coinherence of the one in the other."[14] In this light, there need not be a contradiction between "relationship" (accenting the church as fallen and in covenant relation with Christ) and "substantial identity" (highlighting the mystery of the church in real union with Christ and participation in him as his body) (as Simon Chan tells us).[15] Moltmann's application of coinherence helps us to understand how both difference and identity are true. We will explore the institutional realities of the church in our next chapter. Suffice it to say here that the church has an inner mystery in the presence of Christ and the Spirit that its visible reality can point to as a sign but not yet fully bring to expression until the ultimate baptism in the Spirit when this mortality is swallowed up in immortality (2 Cor. 5:4). Christ in us is indeed the "hope of glory." We are thus a pilgrim people who in loving God above all else yearn for the new creation to come, never satisfied with things as they are. In loyalty to the kingdom of Christ we strive to signify the new creation in the world in every way possible.

## Models of the Church

We struggle to formulate an understanding of the church in distinction from extremes on both sides (over- and under-realized versions of the fulfillment of the kingdom in our midst). Throughout such a search, one will in fact be hard-pressed to find abstract definitions of the church in the New Testament. One finds instead various models that are richly suggestive for understanding the relationship between the "now" and the "not yet" elements of the fulfillment of the kingdom in the church. The theologian seeks to tease out their implications. Herein lies the creative challenge. As I proceed, I will note that each model is both a gift ("you are . . .") and a task ("become!"). To more fully explore the theological issues implied by these models, I will conclude by discussing the classical marks of the church as they are given for us in the Nicene Creed (one, holy, Catholic, and apostolic).

### Field of God

As we noted in our previous chapter, Christ is the wellspring of the Spirit, mediating the Spirit to all flesh from the heavenly Father. He is the visible point of reconciliation

---

[14] Moltmann, *The Church in the Power of the Spirit*, 27.
[15] Chan, *Pentecostal Ecclesiology*, 42.

and mediation where the Triune God abundantly self-imparts through the presence of the Spirit, the Spirit that nourishes the life fashioned in the image of the faithful Christ. There is a cluster of agricultural metaphors of the church in the New Testament that stress the fact that the church belongs to God and is nourished by the Spirit from God and through Christ. "You are God's field" (1 Cor. 3:9). This is a statement of fact, a wonderful gift. And, yet, we are also told to bear fruit, or to *be* those fruitful vine branches or that fruitful field as a visible reality (Jn 15:1-4). Our unity, holiness, catholicity, and apostolicity from Christ (to be discussed below) are to be manifested as fruit for the world to see as its own hope for the future.

Paul informs the Corinthians that they are the field of God in answer to divisions in the church that involved a kind of hero worship, focusing on a favored apostle. Paul addresses the situation in chapter 1: "What I mean is this: One of you says, 'I follow Paul'; another, 'I follow Apollos'; another, 'I follow Cephas'; still another, 'I follow Christ.'" It could be that the divisions were between house churches, each one tending to favor a chosen leader.[16] If the final slogan ("I am of Christ") was meant to be included alongside the rest as descriptive of a faction, the arrogance involved in the conflict would come forth with special force in this one. This faction would in effect be saying, "Well, *we* belong to *Christ*. Top *that*!" In this case, believers may even seek to reduce Christ to a tribal Lord who only represents the interests of a favored group. But Christ cannot be so reduced. He is the Lord of the entire church, of the entire creation, and he is the sovereign Head whose mission should unify us and determine our course. Congregations and families of churches in the world need each other to glimpse Christ and experience the Spirit in greater diversity and fullness. As important as they were to the witness of the church, the apostles were not to be elevated to wise sages or teachers who command loyalty from adoring disciples. The same is also true of pivotal figures in the history of the churches, whether it be St. Thomas Aquinas, St. Gregory Palamas, Martin Luther, John Calvin, Menno Simons, John Wesley, or William Seymour (as well as all of the bishops and leaders of the church). There is one Lord and only one foundation for the church, and that is Christ Jesus. And he is Lord of all. Under him, these figures are mere servants, as are the rest of us to be, and they belong, each and every one of them, to all of us.

Paul's retort to these divisions is thus swift and rhetorically effective, "Is Christ divided? Was Paul crucified for you? Were you baptized in the name of Paul?" (1 Cor. 1:13). Dividing the church into competing factions makes as much sense as Christ himself being torn asunder. Paul is introducing here "the body of Christ" model for the church, which we will discuss shortly. The point we wish to make here is that elevating the apostles to adored masters borders on blasphemy. Who else but the one crucified and risen for us all can claim our ultimate loyalty? We were joined to Christ by way of the Spirit as signified in water baptism. We are thus "planted" into him, belong ultimately only to him, and drink the Spirit only from him. Such insights reduce the

---

[16] Richard Hayes, *First Corinthians*, IBCTP (Louisville: Westminster John Knox, 2011), 21–25.

apostles to mere servants in the field on Christ's behalf. Paul's entire discourse on the matter is worth quoting in full:

> [5] What, after all, is Apollos? And what is Paul? Only servants, through whom you came to believe—as the Lord has assigned to each his task. [6] I planted the seed, Apollos watered it, but God has been making it grow. [7] So neither the one who plants nor the one who waters is anything, but only God, who makes things grow. [8] The one who plants and the one who waters have one purpose, and they will each be rewarded according to their own labor. [9] For we are co-workers in God's service; you are God's field. (3:5-9)

The church does not belong to the servants who proclaim the word and nurture others in it on their master's behalf. They belong to the church. It is not *their* church, *their* possession, under *their* authority to fulfill *their* needs and ends. The church is *God's* field. *God* is behind the work. *God* provides the seed and the water that the servants use to mediate grace. And only *God* can make these plants grow. God's ends are the only ones to be accomplished. The leaders are mere servants, laborers in God's field. God's word alone commands allegiance; God alone receives the glory. Both the servants and the believers who become servants themselves under their ministry are thoroughly dependent on God alone for all that makes them a field of God's planting and God's nurturing.

Jesus was aware that arrogantly elevated leadership is not the only temptation the church faces. Discouraged and despondent leadership is a challenge as well. Jesus taught the parable of the sower to meet this need. Jesus's disciples were learning very quickly that they would face mixed and disappointing results. And the future held for them many trials. To address their growing disappointment, Jesus tells them about the uneven results that every hard-working farmer typically faces. Birds may steal some of the seed before it has the chance to take root. Some seed falls on rocky ground with soil too shallow for the plant to come to fruition. The harsh rays of the sun will scorch the plant before it can grow. Seed that falls among thorns will be choked of life. Even seed that falls on good soil will yield at best mixed results: "thirtyfold and sixtyfold and a hundredfold" (Mk 4:1-8). But that hundredfold, though relatively rare, will be cause for rejoicing. In fact, one learns to celebrate *every* gain as a gift from God. Jesus seems to be telling his followers not to grow discouraged. Keep at it; be faithful, regardless of the hardship and the discouraging results that often come. It is God's work in which the servants have the privilege of participating. Results are not guaranteed or predictable, but all will still have reason to glorify God and be grateful. All participation is a privilege, and it will all prove worthwhile in the end.

The realism of mixed results in ministry, however, does not lead Jesus to be casual about the need to bear fruit. Israel had become a wild vine (Jer. 2:21), but their Messiah came as the true vine in which Israel would regain its God-intended purpose (Jn 15:1-17). He is the vine and we are but the branches. But the branches have a role to play in their drawing from the vine in a way that leads to fruitfulness. And the responsibility is great. Bearing fruit is not automatic; the branches need to draw nourishment and strive to give forth fruit. Leadership needs to spread the seed, water, and cultivate the crops. Ultimate failure due to inaction or self-serving action is dire in its consequences. All those in him who do not bear fruit will be cut off and thrown into the fire (15:1-6). Christ bore this baptism of fire for us all, so that we could escape it and be planted in the messianic vine for fruit bearing instead. Those that bear fruit will be pruned so as to flourish even more. Christ prunes the church through various ministries. But Christ is clear that *he* is the source and we are totally dependent on him alone, "Apart from me you can do nothing" (v. 5). Jesus explains, "As the branch cannot bear fruit by itself, unless it abides in the vine, neither can you, unless you abide in me" (v. 4). Jesus is the wellspring of the Spirit. Only united to him by faith can the branches receive the nourishment they need so as to have fruitful and meaningful lives that bless others and leave a legacy behind. The key to fruitful growth is remaining in him and having him and his word remain deeply in us (v. 7). His words are life-bearing; having his words dwell in us is transformative. Only in him can we serve each other in love and rejoice together at the results that we witness in changed lives and fruitful ministry (vv. 10-11). The Father is glorified by what blossoms forth in us because of what Christ does in and through us (v. 8).

Israel is featured as a barren fig tree that is given another chance to repent and bear fruit at the first coming of Christ. The servant is allowed by the owner to dig deeper into the soil around the tree and to add fertilizer hoping to spare the tree from being cut down (Lk. 13:6-9). God digs ever deeper in hopes that withering trees may yet take on life! But the divine patience is not to be taken for granted. In another text, Jesus ends up cursing a fig tree declaring that it won't bear fruit again (Mk 11:12-14). The text containing Jesus's cleansing of the temple follows (11:15-18). The implication is that judgment is falling upon Israel for their unbelief. Still, Paul is convinced that they have not fallen beyond recovery (Rom. 11:11). As we noted in our previous chapter, Paul hopes for a future return of Israel to the olive tree that is nourished by Christ. God has relegated all (Gentile and Jew) to disobedience that God may have mercy on all (Rom. 11:32; 3:23-24). At the final judgment there will be a great harvest and only true participants in Christ will gain access to God's kingdom. The tares will be weeded out and only those devoted to Christ will remain (Mt. 13:24-30). Until then, the visible church is a mixture of wheat and tares.

## Body of Christ

As the Spirit Baptizer, Christ binds himself to his people by bearing flesh, dying in their place, and imparting his Spirit to them. This impartation of the Spirit incorporates a diversity of believers united by their faith, their corporate drinking together of the one Spirit, and their ministry to one another as a united body. "For we were all baptized by one Spirit so as to form one body—whether Jews or Gentiles, slave or free—and we were all given the one Spirit to drink" (1 Cor. 12:13). This fact forms the basis of the church as the body of Christ model. There is no model of the church more basic to the ecclesiology of the New Testament than the body of Christ. Paul tells them that they are the body (12:27). And, yet, the church is told to grow into being the body (Eph. 4:15). Here is both the gift and the task of being the people of God.

If the agricultural metaphors highlighted God's ownership of the church and the church's absolute dependence on God for all things, "the body of Christ" model uniquely accents our dependence together on Christ our Head and on one another in him. We also seek together to become more like him in charismatic or spiritually gifted ministry and mission. We are to be vessels of Christ to each other, submitting to one another out of reverence to Christ (Eph. 5:21). Of course, our dependence is always primarily on Christ. Indeed, "in one Spirit we were all baptized into one body . . . and all were made to drink of one Spirit" (1 Cor. 12:13, ESV). There is to be a broad diversity of giftings among the people of God for the edification of one another in the Spirit. And all of the gifted members are to be cherished and upheld as vital to the body. Though the Corinthians had a tendency to glorify certain members who they considered to be paragons of wisdom and knowledge, Paul extols love instead as supreme ("knowledge puffs up while love builds up," 8:1). While most were seeking through speaking in tongues to display before others privileged access to heavenly mysteries, Paul urged instead prophetic speech that all could comprehend and take in as a source of repentance and building up (14:23-24). Though Paul heard indescribable mysteries during his heavenly vision, he realized that strength in the midst of debilitating weakness was far more important (2 Cor. 12:1-10), for from such comfort he could comfort others (1:3-7). Speaking in tongues brought to expression a deep yearning for God or gratitude for grace that is not understandable except through a spiritual interpretation (1 Cor. 14:14-15; 14:18; Rom. 8:26).[17] Such utterances in the Spirit have their place primarily for private edification (1 Cor. 14:2), which is important. But for Paul, speaking in tongues should be allowed in public if interpreted for the sake of the common good (vv. 14-15). There is to be a diversity of gifts, dispersed according to the will of the Spirit (1 Cor. 12:11) and geared to meeting a variety of needs.

The love of Christ governs all of the spiritual activities of the members of the body. There is no absolute knowledge, so prophets are to speak with humility. Knowledge is limited, since believers seek to build faith in the absence of sight and participate in a living hope that is not yet fulfilled. All of these spiritual gifts are limited and will pass away when believers see Christ face to face and know as they we are fully known (1 Cor. 13:8-13). Face-to-face communion fulfills knowledge; love fulfills in fact all of the spiritual gifts. Thus the greatest of all is love, the love that believers share in living communion with both God and others and extend to the world (13:14). Following Christ who emptied himself out as a servant for the sake of others, the love that governs the interactive life of Christ's body causes them to pay closest attention to the members deemed by society to be less honorable ("But God has put the body together, giving greater honor to the parts that lacked it," 12:24). No patronizing here, only genuine respect. The members bear one another's burdens as Christ bore the burdens of all. The communion of saints is not removed from the grief and suffering of particular members. All suffer with those who suffer. Members are not afraid to expose themselves to vulnerability and sacrifice. It means being vulnerable to the sorrows of others, willing

---

[17] Ernst Käsemann has convinced me that Paul in Rom. 8:26 is describing unutterable rather than unuttered expressions of the inner soul in the church. "The Cry for Liberty in the Worship of the Church," in *Perspectives on Paul* (Philadelphia, MN: Fortress, 1971), 122–24 (122–37).

to join them in their grief or hardship as a support in every way. The body also rejoices with those who celebrate; members are not envious or jealous when others are blessed (v. 26). This sharing of life is both a gift and an awesome responsibility.

Upon his outpouring of the Spirit, Christ imparts the many gifts to the body (Eph. 4:7-8). The body has one Head, which is Christ alone. As noted earlier, leaders are but servants, ministers of all others who are themselves called to minister (4:11-13). Though those who exercise oversight no doubt lead in the proclamation and teaching of the Word of God and preside over the sacraments, all members participate. All speak the truth in love so that we "grow to become in every respect the mature body of him who is the head, that is, Christ" (4:15). All share the one loaf and the one cup together in communion with Christ (cf., 1 Cor. 10:16-17). Since Christ incorporated the church into himself by the Spirit, the church is blessed with "the fullness of him who fills everything in every way" (Eph. 1:23). The church has access to the fullness of Christ, though they do not as of yet fully possess or manifest this in themselves as a people united in faith. Let us be reminded that the church as blessed with the fullness of Christ is to conform to this Christ as an eschatological goal (1:10). Thus, Paul adds in Ephesians that the church also needs to "grow to become in every respect the mature body of him who is the head" (4:15). The church has a long way to go to achieve such depth in the Spirit. But we strive "together with all the Lord's holy people, to grasp how wide and long and high and deep is the love of Christ" (3:18). This journey into Christ, this deeper baptism in the Spirit, will span one's entire journey, and the entire history of the church in time.

The Head is mature, but the body still needs to grow. The fact that the body needs to mature while the Head does not implies a significant distinction between the Head and the body that stretches the body of Christ model beyond its limits, qualifying those who wish to overly stress an organic model of the church under the idea of the church as the prolongation of Christ (*Christus prolongatus*) or the total Christ (*totus Christus*). For one thing, the idea of the church as the prolongation of Christ can cause us to underestimate the degree to which those who exercise authority in Christ's name can end up betraying Christ. Hans Küng warns us that despite the good intentions behind the idea of the church as the continuation of Christ, the church in advocating it "is trying to emancipate itself, for all of its pose of humility is trying to be self-reliant, for all its modesty is trying to be autonomous. A knowing church has replaced a believing church. A possessing church has replaced a needy church. Total authority has replaced obedience."[18] Such can be said of the entire church as well.

The stark realization of the possibility of misusing this notion of prolongation requires one to note how Paul blends the "body of Christ" model with the "bride of Christ" model in Ephesians 5. This realization will bring with it a proper emphasis on the covenantal distinction between the Head and his body and the need for the body to be faithful to its Head in order to fulfill its identity. Paul notes in Ephesians 5 that the husband is to love his wife as his own body, just as Christ as the Head of the church loves his own body by loving the church as his bride (5:28-30). The body and the Head are so sharply distinguished in this discussion of the body of Christ model that the two

---

[18] Küng, *The Church*, 239.

are imagined as sharing something akin to a faithful covenant relationship such as one has in a marriage between a man and a woman. So also, in 1 Cor. 6:15, the members of Christ's body are said to be wedded to their Head and not to a prostitute. As Miroslav Volf stated, "Only as the bride can the church be the body of Christ, and not vice versa."[19] Thus, the organic model of the church as Christ's body, really participating in his life and drinking of the Spirit from him, needs to be qualified from the start by the covenantal model of the body wedded to its Head and called to not only enjoy him but be faithful to him.

Similarly, the *totus Christus* (total Christ) idea of the church was advocated by St. Augustine in the fifth century in his criticism of the Donatists, who believed that believers are justified in breaking from churches whose ministers have erred is some significant way. The Donatists regarded the sacraments over which these ministers have presided as invalid. Augustine viewed the Donatists as schismatics or separatists. To counter their separatism, Augustine advocated the idea of the *totus Christus*, namely, Christ is one subject with his church acting through it to accomplish his purposes, even if the minister is unworthy of his task. He wrote, "Let us rejoice then and give thanks that we are made not only Christians, but Christ. Do you understand, brethren, and apprehend the grace of God upon us? Marvel, be glad, we are made Christ. For if He is the head, we are the members: the whole man is He and we."[20] Since Augustine considered any division between the Head and his body (both together as the "total Christ") to be impossible, so was any division of members from each other. The *totus Christus* idea is a potent symbol of the fact that Christ identifies with his church so intimately that he would identify himself as the one Paul was persecuting in persecuting the church (Acts 9:5). In Hebraic thought, "body" refers to "self." So, theologically, Christ is the One who as the Spirit Baptizer includes in his exalted self the diverse many who function as instruments of his self-giving. So Paul warns that to sin against one's brothers and sisters is to sin against Christ (1 Cor. 8:12).[21] Let us not forget here Dietrich Bonhoeffer's provocative insight that Christ exists precisely as concrete community, which inspires the church to identify with him by being the church for others.[22] With the gift of incorporation comes the challenge of joint mission. But what I said earlier about the covenant relationship between Christ and his body needs to be taken into consideration as well, lest those who are ordained to act on behalf of the church claim Christ's authority in ways that attempt to domesticate Christ to their own self-serving ends (or that of the church). Michael Horton helpfully points out that Christ and his body as the *totus Christus* is to be viewed in the context of covenant grace and covenant faithfulness, as "connected with the historical economy." We share in Christ's death and resurrection, "so that what has happened to Jesus will also happen to us." In actuality, "Christ is the representative head in a covenant, not the 'corporate personality' in whom his own identity as well as ours is surrendered

---

[19] Volf, *After Our Likeness*, 143.
[20] St. Augustine, *Tractates on the Gospel of John*, 21, #8, http://www.newadvent.org/fathers/1701021.htm
[21] Richardson, *An Introduction to the Theology of the New Testament*, 254–55.
[22] Jennifer M. McBride, "Christ Existing as Concrete Community Today," *TT* 71, no. 1 (April 2014): 92–105.

to the whole."[23] I do think corporate personality is acceptable terminology if one views it as a complex and differentiated reality that involves mutual communion and faithfulness. We should recall our point in the first chapter that the Spirit is the one for the many, who diversifies the environment of Christ's presence in fulfillment of Christ's self-giving as the One for others. As a diversified people of the Spirit, the church is distinct from Christ though also bound to him in communion. Pneumatology helps distinguish the church from Christology, while at the same time binding the church in mutual communion to Christ as one body—*one body, but not one subject*. Through the Spirit, Christ is one bound to the many. The diverse witness of the Spirit in the church thus helps us to avoid a Christomonistic ecclesiology that collapses Christ into the church as one subject. As Miroslav Volf points out, the church is not a single subject but a communion of persons, a "differentiated unity" in loyalty to their Head. "Christ lives in them through the multiple relations they have with one another."[24] It is not the bishop or the ordained pastor alone who foundationally mediates Christ but the differentiated witness of the entire congregation.

Christ's identity is indeed conditioned by his body. He is the Head, Lord, and elder brother of the community, and they are his body and family. But he is the Subject and we the diverse predicate. He is the Lord who imparts all that makes us the church and conditions his own existence within his self-giving for, to, and through us. I am sensitive to the criticism leveled against those who make the body of Christ a "mere metaphor." Indeed, Spirit baptism implies that the "body of Christ" model is metaphorical in the deepest sense of that term, depicting access to a real union, a real identification of Christ with his body, and a real participation in Christ and in the love of the Triune God. But to say that the body of Christ is *more* than metaphorical can end up denigrating the depth of metaphor as an open window to a deeper reality. As Alan Richardson remarked, "It would surely be wiser to say that such a phrase as 'body of Christ' (meaning the church) is used realistically, ontologically, and therefore metaphorically or symbolically or analogically."[25]

Indeed, the bride metaphor in Revelation highlights the church's faithfulness, for the bride's fine linen are indeed her righteous acts (Rev. 19:8). The bride is wedded to Christ by *his* faithful acts and generous outpouring of the Spirit but then she seeks to please her Lord by how she receives and brings to expression the grace that flows out from him to her. One could view the Last Supper between Christ and his disciples as "the solemnization of the marriage in a sacramental rite."[26] The continued meal within the life of the faithful church looks ahead to the marriage supper of the Lamb (vv. 6-9). The bride's righteous deeds that adorn her dress are primarily to be viewed as gifts. She has appropriated these gifts as her own and channeled them back to her Bridegroom in glory to him. But the larger reality is not deeds of service but communion. The faithful bride celebrates the Lamb, sharing fully in a communion of life with him (19:9). The

---

[23] Michael Horton, *People and Place: A Covenant Ecclesiology* (Philadelphia, MN: Westminster John Know, 2008), 185.
[24] Volf, *After Our Likeness*, 145.
[25] Richardson, *Introduction to the Theology of the New Testament*, 257, fn. 1.
[26] Ibid., 257.

bride is not married to her groom merely for the sake of service but also for mutual enjoyment within communion. This communion is the heartbeat of her mystery in the world. The bride yearns for the Lamb's return and, with the Spirit, invites the Lamb to come (22:17). The church as the faithful bride is contrasted with the "whore" of Babylon, who supports the martyrdom of the saints to the point of celebrating it (drunk on their blood, 17:9). Just as the beast parodies the Lamb, and the unclean frogs spreading lies to the kings of the earth parody the witness of the Spirit throughout the world (5:6; 16:13), the whore who blasphemes God and celebrates the beast's campaign of terror against God's people parodies the faithful bride of the Lamb. The call goes out to God's people: Choose this day whom you will serve!

We should bear in mind also that God's very people are warned of spiritual adultery. The bride cannot sup at the table of the Lord and the table of demons at the same time (1 Cor. 10:21). Though the bride is fallen and weak, she dares not divide her loyalty so. There are moments in history when an "underground church" must oppose a "church" that has allied itself with a state power that opposes the cause of Christ in the world. One recalls the German Christians (*deutsche Christen*) that acquiesced to Hitler's campaign of terror and the confessing church that opposed them. The famous Barmen Declaration of 1934 of the confessing church, an early rejection of Hitler's effort to control the church, vowed obedience alone to "Jesus Christ, as he is attested to in Holy Scripture" in resistance to any other proposed "events, powers, historic figures and truths" (Art. 1). Christ will always warn a seriously errant church and call them to repentance by his word ("If you do not repent, I will come to you and remove your lampstand from its place," Rev. 2:5). God pursued Israel as a man pursues his future bride who has become an adulteress. God blocked Israel's path to her lovers with the thorns of judgment and took this occasion to lead her to the wilderness to speak tenderly to her. She will once more be God's betrothed as at the Exodus. One day, she will call God her "husband" in intimate union and faithfulness (Hos. 2:1-16). So also Paul warns the Corinthians that members of the church are members of Christ's body and, as such, cannot be wedded also to a prostitute (1 Cor. 6:15). The Lord as our Head is wedded to us as his body in the entirety of our being, for we possess his Spirit within our embodied life in union with him (v. 19). We must be loyal in body and soul, politics and spirituality.

In the baptism in the Spirit as signified by water baptism, the entire body puts on Christ (Gal. 3:27-28). Baptism is the ordination service of every Christian. In the Lord's Supper and broader contexts of communion they drink of the Spirit (1 Cor. 10:3-4; 12:13). They submit to mutual ministry in Christ's name or in reverence to Christ (Eph. 5:21). Social markers that depict levels of privilege and access to power no longer divide them hierarchically: male over female, Jew over Gentile, free over bond. These dualisms of power are nullified by the putting on of Christ in the empowerment of the Spirit of communion.[27] "There is neither Jew nor Gentile, neither slave nor free, nor is there male and female, for you are all one in Christ Jesus" (Gal. 3:28). Luke makes much the same point in depicting the church as a community of Spirit-empowered

---

[27] Lisa Stephenson, *Dismantling the Dualisms for American Pentecostal Women in Ministry*, GPCS (Leiden: Brill, 2011), 170–74.

prophets in which male and female, young and old, Jew and gentile participate (Acts 2:17; 11:18). The body of Christ thus models for the world a different way of construing human community and vocational purpose, the way of Christ's self-giving love. The power of the church's witness is not only through word but also through an embodied witness that this word promotes and through which this word continues to speak. The church as Christ's body is with Christ the inauguration of the new humanity. This new humanity respects and preserves differences but unites them in a just communion and a faithful service. The church is the sign and instrument of the kingdom, God's liberating reign, in the world.

## Temple of the Spirit

I accept the conclusion of the international Reformed-Catholic dialogue concerning the nature of the church: "Just as the Spirit came upon Jesus at the moment of his baptism, so the Spirit descended upon the disciples gathered in the upper room (Acts 2:1-12) and on the Gentiles who listen to the word (Acts 10:44-48). These three closely linked 'Pentecosts' belong to the foundation of the church and make it the 'Temple of the Spirit.'"[28] Being filled with the Spirit (Eph. 5:18), the Spirit-baptized church is called to bear the Spirit in the image of Christ as priests offering themselves as living sacrifices, glorifying God, and drawing others to the place of joining such life-transforming access to God. Not only are we as individuals temples of the Holy Spirit, the entire church is also a temple of the Spirit. "God's temple is sacred and you together are that temple" (1 Cor. 3:17). Yet, we are also told that we are being built into a spiritual house, a process in which we participate by grace through faith (1 Pet. 2:4). Here is the gift and the task. As the temple of the Spirit we offer ourselves through worship and acts of love to God's glory. "Therefore, I urge you, brothers and sisters, in view of God's mercy, to offer your bodies as a living sacrifice, holy and pleasing to God—this is your true and proper worship" (Rom. 12:1). Worship is a constant feature of the church as a temple of the Spirit. But notice how worship is to connect with service to others to God's glory: "Through Jesus, therefore, let us continually offer to God a sacrifice of praise—the fruit of lips that openly profess his name. And do not forget to do good and to share with others, for with such sacrifices God is pleased" (Heb. 13:15-16).

There is no place in the temple of God's people for any glory except that which is directed to Christ (to the glory of the Father) or through Christ to the Father (the two major patterns of worship). Against the exaggerated claims about the significance of apostolic leaders, Paul insists that Christ is the only foundation upon which the temple of the church can be built. "For no one can lay any foundation other than the one already laid, which is Jesus Christ" (v. 11). The materials that one uses by God's provision to build on that foundation must be consistent with that foundation itself. Surely "wood, hay, or straw" would not be worthy of this temple of the Spirit's presence and would, therefore, not survive God's eschatological judgment. Only gold, silver, and costly stones would do (v. 12). These are materials ordained of Christ and used in glory to God. The final judgment will reveal the nature of everyone's work (v. 13). God's

---

[28] "Towards a Common Understanding of the Church," Second Phase, 1984–1990, #76, *GW II*, 798.

grace toward workers who build with unworthy materials is nevertheless rich, for they may yet survive "even though as one escaping through the flames" (v. 15). They will be purged of all that contradicts Christ. There is no room for self-glory or glory of anyone besides Christ in the eschatological destiny of the church in the kingdom of God. Even when Paul speaks of the foundation of the church as the Old Testament prophets and the apostles of the new covenant, his emphasis is on their witness to Christ (Eph. 2:20). They will contribute to the Christian canon that functions in the power of the Spirit to convey the good news of Christ to his faithful. Christ himself will speak through these words. Thus their foundational significance is based on him and not themselves. His significance is all encompassing: "In him the whole building is joined together and rises to become a holy temple in the Lord. And in him you too are being built together to become a dwelling in which God lives by his Spirit" (Eph. 2:22-23). We are the temple but we are also growing into a temple through the power of the Spirit. We strive to embody Christ and witness of him in this growth. He has no equals. Those who exercise ministries of oversight are instruments of his word and are held accountable to this word in the most profound way. The church will hold its leaders accountable, for all God's people are to speak the words of Christ in love (4:15). All serve as supportive stones to one another, spiritual stones being built on the shoulders of others into a spiritual house, all serving as priests offering themselves as holy sacrifices unto God (1 Pet. 2:5). The universal priesthood of all believers was an ancient and long-standing belief of the church, being highlighted by Luther and more recently affirmed by the Second Vatican Council of the Catholic Church (except the Council disagrees with the Protestant tendency to view the universal priesthood of all believers including clergy as essentially one continuous priesthood; the Council advocates instead two separate though united priesthoods, with the ordained priesthood established to participate uniquely in sacramental mediation).[29] Pentecostal author, David Lim, emphasized the priesthood of all believers as well and showed that the Pentecostal emphasis on the spiritually gifted church brings this biblical teaching to bold expression.[30] Though I agree wholeheartedly with the Protestant advocacy of one universal priesthood of believers (which includes clergy and laity alike), there is no denying that the congregation is also to pay special respect to those who strive sacrificially to exercise oversight and to lead in the ministry of word, sacrament, and charismatic edification: "Have confidence in your leaders and submit to their authority, because they keep watch over you as those who must give an account. Do this so that their work will be a joy, not a burden, for that would be of no benefit to you" (Heb. 13:17). The universal priesthood of believers is not to lead to individualism or the denial that some are ordained to lead in the word, sacraments, and charismatic life that mediate Christ's presence to us. Each of us is not simply our own priest, for we are dependent on the mediation of others, especially those who lead us. Note Lutheran theologian Paul Althaus:

> Luther never understands the priesthood of all believers merely in the sense of the Christian's freedom to stand in a direct relationship to God without a human

---

[29] LG, #10.
[30] Lim, *Spiritual Gifts*.

mediator. Rather, he constantly emphasizes the Christian's evangelical authority to come before God on behalf of the brethren and also of the world. The universal priesthood expresses not religious individualism but its exact opposite, the reality of the congregation as a community.[31]

The church as a *people* is the temple. The temple is no longer essentially a physical dwelling like the temple in Jerusalem. John the Baptist had already baptized people unto repentance and the forgiveness of sins apart from the temple cult. God was already acting outside of official channels. Christ cleansed that temple, implying that God's judgment was already resting upon it. When questioned as to the authority by which he took such action, Jesus responds that if they destroy "this temple" (meaning his body) in three days he will raise it up (Jn 2:19-21). The irony here is clear. The temple to which the Jewish leaders cling will not last, and the temple that they will seek to destroy, God will raise up. The locus of God's presence and favor, of access to God, was shifting from the temple to Christ. When rising up and bestowing the Spirit to others, he opens his temple identity to his people. He becomes the foundation of the new temple of God and the people become a temple in him. John the Revelator writes of the eschatological new Jerusalem: "I did not see a temple in the city, because the Lord God Almighty and the Lamb are its temple" (21:22). The communion of saints joined by the new creation becomes the final dwelling place of God as they are transformed to serve in giving God glory. This reality is anticipated already in this climactic doxology early on in Revelation:

Then I heard every creature in heaven and on earth and under the earth and on the sea, and all that is in them, saying:

To him who sits on the throne and to the Lamb
be praise and honor and glory and power,
for ever and ever! (5:13)

The church as the temple in Christ is not to be construed to mean that the church in any way completes Christ's redemptive work that opens access to God for the world. Christ "appeared once for all at the culmination of the ages to do away with sin by the sacrifice of himself" (Heb. 9:26). The Father provided an anointed body for the faithful Son through which the Son can offer himself on behalf of all ("a body you prepared for me," 10:5). Christ said to the Father, "Here I am. I have come to do your will" (v. 9). "And by that will, we have been made holy through the sacrifice of the body of Jesus Christ once for all" (v. 10). He entered the holy of holies in heaven to offer his embodied life, his faithful life, as a sacrifice of glory to the Father on humanity's behalf so as to cancel humanity's debt and open a path for sinners to God. The temple cult of offerings given by human hands could not provide such passage, for only the faithful Son incarnate can cancel our debt, remove sin and death, and fulfill divine glory. No

---

[31] Paul Althaus, *The Theology of Martin Luther* (Philadelphia, MN: Fortress, 1966), 314, I am grateful to Timothy George for drawing my attention to this quote and for the overall point that I am making here: "The Priesthood of All Believers," *First Things*, October 31, 2016, https://www.firstthings.com/web-exclusives/2016/10/the-priesthood-of-all-believers

such path is possible for us: "It is impossible for the blood of bulls and goats to take away sins" (v. 4). All that the temple cult could do is foreshadow what Christ would come to do. The church as God's temple are servants of Christ's self-offering by seeking in all of their weakness to be an effective sign of it. In this instrumental role, they serve through practices like proclamation, sacraments, and cultivation of gifts to be instrumental in drawing people to Christ as participants in his access to the Father. But he is the one who acts by the Spirit through this fellowship and other practices. The end toward which this witness is directed is a cruciform self-giving by all of God's people, which serves to bring glory to God and to expand the church's witness (Rom. 12:1).

As the temple of God, we are indeed the dwelling place of the Spirit: "Don't you know that you yourselves are God's temple and that God's Spirit dwells in your midst?" (1 Cor. 3:16). Through the Spirit the ascended Christ dwells in us, using us to further his mission in the world ("Christ in you, the hope of glory," Col. 1:27). The church grows in its capacity to mystically grasp this love that they have in him and exercise for him (Eph. 3:17-19). One also thinks of a sacred dwelling place: "God's temple is sacred, and you together are that temple" (v. 17). We are sacred by God's grace "through the sanctifying work of the Spirit, to be obedient to Jesus Christ and sprinkled with his blood" (1 Pet. 1:2). But we are also called to be a holy people in practice, offering ourselves in the image of the crucified Christ as living sacrifices in communion with God and toward the fulfillment of God's cause in the world. In the process, we resist conforming our thinking and outside actions to the "pattern of this world" (Rom. 1:1-2). We seek not only to understand the Word of God but also to embody that word as living letters of Christ written on our hearts by the Spirit (2 Cor. 3:3).

We are the temple, the priests, the sacrifices, the gifts, and the embodiments of the words of Christ that represent the core of temple worship. The Old Testament prophets and the apostles of the new covenant provided the basis for the canon that offers the church the living standard by which the living temple hears from, and seeks to bear witness to, the living Lord. So that canon is foundational, but only because it provides the standard by which Christ is properly heard and obeyed. The Spirit that inspired that canon provides ongoing and variously contextual discernment of its meaning and embodiment. Worship is indeed important to the church as the temple of the Spirit. Our all-encompassing act of worship is offering our entire lives to Christ as a living sacrifice ("This is your true and proper worship," Rom. 12:1). But worship is also a corporate practice that shapes us profoundly and guides our larger obedience to God:[32] "Let us be thankful, and so worship God acceptably with reverence and awe" (Heb. 12:28). As Simon Chan reminds Pentecostals, the liturgy allows the scriptures, and important practices formed around them, to shape the church down through the centuries and provide a framework for interpreting experiences of the Spirit in worship and in private piety.[33] But there is also room in worship for Spirit-led freedom

---

[32] Geoffrey Wainwright, *Doxology: The Praise of God in Worship, Doctrine, and Life* (New York: Oxford University Press, 1980), 1–14.

[33] Simon Chan, *Liturgical Theology: The Church as Worshipping Community* (Downers Grove, IL: InterVarsity Press, 2006), 21–100.

and innovation.[34] In worshipping, we join the heavenly hosts, in fact, all of creation, in exalting Christ as Lord in the power of the Spirit and to the glory of the Father (Phil. 2:9-11; Rev. 5:6-14). For such a destiny we were created. Sin causes us to fall short of God's glory (Rom. 3:23); worship by the Spirit allows us to participate in the restoration.

## The Army of God

In witness to Christ in the power of the Spirit, the Spirit-baptized church will encounter opposition. In the demonic forces, we have an enemy that is bent on our destruction. The global Pentecostal emphasis is rightly on spiritual warfare through empowered witness, acts of love and justice, and signs and wonders of the Spirit. We are the army of God by the grace of Christ's victory and in the power of his Spirit, but we are also told to put on the armor so as to prepare for battle (Eph. 6:10-11). Here's the gift and the task. Christ's work is the basis of victory. Gustaf Aulen has convincingly made the point that Christ's death and resurrection were interpreted in the New Testament, the church fathers, and Luther as a victory over the dark powers, sin, and death.[35] Christ bore human flesh to "break the power of him who holds the power of death—that is, the devil" (Heb. 2:14). Christ disarmed the powers and authorities, "triumphing over them by the cross" (Col. 2:15). The last enemy to be conquered is death (1 Cor. 15:26). Christ pours forth the Spirit of life as the inaugural act of his triumphant ascension to the throne to reign:

> When he ascended on high,
> he took many captives
> and gave gifts to his people (Eph. 4:8).

Note also Acts 2:33-36:

> [33] Exalted to the right hand of God, he has received from the Father the promised Holy Spirit and has poured out what you now see and hear. [34] For David did not ascend to heaven, and yet he said,
> "The Lord said to my Lord:
>   "Sit at my right hand
> [35] until I make your enemies
>   a footstool for your feet."
> [36] "Therefore let all Israel be assured of this: God has made this Jesus, whom you crucified, both Lord and Messiah."

---

[34] A point made throughout in Daniel Albrecht, *Rites of the Spirit: A Ritual Approach to Pentecostal-Charismatic Spirituality*, JPTS (Edinburgh: Bloomsbury T & T Clark, 1999).

[35] Gustaf Aulen, *Christus Victor: An Historical Study of the Three Main Types of the Idea of Atonement* (Eugene, OR: Wipf & Stock, 2003).

Indeed, the victorious and reigning Lord opens his victory to his church by bestowing his Spirit, his kingly anointing, on them. According to Revelation 19, Christ will return to earth as a conquering warrior ("King of kings and Lord of lords," v. 16) to fully bring the kingdom of God to earth (19:11-21).

But this final fulfillment has not yet come. The victory of Christ is both an established fact and a fulfillment that is yet to come and for which we must now struggle. When G. C. Berkouwer charged that Karl Barth had been too one sided in his emphasis on the victory of Christ as an established fact, Barth used the clarion call "Jesus is Victor" from Johann Blumhardt to emphasize just as much that this victory has a teleological realization in history. This present age is marked by genuine conflict against all that opposes Christ.[36] In this age, the church is to be discerning, alert to the deception of the enemy. If one is not careful, one can be completely taken in by the lies of hate, pride, and social privilege. "Be alert and of sober mind. Your enemy the devil prowls around like a roaring lion looking for someone to devour" (1 Pet. 5:8). Sin can eat one alive from within: "Sin is crouching at your door; it desires to have you" (Gen. 4:7). This warning and the promise of victory in Christ form the basis for the model of the church as a "military" force. But since Christ has won the decisive victory and reigns already, we are "more than conquerors through him who loved us" (Rom. 8:37) for we are now strong "in the Lord and in his mighty power" (Eph. 6:10). Indeed, we must still stand our ground firmly in Christ against evil (vv. 13-14). And we actively take on righteousness (the breastplate), the glad tidings of Christ (as armor on our feet), faith (as our shield), salvation (as our helmet), and the Word of God (as the sword of the Spirit in our hands). Of course, all of the armor is "of the Spirit," because they are all of Christ and for him. He is the one who acts through us as we struggle. Hence, the victory belongs to him.

Before we proceed, it is necessary to point out that Christ did not conquer in the usual fashion known to us from social contexts, or in the way typical of worldly powers. He assumed humble and weak flesh, taking on the form of a servant (Phil. 2:7). He did so to offer his life as a ransom for sinners (Mk 10:45). His resurrection, ascension to the throne, and Spirit impartation were not greeted by the original followers of Jesus with flag waving, boasting, and efforts at conquering others in the name of Christ. Christ's victory was met rather with worship, humble service, and a hospitable table fellowship. "They devoted themselves to the apostles' teaching and to fellowship, to the breaking of bread and to prayer" (Acts 2:42). Empowered by the Spirit, their witness proclaimed grace to all to repent, even (and especially) among those who crucified Christ (and we all contributed in some way to that crucifixion). In the book of Revelation, the saints triumph by the blood of the Lamb, the poured out blood of Christ's life given out of love for humanity, and the word of their testimony (to the gospel of Christ) even to the point of death (12:11). Christ returns to bring his victory to fulfillment in creation but he does so, not by military weaponry but rather by the sword of truth by which he brings the nations to their knees. He does "strike down the nations," not to destroy them but rather to humble them so as to rule them in justice and peace (19:15).

---

[36] Karl Barth, *CD, The Doctrine of Reconciliation*, Vol. IV, pt. 3, Second Half, ed. G. Bromiley (Edinburgh: T & T Clark, 1963), 165-274 (esp. 173f).

Revelation utilizes warlike imagery to depict the victory of Christ and the church but does so in a way that subverts and critiques it as it was commonly known.

Some words are in order here about the prevalence of spiritual warfare ministries in Pentecostal contexts worldwide. I agree entirely that we in the rationalist West must remain open to the legitimacy of numerous testimonies of freedom made by those who have been blessed by these ministries. If there is a psychosomatic dimension to their healing, so what? Is it not healing nonetheless? But the deeper theological question has to do with how we understand the demonic. Human bondage and torment are a complex reality. Many ask, how does it help to bring the devil into it? Does not doing so cause us to overlook research into the natural causes of human illness and moral corruption as well as the strategies for dealing with them that have proven to be effective? No doubt, this is a genuine concern. The Spirit-empowered church cannot regard every problem as solvable simply by binding and resisting demonic involvement in the situation. Indeed, the scriptures make a distinction between physical illness and sins of the flesh on the one hand and direct demonic activity on the other. For example, Mk 1:34 states that "Jesus healed many who had various diseases. He *also* drove out many demons" as though disease and demonic oppression were two different things. As for sin, James is clear that "each person is tempted when they are dragged away by their own evil desire and enticed" (1:14). Whatever the demonic does, humans can pursue evil and injustice in devastating ways from within their own internal corruption.

Perhaps we have thought too exclusively on the demonic in personalistic and individualistic terms. Pauline language about the demonic seems more prominently cosmic and social, broadly eschatological in significance: "For our struggle is not against flesh and blood, but against the rulers, against the authorities, against the powers of this dark world and against the spiritual forces of evil in the heavenly realms" (Eph. 6:12). Walter Wink has maintained that the demonic in scripture highlights the corporate "spirit" that legitimates and preserves dehumanizing or evil practices within a community or an institution, even if there are individuals who might wish something else but are eventually pressured to conform.[37] This corporate spirit may be said to incarnate evil powers, placing the onus of responsibility on the humans who construct and give themselves over to such corporate and institutional structures. Prayer, corporate witness and resistance, and structural change are all needed to combat such evil. The stakes are high, for this evil "possession" is more destructive than the individual cases that often become the subject of deliverance testimonies (as important as they are). Even individual cases of demonic torment are typically tied to long histories of abuse and institutional abandonment. Additionally, the scriptures speak of the demonic as eschatological in significance. The mystery of evil will only be fully disclosed at the conclusion of the age when the full light of truth in all of its brightness exposes it. This is why the demonic, which plays only a minor role in the Old Testament, is divulged more explicitly and glaringly with the coming of Christ and the inauguration of the kingdom of God in the power of the Spirit (e.g., Mt. 12:28-29). When confronting evil and its legitimation in our world, we are made to deny Satan

---

[37] A good place to start is Walter Wink, *Naming the Powers: The Language of Power in the New Testament* (Philadelphia, MN: Fortress Press, 1984).

and his works, because we realize that there is more at stake than one particular case of evil oppression or cluster of them. Since evil is primarily corporate and eschatological, the inauguration of a new humanity in the communal life of the church is the most effective force against it. God is still sovereign over all, but the victory that God has granted in Christ and the presence of the Spirit forms a new communal spirit of mercy and justice that overturns the conditions from which evil power can gain momentum and have its way in the world. This is only possible in God, to be sure, but a firm stance and resistance are still required on our part.

So the people of God are an army in the sense of resisting the powers of darkness and death and humbly serving the cause of Christ's love in the world in the power and liberty of the Spirit. As soldiers trained and disciplined themselves, so also the church disciplines their embodied life and struggles for victory using prayer, confession, fasting, scripture reading, evangelism, generous hospitality, acts of service, and working for social transformation, in terms of both changing existing systems and creating alternative ones. They depend on the Spirit of Christ in all things, believing that all things are possible with God. Signs and wonders of the Spirit's work are possible as foretastes of liberty in the midst of our groaning for the kingdom to come, but strength in weakness is needed even more, especially in the absence of such signs. Paul prayed often for the removal of his thorn, only to learn that God's grace was always sufficient for all circumstances to make God's power perfect in weakness (2 Cor. 12:9). The goal is a sanctified embodiment of Christ's faithfulness in the world. This is core to the church's overcoming witness.

We as God's people are also like athletes, as were a number of the soldiers of ancient Rome. Soldiers were often drawn from the ranks of athletes. As "athletes of piety"[38] we strive for the "prize" of faithful service and we discipline ourselves for this purpose (1 Cor. 9:24-27). We bring our bodies under subjection lest we be disqualified (1 Cor. 9:27). We run the race cheered on by the cloud of faithful witnesses who have gone before, letting go little by little of the sin that hinders us from moving forward effectively. We fix our eyes on Jesus, the pioneer and fulfillment of our race, for we run and finish in him and by his powerful endurance, comforted by the joy (even in the midst of sorrow) of attaining the prize (Heb. 12:1-2). The military metaphor has the advantage of accenting the cooperative work of the church, supporting one another in our shared witness. If a brother or sister falls, we seek to lift them up and restore them. But the athletic metaphor has the advantage of a single focus on the goal that is attainable for a pilgrim church that is driven forward by the vision of a better world ahead (Heb. 11:16). The cloud of witnesses that has gone before us (12:1-2) is still waiting for the resurrection of the dead and the new creation, for God willed that they should not be perfected in the image of Christ the Victor without us (11:40). God willed for the church triumphant to attain the prize together, the communion of saints from all times and places! As the final words attributed to Paul put it:

---

[38] So St. Basil described those given over to the contemplative life in his letter to Gregory Nazianzen, Letter II, no. 6, http://www.newadvent.org/fathers/3202002.htm

I have fought the good fight, I have finished the race, I have kept the faith. Now there is in store for me the crown of righteousness, which the Lord, the righteous Judge, will award to me on that day—and not only to me, but also to all who have longed for his appearing. (2 Tim. 4:7-8)

## Marks of the Church

There are a number of critical issues raised in the discussion of the major models of the church given earlier that I wish to explore under the classic marks of the church as given to us in the Nicene Creed: "We believe in one, holy, catholic, and apostolic church." The classic marks of the church are thus unity, holiness, catholicity, and apostolicity. We confess our belief in the church because the life of the church is not entirely in our grasp. We cannot create or manipulate it. We can only confess it as a reality that has its origin and destiny in God. Yet, the church is still something in which we participate and stoke into flame by the grace of God. We begin with unity.

### Unity

The Pentecostal Movement was born from the conviction that the unity of the church is ever-expanding because it occurs in the Spirit of God, who overflows all boundaries. Note this early statement in William Seymour's *The Apostolic Faith* paper: "Jesus was too large for the synagogues. He preached outside because there was not room for him inside. The Pentecostal Movement is too large to be confined in any denomination or sect. It works outside, drawing all together in one bond of love, one church, one body of Christ."[39] This quote views Pentecostalism as transcending denominations and sects so as to provide a larger unity in the outpouring of the Spirit. There is, of course, hidden within this statement a somewhat naive and exaggerated sense of the movement's significance, potentially leading to a new confinement of the Spirit within prescribed boundaries. But aside from this potential (which is not exclusive to Pentecostalism by any means), there is nevertheless a valuable insight. The Christ who was too "large" for the synagogues to contain is also too large for the institutional church. The Spirit in witness to Christ also overflows the church, beckoning the church to follow. The unity of the church cannot ever serve the goals of only one church family; nor can boundaries be erected for it. Thus, unity serves the larger purposes of the kingdom of God in the world. The church can never rest secure in it but must always find it to be a challenge that breaks us out of our secure boundaries. The churches today cannot contain Christ nor his Spirit any more than the synagogues could, or the church of Jerusalem, Rome, the East, the Reformation, Pentecostal renewal, etc. Unity is not of the Spirit of Christ if it does not surprise and even disturb us. We are tribal by nature. The Spirit is not. True unity will always be a threat to us, which is why we must work

---

[39] No author, *AF* 1, no. 1 (1906): 1.

so hard at it, and which is why its full attainment can only come with the advent of the kingdom of God in fullness.

Our only hope for significant fulfillment of unity this side of eternity is the Spirit of Christ. "The Spirit alone can lead the churches from their present state of division into unity."[40] All Pentecostals would heartily agree with this statement from ecumenist Lukas Vischer. It can sound to some ears as simplistic and can indeed be believed in a way that sidesteps the hard work that must go into making unity a visible witness of Christ's presence to save. Pentecostals must certainly avoid this danger. But to those like Vischer who have worked hard on the front lines of the ecumenical movement it is a ray of hope. The term "ecumenical" comes from the Greek term *oikoumene*, which refers to the inhabited earth (ecclesiologically, "the household of God"). The ecumenical movement seeks to work toward the visible unity of the entire household of God in the world. There is no question but that the New Testament refers to the unity of the church as a gift from God. Speaking of the baptism in the Holy Spirit, Paul wrote, "For we were all baptized by one Spirit so as to form one body" (1 Cor. 12:13). Not only is this unity congregational but it is also to be interchurch on all organizational levels of church life.

There is thus a sense in which unity is inescapable for the church. There is indeed only one Spirit, not many. So there can only be one shared life in which all members and congregations participate. Though encouraging diversity, the Holy Spirit opposes the partisan and tribal human spirit that divides and wars with one another in the pursuance of self-serving goals. The Spirit of God seeks rather to unify a new humanity through a mutual sharing of life in communion with God. There is also only one Lord, Christ Jesus, into whom we are incorporated by the Spirit through faith and water baptism as members of his body. He is the rock from which we continue to "drink in" the Spirit and eat the spiritual food of the word (1 Cor. 10:4). As one body we commune together by the Spirit with Christ through the Lord's Supper and other contexts that move outward from that participation (*koinonia*) in Christ (10:16). We are members of his body. We can no more be divided than Christ can be torn asunder: "Is Christ divided?" (1 Cor. 1:13). And the Father is the ultimate source of all good things (Jas 1:17) and is the Father of us all: "We are his offspring" (Acts 17:28). Through the Son and the Spirit, the Father's love is all encompassing: "One God and Father of all, who is over all and through all and in all" (Eph. 4:6). It's the Father's will that is accomplished in the kingdom over which the Son reigns and that is experienced in the life-transforming presence of the Spirit (Mt. 6:10; 12:28). The Father is the ultimate source of the Spirit who is poured forth through the Son (Jn 15:26; Acts 2:36). All of the above means that we are "stuck" with each other, for God holds us together in the divine embrace. We might as well discover together the riches of our visible unity in the communion of the Triune God!

The communion of the Triune God values both unity and diversity, for God is one and yet a fellowship of three. So also is the church analogously one body in diverse communion. The many tongues of Pentecost bearing witness to the mighty deeds of God (Acts 2:4f) reveal an expanding plurality that makes up a differentiated unity

---

[40] Lukas Vischer, "Invoking the Holy Spirit: Report on the Unity of the Church," *ER* 2, no. 4 (1974): 578 (578–89).

in the Spirit of Christ. Any movement that focuses on this story has the potential of helping to energize the church toward unity, as Amos Yong has noted.[41] Unity does not mean uniformity, but rather a differentiated communion in the Spirit. Diaspora Jews from many nations gathered to hear the prophetic word in their own diverse tongues. Later in Acts, Luke summarized Paul's sermon in Athens to state that God cannot be contained by temples made with human hands (17:24). God did not crush those who attempted to place God at their disposal through religious means but rather accompanied them in their journeys, marking out their "appointed times in history" and the "boundaries of their lands" (17:25-26). God did this "so that they would seek him and reach out for him and perhaps find him for he is not far from each of us" (v. 27). For in God they all live and move and had their being (v. 28). The attempt to localize or provincialize God through religion is disrupted in order to open space for a living encounter with God in history on God's terms. Echoes of the Tower of Babel incident are thus indicated in these verses, implying that the diverse tongues featured in the first outpouring of the Spirit in Acts 2 was the fulfillment of the promise implied in the diversification of tongues that occurred at Babel in Genesis 11. The confusion of tongues at Babel was God's judgment against the idolatrous effort at legitimizing power. They sought "with a tower that reaches to the heavens" to "make a name" for themselves (11:4). But this judgment also contained a promise that the diverse tongues that dispersed them would play a role in the future possibility of human freedom for God within a differentiated fellowship.[42]

I like Daniela Augustine's description of God's diversification of tongues at Babel: "He acts in conformity to his nature of creating and affirming diversity. He extends self-giving by opening space and time for the other and thereby creates the possibility of an authentic human community, one in which life can be shared in a multiplicity of forms and locations."[43] Through the diversification of tongues, "the monotone superiority of imperial culture is challenged by the polyphony of human speech as the inaugural address of a multicultural human reality."[44] Acts 17 tells us that God never lets go of the diversified peoples, for it is in God that they are sustained and guided. God never leaves them but rather leads them to the climax of history that will occur with the coming of the Messiah and the outpouring of the Spirit. This striking interpretation of history finds its penultimate fulfillment in Acts 2 when on the lips of Jesus's followers the tongues of the nations glorify God. The body of Christ, baptized in the Spirit so as to form one body, embraces diversity: "For we were all baptized by one Spirit so as to form one body—whether Jews or Gentiles, slave or free—and we were all given the one Spirit to drink. Even so the body is not made up of one part but of many" (1 Cor. 12:13). Acts 2:17-18 reiterates much the same point, adding that both

---

[41] See, for example, Amos Yong, *The Spirit Poured Out on All Flesh: Pentecostalism and the Possibility of Global Theology* (Grand Rapids, MI: Baker Academic, 2005), 167ff.
[42] See Frank D. Macchia, "Babel and the Tongues of Pentecost—Reversal or Fulfillment? A Theological Fulfillment," in *Speaking in Tongues: Multi-disciplinary Perspectives*, ed. M. Cartledge, SPCI (Milton Keynes: Paternoster, 2006), 34–51.
[43] Augustine, *Pentecost, Hospitality, and Transfiguration*, 31.
[44] Ibid.

sons and daughters, rich and poor, old and young participate equally in the life and mission of the Spirit.

The one Father, Lord, and Spirit, the one God as a diverse communion, implies and necessitates the unity of the church. Yet, even in the pages of the New Testament it appears that unity is finite and fragile, vulnerable to being broken. As we noted earlier, Paul dealt with divisions in the young Corinthian congregation, as is evident in the first three chapters of 1 Corinthians. Moreover, Paul sought to confirm his unity with the leadership of the Jerusalem church lest he discover he had run his own race in vain (Gal. 2:2). The Jerusalem Council convened to stave off threats to the unity of the infant church. In affirming uncircumcised Gentiles as part of God's elect people, they unified around the words of the prophets ("The words of the prophets are in agreement with this," Acts 15:15) as revealed in the new work of the Spirit ("It seemed good to the Holy Spirit and to us," 15:28). The threat of disunity also lies behind Paul's admonition that the Ephesians "make every effort to keep the unity of the Spirit through the bond of peace" (4:3). And he described the ultimate attainment of that unity as an eschatological reality, something toward which to grow, "until we all reach unity in the faith and in the knowledge of the Son of God and become mature, attaining to the whole measure of the fullness of Christ" (4:13). Unity is not static but dynamic and multifaceted, involving a diverse sharing of life and vocation in God. It must grow in both depth and breadth, in quality and quantity. We strive with all of the pilgrim people of God to grasp the breadth, height, and depth of the love of Christ (Eph. 3:18-19). Such a goal in Ephesians is meant to eventually include the new humanity, indeed, the entire new creation, for the goal is "to bring unity to all things in heaven and on earth under Christ" (1:10). The church is to bear witness to the new humanity in the here and now, especially in overcoming and seeking together by grace to heal divisions that are self-serving, unjust, and dehumanizing. In an ongoing effort to strengthen and expand our shared communion in the Spirit, we realize that our life together in God is but "a provisional embodiment of an eschatological unity."[45] Unity is both a gift and an ongoing task.

How much more is unity an ongoing task in *our time*, given the deep fractures that exist in the church. What the New Testament says about the one God and one gospel makes a divided church unthinkable, intolerable, and devastating to the integrity of the church and its witness. "What kind of strange, enigmatic reality is it that we call the 'divided' church?"[46] The strangeness should never become normal. We should never tire of rejecting it. Even where it is necessary, it should grieve us. The church's unity is indeed a gift, but it is also a task: "Make every effort to keep the unity of the Spirit through the bond of peace" (Eph. 4:3). Jesus prayed that his followers be completely one. "Then the world will know that you sent me and have loved them even as you have loved me" (Jn 17:23). The effectiveness of the church's Spirit-empowered witness is at stake in the challenge to pursue unity among God's people. The fact is that Jesus's prayer that his followers be one has not yet been fully answered. This fact should

---

[45] As noted in the Anglican-Reformed dialogue, "God's Reign and Our Unity," 1984, #106, *GW II*, 145.
[46] G. C. Berkouwer, *The Church* (Grand Rapids, MI: Eerdmans, 1976), 30.

motivate us to pray and to act in ways that open up new possibilities for communion across confessional divides.

Division in the embrace of the Triune God is indeed unthinkable, theologically absurd. And, yet, we as the people of God *are* divided. Fortunately, however, our divisions as believers are not absolute. Nor can they be. One could argue that the foundation of Christ's prayer for our unity is spiritual in the sense that the one God as Father, Son, and Spirit does embrace the church as one spiritually and, thus, invisibly. As the World Council of Churches-Roman Catholic Joint Working Group pointed out, "Because ecclesial communion is a fellowship inspired by the indwelling Spirit, we can say that the barriers of our divisions do not reach to heaven."[47] Our divisions do not reach to heaven; nor can they be absolute here on earth. In speaking of the "invisible unity" of the global church, we do not speak of an abstract reality apart from the visible church, a platonic ideal. We refer rather to the spiritual reality of the baptism in the Spirit and incorporation into God that binds members together concretely within a congregation or congregations together in Christ. As John Webster noted, those who focus on the church as a visible community of practices "would do well to recover a proper sense of the church's *invisibility*—that is to say, of the invisible character of the church's visible life."[48] Reference to the invisible unity of the church is meant to wake up a complacent church that trusts only in institutions rather than fundamentally in the Christ in and for whom they arise in the Spirit to function as an instrument of Christ's incorporating and uniting presence and action among us. Indeed, the invisible church reference does more than point to the visible church's inner life; it also points to the inadequacy of its visible boundaries to account for its true membership. Reference to this "invisible unity" serves to remind the visible church that not everyone among them are truly incorporated into Christ by the Spirit and by genuine faith in Christ. It is also meant to remind them that their visible boundaries are not absolute, that there are others who belong who are outside of those boundaries, even among those that do not yet consciously name the name of Christ, as Amos Yong reminds us.[49] But the church is nevertheless visible, with all of the ambiguity and complexity involved in saying that, for it is Spirit baptized to be the effective sign and instrument (the embodied witness) of salvation in the world. Downplaying or denying the church's visibility "destroys the real content of revelation and the historical character of the church."[50] There is no church without its visible presence and vocation in the world.

Shared experiences of the Spirit across denominational lines can be a dramatic reminder of the deep bonds that hold the churches (and members within churches)

---

[47] "The Church: Local and Universal: A Study Document Commissioned and Received by the Joint Working Group," World Council of Churches-Roman Catholic Church, 1990, Section IV, no. 2, #51, *GW II*, 873.

[48] Emphasis is original. John Webster, "The Visible Attests the Invisible," in *The Community of the Word: Towards an Evangelical Ecclesiology*, ed. Mark Husbands and Daniel J. Treier (Lombard, IL: InterVarsity Press, 2005), 142.

[49] Notice how he develops this insight using a pneumatologically informed theology of religions: Amos Yong, *Beyond the Impasse: Toward a Pneumatological Theology of Religions* (Grand Rapids, MI: Baker Academic, 2003).

[50] From the Old Catholic-Orthodox conversation, "Ecclesiology," Agreed Statement, Chambésy, 1977, Bonn, 1979, and Zagorsk, 1981, #7, *GW I*, 402.

together. William Seymour's *The Apostolic Faith* paper announces greater unity on the horizon because of shared experiences of the Spirit: "God is drawing his people together and making them one. No new church or division of the body of Christ is being formed. Christ never had but one church. We may be turned out of the big wood and brick structures but 'by one Spirit are ye all baptized into one body.'"[51] This author is right: Shared experiences of the Spirit among Christians in interchurch settings can lead to a renewal of passion for unity among Christians of different church communions.

The ecumenical movement has found a place for a spirituality that prepares churches for greater unity. Since unity comes through communion, there is a spiritual preparation needed for breakthroughs to occur. Spiritual ecumenism accents a spiritual posture of repentance, godliness, humility, and reaching out to other churches, recognizing the bond that they share in the Triune God is real, even in the midst of a visibly broken communion. Spiritual ecumenism has gained traction in the ecumenical movement. It starts by invoking the Holy Spirit. Pentecostals are right to point to the outpouring of the Spirit as key to renewal. But this outpouring is an occasion not only for passionate praise or ecstasy but also of deep repentance and *metanoia*. As Lukas Vischer notes, "To call upon the Holy Spirit is a radically dangerous and even explosive thing. The Spirit pleads Christ's cause in our midst and, in doing this, inescapably calls us and our lives in question. When the Spirit breaks in, Christ is present, His preaching, His suffering, His cross, His victory over death and the power of death." Vischer then adds,

> He is the Spirit of freedom who can therefore never be involved to justify bondage of any kind. But He creates freedom not by allowing us to evade the realities of our world; not even the realities of our divided churches with their antagonisms, anomalies and contradictions. The very fact that He opens our eyes to the future, to the coming of the Kingdom of God, means that He is also the Spirit of change, of change here and now.[52]

Spiritual ecumenism starts when churches at all levels of their life come together with other churches and call together on the Holy Spirit with total yielding of mind and soul. In the presence of the Spirit, ecumenism cannot simply be a game we play. We have to be willing to work hard at the front lines of mutual understanding and be willing to be changed by what we learn, both of them and of ourselves.[53]

A 1980 Lutheran-Roman Catholic conversation noted that spiritual ecumenism involves remorse for our divisions without one-sidedly shifting the blame to the other side.[54] We should seek to overcome all traces of self-righteousness.[55] We should study one another's traditions in search of spiritual treasures that they offer us. Such study will remove prejudicial assumptions toward the other and provide a fairer evaluation of the other's tradition. Spiritual ecumenism, however, seeks personal encounter. We

---

[51] No author, *AF* 1, no. 2 (1906): 4.
[52] Vischer, "Invoking the Holy Spirit," 579.
[53] Ibid.
[54] Lutheran-Roman Catholic Conversations, "Ways to Community," 1980, #57 (57–60), *GW I*, 227.
[55] Ibid., #60.

need to seek beyond books to "an ever more intensive and direct knowledge of the life of other churches, which will inspire greater desire for fellowship between us."[56] We will hopefully discover that despite those divisions caused by sin, "the Spirit has maintained through its work in our churches a fundamental fellowship which constitutes the primary precondition for all our striving for the visible unity of the church."[57] I would add that diversification among different ecclesial communions can be viewed as a natural development that is not in and of itself necessarily a result of sin. But the toxicity of division is. Spiritual communion strikes at the root of that divisiveness.

It is not only in ecumenical conversations that Christians discover a unity that lies deeper than their divisions. This discovery tends to happen even more often in times of joint prayer and common witness, especially on the mission field or in other times of challenge to the Christian faith. I am grateful to Timothy George for this account of how the Lutheran pastor Paul Schneider and the Catholic priest Otto Neururer were able to bear common witness in a German concentration camp. It's worth quoting in full:

> At Buchenwald, there was one block of cells reserved for prisoners deemed especially dangerous or notable. In cell 27 they placed Paul Schneider, a Lutheran pastor, who was called "the Preacher of Buchenwald" because, even from the small window in his cell, he loudly proclaimed the gospel of Jesus Christ in defiance of the orders of the Gestapo guards. In cell 23, they placed Otto Neururer, a Catholic priest, whose work on behalf of the Jews and other so-called "undesirables" had made him a threat to the Nazi warlords. He too ministered in Jesus' name to his fellow inmates in the concentration camp. In Buchenwald, a son of Rome and a son of the Reformation, separated no longer by four centuries but only by four cells, walked the via crucis and bore witness together to their common Lord, Jesus Christ, the sole and sufficient redeemer.[58]

As important as spiritual ecumenism is to unity, it is not enough. The lack of attention to institutional divisions would represent an abuse of the concept of spiritual union.[59] And those who stress the role of the church as the visible means of grace in the world find a one-sided emphasis on the church as an inward, spiritual fellowship to be lopsided, eclipsing "the real content of revelation and the historical character of the church."[60] I thus appreciate Chris Green's drawing the attention of Pentecostals to the fact that such things as the "call of special apostles, the teaching of the 'Our Father,' and the events by which the Eucharist and baptism were initiated make the church the community that she is."[61] Thus the church must still take concrete steps toward visible

---

[56] Ibid., #58–59.
[57] Ibid., #59.
[58] Timothy George, "Toward an Evangelical Ecclesiology," *ERT* 41, no. 2 (2017): 117–18 (100–18).
[59] See Berkouwer, *The Church*, 37–39.
[60] Note the Old Catholic-Orthodox Conversations, "Ecclesiology Agreed Statement," Chambésy, 1977, Bonn, 1979, Zagorsk 1981, III/1, #7, *GW I*, 402.
[61] Green, "The Body of Christ, the Spirit of Communion," 20–36.

unity, and the path will never be easy. The unity of the churches must be embodied. Christ prayed that his followers be one for the sake of their public witness to him: "That all of them may be one, Father, just as you are in me and I am in you. May they also be in us so that the world may believe that you have sent me" (Jn 17:21). The prayed-for unity is not static but rather dynamic: "Father, just as you are in me and I am in you. May they also be in us." This unity is not merely social (a mere sharing of values or a common cause) but a real communion (*koinonia*) together in the life of the Triune God through the visible means that God has provided. We briefly discussed the nature of *koinonia* in our first chapter. Lorelie F. Fuchs's thorough treatment of this concept shows that its rediscovery has helped enormously to provide the churches with a concrete path toward unity and, especially, to help them all to understand the degree to which they are already enjoying unity even while in their divided state.[62] Unity through *koinonia* has degrees; just because it is not visibly full does not mean that it does not exist at all. As the 1980 Lutheran-Roman Catholic conversation noted, "Living unity in Christ is essentially manifold and dynamic."[63]

There are churches that think of unity first as a local church phenomenon, and understandably so. Believers gathered together in Christ have been incorporated into Christ by the Spirit. This congregation is the primary context in which the challenges and witness of unity in communion with the Triune God and one another are directly encountered. As we will note when discussing catholicity, the local church is not to be viewed as simply a part of the global church. It is the church in communion with Christ in the Spirit. The church is in a sense the entire church present, but it is "*an* entire church, it is not *the* entire church," as Hans Küng reminds us.[64] And when saying that Christ is present "wholly and entirely" in the congregation's life or sacred meal,[65] one must immediately qualify that so as to preserve Christ's transcendence and freedom vis-à-vis the local church, which points to grander global and eschatological realization of Christ's presence. As Küng put the matter, "Christ gives himself to the church but is not wholly contained within it."[66] Such a qualification refers to the global church as well.

Catholicity does indeed point to the church throughout the world and even throughout time. How this unity through *koinonia* relates to the church on other levels, such as on the broader level of a denomination (or family of churches), or even the churches in their global presence is a complex issue. It is not that communion cannot exist on these levels too, especially through church leaders or bishops who gather collegially, it is only that speaking of the church on these levels requires careful consideration, which we will do under the topic of catholicity. Suffice it to say here that the challenge of unity through *koinonia* exists on every level at which the church exists, at every level at which some kind of shared life or *koinonia* is possible. Thus, Paul's stunning prayer in Ephesians 3 that believers grasp together the breadth, height, and

---

[62] Fuchs, *Koinonia and the Quest for Ecumenical Ecclesiology*.
[63] Lutheran-Roman Catholic Conversation, "Ways to Community," 1980, #33.
[64] Küng, *The Church*, 300.
[65] As is stated in the Report of the Joint Lutheran-Roman Catholic Commission, "The Eucharist," 1978, #7, *GW I*, 194.
[66] Küng, *The Church*, 236.

depth of Christ's love refers to "all the Lord's holy people" (v. 18) and is prayed to the heavenly Father "from whom every family in heaven and on earth derives its name" (vv. 14-15). Surely this prayer is not limited to the local church.

One must add here that the church catholic includes both the dead and the living. Indeed, "whether we live or die, we belong to the Lord. For this very reason, Christ died and returned to life so that he might be the Lord of both the dead and the living" (Rom. 14:8-9). God willed concerning all of the people of God from all times, "that only together with us would they be made perfect" (Heb. 11:40). The resurrection of the dead will be the grand reunion of all the saints, of all times and places. At the Lord's return, we "will be caught up together with them in the clouds to meet the Lord in the air" (1 Thess. 4:17). This is why we presently have a great cloud of witnesses cheering us on as we run the race to the high calling that God grants to us all (12:1). The connection between the pilgrim church and the church triumphant in heaven is not a strong theme in Protestant theology, though it is dramatically pictured for us in the book of Revelation, where John beholds and hears in the Spirit the worship of the saints in heaven (ch. 5). The elders in heaven are even beheld as having "golden bowls full of incense, which are the prayers of God's people" (5:8). I need to point out here that an emphasis on praying to saints in heaven creates a danger of deifying them and of eclipsing the immediacy of our direct access to Christ our only High Priest and mediator (Heb. 4:14-16). Still, the thought that the church triumphant stands in solidarity with us as we await together the fulfillment of the kingdom of God on earth enriches our understanding of the church's expansive unity.

Moving outside of the local church makes the reality of the church's disunity in my view impossible to deny. If we seek to escape this reality by clinging to an "invisible" unity of a spiritual nature, are we not forced to downplay the seriousness of visible disunity? Connecting unity to *koinonia* helps us to view the church's visible disunity as serious, but not necessarily devastating or of ultimate significance. Unity can then be viewed as multifaceted, multilayered, deep, and expansive, a journey with an eschatological goal. *It can exist in degrees.* The growing measure of visible communion attained between churches is to be viewed as the necessary "fruit" of the invisible communion that we share in the life of the Triune God as the Spirit-baptized people of God. This notion of invisible communion bearing visible fruit is helpful for understanding the relationship between invisible and visible unity, showing the connection also between the church's growing unity and growing experience of sanctification (as we will see, catholicity and apostolicity as well).[67]

This notion of unity as united communion and, therefore, as growing and multifaceted has gained broad ecumenical support. For example, the Catholic Church has recognized that other churches or communities of faith share one gospel and one baptism with them. Yet, these churches are not united to the pope and others ordained in the Catholic Church to preserve unity and thus do not share in the meal of unity, the Lord's Supper. So, from a Catholic perspective, there is a degree of unity possible with other churches and communities of faith but this unity is imperfect.

---

[67] The notion of fruit here is taken from the report of the international Anglican-Roman Catholic dialogue, "The Church as Communion," Dublin, Ireland, 1990, V, #52, *GW II*, 341.

The 1972 Lutheran-Roman Catholic conversation thus notes, "Our common baptism is an important starting point in this matter of Eucharistic fellowship."[68] So also, the Evangelical-Roman Catholic Dialogue states, "There is therefore between us an initial if incomplete unity."[69] The Catholic document, *Unitatis Redintegratio* (no. 4), elaborates concerning baptized Christians who are not Catholic or are not united to the bishops of the Catholic Church nor share in the eucharist over which they preside:

> For men who believe in Christ and have been truly baptized are in communion with the Catholic Church even though this communion is imperfect. The differences that exist to varying degrees between them and the Catholic Church— whether in doctrine and sometimes in discipline, or concerning the structures of the church—do indeed create many obstacles, sometimes serious ones, to full ecclesial communion. The ecumenical movement is striving to overcome these obstacles.

In Catholic ecclesiology, there is room for seeing in other churches or communities of faith a degree of catholicity or the grace and virtue present in the church as an expanding and diverse communion. Significant here is the Catholic recognition that there is no exclusive identification of the church of Christ with the Roman Catholic Church. Paragraph 8 of *Lumen Gentium*, the dogmatic constitution on the church for the Second Vatican Council, states, "This Church constituted and organized in the world as a society, subsists in the Catholic Church." The church constituted in the world "subsists in" rather than simply *is* the Catholic Church, implying that there is not an exclusive identification between the two. In the same paragraph, *Lumen Gentium* then draws the conclusion concerning the Catholic Church that "many elements of sanctification and of truth are found outside of its visible structure. These elements, as gifts belonging to the Church of Christ, are forces impelling toward catholic unity." The Catholic team of the 1972 Lutheran-Catholic conversation quoted earlier concludes that the "one church of Christ is actualized in an analogous manner also in other churches. This conclusion also means that the unity of the Roman Catholic Church is not perfect but that it strives toward the perfect unity of the church."[70] The Catholic team even notes that, since these other churches or communities of faith do not participate in the Catholic Church's Lord's Supper, "the eucharistic celebration in the Catholic church also suffers from imperfection. It will become the perfect sign of the unity of the church only when all those who through baptism have been invited in principle to the table of the Lord and are able in reality to partake."[71]

The role of the bishops in maintaining the unity of the church (and the Catholic support of the office of the pope or the Petrine Office as a focal point of unity) is an issue that we will raise under the apostolicity of the church. What is significant about the Catholic affirmation of degrees of unity (in communion or *koinonia*) is its refusal

---

[68] Report of the Joint Lutheran-Roman Catholic Study Commission on "The Gospel and the Church," 1972 ("Malta Report"), 1972, #70, *GW I*, 183.
[69] "The Evangelical-Roman Catholic Dialogue on Mission," 1977–1984, Section 7, #1, *GW II*, 431.
[70] Lutheran-Roman Catholic conversation, "Malta Report," 1972, #71, *GW I*, 183.
[71] Ibid.

to say that unity must be an "all or nothing" reality (as some churches may assume). Unity is thus not exclusively internal to a particular communion. The Catholic Church has resisted this conclusion. And even though the Catholic Church views itself as the central locus of unity, it is willing to recognize a degree of unity with and in other churches and to regard the Catholic Church as on the way toward a more perfect unity that would hopefully include them. This is the pilgrim church highlighted in *Lumen Gentium*. Connecting unity to the concept of communion (*koinonia*) allows for this kind of complexity when it comes to discerning the unity of the church. What is compelling is the recognition shared by the 1981 Anglican-Catholic conversation that Spirit baptism under the sign of water baptism is the point of departure for the path toward full communion or unity in the richest sense of that term. To quote from the "Final Report": "Those who have received the same word of God and have been baptized in the same Spirit cannot without disobedience acquiesce in a state of separation."[72] The Spirit's presence as the environment of Jesus Christ, or our differentiated communion with and in Christ, must be the context in which a more perfect unity is attained. The church is united essentially as the Spirit-baptized church.

In my view, the Catholic Church should not exclude from the sacred meal those who have been incorporated into Christ by the Spirit under the sign of water baptism. After all, it is first and foremost the *Lord's* Supper and not the church's. The eucharist as a meal of unity is a meal of hope. It is to be shared on the basis of the unity already present in baptism and shared with the hope of a more perfect unity to come (as a foretaste of it). In order to arrive at this conclusion, the episcopal office as a necessary condition of eucharistic hospitality would need to be addressed. I will tip my hand here and side with Protestants who subordinate ministry to the gospel and maintain that the churches should move toward a mutual recognition of ministries of oversight across confessional boundaries based on a shared gospel and a shared sacrament.

Among Protestant churches, the road to full communion has become particularly important. There is no fully accepted meaning of full communion in the ecumenical movement. There is rather a "patchwork quilt of meanings."[73] Typically included, of course, is recognition of communion together with and in the Triune God, but then, within that communion, other elements are included. Helpful is the description of the elements of full communion given for us by the 1990 Joint Working group of the World Council of Churches and the Roman Catholic Church: "The ecclesial elements required for full communion within a visibly united church—the goal of the ecumenical movement—are communion in the fullness of the apostolic faith; in sacramental life; in a truly one and mutually recognized ministry; in structures of conciliar relations and decision-making; and in common witness and service to the world."[74] First, there is communion in like faith (faith, hope, and love). The fullness of apostolic faith does not mean total agreement in all matters of faith; it refers to a

---

[72] Anglican-Roman Catholic Conversation, 1981, "Final Report," Intro. #1, *GW I*, 64.
[73] Joseph D. Small, "What Is Communion and When Is It Full?," *Ecclesiology* 2, no. 1 (2005): 72 (71–87).
[74] "The Church: Local and Universal: A Study Document Commissioned and Received by the Joint Working Group," World Council of Churches and Roman Catholic Church, 1990, Section III, #25, *GW II*, 868.

grasping together in unity the depth of the gospel. It becomes important within this grasping that disagreements are not regarded as church dividing in significance. Not all doctrinal agreements are vital enough to the gospel to be church dividing in the case of unreconcilable disagreement. The ecumenical movement uses the concept of the "hierarchy of truth" to determine which doctrines are potentially church dividing (high enough on the hierarchy of truth) and which are not, and, additionally, which elements of belief within a dogma or vital doctrine are most important to it (most in need of agreement). Ecumenical milestones such as the Nicene Creed function as a basis for such a shared faith. Areas of dogma (those doctrines deemed most important to the gospel) would typically include salvation by grace alone, the deity of Christ, the unity of Christ's person, and salvation only by way of Christ's atonement. Within Pentecostalism there is a division over the doctrine of the Trinity, with at least a quarter of the movement advocating a Christocentric modalism that rejects an eternal relation of persons in the Godhead. Ecumenical conversations between the two sides have found unity on the deity and lordship of Christ and the empowerment of the Spirit in the life and ministry of the church to make Christ present to us. Though both sides would see the other as defective theologically, both have shown ecumenical openness to the faith of the other.[75] Besides strictly doctrinal issues, ethical values such as the dignity and worth of all human beings, since they are all made in God's image, would also be worthy of attention as an area of commonality among the churches. Besides shared faith, there is also communion in the sacraments (principally baptism and Lord's Supper), and mutual recognition of ordained ministry. Lastly, there is a sharing of public witness to the gospel and the justice of the kingdom of God.

There are currently Protestant churches that have full communion agreements, which does not mean that there is not still room for deeper forms of unity even within such agreements. Indeed, the idea of degrees of unity through degrees of *koinonia* has become important to those working at the forefront of the church's growth in unity. The fact that in many cases a degree of unity already exists grants churches a deeper sense of solidarity with each other and a path along which they could work toward greater fullness of communion. Of course, ultimate communion is an eschatological goal realizable only at the final gathering of the church unto Christ at his return. But a kind of penultimate full communion is still a goal worth striving for this side of eternity. We must along the way be cautious that we do not come to feel comfortable with our arrived-at level of unity. As greater sacrifice is required, it may become easy to be satisfied with our arrived-at degree of unity, growing insensitive to the scandal of our divisions and using the ecumenical status quo to justify avoiding bolder moves.[76] We dare not be lulled into complacency.

The kingdom vision of full communion among churches on a global scale must remain at the forefront of the ecumenical movement. The 1984 Lutheran-Roman Catholic Dialogue highlights models for comprehensive or full communion.[77] I will

---

[75] See Frank D. Macchia, "The Oneness-Trinitarian Pentecostal Dialogue: Exploring the Diversity of Apostolic Faith," *HTR* 103, no. 3 (2010): 329–49.

[76] I am grateful here to Joseph Small for this insight, "What Is Communion and When Is It Full?"

[77] Lutheran-Roman Catholic Dialogue, "Facing Unity," Rome, Italy, March 3, 1984, Part 1, Section C, #13–34, *GW II*, 446–50.

discuss a few of the major ones. The reader will detect throughout a sliding scale of independence among different churches or communions. The first model of comprehensive union is not only the boldest but also the one that allows for the least amount of independence among different churches, namely, the "organic model." This model seeks a world communion that abandons all denominational or confessional loyalties and divisions. It would be comprised of "the working out of a common confession of faith, agreement about sacraments and ministry, and a homogeneous organizational structure."[78] Denominational loyalties are to be abandoned but only to make way for the adoption of something far grander and more satisfying. In my view, this model needs to be admired for its boldness. Yet, it is surely unrealistic. Confessional loyalties have long histories and are baked into the historical consciousness and life of the church. One cannot put this kind of toothpaste back into the tube, nor should one try, since this diversification is to an extent a normal development and is even to be cherished. As Oscar Cullmann argued, the different confessional accents in the recent history of the church function in a way that is analogous to how different spiritual gifts function within a local congregation. They enrich the landscape of the church and can edify the whole in unique ways.[79] However, one cannot deny that denominational and confessional loyalties have divided the church in a way that denigrates one another and harms the church's public witness. Will not full communion on a vast scale unite us visibly in a way that radically alters how these confessional differences are preserved institutionally and how they function in relation to others? There is indeed some level of diversity of traditions and ministries within large churches already. Such a diverse reality could perhaps be allowed to expand considerably within an organic unity model, so that diverse loyalties are not dissolved entirely. Still, one has a right to be wary of a world church this side of eternity that seeks to eliminate all sense of independence among major confessional bodies.

A second model, termed "corporate union," would be a variation of the organic model, except a diversity of confessional loyalties and even institutional commitments would be emphasized and cherished more, even to the point of allowing relative autonomy among participating bodies of churches. A merger or "mutual absorption" of communions would be rejected, but neither would they exist with total independence. A differentiated organic unity would be embraced in which different churches still have relative autonomy. Of course, this model is superior to the previous one for reasons stated earlier.

A third model is that of a "conciliar fellowship." This model strives for maximum independence of churches or communions within a full communion sharing of life and ministry. It would be a global fellowship of autonomous churches that would exist within a full communion agreement. They would "confess the same apostolic faith, have full communion with one another in baptism and eucharist, recognize each other's members and ministries." They would also be "one in witness and service

---

[78] Ibid., #16–17, 447.
[79] Oscar Cullmann, *Unity through Diversity: Its Foundation and a Contribution to the Discussion Concerning the Possibilities of It Actualization* (Minneapolis, MN: Fortress Press, 1988).

before the world."⁸⁰ It would be close in nature to the "corporate union" model just discussed because of the varied richness of communion shared among the churches, except there would be more independence institutionally among the churches, and a greater level of diversity allowed and even cherished. Different communions would be free to continue to cultivate and celebrate their varied uniqueness. Some fear that the conciliar fellowship model still resembles a world church too much and that diversity would be hindered to an extent. They thus prefer to call this model "unity by reconciled diversity" so as to highlight the preservation of independence and unique identities among all churches as they share full communion with one another.⁸¹

In my view, this latter option seems to strike the right balance between unity and diversity. But the churches have a long way to go before they can realistically reach this level of communion. I currently cannot imagine all churches joining, even most. Are our differences too great to make such a diversified union realistic? For this reason, Pentecostal theologian Miroslav Volf limits unity to the local congregation and advocates for the much more modest "openness" of different congregations to each other as the goal to be achieved for global Christianity this side of eternity.⁸² He makes us ask, does a global "full communion" agreement tilt us too far in the direction of an unattainably realized eschatology? Indeed, even if such a global attainment of full communion can be realized this side of eternity, our unity in communion will still be imperfect.

Yet, I cannot let go of the dream of full communion on a global scale. Ecumenical openness is not enough for me, although it is a welcomed beginning. It at least begins to help us answer Amos Yong's question, "How do Pentecostals make connections with Evangelical and other non-Pentecostal Christians beside proselytizing them?"⁸³ Yong notes that Pentecostals have the potential to be an ecumenical force. They have essentially functioned as a restorationist movement with an ecumenical appeal to come together under a new outpouring of the Spirit.⁸⁴ As Cecil Robeck maintained, they are implicitly ecumenical but do not yet fully realize it.⁸⁵ It only takes the right encouragement and contextual experiences to move them in the direction of realizing their ecumenical potential. Perhaps it's time to think boldly about the possibilities, not only for them but also for other church families that are not ecumenically involved and are perhaps pessimistic about being so. Paul's vision of what can be grasped together by the Spirit among all of the church families named by the Father is truly bold:

> ¹⁶ I pray that out of his glorious riches he may strengthen you with power through his Spirit in your inner being, ¹⁷ so that Christ may dwell in your hearts through faith. And I pray that you, being rooted and established in love, ¹⁸ may have power,

---

80. Lutheran-Roman Catholic Dialogue, "Facing Unity," 1984, #27–30, *GW II*, 449.
81. Ibid., #31–34, *GW II*, 449–50.
82. Volf, *After Our Likeness*, 225–26.
83. Amos Yong, "The Marks of the Church: A Pentecostal Re-Reading," *ERT* 26, no. 1 (2002): 46 (45–67).
84. Yong, *The Spirit Poured Out on All Flesh*, 144–45.
85. Cecil M. Robeck Jr., "Taking Stock of Pentecostalism: Reflections of a Retiring Editor," *Pneuma* 15 (1993): 39ff.

together with all the Lord's holy people, to grasp how wide and long and high and deep is the love of Christ, [19] and to know this love that surpasses knowledge—that you may be filled to the measure of all the fullness of God. (Eph. 3:16-19)

Unimaginable? Paul does not stagger at the thought of it: "Now to him who is able to do immeasurably more than all we ask or imagine, according to his power that is at work within us, to him be glory in the church and in Christ Jesus throughout all generations, for ever and ever! Amen" (3:20-21). Surely what remains imperfect in this world will be perfected in the next. As Ernst Käsemann noted, "The unity of the church was, is, and remains primarily an eschatological property."[86] Volf would agree. But my question is, can we not in the meantime make every effort together to strive for unity as we let God have God's way among us? Who knows what the Spirit can accomplish? And since the church's divisions in history have contributed to the division of humanity, the church has a compelling reason to seek unity for the sake of a new humanity united at the *eschaton* under Christ by the Spirit of God (Eph. 1:10). The unity of the church serves the coming kingdom of God.

## Holiness

The church is holy. Lack of involvement by Pentecostals in the ecumenical movement has perhaps more to do with personal holiness than strictly doctrinal issues. As was typical of the holiness revivalism from which Pentecostalism came, there was a shared feeling that the mainline churches had compromised personal holiness and spiritual fervor. Even though Pentecostals over time came to emphasize the power of the Spirit in ministry over personal purity, the background of Pentecostalism in the Wesleyan Holiness revival did leave a permanent stamp on the ethos of the movement. Their eschatological zeal for the soon return of Christ caused them to seek to wake up the sleeping churches to personal holiness before Christ returns. Their zeal tempted them to see the true church as a little flock and the rest of the church as seriously compromised in the sense of being too worldly. In the first half of the twentieth century, the rapture doctrine was popularized throughout the evangelical churches advocating a secret return of Christ to rapture or snatch away the faithful remnant leaving the apostate church to go through the time of tribulation. Visions of a world church headed by the antichrist during the time of tribulation made the ecumenical movement look especially dangerous. Many Pentecostals found that the preaching of the rapture to wake up the sleeping church fit well with their ecclesiology and they became loyalists, even though other aspects of this teaching were incompatible with Pentecostal hermeneutics, theology, and mission.[87]

The idea of the faithful little flock waiting to be raptured, however, was out of sync with Pentecostal optimism concerning a latter-day outpouring of the Spirit to

---

[86] Report of Section 1: "The Holy Spirit and the Catholicity of the Church," Fourth Assembly of the World Council of Churches, Uppsala, 1968, *EM*, 98.

[87] Frank D. Macchia, "Pentecostal and Charismatic Theology," *Oxford Handbook of Eschatology*, ed. Jerry Walls (New York: Oxford University Press, 2008), 280–94.

prepare the bride for her returning Christ. In the 1960s and 1970s, the charismatic movement among the mainline churches, including the Catholic Church, put Pentecostal optimism to the test, shaking a number of Pentecostals at their core, and calling into question their understanding of the inner life of these churches. Vinson Synan's admission in his classic, *Charismatic Bridges*, is a case in point. Commenting on his attendance at the Sixth International Conference on the Charismatic Renewal in the Catholic Church (1972), Synan noted that he was so overtaken with emotion at that meeting that he had to temporarily leave the assembly of worshipping Catholics to regain his composure. In describing the incident, Synan exclaimed, "They were singing 'our' songs and exercising 'our' gifts. It was more than I could take!"[88] Similarly, Assemblies of God Pentecostal pioneer Joseph Flower wrote during the heyday of the charismatic movement, "It is extremely difficult for many, especially those who have adopted inflexible standards of doctrine and behavior, to see how God can be in the present, seemingly confused, situation."[89] God often confuses us by confronting us with living streams flowing out from churches that we have denigrated with one-sided or prejudicial assumptions.

Personal holiness is indeed a challenge to all of the churches. The existence in the churches of those who are only nominally connected to Christ or who are too carnal in their witness when considering the length of time they have believed is a problem as old as the scriptures ("Are you not worldly?" 1 Cor. 3:4) and affects all churches to some degree. It is possible for zealots in the area of personal holiness to call their congregations or larger communions of churches into question, and their voices need to be heard as an occasion for repentance. Yet, this zealotry can also be a threat to the ongoing life of the church when it morphs into intolerance, elitism, and divisiveness. This is an ecumenical problem. Note for example John Zizioulas's response to those who criticize the Eastern Orthodox Churches from within their ascetical tradition.[90]

The call to personal holiness is especially challenging to historic churches that put their ecclesiological emphasis on external means of grace rather than on the faithful responses among congregants. In the final report for the third quinquennium of the Roman Catholic-Pentecostal dialogue, the Pentecostal team observed that "it seems possible for some Roman Catholics to live continuously in a state of sin, and yet be considered members in the church. This seems to Pentecostals to undermine the concept of Christian discipleship."[91] The Catholic team responded by wondering what means Pentecostals have at their disposal for bringing those who have fallen into sin into a process of repentance.[92] Interestingly, while Pentecostals emphasized the personal discipleship of the church's members, the Catholics responded by shifting attention to the external means of grace. Though nominal Christianity and Christian

---

[88] Vinson Synan, *Charismatic Bridges* (Ann Arbor, MI: Word of Life, 1974), 25.
[89] Joseph Flower, "The Charismatic Movement: Some Problem Areas and Solutions, Pt. 2," *Advance* 8 (1972): 11.
[90] John D. Zizioulas, *Lectures in Christian Dogmatics* (New York: T & T Clark, 2008), 124–25.
[91] "Perspectives on Koinonia," Report from the Third Quinquennium of the Dialogue between the Pontifical Council for Promoting Christian Unity and Some Classical Pentecostal Churches and Leaders, #78, *GW II*, 746.
[92] Ibid., #79, *GW II*, 746.

worldliness is a problem across ecumenical boundaries, it is a particular problem for communions that practice paedobaptism and stress the nature of the church as an external sacramental means of grace rather than as a community of personally committed disciples.

Yet, one cannot understand the Nicene belief in the holiness of the church without a focus first on the external means of grace, for this belief refers first and foremost to that which is given by grace to the church, and not to that which is visibly realized among its members. Christ binds himself to us by the Spirit in the proclamation of the gospel, baptism, eucharist, and the many forms of witness and service among a diversity of members. Even the significantly flawed Corinthian church is described as mediating the work of the Lord and the Spirit through its charismatic life (1 Cor. 12:4-6). The church is the environment of the Spirit, and, as such, the environment of Jesus Christ who takes us into his life, which is the life of the Triune God. In receiving Christ by repentance and faith, we are justified and sanctified "in the name of the Lord Jesus Christ and by the Spirit of our God" (1 Cor. 6:11). The church is holy primarily in the presence of Christ by the Spirit. This is a holiness that is offered as a gift and is not the result of the church's own spiritual attainment. The church is holy precisely as fallen.

But holiness is a faith commitment that bears spiritual fruit as well. When looking at the doctrines of justification and sanctification, we can appreciate the holiness of the church as both a gift and a way of life. This is because they are received by faith and in the Spirit as transformative realities. In justification we have peace with God (Rom. 5:1); we are set in right covenant relation with him. Christ himself is our peace, both with God and with one another (Eph. 2:14). But justification as a divine declaration is powerful and transformative. In Christ's righteousness, "God makes his cause triumph in the world."[93] Christ was condemned in crucifixion but justified by the Spirit in resurrection (1 Tim. 3:15). In resurrection, he was declared the Son of God in power by the Spirit (Rom. 1:4). The gift of righteousness that triumphs in Christ's life, death, and resurrection is offered to us through the gospel, which is the power of God unto salvation (Rom. 1:16). We are justified by faith through union with Christ, or by the baptism in the Holy Spirit.[94] I thus agree with Article 15 of the Lutheran-Catholic Joint Declaration on the Doctrine of Justification (1999): "Justification thus means that Christ himself is our righteousness, in which we share through the Holy Spirit in accord with the will of the Father." Justification occurs "in the Spirit" in union with Christ, allowing for a relationship of communion through the baptism in the Spirit. The wedge between a forensic and a transformative understanding of justification by faith is thus overcome.[95] This earlier statement from the Lutheran team in the 1972 Lutheran-Roman Catholic study commission (the Malta Report) says something similar: "Lutheran theologians emphasize that the event of justification is not limited to individual forgiveness of sins and they do not see in it a purely external declaration of the justification of the sinner. Rather, the righteousness of Christ actualized in

---

[93] Ernst Käsemann, *Perspectives on Paul* (Mifflintown, PA: Sigler Press, 1998), 180.
[94] See how I develop this idea in Frank D. Macchia, *Justified in the Spirit: Creation, Redemption, and the Triune God* (Grand Rapids: MI: Eerdmans, 2010).
[95] Ibid.

the Christ event is conveyed to the sinner through the message of justification as an encompassing reality basic to the new life of the believer."[96] The gift of righteousness through Christ that justifies us is thus "inseparable from the Giver."[97] Justification in Christ by the Spirit opens up for us communion with Christ, not only as individuals but also as communities bound together by Christ who is our peace. We will also be ultimately justified in resurrection, which is the righteousness for which we hope (Gal. 5:5).

So we are also sanctified by Christ who sanctified himself that we may be sanctified in him (Jn 17:19). His baptism in fire on our behalf made our passage through the fire a sanctifying rather than a destructive force. Under the sign and seal of baptism we pass from death to life accompanied by Christ. Christ's goal is to impart the Spirit to us so that we in him could be set apart for a life of fruit bearing and service. We are sanctified by the Spirit in Christ (2 Thess. 2:13), which means set apart from sin for the holy life, to fulfill a holy purpose. Again, it is through the baptism in the Holy Spirit that we are sanctified and empowered for witness (Acts 1:8; 15:9). Like Christ, the church is sanctified for the sake of others, to provide a witness to truth, beauty, and virtue before the world. But sanctification is first a gift before it is ever a challenge and a task: "for we are God's handiwork, created in Christ Jesus to do good works" (Eph. 2:9). The sanctified Christ whose presence in the Holy Spirit speaks to us and unites himself to us as the wellspring of the sanctifying Spirit is the source of the church's holiness. Indeed, though the church is fallen, Christ through the Spirit still indwells as the source of goodness and life. The church is simultaneously just and sinner in both its justification and sanctification. But in both we are confronted and transformed as well.

Thus, though holiness is through and through a gift, the church dare not become complacent in its confession of its own holiness. "Shall we go on sinning that grace may increase? God forbid!" (Rom. 6:1-2). The same baptism by which Christ is embraced so as to set us all apart by grace unto divine communion is also a transformative commitment to "live a new life" (6:4) and to crucify "the body ruled by sin" (v. 6). Moreover, the church shares in Christ during the Lord's Supper (1 Cor. 10:16), which surely involves a commitment to share in his crucified life for the sake of the world ("I am crucified with Christ," Gal. 2:20). We seek as living letters of Christ to embody him in the world (2 Cor. 3:3). Toward these ends, the church must always hear Bonhoeffer's stinging warning against cheap grace: "Cheap grace means grace sold on the market like cheapjacks' wares. The sacraments, the forgiveness of sins, and the consolations of religion are thrown away at cut prices."[98] Grace becomes an "inexhaustible treasury" that the church doles out without the expectation of repentance or new commitment: "grace without price; grace without cost!"[99] This grace becomes an abstract idea to which one is merely expected to offer assent. The Church is assured of forgiveness without repentance or striving, "Let the Christian rest content with his worldliness!"[100]

---

[96] Lutheran-Roman Catholic conversation, "Malta Report," 1972, #26, *GW I*, 174.
[97] Käsemann, *Perspectives on Paul*, 174.
[98] Bonhoeffer, *The Cost of Discipleship*, 43.
[99] Ibid.
[100] Ibid., 43–44.

Over against such misconceptions is costly grace that sets one on the path of the crucified Christ for the sake of the world. Note Paul's admonition that the church as the dwelling place of the Spirit should offer not just the praises of their lips but of their entire lives as living sacrifices, for "this is your true and proper worship." They make every effort to resist conforming to the world, conforming instead to Christ (Rom. 12:1-2). They seek together to embody Christ crucified and risen before the world (Gal. 2:20). The holiness offered as a gift to the church is to transform the church and set it on its path of Christlikeness. As Berkouwer pointed out, the marks of the church such as holiness were meant not only to be confessed as a gift but also to function as tests that constantly call us to repentance and obedience. We are to strive toward making the mark an attribute.[101] The church is to be comforted in its striving but challenged in its complacency. Such is the confession of the church's holiness.

John Wesley in his *Plain Account of Christian Perfection* challenged the church to strive for "simplicity of intention" and "purity of affection" in all things.[102] Simplicity of intention meant that all of our goals are to be submitted to one overriding intention, which is the redemptive purpose of divine love in Christ. And in this conformity in all things, one finds the affections being purged of selfishness, lust, and pride. Perfection for Wesley is the attainment of this simplicity and purgation. Wesley did not describe this attainment in terms of absolute perfection in this life, for the Church continues to have battles to win in its resistance to challenges that it must confront. Galatians 5:16 exhorts Christians to walk by the Spirit in conformity to Christ as the way of not fulfilling the desires of the flesh. Yielding to desires of the flesh strengthens those desires, while walking by the Spirit cultivates the desires of the Spirit implanted by the word of Christ. Yet, Wesley's understanding of Christian perfection, though not absolute, is a perfection for which the church is to strive nonetheless, even though its full depth can only be realized in the *eschaton*. In this light, Steven J. Land urged Pentecostals to see their transformed affections as passions for the coming kingdom of God in all of life.[103] The inward transformation is to manifest itself outwardly in good works: "We are God's handiwork, created in Christ Jesus to do good works" (Eph. 2:9). These deeds are the fine linen that adorns the wedding gown of Christ's bride at his return (Rev. 19:8). She is clothed primarily with Christ, indeed, but with the outward linen she also wears her acts of conformity to him. The end goal is described by Wesley in moving terms: "Let the Spirit return to God that gave it, with the whole train of its affections. Other sacrifices from us he would not: but the living sacrifice of the heart hath he chosen. Let it be continually offered up to God, through Christ, in flames of holy love."[104]

---

[101] Berkouwer, *The Church*, 14–15.
[102] John Wesley, *Plain Account of Christian Perfection*, #3. http://wesley.nnu.edu/john-wesley/a-plain-account-of-christian-perfection/
[103] Steven J. Land, *Pentecostal Spirituality: A Passion for the Kingdom* (Cleveland, TN: CPT Press, 2010), esp. 120–80.
[104] Wesley, *Plain Account*, #6.

## Catholicity

The church is also confessed as Catholic. Catholicity is the other side of unity, describing its substance of *koinonia* with richer detail. Catholicity refers to the church's fullness of life and virtue in Christ and in the Spirit, as well as to its vast diversity and universality throughout the world. Indeed, catholicity is eschatological, for the reality of Spirit baptism reaches for ultimate eschatological depth in the fullness of life when mortality is "swallowed up" in immortal life (2 Cor. 5:4) and eschatological expanse when the church's mission reaches the ends of the earth (Acts 1:8). Geoffrey Wainwright rightly points to the exalted Christ in Philippians 2 who is to be worshipped by every tongue as the Christological explanation for the church's catholicity.[105] Christ is the fullness of unfathomable love at the heart of the church's life (Eph. 3:18-19), and he is the one who draws all people everywhere to himself (Jn 12:32). Indeed, Christ is worshipped in the depth of the Spirit by every tongue, for it is only by the Spirit that the church can confess Christ as Lord (1 Cor. 12:3). Exalted to the throne, Christ poured out the Spirit upon *all* flesh (Acts 2:17, 33-35). The disciples will thus be driven by the Spirit to the very ends of the earth in witness to Christ (1:8). Because of all this: "The ultimate scope of the church cannot be anything less than universal."[106] It can also be nothing less than reaching and groaning for the Spirit's ultimate fullness in the *eschaton* to come (Rom. 8:22-23).

Catholicity is a term that most Pentecostals and their evangelical siblings would not typically use. Interestingly, Timothy George makes the point that the Reformers of the sixteenth century and the Puritans of the seventeenth, including Baptists, did not always have a problem using the term. Their complaint about the church of Rome was not that it was too catholic "but that it was not catholic enough."[107] The church of Rome in their view had tended to draw the boundaries at that time too narrowly when it came to judging who was allowed to share in the church's catholicity. The term "Catholic" is richer in connotation than the word "universal" (which is a weak substitute for it) and should perhaps find its way back into the vocabulary of those who are not accustomed to using it.

As implied earlier, the term "Catholic" has qualitative and quantitative meanings. Qualitatively, the term can refer to the fullness of grace, truth, or spiritual gifts. Such fullness can be viewed fundamentally from the vantage point of the church's participation in the Lord's Supper but not exclusively so. Though catholicity is not commonly used among Pentecostals, the term, qualitatively defined, would be understood among them primarily in the shared experience of the Holy Spirit evidenced supremely by love and also in the outward sign of speaking in tongues or other extraordinary gifts of the Spirit. They would view catholicity in the light of Paul's point in 1 Cor. 1:7 that the church not lack any gift while waiting for the appearance of Jesus Christ. In accenting the works of the Spirit, Pentecostals would agree with Irenaeus: "For where the church is, there is the Spirit of God; and where the Spirit of God is there is the church, and every kind

---

[105] Wainwright, *Doxology*, 132.
[106] Ibid., 133.
[107] George, "Toward an Evangelical Ecclesiology," 112 (100-18).

of grace."[108] Early on, however, the term "Catholic" also gained a quantitative meaning, as the church throughout the world. It referred to the diversity and vast breadth of participants in the life of the church. Cyril of Jerusalem combined the qualitative with the quantitative by stating that the church catholic "is called Catholic because it is spread throughout the world" and because it "teaches universally and completely all the doctrines," "subjects to right worship all humankind," and "possesses in itself every conceivable virtue, whether in deeds, words or in spiritual gifts of every kind."[109] This bold assumption that the church "possesses in itself every conceivable virtue" can seem on the surface as a kind of realized eschatology. The assumption by any one church family to possess this can seem especially problematic.

With Vatican II, the Roman Catholic Church clarified its position on catholicity in helpful ways. Most significant is the recognition of elements of catholicity outside the visible boundaries of the Catholic Church among separated brothers and sisters: the written Word of God; the life of grace; and faith, hope, and charity, along with other interior gifts of the Spirit. These elements can contribute to the edification of the Catholic Church.[110] If non-Catholic churches are thought to possess genuine elements of catholicity, are not these churches essential to the Catholic Church's realization of catholicity? Implying an affirmative answer to this question, the "Decree on Ecumenism" stated further that the "separated brethren" prevent the Catholic Church "from effecting the fullness of catholicity proper to her."[111]

Yet, though elements of catholicity are thought to exist among separated churches or communities of faith and the Catholic Church seeks unity with them so as to fully "effect" the catholicity proper to her, the Decree on Ecumenism also stated that the elements of catholicity in separated churches "derive their efficacy from the very fullness of grace and truth entrusted to the Catholic Church." It stated further that "it is through Christ's Catholic Church alone, which is the all-embracing means of salvation, that the fullness of the means of salvation can be obtained." Christ established this Catholic Church by entrusting all of the blessings of the covenant "to the apostolic college alone, of which Peter is the head."[112] Miroslav Volf responds critically to these assumptions by shifting the locus of catholicity to the local church as mediated by the congregation's differentiated but united life of faith rather than primarily by an episcopate that is tied to a particular church communion. He adds, however, that not everyone participates in the same way or with the same intensity in the mediation of faith. He refers also to the "pre-eminent place of officeholders" who have an "indispensable role" in the church. But the whole life of the church is not ordered around them. Mediating catholicity is a diversely communal action.[113] Volf helps us to arrive at a pneumatological ecclesiology that respects the freedom of the Spirit to honor the word, the sacraments, the gifts, and the mission, wherever they are practiced in genuine witness to Christ.

---

[108] Irenaeus, *Against Heresies*, III, 24, no. 1, http://www.newadvent.org/fathers/0103324.htm
[109] Cyril of Jerusalem, *Catechetical Lectures*, Lecture 18, #23, in *WCJ*, Vol. 2, 132.
[110] "Decree on Ecumenism," chap. 1, #3–4.
[111] Ibid., #4.
[112] Ibid., #3.
[113] Volf, *After Our Likeness*, 226.

In an effort, in part, to be true to his Pentecostal heritage, Volf also locates catholicity ultimately in the eschatological gathering of the people of God and their full participation at that time in the intra-Trinitarian fellowship of God.[114] It is only then that the ends of the earth will become the possession of God's anointed (Ps. 2:8; Acts 1:8). Only then will all mortality will be swallowed up in the immortal life of God (2 Cor. 5:4). Individuals and local churches will have experiences through the Spirit that are analogous to this final Catholic reality, but this reality is not realized until the eschaton. Interestingly, Catholics and Pentecostals have agreed that the church is "a sign of the eschatological unity" to which the people of God are called and functions as a "counter sign" in its divisions.[115]

The relationship of the local church to the church(es) on a global scale is part of the complexity of catholicity. If catholicity is qualitatively most essentially connected to the presence of Christ in the Spirit, then one could say that the local church experiences catholicity as they gather around the preached word and the table of the Lord, and serve one another in the love of Christ. Qualitatively speaking, the local church does not share in a "limited part" of Christ; rather, Christ himself is present by the Spirit in the fellowship of the saints around the Word of God, the sacraments, and gifted service. "For where two or three are gathered in my name, there am I with them" (Mt. 18:20). But we must be reminded of Küng's distinction, which applies to the local church as well: Christ gives himself to the local church but is not wholly contained within it.[116] The local church must be open to other churches to remain open to Christ. Quantitatively, catholicity has pointed especially to universality, to all those that have been incorporated into Christ by the Spirit in every place and even across the span of time. The breadth of catholicity requires embracing an incredibly vast diversity. Male and female, bond and free, Jew and gentile, old and young (Gal. 3:28; Acts 2:17-18), all God-given identities are granted the full dignity of embodying Christ in the Spirit in ways that are unique and valued. Any marginalization or unjust privilege undercuts catholicity and the entire church suffers loss as a result. Catholicity is open and differentiated, embracing an ever-more diverse receptivity and mediation that enhances the shared experience of God among all. It reaches for the fulfillment of the kingdom of God, and the inclusion of all of humanity in the new society brought together by the just and loving communion of saints.

## Apostolicity

Veli-Matti Kärkkäinen stated succinctly: "There can be no church without apostolic continuity."[117] The church is indeed apostolic, united by the life and mission of the original church of the apostles. The term "apostle" translates the Greek term ἀπόστολος, which means those who are *sent* as messengers or ambassadors. Christ is *the* "Apostle" of the church (Heb. 3:1), the one sent of the Father under the anointing of the Spirit

---

[114] Ibid.
[115] "Perspectives on Koinonia," #91, *GW II*, 748.
[116] Küng, *The Church*, 236.
[117] Veli-Matti Kärkkäinen, "The Apostolicity of Free Churches," *Pro Ecclesia* X, no. 4 (2001): 485 (475–86).

to redeem humanity and impart the Spirit's anointing and God's calling to them, thus opening *his* apostolicity to *them* (Jn 20:21). "Because Christ is thus 'apostled,' the church is therefore apostolic."[118] His commission and his presence are most essential to the church's ongoing apostolicity. He is thus the only foundation of the church (1 Cor. 3:11), upon which there are foundational builders—the Old Testament prophets and the New Testament apostles (Eph. 2:20). The twelve apostles were chosen by Christ as his disciples to follow him and guide others in following after him as well. Christ commissions and sends them: "Therefore go and make disciples of all nations, baptizing them in the name of the Father and of the Son and of the Holy Spirit, and teaching them to obey everything I have commanded you. And surely I am with you always, to the very end of the age" (Matt. 28:19). The setting of this text is Christ's appearance to his disciples after his resurrection. Though they had failed him initially, he stayed true to them and commissioned them as his ambassadors, sent by him as he was sent of the Father. Their commission was thus based on the good news of Christ's acceptance of them and incorporation of them into his life by grace. Christ tells them of his authority and then exercises it in commissioning them. Implicit is the fact that the disciples will fulfill their commission in service to (and in the power of) his liberating lordship. The lordship of Christ is not to be used to justify the dominance of the disciples over others, which Christ disallows: "Instead, whoever wants to become great among you must be your servant" (Mk 10:43). In service, they were to be an instrument in the Lord's incorporation of others into communion with himself and them. Christ has promised to be with them as they carry out their tasks of witnessing, teaching, and baptizing to the ends of the age. This text thus raises the issue of the continuity of apostolic mission and identity throughout the era of the church and locates its essence in the ongoing presence and activity of Christ through the Spirit.

Others were added to the twelve, such as Paul, to whom the risen Christ also appeared (1 Cor. 15:3-6). Paul ranked himself among the inner apostolic circle that was commissioned and taught directly by the risen Christ ("I did not receive it from any man, nor was I taught it; rather, I received it by revelation from Jesus Christ," Gal. 1:12). That Paul "received" what he handed down to the Corinthians as part of the deposit of faith committed to the church by Christ (1 Cor. 15:3-6) only refers to the fact that Paul did indeed visit the pillars of the church in Jerusalem to confirm his continuity with what they had also received ("I wanted to be sure I was not running and had not been running my race in vain," Gal. 2:2). To defend his gospel and its absolute authority, however, he went to great lengths to highlight his direct commissioning and instruction from Christ alone in Galatians 1 (adding in 2:6 that the Jerusalem leadership "added nothing to my message"). These original apostles were unique among the community of sent ones, because they proclaimed words inspired by the Spirit (1 Cor. 2:13). This function does not seem to have been universally shared in the churches at that time. Interestingly, some esteemed leaders do not have the title of apostle applied to them, such as Apollos (1 Cor. 3:5), Timothy (2 Cor. 1:1; Phil. 1:1; Col. 1:1; 1 Thess. 3:2; Philemon 1:1; 1 Tim. 1:2; 2 Tim. 1:2), and Titus (Titus 1:4). "Obviously in the NT period the title

---

[118] Richardson, *An Introduction to the Theology of the New Testament*, 292.

of apostle was not bestowed lightly."[119] In the *Didache*, itinerate evangelists are called apostles, but such a loose use of the title is not found in the New Testament.[120]

With the title came a unique authority. When challenged by prophets active in the churches of Corinth, Paul assumes authority over them (1 Cor. 14:37), but only in his witness to Christ, which he originally gave at Corinth "in weakness and with great fear and trembling" (1 Cor. 2:3). The words of the Corinthian prophets must be evaluated by others who are gifted with prophetic discernment and the spirits of the prophets evaluated must submit to the judgment of their peers (v. 32). By contrast, what Paul wrote is the "Lord's command." If anyone ignores this, "they will themselves be ignored" (v. 38). Not surprisingly, it was not long before Paul's writings were regarded as bearing the same authority as Israel's Scriptures (2 Pet. 3:15-16). Historically, the New Testament canon was confirmed as the privileged voice of the Spirit in the churches, because it was thought to be quintessentially apostolic, at least in its message. The foundational role played by the inner circle of the original apostles was once and for all, granting a faith "once and for all" given to the church (Jude 3). There were those appointed by the church as special ambassadors to other locations who were called "apostles" (2 Cor. 8:23), but Paul implicitly distinguishes himself from them by stressing that *his* apostolicity was not by the hands of any man but solely by Christ (Gal. 1:1). I accept Alan Richardson's conclusion that the only ones in apostolic times who were regarded as apostles "in the full and primary sense" ("apostles of Christ") were the twelve including Matthias "together with St. Paul and perhaps St. James."[121] Their time, however, has passed. "The apostles are dead; there are no new apostles. But the apostolic mission remains."[122] And so does their witness in the scriptures and the life of the church empowered by the Spirit.

What the apostles hand down to the church is their witness, which the Spirit uses to overcome evil so that the church could be a living sign and instrument of the kingdom of God breaking in to the world. Matthew tells us that the apostles will bind the evil powers and loose those who were held in their grip (Mt. 18:18-19).[123] They have with Peter the "keys" of the kingdom in their witness to Christ (Mt. 16:19), which is Peter's confession in representation of the twelve: "You are the Messiah, the Son of the living God" (v. 16). Their confession is not only with lips but with their very lives, which they will give for Christ in their faithfulness to the gospel. Paul as a sent ambassador for Christ is in chains for the sake of this gospel (Eph. 6:20). It is in this sense and this sense only that Peter with the other apostles form the rock given by Christ upon which the church is placed as living stones (1 Pet. 2:5). Christ told them, "Whoever listens to you listens to me; whoever rejects you rejects me" (Lk. 10:16) but this statement is not absolute or unqualified but rather descriptive of their role by the Spirit as witnesses. The same is true of their task in forgiving others or excluding those who are obviously not aligned with Christ (Jn 20:23). In unique leadership, they do things in which the

---

[119] Ibid., 320.
[120] Ibid.
[121] Ibid., 321.
[122] Küng, *The Church*, 355.
[123] This meaning of the terms is often overlooked. See Richard H. Hiers, "'Binding' and 'Loosing': The Matthean Authorizations," *JBL* 104, no. 2 (1984): 233–50.

whole church participates as apostolic, or as sent witnesses of Christ. The whole church is built upon the apostolic witness as living stones, a universal priesthood in God's temple offering themselves as living sacrifices and interceding for others, for the entire world. Empowered by the Spirit to bear witness, they are also a universal prophethood (Acts 2:17-18).[124] The book of Revelation stresses this identity of the church: "For it is the Spirit of prophecy who bears testimony to Jesus" (19:10). The church gathers to discern what the Spirit is saying through the word of Christ and strives together to bear witness to this in the world.

The church is all of these things (apostolic, priestly, prophetic) with the important supervision of those especially called to exercise oversight in the churches. Beyond the inner circle of apostles, the pastoral epistles make reference to ministers (bishop or ἐπίσκοπος and elder or πρεσβύτερος) who lead congregations and are "ordained" by the laying on of hands to do so (e.g., 1 Tim. 4-5). Yet, there is no indication at this early stage of a clearly defined difference between these ministries. They do exercise authority (Heb. 13:17) but submission to it is justified with reference to its benefit to the church: "Do this so that their work will be a joy, not a burden, for that would be of no benefit to you." The authority exercised by those not directly commissioned by the risen Christ seems derivative and accountable to discernment by the congregation: "Whoever has ears, let them hear what the Spirit says to the churches" (Rev. 2:11). There is no indication that their words could be ranked as Paul's were on the same level as scripture. These overseers or elders do not seem to be as foundational to the church as was the original circle of apostles mentioned earlier. This fact lends credence to the Protestant idea that the witness of the original apostolic circle lives on in the church in the canon of the New Testament, especially the gospel that speaks through its pages, rather than through living overseers (bishops) and elders. But one is not to underestimate the enduring role of pastoral authority in the church down through the ages. As Hans Küng warned, one is not to attempt "to set up a community without system or organization, characterized by arbitrariness and charismatic license."[125]

According to Luke's account, Christ said that all of his followers, which includes a community of 120, would be baptized in the Spirit (Acts 1:5) to be his witnesses to the ends of the earth (v. 8). The church was indeed guided by apostolic teaching and leadership (2:42). But there was also a sense in which the entire church was "apostolic." As the sent one of all who are sent, Christ would speak through everyone as they serve in faithfulness to him. As Acts 1:1 tells us, Luke's Gospel was only an account of what Christ "*began* to do and to teach" as though Christ continues to act and to teach centrally through those whom he sends forth in the power of the Spirit. They are commissioned to be his instruments as they bear witness to the very ends of the earth (1:8).

As a renewal movement, Pentecostals often used the term "apostolic" in order to identify themselves as faithful to the original church that was aflame with the Spirit

---

[124] Roger Stronstad, *The Prophethood of all Believers: A Study in Luke's Charismatic Theology* (Cleveland, TN: CPT Press, 2010).
[125] Küng, *The Church*, 294.

as depicted in the book of Acts and elsewhere in the pages of the New Testament.[126] They classically emphasized the fact that they seek the restoration of "apostolic faith" to the church by which they meant an understanding of the gospel that opens space for the presence of Christ through the Spirit to sanctify, empower, heal, diversify gifts, empower mission, and inspire a fervent hope for the fulfillment of the kingdom of God. The goal is to restore not only apostolic belief and practice but also apostolic experience, to return to the vibrant and transformative life of the Spirit that is evidenced in the pages of the New Testament. British Pentecostal pioneer Donald Gee wrote, "When we 'came out' for Pentecost, we came out not merely for a theory, or a doctrine: we came out for a burning, living, mighty *experience* that revolutionized our lives."[127] Like all renewal movements, whether they be monasticism, the Reformation (all wings), revivalism, or pietism, Pentecostalism viewed a rediscovery of the original witness of the Apostolic church as key to the church's renewal and continued faithfulness. In every case, something essential to the apostolic life and witness was regarded as lost and in need of recovery. The best way forward for the church was definitely viewed as a going back and rediscovering that which was lost. Rather than continuity of church office or institution, Pentecostals and other restorationist movements stressed instead a lost gospel and a lost expansiveness and vibrancy of faith. Importantly, the very fact that some aspect of apostolicity was thought to have been significantly lost and in need of recovery implies a negative view of those commissioned with the charge of oversight in the mainline churches but who were judged to have resisted the winds of change and renewal. The tendency was to highlight the ability of Christ through the outpouring of the Spirit to cause the apostolic witness of scripture to come alive again and stay alive through the diverse ministries and mission of the whole people of God. Ordained ministry was also considered as important but apostolicity could be preserved by Christ even in its neglect or absence.

There is much to discuss here in unpacking this issue of apostolicity in the context of ecumenical discussion. First, the apostolicity of the church can in fact refer to a number of essential features of the original apostolic life and witness. The World Council of Churches Faith and Order document, *Baptism, Eucharist, Ministry*, describes the church's apostolicity this way:

> Apostolic tradition in the Church means continuity in the permanent characteristics of the Church of the apostles: witness to the apostolic faith, proclamation and fresh interpretation of the Gospel, celebration of baptism and the eucharist, the transmission of ministerial responsibilities, communion in prayer, love, joy and suffering, service to the sick and the needy, unity among the local churches and sharing the gifts which the Lord has given to each.[128]

---

[126] See Kärkkäinen, "The Apostolicity of Free Churches," 475–86.
[127] Donald Gee, "Tests for 'Fuller Revelations,'" *PE* (1925), quoted in Kärkkäinen, "The Apostolicity of Free Churches," 481.
[128] "Baptism, Eucharist, Ministry," M34, *GW I*, 490–91.

The scriptures and the dogmatic milestones of tradition, especially in the ecumenical creeds, would be important to the apostolic faith of the church as well. The Reformation saw the core of this apostolic heritage as the pure proclamation of the word and the right administration of the sacraments. To be added to this is the horizon of the church's mission fueled by a yearning for the kingdom of God to come. Of interest to Pentecostals is the additional point made by the 1977 Reformed-Roman Catholic Conversation: "It is by the power of the Spirit that the Lord sustains his people in their apostolic vocation. This power manifests itself in a variety of ways which are charismata—gracious gifts of the one Spirit (1 Cor. 12:4ff). Guided by and instrumental to the work of God in this world, the church has a charismatic character."[129] Thus to speak of "apostolic succession" is to refer to the life of the entire church that is to be discerned according to different criteria: spiritual, hermeneutical, dogmatic, and practical. Veli-Matti Kärkkäinen pointed out that the diversity of elements involved in preserving the church's apostolicity opens the door for Pentecostal and other free churches to make a legitimate contribution to the question as to how this apostolicity is to be preserved throughout various times and places.[130]

Second, leadership of oversight has been a part of preserving the larger apostolic witness of the church over the centuries, but this leadership has changed over time to the point of undercutting a notion of "apostolic succession" that focuses on ordination into a fellowship of bishops that then links them in unbroken succession to the original circle of apostles. As the 1987 Anglican-Lutheran dialogue noted, the New Testament does not describe pastoral supervision as carried out by a "uniform structure of government inherited directly from or transmitted by apostles."[131] Allow me to be more specific. As noted earlier, a bishop or overseer (*episcopos*) and a presbyter or elder (*presbyteros*) were functionally equivalent in the New Testament. By the time of Ignatius of Antioch (b. 117) in the second century we find these two terms clearly distinguished as part of a threefold ministry of bishop, presbyter, and deacon, in that order. According to Ignatius, the bishop presided over a local church, especially baptism and the Lord's Supper. He was the focal point of a congregation's unity. The presbyters formed a local church council. They collaborated with the bishop in matters of policy and discipline. Deacons served the needy of the congregation. Moreover, Ignatius does not invoke the principle of apostolic succession, though mention of this can be found somewhat earlier in Clement of Rome.[132]

By the time we reach the fourth century, the common structure of oversight is further developed. The bishop was by then known to take on regional oversight, while the presbyters who earlier had no independent liturgical function now presided over local eucharistic gatherings.[133] It was tempting at this stage to read this later development back into the New Testament, especially in support of the office of the

---

[129] "The Presence of Christ in Church and World," Final Report of the Dialogue between the World Alliance of Reformed Churches and the Secretariat for Promoting Christian Unity, 1977, #94, *GW* I, 457.
[130] Kärkkänen, "The Apostolicity of Free Churches," 484–86.
[131] Anglican-Lutheran Dialogue, "Episcope," Niagra Falls, September 1987, I, #20, *GW II*, 15.
[132] Jay, *The Church*, 32–37.
[133] Anglican-Lutheran Dialogue, "Episcope," 1987, II, #51, *GW II*, 22–23.

bishop as part of an apostolic succession, reaching all the way back to the original apostles. Not only was this move anachronistic but it also leaned upon an assumption unsupported by the New Testament. There is no indication in the New Testament that the original apostles meant to establish a permanent office that would carry forth their level of authority beyond their passing. In effect, the New Testament does this, which we will discuss further in our next chapter. Suffice it to say here that the central role of scripture in the liturgy, hymns, preaching, mission, and dogmatic milestones of the church down through history is key to the church's ongoing continuity with apostolic life and faith. The scriptures are in the life of the church the privileged voice of the Spirit who inspired the apostolic witness. Ordained ministry serves this witness above all else. The bishops did indeed approve the New Testament canon and supervise the struggle that led to the ascendance of ecumenical creeds. Giving voice to an episcopal Pentecostal heritage, Dale Coulter rightly notes that enduring gifts of oversight such as the office of the bishop became prominent at the same time that the canon of scripture was formed to guide the church's charismatic mediation of Christ.[134]

But the churches that cherished episcopal succession in the early centuries went too far in the kind of authority that they claimed for their bishops, sometimes with devastating results. As Jaroslav Pelikan pointed out, due in part to the threat of Montanism, the bishops were elevated to a kind of "aristocracy of the Spirit" whose experience and ministry differed in kind and not only in degree from that of ordinary Christians.[135] Hans Küng observes that "charisms of leadership in the Pauline churches did not at all events produce a 'ruling class,' an aristocracy of those endowed with the Spirit who separated themselves from the community and rose above it in order to rule over it." He notes further that the entire New Testament avoids using secular terms of "office" for such persons, using instead "service" (διακονία).[136] This is not to say that bishops of later centuries did not serve the church at various times and places by preserving important elements of its apostolic identity. But the hierarchical ecclesiology that came from their elevation has arguably impacted the church negatively for centuries.

The more historically credible idea in support of an apostolic succession of bishops that has emerged in the ecumenical movement is based on irreversibility, namely, on the recognition that, though not traceable to the New Testament or the primitive church, the office of the bishop did arise relatively early in the providence of God to supervise the church's preservation of apostolic witness. Since this development has proved to be indispensable to that witness, as is evidenced in the approval of the New Testament canon and the formation of ecumenical creeds, it is irreversible. This development now shows us that any church without this office lacks the fullness of unity and apostolic continuity.[137] In response, Protestant churches are known for their desire to "reverse" trends or interpretations in history in order to retrieve lost elements of the universal

---

[134] Coulter, "Christ, the Spirit, and Vocation," 335 (318–39).
[135] Jaroslav Pelikan, *The Emergence of the Catholic Tradition, Vol. 1, The Christian Tradition* (Chicago: University of Chicago Press, 1971), 107.
[136] Küng, *The Church*, 187.
[137] See George Lindbeck, "The Church," in *The Church in a Postliberal Age*, ed. James J. Buckley (Grand Rapids, MI: Eerdmans, 2002), 162 (145–65).

church's apostolic witness, of which the universal priesthood of believers is such an element. Though not necessarily rejecting the special leadership of oversight and its God-ordained role in preserving elements of the church's apostolicity over time and throughout the world, they would point to the entire believing church gathered around Christ and around the scripture in such a preservation. Though ordained clergy lead in the hearing of the word, this hearing belongs to all of the people of God. This is an idea that has indeed gained broad ecumenical support.[138] But Protestants typically use this insight to reject the notion sometimes added to it, namely, that the ministry of the clergy "is not an extension of the common Christian priesthood but belongs to another realm of the gifts of the Spirit."[139] Rather, the Protestant tendency would be to say that the ordained ministry belongs to the priesthood of all believers but *functions* in ways that place them in leadership within it. Placing these leaders in "another realm" of spiritual gifting altogether separates them too much from the common priesthood and from accountability to it, inviting the abuses referred to earlier. Abuses of power are possible in any case (just note the power that charismatic preachers sometimes wield), but at least locating the clergy within the priesthood of all believers provides the church with a framework for resisting it.

There is no doubt that various forms of oversight have helped the church maintain some degree of apostolic witness over the centuries of the church's history—an idea that has broad ecumenical support as well. I agree, for example, with the conclusion of the 1987 Anglican-Lutheran dialogue quoted earlier: "Ministries of pastoral leadership, coordination, and oversight have continuously been part of the church's witness to the gospel. Indeed, we may say that the witness of the church required the coherence of its witness in every aspect of its life and that this coherence required supervision."[140] Such supervision was certainly not only a sociological development with a pragmatic purpose but also the Lord's will for the church to be realized with all of its imperfection through the gifting work of the Spirit as poured forth from Christ (Eph. 4:7-8). Ordained ministry and church order can take on different forms (as it does in the New Testament). The historic episcopate cherished in churches with ancient roots can be respected not only for the role that it has played in preserving the apostolic faith but also for their symbolic or sign value, standing for a faith that is meant to endure over time and find expression everywhere. Other forms of ordained ministry in other churches (including free churches), however, should also be respected as well for their work in preserving and especially renewing the substance of that sign. What I reject is the judgment that churches lack the fullness of unity or apostolicity without such a bishop.

Third, the emphasis of ecumenical discussion today has directed attention especially to the faith at the core of an apostolicity that the entire church joins in preserving. Both sides of the 1987 Anglican-Lutheran dialogue agreed concerning the office of bishop: "Oversight is never to be viewed apart from the continuity of apostolic faith.

---

[138] For example, note this insight from the Anglican-Roman Catholic "Venice Statement": "The perception of God's will for his church does not belong only to the ordained clergy but is shared by all its members." "Authority in the Church," Venice Statement, 1976, #6, in *GW I*, 91.

[139] The Anglican-Roman Catholic Conversation, "Canterbury Statement," 1973, #13, in *GW I*, 82.

[140] Anglican-Lutheran Dialogue, "Episcope," 1987, I, #20, *GW II*, 15.

The fact of bishops does not by itself guarantee the continuity of apostolic faith. A material rupture in the succession of presiding ministers does not in itself guarantee a loss of continuity in apostolic faith."[141] It is important to note in this context that the Reformers did not necessarily deny the ecclesiality of the Catholic Church (that the Catholic Church was still in essence a church), though they felt compelled because of resistance to reform by the pope and key bishops to shift the focus of continuity of apostolic faith from episcopal succession to the pure preaching of the gospel and the right observance of the sacraments in the hands of the entire people of God. The entire people of God is charged to preserve these things, though the supervision of the ministry of oversight is certainly important. The Reformers then established their own forms of oversight that they considered more effective in preserving the original faith of the apostles as mediated in word and sacrament.[142] In dialogue with Catholics, Pentecostals sided with this break by the Reformers with the historic episcopacy, to which the Catholic team responded that the necessary role of the bishops in presiding over word and sacrament is not nullified by their personal failures.[143] But what if the failure is judged to be systemic and related to the eclipsing of the gospel? Must there not be a fracture in the church to preserve that which must hold us together? It's a tough question to answer, but one which I believe the Reformation answered rightly.

Lutherans in ecumenical discussion today admit to seeing the hand of the Spirit in the positive role that the historic episcopate played in preserving valuable elements of the apostolic faith but stop short of elevating that episcopate to the level of the means of salvation established by Christ in word and sacrament, which are alone "unconditionally necessary" for salvation and for the church.[144] Justification by grace through faith implies that only the word of the gospel in proclamation and sacrament (or Christ's active presence through these principle means) is essential to the church. As Miroslav Volf maintained, the bishop is for the good of the church (*bene esse*) but is not absolutely essential (*esse*) to the church.[145]

The Catholic response to this Protestant challenge has been to note that ordination is not just a gift but also a sacrament and is thus essential to the church. Yet, the bishop is not essential to individual salvation. Though the ordained ministry is necessary to mediate word and sacrament, only the latter is necessary to individual salvation, which is why Catholics can affirm the presence of salvation in other communions outside of the Catholic Church. The Catholic side of the dialogue can in this light affirm concerning the office of the bishop: "Because of such a differentiation it is possible for Catholics to assert the necessity of this office without thereby contradicting the doctrine of justification."[146] However, does not the necessary role of the bishop in presiding over word and sacrament imply for Catholics that something is lacking within the means of salvation if a church has broken communion with the bishops of the Catholic Church?

---

[141] Anglican-Lutheran Dialogue, "Episcope," 1986, I, #54, *GW II*, 23.
[142] Wainwright, *Doxology*, 124, 137.
[143] "Final Report," 1977–82, #90–91, *GW II*, 733.
[144] See the final report of the Lutheran-Roman Catholic dialogue, "Church and Justification," Wurzburg, Germany, September 11, 1993, #192, *GW II*, 531.
[145] Volf, *After Our Image*, 152.
[146] Lutheran-Roman Catholic dialogue, *Church and Justification*, #201–202, *GW II*, 532–33.

Indeed, by regarding the Lutheran eucharist as not preserving "the total reality of the eucharistic mystery" because the Lutheran churches lack continuity with the Catholic sacrament of orders, do not Catholics still make the historic episcopate honored by Catholics "indirectly" necessary for salvation? Lutherans thus add that it is important for Catholics to recognize "the saving presence of the Lord in a eucharist celebrated by Lutherans."[147] Only in this way can the doctrine of justification not be at stake in the debate over ordination as a sacrament. And so the conversation continues.

In my view, the Lutherans have the stronger argument in this conversation. The ordained ministry, along with all of the gifted ministries of the church, is to be subordinated to the gospel as it comes to us from Christ and in the Spirit. We should not forget the judgment of John Wesley that the end of all ecclesiastical order "is to bring souls from the power of Satan to God, and to build them up in his fear and love."[148] Behind this gospel that comes to us in word and sacrament is the presence of the living Lord in the Spirit among and through us. As *Baptism, Eucharist, Ministry* points out, "The same Lord who sent the apostles continues to be present in the church. The Spirit keeps the church in the apostolic tradition until the fulfillment of history in the kingdom of God."[149] If the church as guided by its leadership lives from this Spirit and is faithful in doctrine, ministry, and mission, the apostolic tradition will remain and flourish. Christ promised it: "And surely I am with you always, to the very end of the age" (Mt. 28:20).

One last point: the Petrine (or papal) Office is a particularly difficult barrier for Protestants. Catholics have classically based this office on Christ's granting Peter the keys of the kingdom and calling him the "rock" upon which Christ will build his church (Mt. 16:13-20). As we noted earlier, this rock is arguably Peter as confessing and embodying his witness to Jesus, a role shared by all of the apostles and, more expansively, the entire body of Christ. Yet, Peter in Matthew 16 still seems to represent something necessary to the whole church. This point is not to be underestimated. Peter does join James and John in occupying a place of honor in the Gospels (e.g., Mk 5:37; 9:2; 13:3; 14:33). Peter is the one who preaches to Jews from all nations on the occasion of the church's birth (Acts 2:14-41), and he plays a central role in the first half of Acts, even representing the first bridge to the Gentiles (ch. 10). Moreover, Paul lists Peter first and foremost when reciting the church's confession of the gospel ("and that he appeared to Cephas, and then to the Twelve," 1 Cor. 15:5). The earliest Gospel has the angel tell the women at the tomb to "go, tell his disciples and Peter" as if he stands out (Mk 16:7). And Jesus in meeting with his disciples after his resurrection singles out Peter to shepherd the flock (Jn 21:15-19).

Yet, how far can one take such things? Paul is concerned to confirm his continuity with the pillars of the Jerusalem Church of which Peter is prominent (Gal. 2:2), but Paul seems not to yield to them any superiority of position over him: "As for those who were held in high esteem—whatever they were makes no difference to me; God does not show favoritism—they added nothing to my message" (v. 6). In fact, he confines Peter's

---

[147] Ibid., #203, *GW II*, 533.
[148] Letter of 25th of June 1746 to John Smith, *WJW*, 81.
[149] "Baptism, Eucharist, Ministry," M34, *GW I*, 490-91.

ministry to the Jews and carves out his domain as the gentile churches (v. 7). At the Jerusalem Council in Acts 15, Peter is one of the major voices but does not preside over the others in any clearly definable way. So, Peter does exercise significant leadership in the early church but not nearly on the level that would come to be attributed to the pope in the Catholic Church, where he is regarded as the universal vicar of Christ on earth, having been granted from Christ juridical authority over the entire church. Even if one allows for legitimate development of truth, this much development radically calls into question its biblical basis.

In current ecumenical discussion, the office of the pope has shifted in emphasis from juridical authority to collegial service. With the work of Walter Kasper as his inspiration, Kilian McDonnell maintains that the early language granting the bishop of Rome primacy in the church is sacramental rather than juridical. The pope is to be an effective sign of the presence of Christ in the church to preserve the church's marks. "Even in Vatican I there are echoes of this terminology," he argues, while admitting that "it must be further unfolded." He concludes, "When this is done then the primacy would appear as a quasi-sacramental effective sign of unity, as a living personal organ and instrument of Christ and of the unity bestowing presence of the Lord, which can always again become an event."[150] The pope's office is sacramental as the sign of unity to which the church does not give rise and over which it cannot legislate. According to Kasper, the Second Vatican Council developed further the collegiality of the pope with the other bishops (working in unison with them). McDonnell elaborates: "On the basis of the sacramental character of ordination the bishop acts 'in the person of Christ' (*in persona Christi*). The bishops are 'vicars and legates of Christ' and are not 'vicars of the Roman Pontiff,' having their own proper fullness of power (potestas propria, LG no. 27)."[151] Though the bishops' representation of Christ must be exercised collegially in unison with the pope and other bishops, "they exercise it in their own right, on the basis of their own responsibility."[152] So apostolic succession is not narrowly focused on the pope in the succession of Peter. "Rather it is the college of apostles which is the successor to the college of the apostles."[153]

The emphasis of the Second Vatican Council on collegiality according to Kasper (as summarized approvingly by McDonnell) comes also with an equally new emphasis on the pastoral nature of the pope's role. McDonnell explains:

> The bishop's office is properly a ministry, and more specifically, the ministry of a shepherd (LG no. 18 f.), and the bishop must model himself on the image of the Good Shepherd (John 10:1-39), leading his sheep into good pastures, keeping them together, and guiding them in the paths of the gospel. This the bishop does by his threefold office of proclamation, sanctification, and leadership (LG no. 24).[154]

---

[150] Kilian McDonnell, "Walter Kasper on the Theology and the Praxis of the Bishop's Office," *TS* 63 (2002): 715 (711–29).
[151] Ibid., 721; The LG in parentheses refers to Lumen Gentium, the dogmatic constitution on the church from the Second Vatican Council.
[152] Ibid.
[153] Ibid., 718.
[154] Ibid., 717.

We can add that John Paul II's encyclical, *Ut Unum Sint* (1995), additionally highlights the weakness and servanthood of the pope. The pope John Paul II presents himself there as the servant of all of the churches, striving in weakness for the full communion of all of Christ's disciples. As Jesus prayed that Peter not ultimately fail but after turning uplift his brothers (Lk. 22:32), so also the pope John Paul II sought prayer for his own constant conversion to Christ that he might help to unify the people of God.[155]

These points help to bring Protestants to the table of dialogue concerning the Petrine Office. Some have been willing to say as a result that the Petrine Office can serve as a sign of the ministry of Christ to unify his church.[156] Peter stood in representation of the other apostles when Christ referred to him in his witness to Christ as a rock upon which others will be placed. Can the Petrine Office serve that role today? Some Lutherans have shown an openness to such a universal sign of unity but only "insofar that is subordinated to the primacy of the gospel by theological reinterpretation and practical restructuring."[157] The problem is that the Petrine Office has not always functioned in this way. Moreover, as the Pentecostal participants in the 1976 Catholic-Pentecostal dialogue noted, collegiality is undercut by this statement from *Lumen Gentium* (from the Second Vatican Council) that by virtue of his office "the Roman Pontiff has full, supreme and universal power over the Church. And he is always free to exercise this power."[158] And though the Council affirms Christ as the sole mediator of all grace in relation to the ordained ministry, one must wonder what could possibly be the intent behind the quote from Chrysostom in *Lumen Gentium* that "he who dwells in Rome knows that the people of India are his members."[159] It hardly needs to be said that the church in India are members of Christ alone! Only he is the Spirit Baptizer who incorporates others into himself. I cannot imagine any context in which that kind of blurring of the line between Christ and the pope could be anything but baffling and offensive to Protestants.

Lastly, concerning papal infallibility, a minimalist definition would note that infallibility is "not attributed to the pope nor to the teaching but rather to a particular act of teaching. It means that in speaking from his office on matters related to salvation he has been prevented by God from teaching error. It does not mean that a particular teaching has been presented in the best possible way, nor does it mean that every time he teaches he does so infallibly."[160] Even qualified in this way, the notion, as Hans Küng as shown, is problematic both as a historical thesis and as a theological presupposition.[161] The weakness under which the pope serves the church, which is so wonderfully described in *Ut Unum Sint*, belongs to all that the pope says and does,

---

[155] *Ut Unum Sint*, #4.
[156] See the World Council of Churches-Roman Catholic study, "The Church: Local and Universal: A Study Document Commissioned and Received by the Joint Working Group," #47, *GW II*, 873.
[157] Lutheran-Roman Catholic conversation, "Malta Report," 1972, #66, *GW I*, 184.
[158] *Lumen Gentium*, no. 22.
[159] Ibid., no. 13.
[160] From the Catholic side of the Methodist-Roman Catholic Dialogue, "Towards a Statement on the Church," Fourth Series, 1982–1986, Nairobi, Kenya, 1986, #71, *GW II*, 595.
[161] Hans Küng, *The Church Maintained in Truth: A Theological Meditation* (New York: Vintage Books, 1982).

indeed, to the church in general as it strives in mortal flesh to witness to Christ in the power of the Spirit. That witness is always strength revealed in weakness. Always.

## Conclusion

The Spirit-baptized church is also the pilgrim church that is on its way from the gift of being the church in the presence of the Spirit and in communion with Christ to the full visible realization of that gift at Christ's return. The way that it takes is the way of Christ, the way of the Spirit. In every model of the church, the truth is driven home that the church lives from a reality that it has not yet fully realized. As branches of Christ (who is the true vine of the Spirit), the church seeks to bear fruit worthy of that vine. The day will come at the time of its glorification when the church by grace will manifest a beauty that will be ripe and full enough to be fitting to Christ as its vine. The church as the bride and body of Christ is not yet as "mature" as its Head, not yet conformed to Christ. The day will come when it will be. The church as the temple of the Spirit is not yet conformed and yielded to its occupant, not fulfilled in its personal holiness and priestly self-offering so as to grant the glory that matches its Lord. But it will one day be so by his grace. Putting God's kingdom above all else, the church currently seeks to live faithfully from the Spirit and the promise of future fulfillment. As Jürgen Moltmann wrote, the church is "driven out beyond every historical form" while living "from the surplus of promise over its own realizations of the promise."[162]

In this time in between, the marks of the church—unity, holiness, catholicity, and apostolicity—are not yet attributes, but they will one day be such when glorified fully by Christ's Spirit. Right now, they are marks that are both a gift and a *challenge*, even a test of authenticity. The church celebrates them because they have been granted in the baptism in the Holy Spirit. But the church also uses them to test themselves. We are united invisibly in the Spirit, but the challenge is to bear visible fruit of that unity by manifesting it for all to see. We are holy by justification and sanctification in the Spirit, in union with Christ. But though grace in the Spirit is free, it is not cheap. It calls us to realize visibly our holiness more and more with both courage and hope. We are Catholic in that the church occupies an expanding diversity of people throughout time and throughout the earth. The church also journeys into Christ by grace with unimaginable depth. This Catholic reality encourages us to continue crossing boundaries to new levels of faithfulness to the kingdom, both geographically and culturally, and every other context of life. We are apostolic, grateful for the arrival of Christ as the Chief Apostle from the Father and for the gift of the Spirit that opened his apostleship to us. We are grateful for gift of the life and witness given to and through the original apostles, deposited in the church as sacred scripture, and actualized among us by the Spirit through the participation of the entire church today. We are determined to be one with this living heritage in our world in every way conceivable. Most essential to this continuity over time is Christ's promise to be with his church as they bear witness,

---

[162] Moltmann, *The Church in the Power of the Spirit*, 24.

teach, baptize, share a table, and minister through many gifts of the Spirit (among other things). Though the supervision by ordained ministries of oversight are willed by Christ and gifted by his Spirit, no single form of this ministry is dictated by scripture, and the task of apostolicity is entrusted finally into the hands of the entire people of God. It can continue, even in the temporary absence of ministerial oversight, though such oversight is certainly important to the overall history and current life of the church. Apostolicity encompasses different aspects of the church's life (spiritual, kerygmatic, doctrinal, sacramental, charismatic, missional); different church traditions with their various accents historically have something valuable to contribute to it. As for all four of the marks of the church, we are to be grateful for the role that the ancient churches have fulfilled for us all in their preservation of the scriptures and dogmatic milestones as well as their passion for the sacramental life of the church. But the evangelical and free churches, including Pentecostal churches, have something to contribute as well. I deeply appreciate what Avery Dulles has written about all of the marks of the church:

> Unity, holiness, catholicity, and apostolicity are dynamic realities that depend on the foundational work of Christ and on his continued presence and activity through the Holy Spirit. Evangelical communities that excel in love for Jesus Christ and in obedience to the Holy Spirit may be more unitive, holy, Catholic, and apostolic than highly sacramental and hierarchically organized churches in which faith and charity have become cold.[163]

---

[163] A. Dulles, "The Church as 'One, Holy, Catholic, and Apostolic,'" *ERT* 23, no. 1 (1999): 27, quoted in Kärkkäinen, "The Apostolicity of Free Churches," 486.

# 4

# The Witnessing Church

Clark Pinnock noted, "The main rationale of the church is to actualize all implications of the baptism in the Holy Spirit."[1] In the church's charismatically gifted witness, it serves by the Spirit as instruments of Jesus's Spirit-baptizing work among all flesh. In speaking of this "mediation" of the Spirit, we must recall that Jesus is in his fleshly sojourn on earth the Word of the Father for all time revealed. He is thus the Word proclaimed for all time by the Father in the Spirit. The church proclaims the gospel fundamentally by proclaiming him. In proclamation, we as the church are but instruments of his self-impartation to us, his incorporation of us into his body. In proclamation, we depend on this; we bear this burden. Also, he is in his embodied and faithful sojourn on earth the sacrament of the Spirit for all flesh. In celebrating the sacraments, we celebrate him; we as the church are but instruments of his presence and self-impartation, his deepening work as the Spirit Baptizer. The church's role as instruments of his presence and work is the main theme of this final chapter. We will begin by discussing the issue of the church's "mediation" of the Spirit (or of grace).

## The Church and Ecclesial Mediation

Recent Pentecostal scholarship has shown us that Pentecostals do indeed have a liturgical tradition of sorts, although it is not generally prescribed through written guidelines and is, therefore, more innovative than those traditions that are known to be liturgical.[2] The same can be said more or less of any family of churches that is not known to follow an established liturgy in the worship services. Walter Hollenweger has noted that Pentecostals in the global South rely heavily on music and spiritual expressions like glossolalia to establish the worship context as one in which God is present. He calls speaking in tongues the "cathedral of the poor," for them, establishing the worship environment as one in which God is present. Their "liturgy" consists of song, movement, and dance, interspersed with testimonials of God's goodness, cries for more of the Spirit in times of need, prophetic and glossolalic utterances, and

---

[1] Clark Pinnock, *Flame of Love: A Theology of the Holy Spirit* (Downers Grove, IL: InterVarsity Press, 1996), 114.
[2] This is Dan Albrecht's major thesis in, *Rites of the Spirit*. See also, Walter Hollenweger, *Pentecostalism: Origins and Developments Worldwide* (Grand Rapids, MI: Baker Academic, 2005), 269–87.

prayers for healing.³ Speaking analogically, glossolalia and other gifts, like laying on of hands for divine healing, function sacramentally or as a visible sign of invisible grace.⁴ Even the sermon tends to function more like an extended prophecy than an exegetical exposition. The aim is to open up a text for the congregation, but it is done more as an effort to open up the life in the Spirit indicated in the text than a rational exposition of the text's intellectual meaning. The entire worship service is intended as an event in the Spirit's witness to Christ, so its effectiveness is typically judged by that expectation. The chief question becomes, was the power of the Spirit's presence evident? Was Christ glorified? Were lives impacted? Though such questions can place too much emphasis on the visible effects of the Spirit's witness, not recognizing enough the Spirit's hidden work (especially in times of hardship when experiences of the Spirit are not so easy to detect), the expectation that the worship service should be all about the Spirit's impactful witness to Jesus can offset what could otherwise be a dominantly cerebral worship experience. Forms of worship like speaking in tongues tap the soul or the subconscious mind, opening worshippers to a more in-depth worship experience. Healing rituals can bring the promise of salvation more profoundly to one's embodied life. But some Pentecostals could expand beyond the cognitive even more effectively than they do. As Clark Pinnock laments,

> Iconoclasm has impoverished the life of the church, and often reduced worship to a cognitive affair. This means that the Spirit is denied certain tools for enrichment. We are impoverished when we have no place for festivals, drama, processions, banners, dance, color, movement, instruments, percussion, and incense. There are many notes on the Spirit's keyboard, which we often neglect to sound.⁵

In general, however, Pentecostals can use more attention to cognitive understanding, since that is an important aspect of the life of faith too. There is no question but that Pentecostals can gain from mainline traditions further insight into the role of scripture reading in the liturgy and scriptural exegesis in the sermon. Geoffrey Wainwright suggests that glossolalia can have a richer interpretive framework within a prescribed liturgical framework.⁶ More generally, he has made the case that doctrinal teaching in the life of the church can help guide the practice of the liturgy and join with the liturgy in shaping the vision of Christian identity or witness of a congregation. But the corrective and guiding role of biblical doctrine is only one side of the life of the church for Wainwright. There is also the role of the liturgy in granting a creative response to scriptural teaching and providing impetus for fresh insights. There is thus in the church a creative interplay of biblical teaching and worshipful responses that continue to provide the church wisdom in responding to missional experiences in the world that pose new challenges of interpretation. *Lex orandi, lex credendi* ("the rule of prayer and

---

³ Hollenweger, *Pentecostalism*, 269–87.
⁴ Frank D. Macchia, "Tongues as a Sign: Towards a Sacramental Understanding of Pentecostal Experience," *Pneuma* 15, no. 1 (1993): 61–76.
⁵ Pinnock, *Flame of Love*, 121.
⁶ Wainwright, *Doxology*, 115.

the rule of faith") in interplay![7] Worship is the place where the vision of the whole of the church's life "comes to ritual focus"[8] "and it is here that the vision has often been found to be at its most appealing."[9] Pentecostalism at its best highlights the "mediating" role of worship as an event in the Spirit's witness of Christ to the whole person, mind, body, and emotion.

The church is born from the Spirit as a communion geared to the glory of God and the accomplishment of the divine vocation in the world. The church is born of the Spirit with practices that allow it to provide the occasion in which God self-imparts and incorporates others into the divine communion of life. The church is thus born of the Spirit "suffering divine things" as Reinhard Hütter put it.[10] This statement is rhetorically effective but requires significant qualification. Hütter uses the term "suffering" to mean "bearing." And, more importantly, the church is born by the Spirit bearing *sanctified* things used by God to self-impart. The church bears the divine only in the sense that God freely dwells among us and acts through our "institutions" of proclamation, sacraments, and gifted ministries. In bearing divine things in this qualified sense, the church finds God at work through them. Indwelt by the Spirit and bearing word, sacrament, and gifted ministries, the church as a missional communion is born and thrives from Spirit baptism, for "we were all baptized by one Spirit so as to form one body . . . and we were all given the one Spirit to drink" (1 Cor. 12:13). Pinnock is right: The entire church is an event "in the history of the Spirit."[11] It is an event with practices that grant it continuity over the span of time and place, but it is still sustained as an ongoing event by Christ as its faithful source and the Spirit as its ongoing sustenance.

Simon Chan has made the point that Pentecostals tend to view Spirit baptism too individualistically, not recognizing how the practices of baptism and Lord's Supper function to provide the ritual frameworks for celebrating its reception and cultivating its ongoing reality in life.[12] The proclamation of the word brings Christ as the Word of the Father to us in and by the Spirit, and we by faith receive Christ and are baptized into his Spirit. But this act is arguably confirmed and deepened at water baptism and expanded and enriched in the breaking of bread in communion, as well as through the overall ministry of spiritual gifts and missional empowerment. Notice in 1 Cor. 12:13 how Spirit baptism opens the church to a continuous drinking of the Spirit. This drinking is not additional to Spirit baptism but is rather a deepening of it. We are evermore deeply baptized in the Spirit as we drink in the Spirit, or as we journey with the church more deeply into union with Christ through the church's core practices. The idea of "one Spirit baptism and many fillings" is too discontinuous and doesn't necessarily reflect any sense of progress or deepening. Jesus's metaphor is better: "Indeed, the water

---

[7] Ibid., 1–12, 218–86.
[8] Ibid., 8.
[9] Ibid., 7.
[10] Taken from the title of Hütter's book, *Suffering Divine Things: Theology as Church Practice* (Grand Rapids, MI: Eerdmans, 1999).
[11] Pinnock, *Flame of Love*, 113.
[12] This is Simon Chan's overall thesis in *Pentecostal Theology and the Christian Spiritual Tradition* (Eugene, OR: Wipf & Stock, 2011).

I give them will become in them a spring of water welling up to eternal life" (Jn 4:13). This welling up and overflowing to which Jesus refers is eschatological, culminating in the eternal life that is grasped together in resurrection and the ultimate communion of the saints in God. Paul refers to this eschatological goal as a being "swallowed up" in God's immortal life, of which we only currently have a foretaste in the down payment of the Spirit (2 Cor. 5:4-5). Jesus's baptism in the Spirit culminated in his resurrection, the ultimate welling up of the Spirit to life eternal in communion with the Father. Whether the metaphor is a "welling up" to overflowing or a being "swallowed up" by an ocean of life, the basic meaning is clear. Both converge within a vision of being taken up completely into the communion of divine love, either from above (swallowed up into something beyond) or from below (welling up from within). We are to be wholly permeated by the Spirit of Christ and the life of the kingdom of God. When one thinks of a Spirit "baptism" one typically thinks of a one-time event. And so it is, in a sense, for Spirit baptism is initiatory in significance. We are at the moment of faith incorporated into Christ and his body and have permanent access to the Spirit. But Spirit baptism is unlike any other "baptism" of which we can conceive, for it is *eschatological* in nature. The one-time event initiates us into a fullness that is not yet! The texts about Spirit baptism typically have the coming kingdom as their horizon (Mt. 3:2; Acts 1:1-8; 2:17-18). Its most decisive fulfillment is not *behind* us but rather *before* us, in the resurrection of the dead, the ultimate swallowing up of flesh into the sanctity, freedom, expanse, and richness of communion in the Spirit. So, though initiatory in nature, the ultimate point of initiation for Spirit baptism is the resurrection of the dead. In a sense, the entire spiritual journey of the church is an initiation into Christ's risen life (as water baptism symbolizes, Rom 6:5). God through word and sacrament "initiates" us into this more expansive eschatological initiation. We have been baptized in the Spirit, but we are also being baptized ever-more deeply in the Spirit, swallowed up in the immortal life of divine love.

Thus, we do not entirely possess the life of the Spirit in some kind of realized eschatology—a tempting thought that appeals to our inherent quest for power and influence but one that must be resisted if the church is to be the church in its subordinate and receptive mode, the mode of faith. The forms of mediation "mediate" in passive receptivity, for Christ is ultimately the only mediator whose presence and working we never cease to serve in all that we do. All that we receive in the presence of the Spirit is but the beginning of our foretaste of the Spirit's freedom and sanctity. That foretaste has other decisive breakthroughs, as we will note in our discussion later. But throughout these breakthroughs there is also a gradual growth involved. Throughout our baptism in the Spirit by the indwelling Christ, we gain the power "together with all the Lord's holy people, to grasp how wide and long and high and deep is the love of Christ" (Eph. 3:18). We are ever-more deeply filled, ever-more widely and diversely expanded, and ever-more thoroughly swallowed up in the love of God. Spirit baptism does not occur merely *within* the kerygmatic, sacramental, charismatic, and missional life of the church. Spirit baptism is the more encompassing reality. So it's the other way around. These visible practices that serve as instruments of the Spirit's work occur *within and by* that Spirit baptism. These forms mediate a life that itself gives rise to them and makes them effective. As John Webster warns concerning the church's practices as "means of grace," "Any notion of 'means' . . . has to be purged of the assumption that the mediated divine reality is itself inert or absent until 'presented' by that which mediates."[13] Rather, the life of the Spirit gives rise to the forms and sustains them as its very own avenues of flourishing. The forms mediate but are themselves mediated in the process, for they have their origin and sustenance in the very life that they serve. The Lord is encountered in the institutions of word, sacrament, and gifted ministries as a kind of mediated immediacy. Such complexity belongs to the life of the Spirit.

Thus, in speaking of the church's role in "mediating" the Spirit, we must exercise both profound gratitude and caution. These words must be ever before us: "For there is one God and one mediator between God and mankind, the man Christ Jesus" (1 Tim. 2:5). This statement is both simple and profound. Notice the emphasis on Christ's humanity in this text. The incarnation under the anointing of the Holy Spirit is the act of mediation between God and humanity for all time. Christ is for all time *the* Word or Sacrament of the Spirit (of the Father's love and of the faithful Son). The Spirit gave the Son a sanctified body for precisely this purpose ("a body you prepared for me," Heb. 10:5). Christ's faithful and exalted life served to make him the fitting Word or Sacrament of the Spirit for all flesh ("I have come to do your will, my God," v. 7). Christ's obedient submission to the baptism in fire placed God on the side of the alienated and oppressed. In the Christ event, God overcomes divine wrath (in human alienation and death) so as to reach out to humanity in mercy. God bears up under our baptism in fire so as to remove it as a barrier, creating in its place a passage to sanctified existence in the abundant outpouring of the Spirit. Sinners are forgiven and filled with the Spirit, and hope is offered in the midst of sin's oppressive consequences, everywhere life is denied or mocked. Jesus's baptism in the Spirit opens the path to the Spirit baptism of all flesh, which brings the kingdom of God to earth and creates the standard by which this victory of the Spirit over fallen flesh is spiritually discerned. Our life in the Spirit conforms to his. Christ's act of mediation means that his embodied life under the anointing of the Spirit is the one Word of the Father for all time, the one Sacrament of the Spirit to all flesh. All words and all sacramental moments in the church depend entirely on him, or function as such only because in it he comes to us and is received by faith among us so that we could commune with and in him. In this insight is contained the key to understanding the nature and purpose of the church in the world. A lack of this insight leads to the demise of the church.

In this context of Christ's sole mediatorship, we find the nature of the church as sign and instrument of Christ's role as Redeemer and Spirit Baptizer in the world. Let us unpack this a bit more. As noted earlier, the church's role in "mediation" has no autonomous significance but is entirely derivative and dependent on Christ, on the self-impartation of the Triune God in the world, for only Jesus is the incarnation of the divine Son, identifiable with the Son. Thus, only Christ's and the Spirit's self-mediation is essential to the gospel; the instrumentality of our witness is not essential to the gospel but rather merely serves it in serving by grace as the vehicle of Christ, of his Spirit. To illustrate this point, notice for example the emphasis on Christ as mediator between God and humanity in the book of Revelation. The Christ as bearer

---

[13] John Webster, *Holy Scripture: A Dogmatic Sketch* (Cambridge: Cambridge University Press, 2003), 25.

of the Spirit (symbolized by his seven eyes, which are the seven "spirits," or, better put, the sevenfold Spirit[14]) appears as slain but rises up to the throne to take the scroll from the hands of the heavenly Father, the scroll that contains the revelation of the gospel or God's victory in Christ over sin and death. Christ alone is the chief subject matter of the drama that follows the opening of the scroll in which this gospel withstands all opposition, so only he is qualified to open it so as to reveal it and to bring its victory to fulfillment.[15] This fulfillment will turn the world into the dwelling place of God (Revelation 21). By way of implication, Spirit baptism allows us to participate in the divine reign over creation, bringing the kingdom in its fullness to earth. We will be a kingdom of priests only in his kingly and high-priestly ministry. We will be a community of prophets but only in witnessing to him as the Word of the Father. He is the author and finisher of our faith (e.g., Heb. 12:2).

Baptized in the Spirit, Christ is the faithful witness for all time but his witness is integral to the drama of redemption, the living gospel that represents the very substance of the church's faith. Our witness is not integral to the Word of the Father and the witness of the Spirit in this way. The Spirit of prophecy thus "bears testimony to Jesus" and not to us. His mediation is internal or essential to the gospel, ours is external and nonessential. He brings atonement, we don't; he imparts the Spirit, we can't. As St. Augustine wrote of Christ the Spirit Baptizer, "None of his disciples ever gave the Holy Spirit; they prayed that he might come upon those on whom they laid hands." Though Jesus received the Spirit as a man, Augustine adds, "he poured it out as God."[16] The only way *to* God is *through* God. Christ's mediation is integral or essential to the divine self-giving, ours isn't. Christ's incarnation is unique in part because it identifies him with the divine Son and makes him alone essential to the impartation of the Spirit. It is thus misleading to speak of the church as the extension of the incarnation, perhaps only as analogous to it. Pinnock has it right again: "The church is an extension, not so much of the incarnation as of the anointing of Jesus. Jesus is the prototype of the church, which now receives its own baptism in the Spirit."[17] But we receive even this in and from him. There is no room for adoptionism here, since Christ imparts the Spirit he bore and, with the Spirit, his own life. "What do you have that you did not receive?" wrote Paul, adding, "And if you did receive it, why do you boast as though you did not?" (1 Cor. 4:7).

Our "mediation" is thus instrumental to Christ's and is dependent always on his own self-impartation through the Spirit. The Father saves through Jesus and the

---

[14] The "seven spirits" are the eyes of the Lamb, 5:6. These seven spirits (sevenfold Spirit) function as the Lamb's eyes in the "fullness" of discernment and witness (the number seven implies fullness in Revelation), implying a divine mode of action. This identification of the seven spirits as the Holy Spirit is taken from the fact that these spirits appear in the Triune greeting where we would expect the Holy Spirit to be referenced (1:4-5). Moreover, these spirits as the eyes of the Lamb can behold the scroll, even though the text emphatically states that no mere creature may do so (5:3). And the spirits do not worship the Lamb but as his eyes are on the receiving end of the worship from all of creation.

[15] See Richard Bauckham, "The Apocalypse as a Christian War Scroll," in *The Climax of Prophecy* (Edinburgh: T & T Clark, 2000), 210–37.

[16] St. Augustine, *De Trinitate*, 15.46.

[17] Pinnock, *Flame of Love*, 114.

witness of the Spirit but in a way that involves them both as integral and as essential to the gift of salvation itself. Thus it may also be said that in mediating salvation from the Father Jesus himself saves his people from their sins (Mt. 1:21), or in mediating the Spirit from the Father, he may himself be said to breathe forth the Spirit (Jn 20:22). And in witnessing of Christ, the Spirit may also be spoken of as the gift that wells up to eternal life conforming us to Christ (Jn 4:14). We are thus baptized in the name of the Father, the Son, and the Spirit (Mt. 28:19), because all three are essential to salvation and to its mediation in God's self-impartation and incorporation of us into communion. Only God can save (Hos. 13:4). Our mediation is not integral or essential to salvation in any of these ways. So when we say we "mediate," we do not mean the same thing as when we say Christ and the Spirit mediate. So we mislead when we speak of our mediation as a "prolongation" of theirs. These two "mediations" (theirs and ours) are not categorically the same. The church cannot be said to save from sin, give forth the Spirit, or be the fullness of life that fulfills kingdom existence. Language like this is misleading if applied to the church. But if the church has from Christ and through the Spirit the scriptures, proclamation, sacraments, gifted ministry, and mission, and if the church's shared faith is the place where these instruments become effectual *by the divine action*, "it follows that the church itself is in a derivative sense an instrument of salvation."[18] Indeed, the church "mediates" in the receptive mode of faith, dependent entirely on the divine action, for "the church receives salvation and its very being from Christ and only as recipient does it mediate salvation."[19] This means that "the church does not actualize its own existence through the sacraments"[20] but is always dependent on Christ by faith for that. We can only say that we receive actualization by faith and by grace alone. Grace alone and faith alone toward the fulfillment of perfect charity really is the message by which the church stands or falls. This is the substance of the church's witness, always pointing beyond itself to a source other than itself. The church invites only in Christ's invitation; the church witnesses only in the Spirit's witness; the church incorporates only in the embrace of the Triune God. We are instruments of Spirit baptism but only God Spirit baptizes.

The well-known adage "no salvation outside the church" (*extra ecclesiam nulla salus*) must thus be qualified. Christ needs no such qualification. He is the only path to the Father (Jn 14:6). The church is necessary to salvation not in the sense that the church saves but only in the sense that salvation involves a shared incorporation into Christ and a communal witness to the life that we have in him. When we are born again, we are born into a family. Our mission is shared; our destiny is shared as well. "There is one body and one Spirit, just as you were called to one hope when you were called; one Lord, one faith, one baptism; one God and Father of all, who is over all and through all and in all" (Eph. 4:4-6). Even if we are speaking of the invisible church beyond the

---

[18] As noted by the Lutheran team of the Lutheran-Roman Catholic Dialogue, in the "Church and Justification," Wurzburg, Germany, September 11, 1993, #126, *GW II*, 518.
[19] Ibid., #128.
[20] Ibid.

bounds of the visible church's shared fellowship salvation involves incorporation into fellowship with Christ's brothers and sisters.

All of this said, we should not underestimate the significance of the church's instrumental function as sign and instrument of the kingdom, of life in the Spirit, so as to bring the fullness of the divine presence and reign to our lives and to the world. Notice that John receives his prophetic commission from Christ to serve as his instrument in the world (Rev. 1:17; 10:1-11), overcoming evil by Christ's blood or self-sacrifice (12:11) and bearing witness in the power of the discerning or prophetic Spirit active throughout the church (e.g., 2:7). He eats the scroll which is sour in his belly but sweet to the taste, for the beauty of following Christ requires mimicking the self-sacrifice of the crucified One (10:10-11). John and his church mediate the prophetic ministry of Jesus, having the privilege of sharing in that way in Christ's ministry and calling, for it is he that is integral to the message of the scroll to which they are committed. They have the privilege of bearing witness by the Spirit and, in that witness, becoming instruments of the Spirit's own witness to Christ. The two witnesses of Revelation 11, who symbolize the prophetic church, bear witness with their very lives.[21] Upon making the ultimate sacrifice, the Spirit enters them after three-and-a-half days and they rise from the dead, being caught up to God, vindicated in the Spirit and in the favor of their Lord (11:1-12; cf., 1 Tim. 3:15). They are vindicated in the crucified and risen One (cf., Rom. 4:25). Their bout with death is overcome by the Spirit of life, their witness embodied the journey of the Spirit-baptized Christ. Their witness led to a mass conversion; they mediated grace by being the instrument of Christ's own self-giving in the world (11:13).

The larger reality encompassing the church, its life and its ministry, is the self-impartation of God toward the fulfillment of God's kingdom on earth. "We believe that the church is sent into the world as sign, instrument and foretaste of the kingdom of God."[22] This statement from the 1987 report of an Anglican-Lutheran Dialogue brings to expression an insight of vast ecumenical significance. In our previous chapter, we discussed the marks of unity, holiness, catholicity, and apostolicity. There are indeed further "marks" by which the church is constituted and serves as sign and instrument of God's self-giving and liberating reign throughout the world and at all times. The central means of the church's life in the Spirit are scripture and its proclamation, baptism, and Lord's Supper. Though led by the clergy, these means actively involve the whole people of God. The faith of the whole church is involved in the mediation of proclamation and sacrament. This wider circle of mediating grace thus also involves the church's spiritually gifted ministries and the church's mission in the world. All of these points will be explored under the section entitled Vocation.

---

[21] Richard Bauckham, "The Eschatological Earthquake," in *The Climax of Prophecy: Studies on the Book of Revelation* (Edinburgh: T & T Clark, 2000), 199–209. Bauckham argues convincingly that the two witnesses stand for the prophetic church in Revelation 11. Their attempted defeat by the beast only comes once their mission is fulfilled. Their triumph is in the power of their self-sacrificial witness, for it is their death and its vindication in resurrection that convert many.

[22] "Episcope," Niagra Falls, 1987, #67, *GW II*, 25.

# The Church and the Example of Cornelius

It would help to begin our discussion of the church's practices (or further marks) with a story drawn from Acts 10. This chapter is a pivotal point in the life and mission of the church in the narrative of Acts, for it represents the church's opening up its Spirit-baptized journey to the Gentiles. The story focuses on Peter as the first missionary to the Gentiles (the mantle that Paul would soon bear). Though not his previous practice, Peter enters the home of an uncircumcised Gentile, a God-fearing and well-respected man named Cornelius. According to the text, God had prearranged the meeting, showing Peter a vision of animals that he had considered ceremonially unclean and asking him to eat. When Peter hesitates, God tells him never to call unclean what God had cleansed (10:15). Peter is then told to go to the household of Cornelius, a man that he had considered to be ceremonially unclean. The meaning was clear: God will open the cleansing work of Christ and the Spirit to all flesh by faith alone (15:9). When Cornelius under angelic instruction sent messengers to fetch Peter, Peter accompanied them. It would later become clear that God had prepared the hearts of this gentile household and circle of friends for their ministry. While Peter was yet in the midst of proclaiming the good news of Christ to them, "the Holy Spirit came on all who heard the message" (10:44). Uncircumcised Gentiles received the Holy Spirit by faith. The meeting between Peter and Cornelius ended up bringing them into the community of faith.

To understand this pivotal event, one must go back to Acts 2, where the Spirit was poured out on the Day of Pentecost upon the original community of Jewish believers. In the light of the larger narrative of Acts, it becomes abundantly clear that the overflowing gift of the Spirit given in Acts 2 was meant to be more than a one-time event without significance for the church's ongoing life and eventual mission to the nations. The end was "delayed" in order to make space for a mission that would reach the ends of the earth (1:5-8). Other communities of faith would arise in various places, "in Jerusalem, and in all Judea and Samaria, and to the ends of the earth," for the exalted Lord is pouring out the Spirit upon all flesh, making the Christian faith a global reality (1:8; 2:17-18, 33-35). The converts in Acts 2 receive the Spirit by believing on Christ in response to the proclamation of the word. The proclamation from Peter was backed by the witness of the entire fellowship of believers who were with him, and theirs was all the more striking for it was understood in all of the major languages of the audience of Diaspora Jews who were present (2:3-12). Michael Welker provocatively referred to this tongues phenomenon as an excessive overflow of communication in the Spirit.[23] Peter's message led a chorus of voices heard in a number of different languages that spilled out beyond the pages of Israel's scripture and beyond the boundaries of the nation's history, because it was poured forth from the crucified and risen Christ, who is destined to be confessed by every tongue. Indeed, referring to the tongues event, Acts tells us that the exalted Christ himself "poured out what you now see and hear" (2:33). The original declaration of the wonders of God fulfilled in Christ was too much for one sermon to handle, too much for only one messenger! And so it will always be,

---

[23] Michael Welker, *God the Spirit* (Minneapolis, MN: Fortress Press, 2004), 264ff.

for all members of Christ's body will "speak the truth in love" (Eph. 4:15). In Acts 2, this witness rides the wave of the overflow of the Spirit to involve a rich diversity of witnesses to the "wonders of God" that include all of the tongues of the world (v. 11). The prophetic witness overflows boundaries of social privilege as well, disrespecting them, and creating a prophethood of believers. Male and female, young and old, Jew and Greek, bond and free freely participate (vv. 17-18; cf., Gal. 3:28).

The outpouring of the Spirit in Acts 2 gave rise to core practices that channel the work of the Spirit and serve a cohesive function in the ongoing life of the church throughout the world. These practices involved not only proclamation but also baptism, worship, Lord's Supper, gifted ministries, and mission. The resulting fellowship is marked by a unity among this diversity of believers, who are baptized in water as a sign and confirmation of their Spirit baptism and a foreshadow of its eschatological fulfillment (Acts 2:38). They gather to break bread together to bring their communion to fullness, and to receive the teaching of the apostles, share sustenance with the poor, and worship together (2:42-47). The Spirit continues to overflow and permeate every aspect of their life together so as to reach out beyond them unto the lives of others. They are thus driven out into the world on the tidal wave of the Spirit, for they have inherited the legacy of witness to the nations, which Jesus passed down to his followers in 1:8, and which follows a geographic path that extends from Jerusalem to the ends of the earth: "But you will receive power when the Holy Spirit has come upon you; and you shall be My witnesses both in Jerusalem, and in all Judea and Samaria, and even to the remotest part of the earth."

The original company of believers consisted of Jews from many nations. This is the beginning of the restoration of Israel about which the disciples had inquired in 1:6. But that restoration will also involve a global witness that breaks through the boundaries of Israel in ways heretofore unimaginable for many, but which have their roots in the expanding geography of witness depicted in 1:8. This journey starts with Jerusalem and proceeds outward to include the Spirit endowment of Samaritan believers in Acts 8. It reaches a decisive turning point with the Spirit reception of uncircumcised Gentiles at the household of Cornelius in Acts 10. The breakthrough depicted in Acts 10 is revealed when Cornelius's household showed signs of having received the Spirit too! But in spearheading this breakthrough, the Spirit does not leave behind the core practices involved in the original outpouring of the Spirit in Jerusalem. Peter comes to Cornelius's household on behalf of Christ but also on behalf of his church, showing a will to embrace these potential converts who stood at a cultural distance from the church of Jerusalem. As such, he also comes bearing the core practices that belong to his church as established by Christ and birthed in the presence of the Spirit. In doing this, he becomes the vessel of Christ's very presence among them.

Peter comes bearing the proclamation of the good news through which Christ will address this gentile household. Though the proclamation comes substantially through Peter's preaching, it also comes implicitly in his very presence across the gulf of Jewish bias. Peter's witness is embodied as well as spoken. It is shown in his will to embrace and his concern for their salvation. The Gentiles receive Christ by the Spirit through Peter's proclamation and personal witness. They responded favorably to the message by worshipping God with praises that include speaking in tongues (10:46), the same gift that the original company of Jewish believers practiced in 2:4. Peter is again accompanied by a shared witness in the Spirit, but the fact that they are gentile concretizes the early promise that the Spirit will empower a witness that crosses all boundaries. In addition, the privilege of the church's rite of water baptism, through which the Spirit baptism of the first participants in the life of the church was signified and confirmed, cannot now be denied to these Gentiles! "Surely no one can stand in the way of their being baptized in water" (Acts 10:47). With John's baptism of repentance for a renewed Israel in the background, this ecclesial practice of baptism now offered to Cornelius's household in Acts 10 occasions a foretaste of the eschatological Spirit for which John and the people he baptized had hoped. This life of the Spirit transforms Israel's mission so as to conform it to the broader mission of the Messiah. Christian baptism cancels the necessity of circumcision as somehow a required prerequisite to faith and makes faith in Christ itself the essential and fundamental requirement for inclusion. "The church's continuity and discontinuity with Israel is established and marked by baptism."[24]

The practice of proclamation and baptism among these gentile converts means that the inclusion of Cornelius's household by faith alone stands in visible continuity with the church that began at Pentecost. The Holy Spirit in Acts is free of human control but acts in ways that are faithful, establishing practices of enduring significance in maintaining the continuity and unity of the church as an ongoing event in the Spirit. The gentile reception of the Spirit by faith alone is confirmed as enduring, as more than a passing anomaly. Their life in the Spirit is now enduring, sustained by Christ though also constantly made real by the Spirit. The movement of the Spirit through the witness of the church was promised from the beginning as divinely ordained to reach the ends of the earth. That promise endures and continues to expand beyond all boundaries through proclamation, baptism, eucharist, ministry, and mission. Through these practices, the doors that are opened to the community of Christ by the Spirit stay open. The core practices help to preserve this openness as an enduring part of the church's life. The Spirit is committed to use them in precisely this way. The Spirit is free as well as faithful to the self-impartation of the Triune God in history. The mission eternally elected by God and announced by Christ shall come to pass in the Spirit.

But what if there are factions in the church that would ignore or even rise up to dispute this inclusion of uncircumcised Gentiles in the messianic fellowship and mission? Peter's visit to Cornelius's household was indeed controversial. It was implied at the beginning when the Spirit was foretold as poured forth upon all flesh, but was this to be done in a way that removed circumcision as a necessary precondition? The implications of the gospel itself were at stake, for it would later be revealed that God cleanses the heart by faith in Christ alone (15:9). This removal of circumcision as a precondition was controversial in part because Peter did not go there as a private individual merely to establish a sense of good will between himself and these "God fearers." He went representing Christ and therefore the community that belongs to

---

[24] Robert W. Jenson, *Systematic Theology, Vol. 2: The Works of God* (New York: Oxford University Press, 1999), 195. He notes further that the nations were discipled through proclamation and baptism, Mt. 28:19.

Christ. He came bearing the practices by which members are incorporated into this community by faith in Christ. He came on behalf of the church with the ecclesial will to embrace across the expanding diversity implied in Jesus's commission in 1:8 ("to the ends of the earth").

Members of his church thus questioned his actions (11:1-18). They understood the significance for the church in what he had done. To secure the unprecedented reach of this will to embrace as a permanent feature of the church (because it is judged to be led by God), the Jerusalem Council reached a consensus about these Gentiles that God had indeed "purified their hearts by faith" (Acts 15:9). The acceptance of uncircumcised Gentiles by faith alone may be viewed as having been "institutionalized" through Peter's opening up to them the life of the church through proclamation, baptism, and other core practices. It was also institutionalized through the subsequent approval of the Jerusalem Council of Peter's actions as led of the Spirit (Acts 15). "The Spirit opens the church's frontiers to people of whom the church itself would never have thought."[25] The Spirit provides the authoritative interpretation and confirmation of Jesus's commission to the church in Acts 1:8 through the use of core practices to embody Christ in the world in increasingly expansive and diverse ways. Christ's own life offered to the world in the Spirit is becoming more inclusive through the practices of a community dedicated to witness of Christ's offering, embodying it in speech and action wherever the Spirit leads.

The Spirit was described as willing this outcome: "It seemed good to the Holy Spirit and to us" (Acts 15:28). By the Spirit the Word of God made Christ real to them and gave rise to faith and repentance in their hearts. By the Spirit they spoke in tongues, expressing the wonders of God in the Spirit from deep within, just as the original Jewish followers of Jesus had done. Led of the Spirit they accept baptism and their union with Christ is confirmed and deepened. It seemed good to the Spirit to give rise to such practices and to use them in opening the church's witness to the world, diversifying the church in the process. What the Spirit is doing through the community of Christ draws out the implications of Jesus's redemptive work and allows for its appropriation in faith. Paul indeed wrote that the cross of Christ broke down the barrier between Jew and Gentile, making them one body (Ephesians 2). The Spirit ends up shaping the church in this cruciform way: faithful to the cross and the resurrection. In this way, the church is sanctified to progressively embody Christ in the world. Core practices are vital to the Spirit's formation of the church in history. The Spirit is not confined to them, nor are they marginal or insignificant to the Spirit's work. They appear in Acts as effective means in the hands of the Spirit, granting the Spirit's work continuity over time.

## The Church and the Word

The Word of God gives rise to the church and sustains it. I thus agree with the conclusion of the Lutheran-Roman Catholic dialogue "The Church and Justification"

---

[25] Schweizer, *Church Order in the New Testament*, 69.

concerning the nature and endurance of the church: "As a creature of the gospel and its proclamation, which is always 'external,' creative, and sustained by God's faithfulness, the church exists continuously through the ages: one holy Christian church will be and remain forever."[26] The supremacy of the Word of God and proclamation in the life and ministry of the church (including its sacramental life) is an idea that has gained ecumenical consensus. The participants of the Reformed-Roman Catholic dialogue agreed that the ministerial order of the church "manifests itself above all in the ministry of the word, i.e., in the preaching of the gospel."[27] We all have our spiritual birth from the "seed" of the Word of God. "For you have been born again, not of perishable seed, but of imperishable, through the living and enduring word of God" (1 Pet. 1:23). Such was always the case with humanity, for creation began when God spoke and the Spirit hovered (Gen. 1:1-3). Human community can only be discovered in all of its richness within what this original act of creation symbolizes. The Logos (Word) of creation is the beloved Son of God as the purpose and destiny of creation, and the *pneuma* (Spirit) is the sanctifying flame of love that represents the means toward that purposed end of filiation (sonship) and communion for humanity. Yet, bearing the Spirit as sanctified vessels could be referred to as the purpose and filiation the means. Word and Spirit are mutually defining when it comes to creation. The bottom line is: we were called forth from the emptiness and the darkness by the Word and Spirit of God for communion. This original Word of creation was more than a spoken word, it was the preincarnate Logos who is also the beloved Son of the Father (Jn 1:1-5; 18; cf., Col. 1:15; Heb. 1:3). In him was the light of all humankind, a light that overcomes the darkness (Jn 1:4-5). Our hope remains within the creative power of this Word and Spirit working cooperatively on behalf of the loving Father, who calls us to communion. Throughout redemptive history, the prophetic word spoken in time by the Spirit continued to channel that ultimate divine Word as that which makes possible the hope of God's people for eschatological salvation. The Word of the Father that mediated creation mediates new creation in the Spirit of the kingdom to come. When Israel failed God and felt the utter despair of hopelessness during years of captivity, God did not abandon them. Those dead bones will live again! God sent the prophet Ezekiel to speak forth the word of prophecy under the powerful wind of the Spirit. As a result, Israel is pictured as rising up from a valley of dry bones to live again with a renewed purpose. "I will put breath in you, and you will come to life. Then you will know that I am the LORD" (Ezek. 37:6). In picturesque fashion, God promised that Israel will be reborn through that inspired word of prophecy. The voice of the Son can be heard through all proclaimed words that are consistent with the gospel, for there is no renewing word that does not carry his own self-giving from the Father.

I thus agree wholeheartedly with the joint conclusion of the international Pentecostal-Roman Catholic dialogue: "Together we believe that our Lord Jesus Christ revealed God in a perfect way through his whole ministry, through his words and deeds, his signs and wonders, but especially through his death and glorious resurrection from

---

[26] "Church and Justification," Wurzburg, Germany, September 11, 1993, #174, *GW II*, 527.
[27] Reformed-Roman Catholic dialogue, "Towards a Common Understanding of the Church," Second Phase, 1984–1990, #134, *GW II*, 810.

the dead, and finally by sending the Spirit of truth."[28] This Word in flesh crucified and risen as the source of life is thus the good news of redemption given in the Spirit for all of creation. That outpouring is part of the gospel, for Christ came that we might have life and "and have it to the full" (Jn 10:10). The Word expressed in Christ's faithful life is vindicated and gloried so as to be embodied in the church through the outpouring of the Spirit. The glorified flesh of Jesus that mediates life abundant for all time, to all flesh. This Word is also the Sacrament of the Spirit for all flesh. "And being made perfect, he became the source of eternal salvation to all who obey him" (Heb. 5:9).

The Word of the Father that includes us in the embrace of the Triune God is essentially a person, the divine person of the Son in flesh, crucified and risen, and present as the Lord of life and the wellspring of the Spirit. This is why the Word that we receive is ultimately Christ himself: "To all who did receive *him*, to those who believed in his name, he gave the right to become children of God" (Jn 1:12). The Word that converts us is ultimately *him*. He does not just *show* the way or *speak* the truth that leads to life. He *is* the way, the truth, and the life (14:6)! The heart of the church's witness is the person of Christ, not an ideology, which is why our preaching is not propaganda but rather entry into a liberating covenant of life. Because the Word of God is a person who is declared by the Spirit finally at his resurrection as the source of new life, the church does not give rise to it, and cannot possess it. Revelation in the context of Spirit baptism is the self-impartation of the Triune God through Christ and in the Spirit for the sake of communion. So the church can never master or domesticate revelation, nor should it want to, though the temptation to do so is always present. Revelation "cannot be commodified"; it is the "uncontainable content" that "is not called forth by any reality other than itself."[29] God is committed to the proclamation of the gospel as the means of self-disclosure, but this disclosure is always given in freedom by God. And the discernment that comes as a result of that speaking must always be tested by the measure of Christ crucified and risen for the salvation of humanity. His baptism in the Spirit is the standard for interpreting our own. The church lives by the Word when it travels the path of Christ's self-giving love for others. But how often has the church tried to use the Word to justify its own self-serving understandings of God, faith, mission, or ethical values! Revelation shatters these idols and calls forth a new receptivity to God's self-giving that requires ongoing repentance and conversion. Lay aside your idols to see what God is doing.

To help the church transcend captivity to its own subjectivity, God gave the church the scriptures, the authoritative witness to Christ and his gospel. With the sanctified service of the scriptures to help us, we can indeed share Karl Barth's confidence that the Spirit has a way over time of transcending the limits of our subjective and self-serving understandings (and they are many), in order to lead us beyond ourselves to the purposes of the kingdom. For Barth, the Spirit's speaking through scripture "is objective enough to emerge victorious from all the inbreaks and outbreaks of man's

---

[28] "Perspectives on Koinonia," Report from the Third Quinquennium of the Dialogue between the Pontifical Council for Promoting Christian Unity and Some Classical Pentecostal Churches and Leaders, 1985–1989, #15, *GW II*, 737.

[29] Webster, *Holy Scripture*, 15.

subjectivity."[30] Such is the possibility of genuine repentance and faith, or *metanoia* (conversion). The possibility of true conversion is rooted in the power of the Spirit's witness to Christ in the pages of holy writ, indeed, in the very presence of Christ himself that will always be with and for the church, to the very end of time (Mt. 28:20). The presence of Christ in the Spirit gives us hope that church renewal is always possible. The biblical authors belong to us, leading the cloud of witnesses that preceded us (Heb. 12:1). In fact, they need us, for God willed that they will only partake of the new creation *with us* (Heb. 11:40). The resurrection will be the grand reunion of all of the saints (1 Thess. 4:17). But biblical authors also speak over against us too, since in their witness to Christ, the author and finisher of our faith, they urge us on to shed all hindrances in our journey toward his ultimate victory (12:1-3). They become vehicles of Christ's own address to the church. Their scripture's witness that participates in revelation for our benefit constitutes the church. By the Spirit, the church transcends and corrects itself through the voices of its canon.[31] We should encourage Pentecostal churches to include scripture reading in its services, more exegesis in its preaching and teaching, and more scripture reading and discussion in its general life. I agree with Chris Green's remark, "I suspect that for all their verve, Pentecostal services too often fail to impress upon celebrants the splendor of the gospel and the gospel's God."[32]

As the vehicle for Christ's address to his church the biblical witnesses speak with fresh relevance to every time and place. This is especially true in that their ultimate point of reference is the risen Christ and his coming kingdom. Their witness contains a powerful promise that comforts and challenges the church of all times and places. Christ thus speaks of the biblical witness in its entirety as having its *telos* or ultimate purpose and fulfillment in him. Since the fullness of Christ crucified and risen can never be fully grasped this side of eternity (for we see through a glass dimly, 1 Cor. 13:12), the biblical witness is never fully grasped in the church's hearing in history. Though anchored in Israel's hope and the story of Christ's sojourn on earth, it is fulfilled in his destiny as risen and as the source of life to all flesh. Thus, the biblical witness knows no boundaries in the power of its promise. It can never be exhausted or contained by the church's doctrinal milestones, as important as they are in the church's progress in truth. The Spirit-baptized Christ is the risen Christ, who involves but also transcends historical conceptualities or possibilities.

This eschatological fulfillment of the witness of scripture is particularly clear in the significant discourse from Christ given for us in Mt. 5:17-18:

> Do not think that I have come to abolish the Law or the Prophets; I have not come to abolish them but to fulfill them. For truly I tell you, until heaven and earth disappear, not the smallest letter, not the least stroke of a pen, will by any means disappear from the Law until everything is accomplished.

---

[30] Karl Barth, *CD*, Vol. I, Pt. 2, 534.
[31] Webster, *Holy Scripture*, 42.
[32] Green: "The Body of Christ, the Spirit of Communion," 22 (20–36).

Tellingly, though in the previous quote the law and the prophets pass away at the fulfillment of the kingdom in Christ, Christ said elsewhere that *his* words will never pass away: "Heaven and earth will pass away, but my words will never pass away" (Mt. 24:35). That in scripture most explicitly revelatory of him remains. It is as if this core represents the enduring heart of the biblical witness. All of scripture has its eschatological *telos* in him, his deeds and teaching, his gospel. Until the cause of Christ is fulfilled via the Spirit in the new creation (inaugurated at his resurrection), the witness of this biblical text will always point us to a fulfillment that is beyond our reach. It is always challenging us with a promise that we can realize in the here and now only in the form of a foretaste. We groan for the fullness of liberty to come and reach for it in faith. The biblical witness always calls us to conversion, to a journey that plunges us ever deeper into Christ, his love, his vocation, his righteousness. No one can enter the kingdom at its arrival unless their righteousness has been ignited by this hope of a fulfillment that we were never able to grasp fully. This was Jesus's perceived contrast with those Pharisees who resisted the inbreaking of God's kingdom in the world and the *metanoia* that it constantly required. Such is the meaning of 5:20: "For I tell you that unless your righteousness surpasses that of the Pharisees and the teachers of the law, you will certainly not enter the kingdom of heaven."

As an eschatological witness, the Bible is a medium that is both fixed and dynamic at the same time. As a written text, it is stable and unchanging, for it has its own history in witness to Christ apart from our own. No inflated emphasis on the significance of our corporate or contextual hearing or discernment can be allowed to eclipse the unique particularity of the Bible's own historically situated witness to Christ. There is no way of peering into the scripture's eschatological witness except through the particular lens of the scripture's own uniquely situated voices (both individually and together in chorus), within its own contexts. Yet, as we saw earlier, the Bible is sanctified ultimately to serve the Spirit's witness to the risen Christ. This fact causes the Bible's witness to transcend even its own historical contexts and literary creativity, though not in the sense that such things are stripped away and laid aside. To assume so would be docetic or a removal of the Bible's own unique "flesh" in favor of a divine voice that intrudes upon us strictly from above. The Bible's own diverse particularity as a witness (or chorus of witnesses) in time (what can be known of it) reaches for the fulfillment of history already given in the risen Christ and his impartation of the Spirit. In this reaching, the text's liberating witness to Christ and the kingdom fulfilled in him strives for expression through the weakness of its finite (time-bound) expression as a text. As Karl Barth saw so well, the goal of the interpreter (community of interpreters) is to grasp these witnesses in the particularity of their own contexts in hope for a fulfillment that can only be imagined through eyes of faith. "Is there any way of penetrating the heart of a document—of any document!—except on the assumption that its spirit will speak to our spirit through the actual written words?"[33] The Bible's speaking "spirit to spirit" is not docetic or abstract, removed from the particular context of the Bible as a written text. Rather, this "spirit to spirit" refers to the fact that the Bible at its spiritual

---

[33] Karl Barth, *The Epistles to the Romans*, trans. Edwyn C. Hoskyns (reprint: New York: Oxford University Press, 1977), 18.

core has an eschatological point of reference within its own particular origin as a text. Reading in the Spirit, that point of reference grips us. Only the voice of Christ coming through this text by the Spirit can bring this point of reference to bear on us at the core of our spiritual yearning. The particulars of the wisdom imparted will vary but the overall point of reference to the kingdom of Christ is core to them all. This is what Barth means by the spirit of the text speaking to our spirits.

As the Bible speaks with fresh relevance to all times and places, it is not Christ or his gospel that changes, but there is change and movement in our hearing by faith, as Gerhard Ebeling put it, "in the interpretation of this same Word of God in all of the heights and depths of the world and human existence."[34] And in this movement through spiritual discernment into the heights and depths of creaturely existence in the world, we can appreciate the heights and depths of the gospel of Christ itself. For as the hearing of the church's faith deepens and expands so does the church's appreciation of the liberating heights and depths of the good news which is Christ. Karl Rahner argues that revelation is once and for all (with universal and ultimate significance) given for us in the Christ event and the gospel that bears witness to it in the scriptures. Revelation is in that sense "closed." There is no possibility of going beyond that revelation or that faith once and for all given to the saints (Jude 3), for even the new creation will but more clearly and deeply disclose it. Yet, there is also a sense in which precisely this disclosure of this revelation is ongoing in the sense that it is internally received and externally embodied, "For revelation itself has a history, and necessarily so, and not just because the speaker, God, can in his freedom act historically, but because the hearer, man, is a historical being."[35] It is this distinction in revelation between given with finality and realized historically that is sometimes meant under the distinction between "revelation" (Christ and scripture) and "illumination" (postbiblical tradition). Caution must be exercised here, since this distinction is often used to defend a notion of revelation as simplistically identifiable with the propositions of the biblical text rather than at its essence with the self-disclosure of Christ in and through this text. God continues to bring the church more deeply into himself and his truth in a way that is more interpersonal, dynamic, and transformational than a mere cognitive "illumination" of a proposition. So perhaps a better distinction would be between revelation de jure or once and for all given in the gospel of Christ crucified and risen for the renewal of the world (eschatologically final) and revelation de facto or ever-more deeply and diversely mediated and experienced (which is derivative and eschatologically realized). Since the scripture's gospel is embodied in the risen Christ and the kingdom to come, it cannot be fully grasped in any single community, in any one idiom, in any one context, not even in all of them together. The life promised and called forth by this gospel can only be grasped as a foretaste in our hearing, and always in ways that carry new and deeper nuances of meaning in the context of this sinful and dying world that we inhabit.

---

[34] Gerhard Ebeling, *The Word of God and Tradition: Historical Studies Interpreting the Divisions of Christianity* (Philadelphia: Fortress Press, 1968), 31.
[35] Karl Rahner, "Considerations of the Development of Dogma," in *TI*, Vol. IV (New York: Crossroad, 1982), 8 (3–35).

The Bible is thus a vessel of clay that is sanctified to carry a treasure of glory of which it is unworthy (2 Cor. 4:7). The Bible's witness is strength revealed in weakness too. Hebrews 1 notes that God spoke through our ancestors "in various times and in various ways" but in these latter days through a Son whom the Father appointed heir of all things (vv. 1-2). In the exalted Son alone do we find "the radiance of God's glory and the exact representation of his being" (v. 3). The ancestors of holy writ pointed to this glory but only Christ contains it. That glory shines through the text "whenever Moses is read" when those in their reading "turn to the Lord": "Even to this day when Moses is read, a veil covers their hearts. ¹⁶ But whenever anyone turns to the Lord, the veil is taken away" (2 Cor. 3:15-16). That glory begins to shine forth from us to one another (the beauty of a life given over to the love of Christ) as we are transformed in the text's hearing "from glory to glory" from the Spirit (v. 18). But both the text and we are weak vessels of this glory. Only at the resurrection will our glory mirror Christ's; only then will these vessels be fitting bearers of the glory they bear.

Indeed, the ministries of word and sacrament in the church may be said to convey a taste of the power and beauty of the coming age (Heb. 6:5). This is why we cannot do without the canonical voices of our ancestors in the faith; we cannot decide to replace them with something that we consider more adequate. For this text is "God breathed" in origin and functions to make us as the church wise unto salvation through faith in Christ (2 Tim. 3:16). This text is a reliable witness (2 Pet. 1:19) useful "for teaching, rebuking, correcting and training in righteousness, so that the servant of God may be thoroughly equipped for every good work" (2 Tim. 3:16-17). Any attempt to flee the Bible's weakness as a finite text will cast us headlong into our own more serious weakness, the chief of which would be rooted in a desire to detach ourselves from that cloud of witnesses who speak to us from the foundational history of salvation surrounding Christ's appearance in time to save us.

We cannot do without these foundational witnesses for they were elected from among us to guide us on Christ's behalf. The apostolic proclamation of Christ that dominated the years of the church's existence prior to the writing of Paul's letters guided a much larger witness in the churches. Paul notes that all members of the church in their own way spoke the truth of Christ in love (Eph. 4:15). Before these New Testament texts ever emerged and were accepted as sanctified writ, the message was embodied in sanctified lives. They embodied Paul's preaching in words and deeds as though they were written testimonials of his gospel: "You show that you are a letter from Christ, the result of our ministry, written not with ink but with the Spirit of the living God, not on tablets of stone but on tablets of human hearts" (2 Cor. 3:3). The proclamation of ordained ministry belonged to the larger witness of the church, but it also stood apart from it as its corrective guide, from the beginning. What better way for this proclamation to serve this function throughout the history of the church than to be committed to writing! One could argue that the role this proclamation played in the expanding church over time made the proclamation's inscripturation inevitable. Of course, there were the Jewish scriptures involved in this original proclamation. But the proclamation was still needed to complete it, which in and of itself begged for inscripturation.

This is not to say that the church would ever hand the task of witness completely over to its sacred text. Such an act would turn the church into a passive audience that hears a text read from a distance, unable to be drawn into it as a participant in the story and in the challenge to carry on the inscripturated witness in the world so as to mediate the voice of their Lord to others. I agree with James K. A. Smith that the church resisted the tendency of Judaism to view worship mainly through the lens of the synagogue practice of simply reading and hearing texts. Having texts to mediate and guide revelation is not the same as reducing revelation to texts.[36] The churches became living letters that embodied and reflected a degree of the glory that shown from the text of the old covenant (2 Corinthians 3). Moreover, a wider circle of revelation existed throughout multiple spiritual gifts by which the Spirit spoke. Prophetic voices offered words from the Lord, and the church discerned the significance of that which was said (1 Cor. 14:31-32). "What then, brothers? When you come together, each one has a hymn, a lesson, a revelation, a tongue, or an interpretation. Let all things be done for building up" (14:26). The scriptures were indeed the supreme witness and guide in discerning the voice of the Lord in the churches, functioning at times in asymmetrical relationship with the larger church (representing the church correcting itself through its sacred texts). In belonging to the larger witness of the church, however, the scriptures were also accompanied and received by the larger witness of the church. These texts mediated Christ within churches that heard from God through many different means, both spoken and lived out. No set of texts, no matter how sanctified, could contain the voice of the Spirit. The Spirit who inspired these texts was not removed and far away, only at work among an elite group of leaders and biblical authors, but rather present and active among the entire people of God, with regard to both the formation of Israel's scripture and the formation of the New Testament.

The special role of scripture in leading the church's witness was there from the beginning of its production and throughout its formation as part of that witness. The history of the canon shows that the majority of books that make up our New Testament rose to the top of the church's witness fairly early in the church's life and vocation. Luke tells us that "many have undertaken to compile a narrative of the things that have been accomplished among us" so that "it seemed good to me also, having followed all things closely for some time past, to write an orderly account for you" (Lk. 1:1-2). Luke along with the other three Gospels were not the only accounts written of Christ's teaching and deeds. But the four Gospels do emerge as dominant not long after they were written. Even before the Gospels were written, Paul's letters were in existence; they seemed to have been accepted early on as "scripture" as well (2 Pet. 3:15-16). These letters are deemed "hard to understand" (v. 16), in part, perhaps, because of their limited scope. They emphasize the apostolic proclamation of Christ crucified and risen as the source of new life, the very core of the gospel, as well as practical outcomes of its proclamation. But not much is explicitly given by Paul from the undergirding narrative of Jesus, a lack made up for by the Gospel narratives written somewhat later. Though the boundaries of the New Testament canon in the centuries leading up to the fourth century were unclear, the indisputably Pauline letters and the Gospels were nearly everywhere affirmed from the second century on, representing the backbone of the

---

[36] James K. A. Smith, "The Closing of the Book: Pentecostals, Evangelicals, and the Sacred Writings," *JPT* 11 (1997): 49–71.

new covenant scriptures to which other voices were eventually affirmed as belonging. Though "canon" as a fixed and closed set of books is a later concept in the history of the church (fourth century and beyond) an argument can be made that a "canon consciousness," or a sense that certain texts are "scripture" apart from other texts that aren't, is much earlier, even present within scripture itself.[37] With this broader definition of "canon" in mind, we can recognize a canon formation clearly evident throughout the second century, as Michael J. Kruger has convincingly shown. He disproves the idea that the decision as to which Christian books were "scriptural" prior to the fourth century was wide open, with any number of books competing for acceptance. Such was not the case. Added to this unsubstantiated assumption is sometimes the idea that Irenaeus and others imposed their selection of books on the church in the second century in order to ram through their understanding of orthodoxy. Kruger shows that there is rather broad acceptance as early as the second century for the bulk of the New Testament canon as scripture. The formation of the New Testament canon was not provoked by the narrower selection favored by the second-century heretic, Marcion. His narrower selection (consisting of Luke and a collection of Paul's writings) was but a challenge to an already-gathering consensus which was broader.[38] I agree with John Webster that the Holy Spirit was at work not only in the writing of scripture but throughout its formation and canonical acceptance in the church.[39] Tania Harris reminds us that throughout the process of the New Testament canon's formation and acceptance was a discerning church that listened to the voice of the Spirit and heard it, indeed, the very voice of Christ, in the pages of these books. That same church discerns Christ today in the Spirit when listening to the scriptures.[40] Because of this, we need to point beyond church politics to the discerning work of the Spirit when accounting for the rise of the canon. The church does not form the canon as much as receive it as a gift through their ongoing discernment, "a receptive rather than an authorizing act."[41]

The fact that Christ is the chief subject matter of all scripture means that he functions as the canon within the canon so to speak, the living measure for discerning the meaning of the gospel at the core of scripture and in every text, for every text ultimately bears this burden of serving the gospel in some sense. Christ is the Lord of all scripture, for he imparts the Spirit that gave rise to this text so that it may be sanctified to bear witness to him and to his eschatological salvation. He speaks to us through this witness. There are places in scripture where the witness to Christ may seem eclipsed and must be carefully discerned. But discerned it must, for all scripture is fulfilled in him (Mt. 5:17). Luther even went so far as to write, "And the scriptures

---

[37] I am grateful to Gerald T. Sheppard for impressing this idea on me during my seminary studies at Union Theological Seminary (New York). He was in turn inspired by Brevard Childs. See Childs, "On Reclaiming the Bible for Christian Theology," *Reclaiming the Bible for the Church*, ed. C. E. Braaten and R. W. Jenson (Grand Rapids, MI: Eerdmans, 1995), 1–17.

[38] Michael J. Kruger, *Christianity at the Crossroads: How the Second Century Shaped the Future of the Church* (Downers Grove, IL: InterVarsity Press, 2018), 202–26.

[39] Webster, *Holy Scripture*, 30.

[40] Tanya Harris, "The Impact of Pentecostal Revelatory Experiences on the Theology of Scripture," Paper presented at the 48th Annual Meeting of the Society for Pentecostal Studies, March 2019, Hyattsville, MD.

[41] Webster, *Holy Scripture*, 61–62.

must be understood for Christ, not against him. Therefore a passage of scripture must relate to him or it cannot be regarded as true scripture. If, therefore, our adversaries should use scripture against Christ, we shall use Christ against the scripture."[42] Luther's bold rhetoric has shock value that is provocative! But this statement cannot be taken to mean that we can simply disregard scriptures that present us with an interpretive challenge. As Barth pointed out concerning the scripture, "We are tied to these texts."[43] Barth elaborates: "If a biblical text in its literalness as a text does not force itself upon us, or if we have the freedom word by word to shake ourselves from it, what meaning is there in our protestation that the Bible is inspired and the Word of God?"[44] But Luther's rhetoric is still fundamentally correct. All scripture (precisely as scripture) bears the weight of witness to the crucified and risen Christ as the sole and merciful mediator of life. What they have to say to us is not to be narrowly discerned only in relation to a particular text alone (though its own unique voice is to be recognized); we are rather to discern the meaning of a text or narrative only in relation to other witnesses in the canon and, ultimately, to the good news of Christ crucified and to which all of the original witnesses ultimately point. How every text bears the burden of serving that gospel is the unavoidable horizon of all exegesis and preaching.

The scriptures in their totality are inspired to serve this gospel, to be the vehicle of Christ's own address to the church, for "all scripture is God breathed" or inspired to occasion God's address to us and to grant wisdom for the exercise of faith by way of response (2 Tim. 3:15-16). John Webster notes rightly that inspiration is meant to explain how the scriptures function as a sanctified servant to mediate Christ's own self-disclosure in the Spirit, to bring the gospel of *him* crucified and raised as the life-giver to the world. But the modernist preoccupation with the question of epistemology caused the church to separate biblical inspiration from its sanctified function and to place it instead at the very forefront of theology, as a guarantee of the Bible's truthfulness. To offer us such a guarantee, biblical inspiration is discussed as the first issue of concern at the basis of all doctrine. In the effort to secure this certainty, inspiration became a property of the text, and revelation became an object placed at our disposal rather than the free self-disclosure of God. "The inspired product is given priority over the revelatory, sanctifying and inspiring activities of the divine agent."[45] To overturn this effort to place revelation at our disposal, Webster wished to remove inspiration as a property of the biblical text, since no creaturely property can be the basis of certainty, which is the divine trustworthiness alone. In the process, Webster wished to restore the doctrine of biblical inspiration to its proper role of explaining the service of scripture in mediating revelation and guiding faith in Christ. This is not to say that the product of inspiration in the truths of the canon are not significant in explaining the canon's inspired function in mediating revelation. But inspiration does not make revelation into an object that we can possess as a guarantee of the veracity of our proclamation

---

[42] Quoted in Heinrich Ott, "Protestant Reflections on the nature of the Church," in Evin Valyi Nagy and Heinrich Ott, *Church as Dialogue* (Philadelphia: Pilgrim Press, 1969), 83.
[43] Karl Barth, *CD*, Vol. I, Pt. 2, ed., G. W. Bromiley and T. F. Torrance (Edinburgh: T & T Clark, 1978), 492.
[44] Ibid., 493.
[45] Webster, *Holy Scripture*, 33. For the broader discussion, see 30–39.

or theology. The biblical truths nestled in the canonical witness are indeed granted to the church as essential to the faith once and for all committed to the church's ongoing life (Jude 3). This truth grants our discernment of the Lord's voice wisdom. But, in the end, what do we have in possessing these truths, other than pointers that take on life and become effective only when God uses them in the freedom of the divine self-disclosure? Their function cannot be secured by any property they possess, but only by the Lord who inspired and speaks through them. We cannot commodify revelation, reduce it to a museum parchment, or rank it with mundane artifacts of human knowledge. Webster is right. Inspiration is a sanctified function serving the voice of the Lord in speaking to us in the Spirit; it is not the property of a human witness, even one sanctified for a sacred purpose. God's faithfulness to address us in the gospel is shown to us in many ways but chiefly through this canon, and it rests on God's trustworthiness alone.

Beyond the biblical canon, the church sought to remain true to the gospel through ecumenical creeds. As Pelikan wrote, "Believing and confessing, then, have always been correlatives."[46] Of course, creeds require heart commitment and living faithfulness (creeds *and* deeds). Early Pentecostals wrote of displacing "dead forms and creeds."[47] But living forms and creeds are something else. Those who emphasize personal discipleship above all else (as well they should) will have reason to be disappointed by the politics at work in the formation of the ecumenical creeds and the ways in which their conclusions were enforced. However, those creedal statements were also responsive to theological challenges potentially devastating to the faith of the church. These responses also came with courage of conviction and biblical insight. Those who place deeds over creeds need to recognize that ecumenical creeds are deeds too, helping to guide faith in a biblical direction by giving it greater cognitive or rational content.[48] As Miroslav Volf noted, "Without personal identification with Jesus Christ, cognitive specification of who he is remains empty; without cognitive specification of who Jesus Christ is, however, personal identification with him is blind."[49] The church's creeds and confessions guard the church against heresies and explain why we give the Triune God alone glory for all good things. Because of the letter produced by the Jerusalem Council, the Judaizers were not able to compromise salvation by grace through faith alone by rejecting believing Gentiles, which opened the church way beyond the bounds of Israel. The Apostles' Creed contains important phrases that resisted the heresy of the Gnostics, who were thereby hindered in their rejection of the heavenly Father, who created all things. They were also hindered in their rejection of the link between creation and redemption, opening space for an appreciation for the Spirit of life to anoint the body of Jesus in preparation for his messianic mission to suffer and die so as to bring new life to all flesh. The subordinationists were not allowed by the Council of Nicea to deny that Christ (and at Constantinople, the Spirit) was integral to the self-impartation of God

---

[46] Jaroslav Pelikan, *Credo: Historical and Theological Guide to Creeds and Confessions of Faith in the Christian Tradition* (New Haven: Yale University Press, 2003), 37.
[47] *AF*, 1, no. 1 (September 1906): 1.
[48] Ibid., 278–305 for an excellent discussion of the deeds over creeds protest in the history of the church.
[49] Volf, *After Our Likeness*, 148, quoted in Pelikan, *Credo*, 53.

to flesh (in a way that only God can be). They were prevented in denying that the true God in the Son took on flesh and suffered in the flesh for the redemption of the world. He was the mediator of a river of divine life that entered the world to turn it into the dwelling place of God. Because of the Council of Chalcedon, Nestorius was not allowed to separate the two natures in Christ (divine and human); not allowed to keep God at arms distance from Christ's journey to the cross. The divine-human Christ was one person while being truly divine and truly human without division or confusion. All that he did, he did as the God-man. I can go on, but there are dogmatic milestones in the history of the church that protect the church's worship and confession and undergird the church's understanding of the gospel. These milestones are not on the same level of authority as scripture; indeed, their expressions are open to critical discussion and improvement in the light of the primary text of the church. But their substance has withstood the test of time and have rightly been given a place of honor in the church.

There are also confessions, catechisms, theological treatises, enduring elements of the church's liturgical and vocational life that make up a rich tapestry of what may be termed "tradition." The Spirit is at work in this development to be sure. The tendency in the ecumenical movement is to see tradition as encompassing scripture as well, so that scripture is not alone in its participation in revelation. *Sola scriptura* (scripture alone as the supreme standard for discerning revelation) is not *nuda scriptura* (only scripture participates in revelation). Nor are scripture and tradition two separate sources of revelation. There is broad ecumenical consensus around the idea that scripture and tradition represent one stream of witness that participates in revelation, with scripture having primacy and the remainder of tradition serving scripture (clarifying, developing, interpreting it). Protestants rightly recognize a more critical relationship between scripture and extra-scriptural tradition than do Catholics or the Orthodox tradition, allowing for scripture to play a corrective function with regard to the tradition that exists external to it. However, this critical function of scripture in relation to tradition, which highlights the functional asymmetry between them, should not eclipse the valuable interpretive function of tradition with regard to scripture and the even more prominent continuity between them within the ongoing work of the Spirit's witness to Christ.

Prophecy is not stable or enduring in the life of the church like written tradition, so the interplay between prophetic utterances and scripture is more difficult to facilitate. It behooves leadership to be diligent in encouraging and leading congregational discernment without unduly embarrassing sincere people who may only wish to encourage or admonish a congregation. Moreover, choruses in the musical ministry of the church that tend to dominate free church worship may be catchy in their melodies and become popular, though their theological content may be questionable. Not enough critical scrutiny is applied to them, though they exercise a profound influence on the church's understanding of the gospel. Congregations need to be open to fresh input into their thinking about the gospel from such sources without abdicating their responsibility to discern in the light of scripture how and to what degree these songs can help us in giving proper glory to God.

There are those called to preach and to teach the Word of God on the level of the local church and beyond. Timothy was ordained for this purpose, though it seems that early on he lacked maturity in the use of his gift. It does not take much imagination to read between the lines of this exhortation from Paul:

> Don't let anyone look down on you because you are young, but set an example for the believers in speech, in conduct, in love, in faith and in purity. [13] Until I come, devote yourself to the public reading of Scripture, to preaching and to teaching. [14] Do not neglect your gift, which was given you through prophecy when the body of elders laid their hands on you. [15] Be diligent in these matters; give yourself wholly to them, so that everyone may see your progress. (1 Tim. 4:12-15)

Notice Timothy's youth and how his moral discipline would make up for his lack of experience and preaching skill until he has the chance to progress. Notice that those laying hands on Timothy are referred to as the "eldership" (πρεσβυτερίου), as though they represent an established ministry of leadership in the mediation of the word. But notice also that the prophetic utterance at the event seems most noteworthy as that which conveyed its particular relevance to Timothy as an event involving the Spirit. Timothy's duties revolved around the scriptures (public reading, teaching, preaching)—a skill he had obviously yet to master. He is thus told to keep at it so that people can see his "progress." Apparently, he was growing discouraged and neglecting his ministry. One sees an even more serious admonition in 2 Timothy 1, where Timothy seems in distress (v. 4) and Paul has to remind him to "fan into flame" the gift that is in him. In 3:15-17, Paul tells Timothy to recall how useful the scripture was in opening his wise path of faith to Christ and urges him to believe that the scripture is God breathed to do the same thing in the lives of others. He can rely on God to make the scripture useful for all of his tasks as a minister in the church: "for teaching, rebuking, correcting and training in righteousness" (v. 17). Timothy was to learn to lean on the God-breathed witness of scripture to Christ for his effectiveness as a minister in the church.

Indeed, though the medium of the written and preached word is weak, the Word that comes through it is strong. These external means were given to the church from Christ and by the Spirit to occasion Christ's presence to save. Christ is objectively present through these means to draw people into the embrace of the Triune God, even if the people who hear choose not to believe. The faith of the church does go into the formation of the canon and the practice of proclamation, for the church mediates Christ through such means in the receptive mode of its corporate faith. On an individual level, people present at the reading of scripture or the proclamation of the word (from the pulpit or members of the congregation) need to repent and believe to receive the word of Christ that comes through these means. Their response to this word will determine whether it grants life rather than confirms death (1 Cor. 2:16). So the word from Christ is always strong: the strong arm of the church's ministry, the sword of the Spirit (Eph. 6:17). May all in the church continue to yield to it in its ongoing life and vocation.

We are indeed weak vessels, but the Word is strong. The reality of our weakness, however, can be an ominous thought. When considering the weight of responsibility borne by preaching, there is little wonder that Paul told the Corinthians that he preached to them "in weakness and great fear and trembling" (1 Cor. 2:3), but he adds later: "Not that we are competent in ourselves to claim anything for ourselves, but our competence comes from God" (2 Cor. 3:5). He does not boast in his prophetic insight or abilities, "I will boast all the more gladly about my weaknesses, so that Christ's power may rest on me" (12:9). There are times when preachers will be overwhelmed by their personal weakness. Even when they feel they've done well, they will still breathe a prayer of repentance for presuming to adequately bear the burden of the Spirit's witness through a text. God will comfort us when facing the guilt of our weakness and will continue to feed our passion to move forward and continue sowing the seeds and watering them as a faithful farmer. The church's passion to continue will be received as a gift, one that must be fanned into flame through use, but a gift nonetheless. "For when I preach the gospel, I cannot boast, since I am compelled to preach. Woe to me if I do not preach the gospel!" (1 Cor. 9:16). This passion was like a fire in Paul's bones, the flame of divine love: "For Christ's love compels us, because we are convinced that one died for all" (2 Cor. 5:14). Every preacher is to cultivate love as the driving force of their ministry. In sermon preparation, they should labor with a text until they get the point of it down deep in their souls as something from Christ that they are eager to proclaim to their church. If the preacher does not speak from that kind of conviction, they will not inspire it in others.

Pastors will not lift themselves up as sole custodians of the word, but rather see themselves as equipping the congregation to speak the word in love to one another and to others as witnesses themselves (Eph. 4:15). Ordained ministers are to view themselves as ministers of ministers. Their congregation is not their audience but rather fellow disciples in need of training. Through sanctified embodiment, multiple giftings, and empowered witness, all mediate the truth of the gospel. All will feel the weakness of mortal flesh and all will cultivate the passion of divine love as the only motivation to continue ministering despite occasional discouragements. We all learn to boast about our weakness so that the power of God gets the credit for the fruit we bear.

## The Church and the Sacraments

The Word of God also involves the sacraments of baptism and Lord's Supper, for they convey the promise of the gospel as well. Gerhard Ebeling's description of the difference between Protestant and Catholic emphases is classic to Reformed dogmatics but requires qualification. As he puts the matter, Protestants affirm that the "the Word precedes the Sacrament, and in the Sacrament itself the Word has a determinative function." He elaborates on the Protestant position by noting that this Word comes to us concretely as "essentially the spoken word." The sacraments are included in this mediation of the Word to us but their inclusion is predicated on the assumption that they convey the proclaimed promise of the Gospel to us as well.[50] Ebeling then contrasts this position with the Catholic one that makes the decisive word as coming

---

[50] Ebeling, *The Word of God and Tradition*, 211.

to us in the sacrament. The spoken word is included as well "yet only preparatory, introductory, and following."[51] The key issue is thus whether the Word is primarily spoken in proclamation or enacted in the sacrament. I don't wish to maintain that Ebeling's distinction is no longer relevant at all, but I would only point out that ecumenical consensus has more recently sought to move beyond the difference of which he spoke. Note again the conclusion of the Lutheran-Roman Catholic dialogue report, "The Church and Justification": "As a creature of the gospel and its proclamation, which is always 'external,' creative, and sustained by God's faithfulness, the church exists continuously through the ages: one holy Christian church will be and remain forever."[52] Both sides then refer to "the proclaimed and transmitted external word of the gospel" that "mediates the abiding faithfulness of God in the midst of the history of this world."[53] They continue that "apostolic preaching which has its precipitate in the New and Old Testament canons, together with the sacraments of baptism and Lord's Supper," are "God-appointed means and signs of the continuity of the church." They are "the institutions in which God makes his creative grace and sustaining faithfulness visible and effective."[54] Such formulations agreed upon by Lutherans and Catholic participants seem to grant the canonical message and its subsequent proclamation a certain place of honor among the "institutional" means by which God conveys the divine presence and faithfulness to humanity.

This insight into the priority of the canonical and proclaimed word in the mediation of Christ in the church is important. It frees the sacraments from any notion of a mechanical or magical notion of grace automatically dispensed through ritual actions. Note what Alexander Schmemann says of the Lord's Supper, "The Eucharist is a sacrament. But he who says sacrament also gets involved in a controversy. If we speak of sacrament, where is the Word? Are we not leading ourselves into the dangers of 'sacramentalism' and 'magic'?"[55] The sacraments of baptism and eucharist are signs that are instrumental in bringing Christ to believers in a way that allows them to celebrate together that union forged by faith in Christ and to genuinely experience the gift of that life in a fresh and deeper way, baptism through confirmed initiation and Lord's Supper through an ongoing communion of life. But the core of the sacramental experience is the living Word, Christ Jesus, and his gospel or the promise of new life in him. Without that Word first received through proclamation, the sacraments are either empty rituals or, worse, magical rites that are thought to impart "grace" as a commodity or a thing to possess and distribute. As we have seen, the Bible and proclamation can also be distorted into a commodity that we possess, which is why even this basic reception of the Lord by faith needs to be carefully defined so as to avoid reducing revelation to something that we have at our disposal. But a true understanding of the self-imparting Word at the core of the biblical message proclaimed and received in faith can then set

---

[51] Ibid., 212.
[52] "Church and Justification," Wurzburg, Germany, September 11, 1993, #174, *GW II*, 527.
[53] Ibid., #175, *GW II*, 527.
[54] Ibid., #178, *GW II*, 528.
[55] Alexander Schmemann, *For the Life of the World* (New York: St. Vladimir's Seminary Press, 1973), 26.

the stage for a proper understanding of the sacrament as the sign and instrument of that same word.

But in defining revelation through proclamation in this dynamic and transformative way, are we not implying that proclamation is more than a set of ideas, that they really do serve by grace as effective "signs" of Christ presence and action among us? Are we not implying a "sacramental" function to scripture and proclamation? We are, precisely! Without this additional insight, granting proclamation the place of honor in the "institutions" of word and sacrament can make the sacraments appear as shallow symbols that merely serve as mental reminders of the propositions of biblical revelation. The depth of sacramental experience is lost. Here is where the sacramental experience that we have in baptism and Lord's Supper must also influence how we view the proclamation of Christ. Here is where we must call the proclamation of Christ (first in the scriptures and then from the scriptures) as "sacramental" in nature. The Bible and the proclamation of its message are physical signs, for speech is physical. Proclamation is a physical sign and instrument that by the Spirit brings the living Christ and his promise of life to us in a way that can be received with heart and mind and experienced in a life-transforming way. The Word that comes to us in the proclamation is not just a series of propositions, and faith is not just mental assent. A sacramental view of the Bible proclaimed delivers us from the reduction of revelation to an ideology and faith to the embrace of propaganda. So in granting primary honor to the Word proclaimed, I am not stripping the sacraments of the richness of sacramental experience; I mean to enrich our understanding of proclamation in a sacramental direction. Proclamation and sacraments are mutually illuminating.

Classically defined, a sacrament is a visible (physical) sign of an invisible grace. But much more needs to be said. In more recent Catholic theology, grace has come to be emphasized as personal, as coming to us in the self-giving presence of Christ. Edward Schillebeeckx proposed that the basis for this sacramental experience of Christ is the prior reality of Christ as the quintessential Sacrament of the Spirit to all flesh. Adam's fall gave rise to an alienation between Adam's race and the sanctifying Spirit. Humanity was created to bear the sanctifying Spirit in the image of the faithful Logos or Son of the Father. The messianic mission was to bring humanity back to that path of bearing the sanctifying Spirit toward the *telos* or the perfection of the faithful Son. By dying and rising on our behalf, Christ opened the path of communion with the heavenly Father overcoming the enmity of *pneuma* (Spirit) and *sarx* (flesh). The faithful life of Jesus is vindicated and perfected in resurrection. He shines forth the glory of the Father's transformative love in his risen body (Heb. 1:3). The Son rises from his sacrificial death on our behalf into the full sanctity, liberty, and beauty of a Spirit-transformed body that was ultimately yielded to the Father's love for humanity, which is a fitting description of Christ's risen body. It is from the sacrament of this embodied life that Christ imparts the Spirit—the flame of the Father's love, to all flesh. This is why Christ was not to impart the Spirit until he was glorified (Jn 7:39).[56] As glorified, he is the One from whose innermost being will flow rivers of living water

---

[56] E. Schillebeeckx, *Christ the Sacrament of the Encounter with God* (Kansas City, MO: Sheed and Ward, 1965), 26–27.

(Jn 7:38). Indeed, "once made perfect, he became the source of eternal salvation for all who obey him" (Heb. 5:8). Our destiny in him is to be conformed to his faithful image and to reflect the Father's glorious love as he did. We behold his glory in word and sacrament so that we may be "transformed into his image with ever-increasing glory" by the Spirit (2 Cor. 3:18). But our word and our sacrament are such only in "bearing" his presence. Our institutions of word and sacrament are nothing without him.

As sacrament of the Spirit, Jesus's embodied life is also the sacrament of the Son's personal presence. Karl Rahner notes that personhood is by nature self-expressive. All beings "necessarily 'express' themselves to attain their own nature."[57] Indeed, "a being comes to itself in its expression."[58] In a primal sense, a being is there for itself in the internal self-expression that comes with self-awareness and then freely for others in personal appearance.[59] In Rahner's Trinitarian ontology, the Father is the Father internally in self-expression through the Logos: "The Father is himself by the very fact that he opposes to himself the image which is of the same image as himself, as the person who is other than himself; and so he possesses himself."[60] Following the trajectory of Rahner's thought, we can say that the Father's inward self-expression by the Spirit in the Logos and the Logos's inward self-expression in the Spirit back to the Father is necessary to God's outward self-expression or appearance in history, which corresponds to the inward self-expression.[61] The embodied life of Jesus is the outward self-expression of the Logos, who is eternally the self-expression of the Father. As such, the outward incarnation of the Logos mediates the Logos to others in the power of the Spirit. The incarnate Word crucified and risen "is the absolute symbol of God in the world, filled as nothing else can be with what is symbolized."[62] The embodied Logos is thus the ultimate self-determination of God: "He is not merely the presence and revelation of what God is in himself. He is also the expressive presence of what—or rather who—God wished to be, in free grace, to the world, in such a way that this divine attitude, once so expressed, can never be reversed, but is and remains final and unsurpassable."[63] This direction of thought sounds Barthian, Christ the incarnate Word is God's eternal self-election or self-determination. Christ is thus of ultimate and final significance as the Sacrament or Word of God in history. I would add to this that in bearing the Spirit as the ideal Son of the Father and then opening up that life to others in the overflowing impartation of the Spirit, the Triune God is in outward expression of what God always self-determined to be. There is no way of getting behind this self-determination of God in history to something higher or going beyond this self-determination to something greater. What we behold when we see the crucified and risen Christ open up communion with the Father by bestowing the Spirit on behalf of the Father from the Sacrament of his faithful life is what God freely and

---

[57] Kark Rahner, "Theology of Symbol," *TI* (New York: Crossroad, 1982), 224.
[58] Ibid., 229.
[59] Ibid., 231.
[60] Ibid., 236.
[61] Ibid.
[62] Ibid., 237.
[63] Ibid.

eternally self-determined to be. This revelation is ultimate, final, and unsurpassable. Our sacramental life is nothing without it.

Human nature for Rahner is also created to self-impart in love. As Rahner puts it, "Man *is* insofar as he gives up himself."[64] We could add that humanity was created to bear the sanctifying Spirit so as to be the self-expression of the Logos, the self-expressive love of the Father. So in expressing himself once and for all in bodily form, the eternal Logos was revealing not only God but also true humanity.[65] I would add that humanity was created to be the bearer of the Spirit and, as such, to be in flesh the self-expression, the Word or Sacrament, of the eternal Son. In this light, the human personhood of Jesus needed the Logos to be complete, to be itself, the quintessential person for all time. Humanity was earmarked for incarnation and Spirit bearing. Our personhood is thus fulfilled only in bearing *his* Spirit and bearing witness to *him*, but only *he* is true humanity in the absolute sense of the word. He has no equals. The glory of our humanity will be nothing more than a mirror of his. The church as the sign and instrument of the new humanity requires that in our worship, proclamation, and sacraments we unite to him by faith, commune with him, and bear witness to him.

Since Jesus is the Sacrament for all time, he alone is the foundation of sacramental experience, not the church. The sacraments that constitute the church depend entirely on him, his person, his work, and his presence in the Spirit. The sacraments also depend on a faith that lives from him. Thus the faith of the church is vital to the life of the church as well. How then do our sacraments function? They function objectively in occasioning a divine presence, a divine offer of grace. These sacraments were given to us by Christ and by the Spirit for this purpose. They are a gift, and they function to occasion the gift of Christ. Thus, we do not baptize ourselves and we are not the Lord of the sacred meal, for that would be Christ. Yet, on an individual level, the sacraments as occasions of saving grace depends secondarily but still importantly on whether they are received by repentance and faith. That decision determines whether the sacrament confirms and deepens communion rather than occasions judgment (1 Cor. 11:27-32).

That visible, ritual means are used in Christ's presence in the Spirit to incorporate us into himself and to facilitate communion is not coincidental. Tom Driver argues that there is a deep-seated longing for ritual performance within human community that has deep roots in our history. It also has deep roots within the history of the people of God too. As visible and communicative beings who thrive in communion, we live by ritual practice of all sorts. One recalls the Passover meal. What more potent way for the Israelites to feel the Exodus down in their souls than to relive it by the Spirit of God through ritual practice! When John the Baptist led repentant Israelites into the Jordan, they must have seen themselves as leaving their sins behind in the water and reemerging from the Jordan as a new Israel, in memory of those who first crossed into the Promised Land in Joshua 3. The Promised Land toward which *they* turned their gaze, however, was the era of the Spirit and of the kingdom of God on earth (just as their forebearers implicitly had done, Heb. 11:16). Jesus's own baptism was necessary

---

[64] Emphasis in original, Karl Rahner, "On the Theology of the Incarnation," *TI*, Vol. IV (New York: Crossroad, 1982), 110.
[65] Ibid., 116.

to fulfill righteousness (Mt. 3:15), for in it he took his place with sinners so that at the cross he can take upon himself their debt and their suffering, not only Israel's but also those of the entire world. Since the descent of the Spirit was the key event of Christ's installation as Messiah, his baptism framed that event as one that places him at the forefront of Israel's mission to the world, one that only he as Israel's Messiah can fulfill. This mission will take him to a cross, to bear humanity's baptism in fire so that he could take them up into his baptism in the Spirit. On the eve before his crucifixion, he yearns to share Passover with them. "I have eagerly desired to eat this Passover with you before I suffer" (Lk. 22:15). At the Last Supper, he shifts the focus from the Exodus to the new Exodus and to a new covenant made possible by his self-offering (spilled blood and broken body) and resurrection. His death recalls the offering up of a sacrifice to God, but this one is empowered by the Spirit and reaches the heavenly holy of holies (Heb. 9:14, 24). It is thus the one offering that brings salvation for all time. At the Last Supper, he washed the disciples' feet to indicate that he is the servant at the meal as well as the eschatological banquet to come, a reminder so potent and so significant that it was meant to be practiced after baptism along with the Lord's Supper, which it was in the early church.[66] After his resurrection, he reveals himself to the two disciples on the road to Emmaus through the breaking open of the scriptures and the breaking open of the bread (Lk. 24:13-35). Even his pouring forth of the Spirit from the heavenly Father recalls the pouring forth of the water by the priest at the Feast of Tabernacles. Jesus is the one out of whose innermost being will flow rivers of living water (Jn 7:38) that will well up to life eternal in the resurrection of the dead (4:14). Jesus's entire messianic mission is anchored in, and carried by, ritual performance. These rituals served to seal his identity as Israel's Messiah, who, as the divine Son incarnate, bore the Spirit of renewal and took up the mantle of Israel's calling to fulfill it. He is indeed the Sacrament of the Son and of the Spirit to all flesh, but he becomes this by taking up the rituals of Israel's worship and both fulfilling and redefining them.

In fulfilling and redefining them, he changes them. John's baptism of repentance is now redefined by water baptism in the name of the Triune God that recalls the story of Jesus as sent from the Father under the baptism in the Spirit to save us. The Triune name thus indicates baptism in the Spirit in union with Christ and in communion with the heavenly Father. Baptism allows one to ritually make passage with Christ from bondage to sin and death to the liberty and sanctity of life in the Spirit, ultimately, the life of the resurrection (Rom. 6:5). Christ is present to ritually confirm Spirit baptism and incorporation into his body. Passover is transformed by the Lord's Supper, which causes the church to relive (as they first did in baptism) the new Exodus from death to life, to celebrate the new covenant through a meal. The Lord's Supper highlights remembrance of Christ, giving thanks for Jesus's self-sacrifice, communing with him, and anticipating the marriage supper of the Lamb. Linked to the resurrection (which occurred on the first day of the week, Mk. 16:9), the Lord's Supper is now practiced on the first day of the week (Sunday) rather than the last day of the week (Saturday). The point of all of this is that Jesus's identity as the Sacrament of the Spirit for all time and

---

[66] See John Christopher Thomas, *Footwashing in John 13 and the Johannine Community* (second edition; Cleveland, TN: CPT Press, 2014), 125–88.

place is realized in history within a series of ritual practices that is rich with meaning. He takes up these old rituals from Israel but as the Lord and not just as an Israelite or a man. As such, he fulfills and transforms them.

As James K. A. Smith reminds us, amid all of the frivolous and destructive rituals in society, there is a deep longing for meaningfully transformative ritual within human beings, especially rituals that locate people within a loving and just human community that grants us a new lens through which to view the meaning of our lives, indeed, of the entire world.[67] In the hands of God, rituals locate one within the history of God's faithful sojourn with God's people, especially as fulfilled by Christ and the history of the Spirit as "God with us" (Mt. 1:23). Our sacraments, as celebrations of Christ and vows of faithfulness to him, signify Christ when by the Spirit they make him present and join us to him. In Tom Driver's words, in Christ they point our gaze to the "alternate world" of the kingdom of God and inspire "imaginative visions" of life in service to this kingdom.[68] Likewise, Geoffrey Wainwright notes that through the sacraments, we "celebrate something that is humanly absurd, something that is literally unbelievable and beyond all worldly expectation," namely, the new heavens and new earth in which God dwells.[69] As Calvin tells us, "The sacraments bring with them the clearest promises and, when compared with the word, have this peculiarity that they represent promises to the life, as if painted in a picture."[70] This representation is not just cerebral but occurs in the Spirit in communion with Christ, for in the sacrament "the Spirit performs what is promised."[71] We participate by faith, or "by the energy of the Spirit."[72] Though the sacraments are mediated in the receptive mode of the church's faith, and is to be received in faith to be effective, these sacraments are objectively significant as means used by God in the divine self-impartation. They function as occasions for hearing and embracing the word of the gospel afresh. The church's faith does not rest on itself but rather on the divine self-giving.

There is no question but that water baptism is important to one's entry to union with Christ and the life of the Spirit. Baptism is a public event of celebration, confirmation, and commitment. Baptism confirms and celebrates one's initial union with Christ by faith and in the Spirit. The church witnesses and affirms the baptized person's commitment to join the elect in bearing witness to Christ. Baptism is the means by which this event can occur in the presence of witnesses representing the church (or in the presence of the entire congregation). After all, in uniting with Christ, one is also incorporated into his body. With baptisms occurring within a church's worship or missionary setting, others can join with the baptized in affirming together, "one Lord, one faith, one baptism" (Eph. 4:5). Such an event is not meant to remain hidden within the private room of one's personal piety. People do not baptize themselves. It is a public act that is done by the church as part of its larger witness to Christ and his gospel.

---

[67] See Smith, *You Are What You Love*.
[68] Tom Driver, *The Magic of Ritual: The Need for Liberating Rites that Transform Our Lives and Our Communities* (San Francisco: HarperSanFrancisco, 1991), 9.
[69] Wainwright, *Doxology*, 121.
[70] John Calvin, *ICR*, 4. 14. 1, trans. H. Beveridge (reprint; Grand Rapids, MI: Eerdmans, 1979), 491.
[71] Ibid., 4. 14. 7, 495–96.
[72] Ibid., 4. 14. 9, 497.

I do not wish to overplay the significance of the water rite to one's entry to the life of the Spirit in union with Christ. Faith is after all the one indispensable element, not water (Acts 15:9). Water and Spirit are arguably contrasted in John's announcement ("I baptize you with water, *but* he will baptize you with the Holy Spirit," Mk 1:8). It is the Spirit that brings the believer into the era of salvation and not a water rite. John's Gospel does not even mention Jesus's baptism at the Jordan when describing his anointing by the Spirit. There is no question but that the key event that installs Jesus as Messiah and signifies his election is the descent of the Spirit upon him (Jn 1:33-34). Yet, John's baptism still provides the occasion for understanding the full significance of Jesus's anointing. Jesus's anointing draws meaning in part from Israel's remnant leaving its sins in the Jordan River and looking with hope for the era of the Spirit that the Messiah will usher in, except Jesus's anointing looks even beyond nationalistic understandings of that hope to the outpouring of the Spirit upon all flesh. Moreover, Jesus's commission of his disciples at the conclusion of Matthew includes the baptism of all nations and importantly mentions the Holy Spirit within a triadic formula (Mt. 28:19). The implication is clear: The anointing of Jesus from the Father and by the Spirit at his baptism now provides the theological context for our understanding of water baptism as an ongoing institution in the life and expanding mission of the church. Baptism confirms and deepens one's entry by Christ into the life of the Spirit, the life fashioned and empowered to bear witness to Christ. It confirms and deepens our entry by the Spirit into Christ, in communion with him and in service for him. Baptism is thus important to Spirit baptism. Though Paul did not found the young church at Rome, and never visited there, he uses their baptism in chapter 6 to make a major point about their need to commit themselves to the way of discipleship, just assuming that they had practiced baptism and that it meant a lot to them. Luke also shares this assumption. What comes through loud and clear in Acts is that baptism is an important confirmation of the reception of the Spirit as an event to be witnessed to within the community of faith. Acts 2:38 is clear: "Repent and be baptized, every one of you, in the name of Jesus Christ for the forgiveness of your sins. And you will receive the gift of the Holy Spirit." The fact that this text is not crafted to give us a normative, causal pattern (repentance and baptism results in receiving the Spirit) is evident in chapter 10 when Cornelius's household receives the Spirit and speaks in tongues before they receive baptism as confirmation of their reception of the Spirit. Yet, baptism here as well is important to Spirit baptism as its cherished public confirmation: "Surely no one can stand in the way of their being baptized with water. They have received the Holy Spirit just as we have" (10:47). Baptism functions here as an important confirmation of their belonging by the Spirit to the life and vocation of Christ and his church. Of course, faith *alone* is the essential ingredient in their purification and reception of the Spirit (15:9). "We can also see from this that baptism by itself is of no value. Baptism and metanoia, baptism and faith go together."[73] But both faith and baptism are based on something deeper: "Faith and baptism do not have their basis in themselves, but alike in the saving act of God in Christ."[74] This

---

[73] Küng, *The Church*, 207.
[74] Ibid.

saving act is the referent of water baptism, and baptism confirms one's participation by faith in that act.

To assume that one is actually united to Christ and baptized in the Spirit at the moment of water baptism is simplistic. Not only is this assumption hard to justify biblically (Acts 10:47), it is not consistent with how rituals generally work. Rather than being the moment in which something spiritual or binding suddenly occurs in toto, a ritual of initiation is usually a point of culmination or confirmation of something already entered into in a less formal way. For example, when does a union of "one flesh" in marriage actually occur? Does it suddenly take place at the vows or the marriage pronouncement at their conclusion? Does it happen at the signing of the marriage license, or when the county officially records it? Or does it happen when the marriage is consummated in the sex act as some cultures have held? And what about the engagement or betrothal? In Jewish culture, the betrothal is considered to be part of the wedding, the period leading up to its culmination is then considered as a time of preparation and anticipation. Actual initiations as they are experienced are complex and take time. Rituals simplify the narrative of this lengthy experience so that it may be publicly confirmed and celebrated. A marriage ceremony takes up the entire story of the couple's entry into marital union and presents it before witnesses in one single moment so that it may be confirmed and celebrated as a public act. One caught up in the potent symbolism can meaningfully say that the couple is indeed united as one in this ceremony. And so on a symbolic level that statement would be true. They are symbolically united there in that ceremony. But we all know that the reality is more complex and involved.

So also, analogously, union with Christ and incorporation into his body by the Spirit does not simply begin at the rite of water baptism. It begins at the moment of faith in Christ in response to the gospel, and even that could be a process. The confession of him as Lord either vocally or inwardly is perhaps the first response. A time of preparation ideally occurs thereafter leading up to the ritual water of baptism in which that union is confirmed and celebrated in the embrace of the church. The baptism in the Spirit as an eschatological reality culminates in our resurrection. So the ritual of water baptism presents the entire narrative of this journey into Christ in one ritual moment: "For if we have been united with him in a death like his, we will certainly also be united with him in a resurrection like his" (Rom. 6:5). When the baptized person emerges from the water, the complex story of their initial union with Christ by the Spirit is presented by God to our senses symbolically in simplistic but potent form so as to confirm and deepen it as a public act affirmed by the communion of saints. But that ritual points ahead to an even grander fulfillment. Indicated there is incorporation into the risen body of Christ. This fulfillment overflows the ritual (as well as precedes it) accounting for its relevance throughout life. There is a reason why water baptism is practiced only once. It speaks of an incorporation into Christ that is final and eschatological in significance. To keep the marriage analogy going, our "marriage" with Christ is made official at the marriage supper of the Lamb and the resurrection. It is at the resurrection that our union with the risen Christ is fulfilled, and it is this event of which baptism symbolically grants us a confirmation and a foretaste. Our initiation into *this* union ultimately involves being swallowed up in *life* and not just water (2 Cor. 5:4)!

To shift metaphors, Paul also does not expect our adoption as God's children to occur in fullness until the resurrection: "We ourselves, who have the firstfruits of the Spirit, groan inwardly as we wait eagerly for our adoption to sonship, the redemption of our bodies" (Rom. 8:23). So baptism may be said to confirm our initial participation in the life of the Spirit, but this life is an ever-deepening journey into Christ that does not find fulfillment until the resurrection from the dead. The culmination of our union with Christ as sons and daughters of God occurs only when life overwhelms death in resurrection. It is ultimately *this* culmination that baptism celebrates! Then, we will be taken up into the fullness of Christ in his overflowing love for humanity and the fullness of his glory to the Father. So Paul reminds the Galatians that they have clothed themselves with Christ at baptism (Gal. 3:27). Yet, Paul told the Romans to clothe themselves with Christ anew (13:14). Actually, the clothing with Christ that baptism signifies continues until its fulfillment at the resurrection, when we are "clothed instead with our heavenly dwelling, so that what is mortal may be swallowed up by life" (2 Cor. 5:4). Then the life that we have received by faith will well up to eternal life (Jn 4:14). It is not that the impartation of the Spirit occurs in water baptism; it is rather the other way around. Water baptism occurs within the impartation of the Spirit as received by faith, as the confirmation of one's entry into the life of the Spirit and in anticipation of its culmination at the resurrection. The entire journey into Christ and into the depths of the Spirit of communion are signified at baptism, not fully realized there, but signified, confirmed, and celebrated there. Water baptism occurs within Spirit baptism and not the other way around.

The confirmation and celebration of incorporation into Christ by the Spirit at water baptism is indeed a spiritually significant event. The Pentecostal team of the international Pentecostal-Roman Catholic dialogue noted that without denying the salvation of the unbaptized (since salvation is by faith alone), "Pentecostals would consider baptism to be an integral part of the whole experience of becoming a Christian."[75] They then add, "Pentecostals would even speak of baptism as a 'means of grace.'"[76] And so it is. "The visible sign, like the proclaimed word, makes this saving event present for the believer."[77] Something significant happens at baptism. The meaning is not only rational but more deeply the enacted and transformative bridge-crossing experience of Christ in us and we in him by the Spirit. Christ is present to make it transformative—a confirmation and deepening that makes a difference to both the individual and the celebrating church. Sacraments "are not simply illustrations or depictions but *signs and seals* of God's promise."[78] The seal of the Spirit is indeed granted from the moment of faith: "And you also were included in Christ when you heard the message of truth, the gospel of your salvation. When you believed, you were marked in him with a seal, the promised Holy Spirit" (Eph. 1:14). The seal is symbolic in this text of a mark of belonging to Christ, like a slave branding, a dehumanizing act in the ancient world that was referred to symbolically in this text as the humanizing reality of incorporation into

---

[75] "Perspectives on Koinonia," 1985–1989, #50, GW II, 742.
[76] Ibid.
[77] Küng, *The Church*, 207.
[78] Emphasis in original, G. C. Berkouwer, *The Sacraments*, SD (Grand Rapids, MI: Eerdmans, 1969), 134.

Christ and his body. But the Spirit who seals us as belonging to Christ may in baptism be ritually confirmed and celebrated together with the church, for union with Christ is also incorporation into his body. The inward sealing becomes a public and communal act through baptism, confirming and deepening it as a bridge-crossing experience in which all take part.

Baptism occasions a deepening of the reality that it signifies sacramentally by making Christ as the promise of salvation present to be ritually embraced in faith. Yes, the believer had already done this as an individual and private act. They may have even given a public testimony of sorts. But like a wedding ceremony, ritualizing that reception of Christ and incorporation into him by the Spirit confirms, finalizes, and celebrates that reception and incorporation in a way that makes it potently real as a bridge-crossing event. The one baptized should be told that in that act they are dramatizing their initial entry into the Christ life, which will have relevance for their entire journey into Christ, including its *telos* in the resurrection of the saints. They should be prepared to hear the word of promise of Christ present in and with them until the very end and embrace him with resolve. They should be encouraged through the congregation's response to celebrate and be grateful for it. They should be prepared to feel the embrace of the Triune God that began at the very moment of faith. They should be encouraged in the baptismal liturgy itself to commit themselves to Christ's cause in the world, whatever form it may take in their lives. In the "tomb" of the baptismal water they ritually bury their old selves that were entangled in sin and death. They lay their old selves down by descending with Christ into death, into the baptism in fire. But by descending with him in the fire, they can then rise with him in the Spirit. They then rise from what is now a watery "womb" as new selves defined by Christ, by his destiny under the Father's favor and in the riches of the Spirit's fullness. They can now say with Paul, "I have been crucified with Christ and I no longer live, but Christ lives in me. The life I now live in the body, I live by faith in the Son of God, who loved me and gave himself for me" (Gal. 2:20). Though not essential to salvation, baptism is indeed spiritually enriching and significant to believers and to the church. It is the ordination service of all believers, for connected to it is a spiritual gifting for service (*diakonia*) in the ministry of the church.

I have been assuming throughout this discussion that baptism is normally to be observed as believer's baptism, or baptism exercised for those who have faith on the Lord Jesus Christ through the enablement of the Spirit. In sharing this assumption, we cannot ignore the reality of infant baptism. Luther rightly maintained that the sacraments must be received in faith to be effective. His position assumed that "faith and the word were inseparably interrelated, also in the sacraments."[79] He did not deny the objective significance of the sacraments as conveying in their own way the presence of Christ in the gospel; he merely insisted that the word is effective to save if received by faith. His acceptance of infant baptism, however, appeared to be inconsistent with this position. Pelikan rightly concludes, "Luther's position consistently carried out, would undercut the traditional doctrine and practice of the church regarding infant

---

[79] Jaroslav Pelikan's summary of Luther's view, Jaroslav Pelikan, *Spirit Versus Structure: Luther and the Institutions of the Church* (London: Collins, 1968), 79.

baptism."⁸⁰ This was a point that did not go unnoticed by the anabaptists who drew precisely this conclusion. From the Reformed side, G. C. Berkouwer admitted that, to be logical, the Reformers should have rejected infant baptism, but then he added, "The fact that they did not draw this 'logical' conclusion shows that they were more interested in being guided by the Word of God than in being logically rigorous."⁸¹ But is the biblical evidence for infant baptism so compelling as to warrant such a logical inconsistency? I hardly think so. The Catholic team of the international Pentecostal-Roman Catholic dialogue notes tellingly: "Roman Catholics admit that there is no incontrovertible evidence for baptism of infants in the New Testament." They point only to the baptism of "households" as possibly "having a reference in that direction."⁸² Similarly, the World Council of Churches Faith and Order paper, "Baptism, Eucharist, Ministry," notes, "While the possibility that infant baptism was also practiced in the apostolic age cannot be excluded, baptism upon personal profession of faith is the most clearly attested pattern in the New Testament documents."⁸³ These are hardly ringing endorsements for a compelling exegetical case for infant baptism. G. C. Berkouwer grants us a lengthy argument for the biblical assumption that baptism replaced circumcision in the New Testament, though nearly all of his energy is expended refuting the arguments leveled against using this link to justify infant baptism.⁸⁴ But this hardly establishes his case. A connection between the two is made in Col. 2:11-12:

> In him you were also circumcised with a circumcision not performed by human hands. Your whole self ruled by the flesh was put off when you were circumcised by Christ, having been buried with him in baptism, in which you were also raised with him through your faith in the working of God, who raised him from the dead.

In this light, a connection might also be hidden beneath the "circumcision of the heart" by the Holy Spirit referred to in Rom. 2:28. But in both of these texts circumcision is referred to figuratively as it was in the Old Testament when the "circumcision" of the heart by the Spirit is mentioned (e.g., Deut. 10:16), and in neither case does the context have anything to do with the applicability of baptism to children; the connection is made in the realm of faith. We have no clear indication that the New Testament suggests an application to children. Romans 4:11 defines circumcision exactly as I have defined believer's baptism, as a public sign confirming acceptance by God through faith; of Abraham it is said, "He received circumcision as a sign, a seal of the righteousness that he had by faith." Circumcision here foreshadows baptism precisely as a celebration of a right standing that Abraham had attained by personal *faith* in the promises, an atypical function for circumcision. In other words, in fulfilling circumcision, baptism arguably goes beyond its role among infants who are incapable of faith.

What about the theological arguments for infant baptism? Here is where the argument gets more interesting for me. Referring to Mt. 19:14 ("Let the children come

---

80  Ibid., 77.
81  Berkouwer, *The Sacraments*, 176.
82  "Perspectives on Koinonia," 1985–1989, #42, *GW II*, 741.
83  "Baptism, Eucharist, Ministry," B11, *GW I*, 572.
84  Berkouwer, *The Sacraments*, 166–76.

to me") and John the Baptist's filling by the Spirit in his mother's womb (Lk. 1:44), Luther argued that infants can exercise faith even though they cannot reason or speak.[85] Luther bolstered this argument by appealing to the fact that for over a thousand years infant baptism was the dominant mode of baptism for the church. It was unthinkable for Luther that the church would have lacked a legitimate baptismal rite for the vast majority of its members throughout its history. He added that the covenant of Christ applies to all who belong to the church, including children, meaning that baptism belongs to them also. So the universality of infant baptism to which tradition testified is now confirmed as theologically justified.[86] Luther considered his strongest argument for infant baptism, however, as based on the objective validity of baptism as a means of grace, even if the faith of the infant receiving it were passive and dependent entirely on grace (a commentary, he would say, on us all). He believed that the anabaptists placed too much emphasis on the role of faith in establishing the efficacy of the sacraments. Luther wished instead to stress the power of the Word of God as compensating for the weakness of human faith. In fact, it is for this reason that Luther considered baptism to be the chief of the sacraments, for, with an infant at the receiving end, the effectiveness of baptism is overwhelmingly based on the strength of the word. In times of trial and doubt we can thus exclaim, "Baptisatus sum!" ("I have been baptized!").[87] Reformed theologian G. C. Berkouwer agrees: "This grace precedes all human activity, and one can certainly see in infant baptism that the covenant is not a matter of God and man facing each other as equal parties. The efficacy and the certainty of the promise certainly do not issue from human activity."[88]

I find this argument provocative. And, yet, one must still aver that the weight has shifted too overwhelmingly here in the direction of the divine action, to the point that the human participation by faith is reduced to near insignificance. Yes, all human participation by faith is enabled by God (Rom. 10:17), for grace liberates human response; it does not oppress it. And faith is indeed a yielding to the divine action. However, God does not believe for us. The human yielding to God by grace is still to receive its due in any account of baptism. And the image of the passive infant, even if supported by the faith of its family and its church, is not sufficient to grant that human participation its due in the economy of salvation.

But surely, with this said, one cannot overlook the beauty and truth that comes through a family and a congregation extending the covenant of Christ so as to encompass their infant children! If this ritual is followed by a living witness to the child of the grace of God and, later, by confirmation, in which the older child accepts their baptismal rite for themselves by accepting the gift of Christ, is not the end result in effect the same as baptism among believers? I would say that it is. And I would encourage free churches that practice believer's baptism to take child dedication services with utmost seriousness. Since most people accept Christ prior to the age of eighteen, child dedication that is followed by a discipling of that child is our most effective means

---

[85] Pelikan, *Spirit Verses Structure*, 80.
[86] Ibid., 90–95.
[87] Ibid., 96–97.
[88] Berkouwer, *The Sacraments*, 184.

of evangelism in the church. But I would still hold that a biblical understanding of the relationship between the divine self-impartation and human reception is best preserved by believer's baptism.

But I agree with Luther about the significance of baptism as the chief sacrament, though perhaps for a somewhat different reason. Baptism is indeed the chief of the sacraments, for it points most clearly to our incorporation by grace into Christ and the entire journey of the believer into Christ that deepens and fulfills it. It also for this reason speaks to us of our full baptism in the Spirit. It speaks powerfully and without ambiguity of our descent with Christ into the abyss of fiery judgment (the baptism in fire), and the consequent leaving that condemned and sinful self behind, so as to rise up with him in the Spirit to newness of life, which is ultimately fulfilled in the resurrection of the dead. The members of his body have been baptized together into the love poured out into our hearts by the Spirit (Rom. 5:5) and, as members of his body, we are baptized into communion with, and service to, one another (1 Cor. 12:13, 28). The life leading to that ultimate baptism in the Spirit is a life empowered for sanctified service in Christ's love for the world (Acts 1:8). The entire depth and breadth of Christ given to us as Redeemer and Baptizer in the Spirit is given for us in this sacrament. The water rite presents to the church a potent presentation of the baptized person's entire journey into Christ, into the fullness of the Spirit, into the embrace of the Triune God, for we are indeed baptized in the name of the Father, the Son, and the Holy Spirit, and Christ is with us always until what that formula signifies is eschatologically fulfilled. All of this is why I have chosen as my overarching framework a Spirit-baptized ecclesiology, rather than a eucharistic one. Baptism implies more than mere initiation to the eucharist. It is initiation to the risen body of Jesus and the fullness of the Spirit to be had in that union; it signifies the entire journey of the Christian life, of the church in its totality.

Yet, one is not to downplay the significance of the Lord's Supper (the eucharist) for our understanding of the church, for the very substance of our life together in communion, in the embrace of the Triune God, is presented with clarity there. If water baptism depicts our eschatological incorporation into the embrace of the Triune God, the Lord's Supper adds depth of insight into the substance of this shared life as *communion*. Communion is the ritual context in which we continue to drink of the Spirit and plunge ever-more deeply into the Spirit-baptized life: "For we were all baptized by one Spirit so as to form one body—whether Jews or Gentiles, slave or free—and we were all given the one Spirit to drink" (1 Cor. 12:13). The epiclesis or invocation of the Spirit at the Lord's Supper indicates the life-giving nourishment that is experienced in this act of communion with Christ.[89] As Paul Tillich proposed, the Lord's Supper provides the occasion in which we participate in the power of what the meal signifies, "and, therefore, it can be a medium of the Spirit."[90] We are incorporated into Christ and his body under the sign of water baptism, and we are further nourished by the Spirit in communion with Christ under the sign of the sacred meal. The eschatological goal is total immersion in the life of the Spirit in deeper communion.

---

[89] John H. McKenna, "Eucharistic Epiclesis: Myopia or Microcosm," *TS* 36, no. 2 (1975): 279 (268–78).
[90] Paul Tillich, *ST*, Vol. 3 (Chicago: University of Chicago Press, 1976), 123.

This communion in the here and now is like a banquet with and in our Lord, shared as a church together in unity with a deep sense of contrition and gratitude, but shared also in hope-filled celebration of what is to come. In granting us a deeper look into the substance of the Spirit-baptized life, the Lord's Supper also grants us a more nuanced look at Christ's redemptive journey. The Lord's Supper signifies that the baptism in fire that Christ endured for us was a state of alienation. Christ drank this bitter cup so as to provide us with the cup of communion. So those who are baptized in the Spirit drink from the Spirit of communion as one body (1 Cor. 12:13); they eat the spiritual food and drink the spiritual water of renewal in the Word of God and the Spirit of life (1 Cor. 10:3-4).

There is no question but that this meal depicts a banquet table spread for those of us who *were* enemies of God, far from the Father's household, but are *now* supping together with and in Christ as his brothers and sisters. The faithful Son has gone out into the far country to bring us to the banquet of the Word and of the Spirit of communion in the Father's kingdom. In supping together with and in Christ, we call up before us his sacrifice signified by his spilled blood and his broken body that was necessary to reconcile us to God ("Do this in remembrance of me," 1 Cor. 11:16), and we invoke the Spirit, who is the very substance of communion and the down payment of its future fullness. We rededicate ourselves to full participation (sharing) in his self-sacrifice through worship and vocation: "Is not the cup of thanksgiving for which we give thanks a participation in the blood of Christ? And is not the bread that we break a participation in the body of Christ?" (1 Cor. 10:16). We offer ourselves to God by the Spirit as spiritual sacrifices through the mediation of his sacrifice for us (Rom. 12:1). The meal among the Spirit baptized signifies not only his presence communing with us but also our presence in him, in communion with him and, through him, with his Father. This communion celebrated at the Lord's Supper is constantly opened hospitably to the world in Christ's name. Life in Christ is a thus a communion, a celebration, or a banquet. Like the wedding feast that provided the occasion for Christ's first miracle, God saves the best wine for last (Jn 2:10). Indeed, the Lord's Supper points to the final marriage supper with Christ in the kingdom of God (Rev. 19:7-9). "For whenever you eat this bread and drink this cup, you proclaim the Lord's death until he comes" (1 Cor. 11:26). When he comes, we put on the heavenly tabernacle in the perfect image of the risen Christ and our communion together in him and with him will be so intimate it will be likened to mortal existence being "swallowed up in life" (2 Cor. 5:4). A Spirit-baptized ecclesiology thus also implies a eucharistic ecclesiology.

Though ordained clergy typically preside over the sacraments, all believers participate. The entire believing congregation are witnesses to the event; they all validate and receive the one undergoing incorporation at the hands of Christ. They all represent Christ in receiving the baptized person into their communion as Christ himself receives them. They all help to make that ritual what it is, they all participate in what it mediates. Though God makes it happen, our corporate faith joins with the faith of the one baptized who receives the divine action in welcoming that person to the communion and service of the Lord. The truth of congregational mediation is especially true of the Lord's Supper. We all commune together in unity at the table of the Lord, receiving one another as Christ receives us. The loaf that signifies his body also signifies us in him. Though the pieces of the bread are many, they are all members of the one load as we are members of Christ (1 Cor. 10:17). Again, we all help to make that ritual what it is. We all mediate together the significance of what Christ does there. Though God makes it happen, our corporate faith comes together as one to receive it, not only for ourselves individually but also together for the entire fellowship. In the act of dining together, we all proclaim the Lord's death until he comes (1 Cor. 11:26).

## Vocation: Spiritual Gifts and Mission

The baptism in the Holy Spirit empowers the people of God to overflowing so that they can serve one another in the power of the Spirit. It is anchored in one's initial reception of Christ by faith, which is when the Spirit first takes position of a life (Rom. 8:9). There are also decisive experiential breakthroughs in a believer's life by which the Spirit sanctifies and empowers that life for service. Paul exhorts the Ephesians to be filled with the Spirit "speaking to one another with psalms, hymns, and songs from the Spirit" (Eph. 5:18-19). The Spirit rests on the people of God and out of their innermost being flows forth rivers of living water (Jn 7:38). Described from above it is likened to the filling of a vessel to overflowing; described from below it is like a welling up to overflowing, a release of the Spirit in life service. Viewed eschatologically it is a welling up to life eternal (4:14). In this experience, believers transcend themselves through the energizing work of the Spirit of love and communion. The experience of Spirit baptism as power for witness is both sanctifying and empowering. In the words of Assemblies of God scholar David Lim, it is an experience of "vocational sanctification."[91] Anchored in the reception of the Spirit by faith in the gospel, the experience is ritually confirmed at water baptism. It is continuously nourished in the shared meal. But the experience overflows the meal and is experienced, sometimes dramatically, in times of prayer and seeking God. It is a charismatic experience in the sense that incorporation into the body of Christ by faith under the sign of baptism implies a spiritual gifting. Spirit baptism as an experience of overflowing fans this gift into flame (2 Tim. 1:6). It energizes believers to bring their gifting to expression when they grow weary, granting them boldness when they have reason to be afraid. It wakes them up from complacency or a lack compassion. It strengthens them when they feel weak or discouraged. The believers threatened by persecution are energized to fearlessly proclaim the gospel in public (Acts 4:31). The household of Cornelius magnifies God and speaks in tongues directly upon their initial reception of the Spirit by faith (10:45-46). Prophetic witness appears to be the characteristic consequence of these breakthroughs or moments of the overflowing of divine love (Acts 2:4ff; 4:31; 10:45-46; 19:6; Eph. 5:18-19). Overall, it helps believers to realize experientially their election and calling to serve.

In this overflowing life of the Spirit the church bears instruments of Christ ministering to his church. Luke tells us in the very first verse of his second volume, Acts, that his first volume, Luke, was about what Jesus "began" to do and to teach,

---

[91] Shared with me in person.

as though Jesus is still active in the narrative of the growth of the church (Acts 1:1). In being empowered to bear witness in the world, believers are empowered to serve the household of faith. There is no credible witness to the world if the church is not meaningfully embodying the love of God by serving one another in the unity of love. Jesus prayed "that all of them may be one, Father, just as you are in me and I am in you. May they also be in us so that the world may believe that you have sent me" (Jn 17:21). Believers are sanctified to become living letters of Christ (2 Cor. 3:3). They have spiritual gifts that will lead the church beyond its boundaries to show the love of Christ in multiple ways to suffering humanity in witness to Christ through word and deed. But one must never underestimate the power of witness that comes from a congregation deeply committed to the love of Christ in their service to one another. The church as a result should pulsate with life, with numerous spiritual gifts through which Christ builds up the entire congregation into a ministering body of believers:

> Instead, speaking the truth in love, we will grow to become in every respect the mature body of him who is the head, that is, Christ. From him the whole body, joined and held together by every supporting ligament, grows and builds itself up in love, as each part does its work. (Eph. 4:15-16)

The Spirit-baptized church constantly opens up into a wider circle of grace-filled exchanges in the Spirit in which the living Christ and his word of promise received in proclamation and sacrament gives rise to and guides mutual edification: "What then shall we say, brothers and sisters? When you come together, each of you has a hymn, or a word of instruction, a revelation, a tongue or an interpretation. Everything must be done so that the church may be built up" (1 Cor. 14:26). Clark Pinnock describes this reality well:

> As well as receiving the sacraments from the Spirit, we need to cultivate openness to the gifts of the Spirit. The Spirit is present beyond liturgy in a wider circle. There is a flowing that manifests itself as power to bear witness, heal the sick, prophecy, praise God enthusiastically, perform miracles and more. There is liberty to celebrate, an ability to dream and see visions, a release of Easter life. There are impulses of power in the move of the Spirit to transform and commission disciples to become instruments of the mission.[92]

Not only do we in the Spirit celebrate together the power of Easter life, we also in that renewing power help bear one another's suffering and burdens. There are also gifts like speaking in tongues and intercessory prayer that allow members to groan together in ways too deep for words for the liberty of the Spirit to come (Rom. 8:26), groaning that helps them to bear the suffering of others so as to comfort them with the hope at the horizon of our shared faith. We suffer with those who suffer and rejoice with those who rejoice (12:26). There are gifts of the Spirit to meet multiple needs. The Spirit knows the needs of a congregation and will diversely give rise to the gifts that are needed for

---

[92] Pinnock, *Flame of Love*, 129.

the common good (1 Cor. 12:11). We serve the Spirit by encouraging one another to "stoke into flame" the gift that God has given each one (2 Tim. 1:6). We should be a "gift-evoking fellowship."

Jesus's own Spirit-empowered ministry involved various supernatural gifts of the Spirit that served as signs of the coming kingdom in power. These gifts grant us a foretaste as "powers of the age to come" (Heb. 6:5) and overcome the dark powers, bringing the kingdom of God closer to human experience. "But if it is by the Spirit of God that I drive out demons, then the kingdom of God has come upon you" (Mt. 12:28). The entry of Christ into flesh by the Spirit was followed by signs and wonders of the Spirit that testify of Christ and open people to receive him at their points of need. His ultimate victory over sin, death, and the devil on the cross and in the resurrection is made available to the church in the bestowal of the Spirit, the ultimate gift active in all lesser gifts. The church bears witness to Christ in the power of the Spirit, with powerful signs following. The church in fact is to be diversely gifted of the Spirit to build up the body in the love of Christ (1 Cor. 12:11; Eph. 4:16). The mediation of the word in proclamation and sacrament occurs in a way that involves the faith of the entire congregation. This means that proclamation and sacrament open up to a larger field of the Spirit's work that involves manifestations of the Spirit in power and empowered ministries. They are all signs and instruments of the Spirit that confirm the word and open the church to receive that word at their different points of need. There is a "kerygmatic" quality to spiritual gifts like prophecy, discernment, words of wisdom, words of knowledge, and also a "sacramental" quality to spiritual gifts like speaking in tongues and the laying on of hands for divine healing that function as physical signs of a work that is too deep for words or rational comprehension.[93]

I would like to propose seven characteristics of spiritual gifts. The first is that these gifts are specific manifestations of grace that address human needs. The term that Paul prefers for these gifts, χαρίσματα (*charismata*), indicates that these gifts mediate actions of the grace (*charis*) or Spirit of God through human vessels. These gifts are not acts of human heroism deserving of praise ("What do you have that you did not receive?" 1 Cor. 4:9). Nor are they exercised only toward those we might consider as deserving of them. No one is deserving. Spiritual gifts are avenues of grace. Second, these gifts are marked by their doxological direction; they encourage the confession of Jesus as Lord (1 Cor. 12:1-3). Again, they are not part of a competition for adulation from others. So in seeking to discern one's gifting in the pursuance of the sanctified life, we heed this admonition: "Do not think of yourself more highly than you ought, but rather think of yourself with sober judgment, in accordance with the faith God has distributed to each of you" (Rom. 12:3). We should dream big but also think soberly. Each qualifies the other. Third, these gifts are diverse. "If the whole body were an eye, where would the sense of hearing be?" (1 Cor. 12:17). The gifts that place people more prominently in the public limelight tend to attract the most interest. But the goal of one's gifting is serving the common good in whatever capacity God should will. Fourth, spiritual gifts come from the same Father, through the same Son, and occur in one and the same Spirit (1 Cor. 12:4-6). They thus serve to unify the body of Christ around

---

[93] See Macchia, "Tongues as a Sign."

divine purposes. The church cannot fragment into a chaos of competing interests. Yet, the unity is not a uniformity, but is rather a unity in diversity. Creative tensions will emerge in serving the kingdom of God but through prayer and dialogue these tensions can morph into an enriching experience for all in the reconciling work of the Spirit. Fourth, the gifts are to be exercised by all: "From him the whole body, joined and held together by every supporting ligament, grows and builds itself up in love, as each part does its work" (Eph. 4:16). There are to be no bench warmers in the church. Everyone has something to offer in serving others. Whether using a natural talent blessed by the Spirit, or being used in a more supernatural manifestation, everyone is spiritually gifted to serve. Fifth, all gifts function according to the standard of divine love. Paul is adamant on this point. He does not say that spiritual gifts are merely defective without love; his insistence is more radical than this. Without love, he insists, there is no spiritual gifting at work. Speaking in tongues is reduced to mere noise; bursts of exuberant faith amount to nothing (1 Cor. 13:1-3). Have we grasped the power of this insight? When Christ appears and the spiritual gifts are no longer needed, love will remain as the power and purpose involved in them all (13:13). Sixth, all of the gifts have as their purpose the building up of the body in love (14:26; Eph. 4:16). Self-fulfillment is secondary. Self-edification is primary in private prayer and spiritual discipline (1 Cor. 14:2). The benefit to others is only the horizon in such a setting. But in the church, the common good is the immediate priority of the gifts. Perhaps families should seek out a church according to where they are most needed rather than where that are most effectively served. Though the latter is important too, the former should have the priority. Otherwise, we are reducing ourselves to consumers of a church that functions as a "salvation machine." Seventh, all gifted activity is to respect decency and order. One is not attempting to draw attention to oneself. Respect for those gifted to be in leadership is to be present. Respect for the order of worship is to be evident. Moreover, biblical teaching is the living measure that tests activity purporting to be in the Spirit. For the scriptures are the privileged voice of the Spirit in the church.

An emphasis on spiritual gifts helps to energize *all* of the people of God and to involve them *all* in the mediation of Christ in the church. We all function as Christ to one another, submitting to one another out of reverence to Christ (Eph. 5:21). Without this congregational mediation of grace, the ministry of word and sacrament can become reduced to a function of the ordained clergy, with the "laity" reduced to an audience or, at best, passive receivers who say nothing more than "amen." Such a vision of the church is foreign to the New Testament. This is not to say that there is something wrong with seeing the church as the congregation that says "amen" to all of the promises of God given in Christ (2 Cor. 1:20). The corporate "amen" is indicative of a church in the receptive mode of faith facing God, always receiving what they give, always dependent on grace for their mediation of grace. The "amen" is said by all to God. It is not said to clergy as a means of distinguishing between them and a passive laity. I agree with Lisa Stephenson who rightly argues that the Spirit is experienced in Acts 2 is an Isaianic new exodus that resulted in a "radical democratizing" of its members, a "pneumatologically constituted discipleship of equals."[94] This is not to deny

---

[94] Stephenson, *Dismantling the Dualisms for American Pentecostal Women in Ministry*, 168.

that there are moments when an ordained minister will address a congregation with the Word of God and in doing so there is momentarily a functionally asymmetrical distinction between them and their congregation. Yet, the word proclaimed by the minister applies to the minister in those moments too. So even in such moments there is a sense in which the minister and the entire congregation stand together listening obediently to the voice of Christ.

The church's internal ministry in building up the saints is not only internal. Guests who are unlearned in the gospel will visit. There is indeed to be "seeker sensitivity" at work, though not in the sense of watering down the cost of discipleship: "Whoever does not carry their cross and follow me cannot be my disciple" (Lk. 14:27). Here's a seeker-sensitive text for you: "So if the whole church comes together and everyone speaks in tongues, and inquirers or unbelievers come in, will they not say that you are out of your mind?" (1 Cor. 14:23). If a church is hospitable to those outside the faith, should we not treat them with the same respect and sensitivity that we would treat guests to our home? Would we not make sure that foreign guests in our home understand the meaning of customs we observe that may not be familiar to them? The church should be a hospitable family that opens its doors to strangers. The church will evangelize within its four walls.

Yet, this is not the only entry point of the church into its vocation. The church cannot remain cloistered away from the world. Such isolation is difficult anyways, since church members are involved with co-workers and neighbors who do not belong to a church. They can use guidance in how to be a source of spiritual wisdom that points to Christ. The church also needs to seek out community needs and strategize about getting involved as a witness. As Jesus prayed for his church, "My prayer is not that you take them out of the world but that you protect them from the evil one" (Jn 17:15). We don't love others insincerely as part of a propaganda campaign. Rather, we love sincerely regardless of their openness to partake of our hospitality of faith. To love properly, we need to be willing to cross boundaries as Peter did in entering the household of Cornelius, to be a presence for the welfare of the other. Metaphorically, the church gathers together in the divine inhale. The Spirit as the divine breath draws us together around Christ. But then comes the divine exhale, which drives the church outward into the world.[95] As Christ the anointed Messiah was sent to seek and to save the lost, so also does he send us under his anointing to bear witness in his name: "As the Father has sent me, I am sending you" (Jn 20:21). We bear witness to Christ, for salvation "is found in no one else, for there is no other name under heaven given to mankind by which we must be saved" (Acts 4:12).

One can indeed make the case that mission is essential to the church's identity and very reason for being in the world. The earliest disciples were taught by the risen Christ about the kingdom of God that is coming to the earth (Acts 1:1-5). Receiving a discourse by the risen Christ on the coming kingdom must have brought their eschatological fervor to a fever pitch. The presence of the risen Christ alone was proof positive that the end is right around the corner. After all, resurrection and new creation

---

[95] Jürgen Moltmann, *The Spirit of Life: A Universal Affirmation* (Minneapolis, MN: Fortress Press, 2001), 45.

were considered to be God's final act of salvation. So the disciples understandably ask an eschatological question: "Then they gathered around him and asked him, 'Lord, are you at this time going to restore the kingdom to Israel?'" (1:6). In other words, is the fulfillment of the kingdom of God and of the promises to Israel about to be fulfilled? Jesus's answer is twofold. First, the times and seasons are in the Father's sovereign will and are not accessible to us (1:7). It's not for us to know. Second, our attention is to be directed instead to the mission that must be fulfilled before the end will come: "But you will receive power when the Holy Spirit comes on you; and you will be my witnesses in Jerusalem, and in all Judea and Samaria, and to the ends of the earth" (Acts 1:8). The ends of the earth must become the possession of the Messiah for his reign to be fulfilled: "I will make the nations your inheritance, the ends of the earth your possession" (Ps. 2:8). So Christ's inaugural act upon his enthronement at the right hand of the Father was to pour out the Spirit upon all flesh so that he may claim as his treasured possession the ends of the earth as his elect people. The times and seasons in the sovereign will of the Father will include God's drawing of the nations to the knowledge of salvation (Acts 17:26). The promise God gave to Abraham was that through his seed (Christ) all nations will be blessed, and God never forgets a promise. "And this gospel of the kingdom will be preached in the whole world as a testimony to all nations, and then the end will come" (Mt. 24:14). Only after the Gentiles occupy the tree of God's people can Israel then be restored. It can be said that God delays the end for the sake of the mission. In making the gentile mission essential to the fulfillment of Israel's restoration and the fulfillment of the kingdom on earth, God made the mission vital to the church's history, to its reason for being in the world. One should not overplay this point. The church is a communion first, for the bride is not chosen by the groom simply to serve him or his cause. We are chosen first for communion. But this relationship is not symmetrical. He alone is Lord. We are chosen to be instruments of his cause in the world, to bring glory to his name throughout the earth. Mission is not just something we *do*; it is what we *are*. Many of the earliest Pentecostal churches were appropriately called "missions" (e.g., the Apostolic Faith Mission). I wish they still were. It would be difficult to neglect mission if the term is in our name!

The challenges of a missional ecclesiology could be viewed as the new frontier of Pentecostal ecclesiology. Andrew Lord notes that "it is impossible to deal with Pentecostalism without considering its missionary heart."[96] He strives for a "Spirit-shaped" missional ecclesiology that correlates the Pentecostal confession of faith and cultural challenges.[97] Gary Tyra recognizes rightly that a Spirit-shaped, missional ecclesiology calls for a focus on prophetic empowerment shared by all of the people of God. Prophetic discernment and speech are not merely for an elite group in the church but rather should characterize the church in general. According to Tyra, reclaiming its prophetic heritage from Acts will set the church on the path of "missional faithfulness," something that is sorely needed to consistently speak the truth of Christ to our

---

[96] Andrew Lord, *Network Church: A Pentecostal Ecclesiology Shaped by Mission*, GPCS (Leiden: Brill, 2012), 10.
[97] Ibid., 21–22.

relativistic postmodern era.[98] Similarly, Wonsuk and Julie Ma developed a Pentecostal theology of mission as well, except the context that they had in mind is Asia. They also sought to develop the biblical roots for a prophetic church in which all consider themselves empowered to be prophets. They characterized the distinctives of this missional ecclesiology as consisting of a deep zeal and commitment for mission, a prophethood of believers that encouraged a "democratized theology of mission and ministry" in which all are empowered to serve, a worldview in which healing and miracles are expected to occur for victory in spiritual warfare, the prioritization of evangelism and inner change without neglecting outward care in challenging social circumstances, and ecumenical and racially diverse participation in mission and congregational life.[99] Intriguingly, Gary Tyra also wrote an entire systematic theology with the church's missional challenge at the horizon.[100] More extensively, Veli-Matti Kärkkäinen wrote a systematic theology in conversation with world religions, which will sure serve a missionally aware church.[101]

Pentecostal missional ecclesiologies tend to prioritize the world as the area of God's redemptive concern, with the church as the means toward which this concern is fulfilled. Peter Althouse goes so far as to view the church exclusively as the means toward a greater end: "The Church is not the focus of God's redemptive activity *per se*, the world is. The Church is the place where God engages and brings people into redemptive participation for the sake of the world."[102] However, Simon Chan criticizes this ecclesiology as instrumentalist, arguing instead that the church is the arena of salvation into which the world will one day be drawn. All of creation will be shaped into the image of ecclesial communion, for the Spirit is the "ecclesial Spirit."[103] I'm inclined to see the church and the world as having mutual significance. Chan is right: the church is the focus of redemptive activity for the sake of communion with God, and the world is made for that communion. On the other hand, Althouse is also right: The world is also the focus of redemptive activity (Christ hidden among all who yearn for redemption and liberation) and the church is created to serve its awakening to Christ. Missional ecclesiologies that share the one-sidedness of placing the priority on the world help to jolt institution-based churches that live only for themselves out of their self-indulgence and call them to a cruciform existence that is there for others. Throughout this book I have stressed that communion is at the heart of the church's mystery, since the bride of Christ is joined to him not just to serve him or his mission but to communion with him and to enjoy him forever. Yet, this communion is hospitable and missional in its reach.

---

[98] Gary Tyra, *The Holy Spirit in Mission: Prophetic Speech and Action in Christian Mission* (Downers Grove, IL: IVP Academic, 2011), 11–38.
[99] Julie and Wonsuk Ma, *Mission in the Spirit* (Eugene, OR: Wipf & Stock, 2011), 8–9.
[100] Gary Tyra, *Missional Orthodoxy: Theology and Ministry in a Post-Christian Context* (Downers Grove, IL: IVP Academic, 2013).
[101] A helpful summary of his much larger work is found in his book *Christian Theology in a Pluralistic World: A Global Introduction* (Grand Rapids, MI: Eerdmans, 2019).
[102] Peter Althouse, "Towards a Pentecostal Ecclesiology: Participation in the Missional Life of the Triune God," *JPT* 18 (2005): 231 (230–45).
[103] Chan, *Pentecostal Ecclesiology*, 42.

Our gospel is to be holistic, speaking of atonement and the fullness of life in ways that address a variety of human needs, both personal and social. If the kingdom of God on earth is the horizon of our message, how can we restrict it to the forgiveness of sins or to the individual quest for heaven? Pentecostal theologians from Walter Hollenweger to Miroslav Volf have drawn attention to the fact that Pentecostalism globally tends to connect divine healing to a broader understanding of salvation that is "embodied" or "material," overcoming the typically western dualism of spirit and body and at least implicitly connecting mission beyond personal evangelism to social justice and transformation as well.[104] Though this view of salvation can (and has) become too focused on prosperity it can (and has) also taken on more liberating forms. There is no eclipsing the commission of our Lord to disciple all nations with the gospel of salvation through Christ as Redeemer and giver of life. But we must also recognize that this giving of life is concrete and holistic. The gospel thus confronts various populations differently depending in part on their social context. The Pharisee and the outcast in Jesus's parable of the prodigal sons in Luke 15 are both confronted with the gospel but in different ways, the outcast in a context of squandered potential and the elder son in a context of self-righteous privilege. Both are sinners, alienated from communion with the Father and one another. But their different social contexts influence how the gospel comes to them and the particular forms that their repentance will take. Personal evangelism remains important and basic. But how can we say we love the lost if we lack compassion for their source of suffering and fail to take responsibility for our role in it? How can we preach against sin and for righteousness if we ignore the most powerful and devastating social and cultural forms of oppression caused by sin in the world? And how can we push back against the source of peoples' suffering without pushing back against sin as it takes concrete shape and is preserved in social structures and cultural attitudes? The church's righteousness and liberating activity are preserved through its institutions of canon, proclamation, sacraments, and gifted ministries. The world preserves its unrighteousness and oppressive activity (e.g., racism) through institutions too (the media, politics, education, etc.). The church needs to present itself as an alternate community that subverts the world and offers prophetic discernment into its destructive ways. The church needs to model this new humanity for the world, for there is no better critique of an oppressive system than one that models the alternative. "Do not conform to the pattern of this world, but be transformed by the renewing of your mind. Then you will be able to test and approve what God's will is—his good, pleasing and perfect will" (Rom. 12:2-3).

In pursuing social protest and transformation, we do so as part of our witness to Jesus Christ as the Savior of the world. For example, the proclamation of Christ crucified and risen for the salvation of the world means that the terror of worldly powers was absorbed by Christ on the cross and overcome so as to open up the path to a different form of existence, one that is given over to the justice and peace of the kingdom of God in the fullness of life. The oppressed are comforted and the oppressors

---

[104] For example, Walter J. Hollenweger, "The Critical Tradition of Pentecostalism," *JPT* 1 (1992): 7–17; Miroslav Volf, "Materiality of Salvation: An Investigation in the Soteriologies of Liberation and Pentecostal Theologies," *JES* 26, no. 3 (1989): 447–67.

are put on notice that the terror by which they live has fallen under divine judgment and is passing away. The oppressed repent of their acceptance of this terror as the final and all defining reality and embrace a different future in hope, and the oppressors can repent of their embrace of this terror for the sake of social privilege and seek a path consistent with the kingdom as well. Both oppressed and oppressor (perhaps to some extent both are in all of us) can lay down the destructive ways of the world so as to take up the life of the Spirit in witness to Christ. The sacraments bear witness to this path of hope in Christ and the Spirit of life as well. Note what William T. Cavanaugh wrote of torture in the light of the Lord's Supper:

> If torture is essentially an anti-liturgy, a drama in which the state realizes omnipotence on the bodies of others, then the Eucharist provides a direct and startling contrast, for in the Eucharist Christ sacrifices no other body but His own. Power is realized in self-sacrifice; Christians join in this sacrifice by uniting their own bodies to the sacrifice of Christ. Christians become a gift to be given away to others.[105]

There are no words that can add anything to the truth and beauty of the above statement.

One could also point to the significance of Pentecost, where God took a major step in the direction of claiming the world as the divine household. All are born into this household through the baptism in the Spirit so as to become siblings of Christ. All of humanity belong, including those still in the far country. They are all created as God's offspring (Acts 17:28). The message of Jesus the Spirit Baptizer thus grants us a framework for social ethics. Note Daniela Augustine's description of Pentecost, "It opened the eyes of the ones who embraced the message of Pentecost to see the image of God in the strangeness of the other and to recognize him/her as belonging to the same family."[106] Indeed, this communion in the Spirit allows us to recognize Christ in one another, for we have put on Christ through faith under the sign of water baptism (Gal. 3:27). In the Spirit and in embodied witness to Christ, the community of the church thus resists privilege based on race, sex, or social status, replacing it with the cruciform image of Jesus that all put on in service to one another (Gal. 3:27-28). The deeper a community journeys into Christ and his liberating message, the deeper the potential for subverting what is wrong with the world. That witness to Christ implies a fundamental criticism of the injustices of our world. There is nothing wrong (and everything right) about a church that extends its gospel message to include pointing that out. The kingdom of God in its coming will set the captives free (Lk. 4:18). The church needs to make that point clear and in a way that contextualizes it for our time and place. On the other hand, God is involved by the liberating Spirit in the world beyond the ministry of the church too. And there are times when the church may prove to be less enlightened than movements in the world may be with regard to issues of mutual regard and social justice. Walter Hollenweger noted that church should in this

---

[105] William T. Cavanaugh, *Torture and Eucharist*, CCT (Oxford: Blackwell Publication, 1998), 279. I am grateful to Ekaputra Tupamahu for drawing my attention to this quote.

[106] Augustine, *Pentecost, Hospitality, and Transfiguration*, 142.

case humbly listen, just like Peter had to listen to what God was telling him through the piety and yearnings of Cornelius.[107] Note what Peter learned when seeing Cornelius through God's eyes: "I now realize how true it is that God does not show favoritism but accepts from every nation the one who fears him and does what is right" (Acts 10:34-35).

With regard to mission and interreligious dialogue, it is important to note that one cannot evangelize people of other religions charitably if they don't understand what these people believe in its best light. For that, we need to talk to them and learn from them, respectfully and with an openness to be blessed. Beyond this, Samuel Solivan grants us several points to consider when approaching believers of other religions:

> (1) the fact that the Holy Spirit is the one who leads Christians to all truth; (2) the importance of identification with the poor of the world and the need to bring their distinctive voice into the dialogue; (3) the conviction of the prevenient workings of the Holy Spirit in every human being; (4) the empowerment of believers for witness by the Spirit; and (5) the diverse and pluralistic character of the Spirit's manifestations across racial, class, gender, language, and religious boundaries.[108]

Amos Yong has helpfully maintained that a pneumatological approach to a theology of religions creates breathing room to recognize elements of the liberating gospel of Christ in other religions, since the Spirit who created all things, including people's penchant to thirst for God and reach for grace, is everywhere at work.[109] Of course, there is no compromising the point that atonement and Spirit baptism come only through Jesus Christ. He alone is the pioneer and perfecter of faith (Heb. 12:2).

The eschatological goal of the church and its mission is the turning of the entire world into the place of God's dwelling:

> Then I saw "a new heaven and a new earth," for the first heaven and the first earth had passed away, and there was no longer any sea. ² I saw the Holy City, the new Jerusalem, coming down out of heaven from God, prepared as a bride beautifully dressed for her husband. ³ And I heard a loud voice from the throne saying, "Look! God's dwelling place is now among the people, and he will dwell with them. They will be his people, and God himself will be with them and be their God" (Rev. 21:1-3).

The ultimate goal is not going to heaven but bringing "heaven" to earth ("your kingdom come, your will be done, on earth as it is done in heaven," Mt. 6:9). There will be no need for a temple in the new Jerusalem, for God and Christ are the temple. We are all

---

[107] Note what Walter Hollenweger has to say about this in *Evangelism Today: Good News or Bone of Contention?* (Belfast: Christian Journals, 1976).

[108] This summary from Samuel Solivan is quoted from Veli-Matti Kärkkäinen, "Mission in Pentecostal Theology," *IRM* 107, no. 1 (2018): 20 (5–22); Samuel Solivan, "Interreligious Dialogue: An Hispanic American Pentecostal Perspective," in *Grounds for Understanding: Ecumenical Responses to Religious Pluralism*, ed. S. Mark Heim (Grand Rapids, MI: Eerdmans, 1998), 37–45.

[109] A good place to start in reading Yong is Amos Yong, *Beyond the Impasse: Towards a Pneumatological Theology of Mission* (Eugene, OR: Wipf & Stock, 2014).

held by the divine presence and live by the divine light of it. We are with and in him the temple to enjoy forever. The kings of the nations will walk by the light of the Lamb and the glory of the nations will be revealed. At no point will the gates ever be shut (Rev. 21:22-27). And those who wash their robes in Christ will be allowed to enter (22:14). The water of life will be in abundant supply: "Let the one who is thirsty come; and let the one who wishes take the free gift of the water of life" (22:17). The goal of the church is to become so swallowed up by the life of the Spirit as to become one with it.

## Conclusion

The church is the sign and instrument of Christ and of his kingdom in the world. The church is constituted by the means used by Christ to baptize others in the Spirit, to address others with the gospel and to incorporate them into communion and vocation. The institutions of canon, proclamation, sacraments, spiritually gifted ministries, and mission are established by Christ and birthed in the Spirit to be used as the means by which the Triune God self-imparts to the world and draws the world into the divine embrace. God freely and faithfully self-imparts through these means and others. The element of divine freedom implies that God is not simply placed at our disposal to be used in any way we wish. Revelation is not reducible to a commodity. The church is not a salvation machine that can be used by religious consumers to satisfy their perceived spiritual needs. Biblical inspiration thus functions to explain how scripture functions as the living measure of our practices. The spiritually discerning church gave the constant "amen" through the formation and canonization of scripture; and today as well, the church discerns and conveys the truth of Christ in many ways. Yet, the scripture, interpreted in a way that conforms to God's self-disclosure in Christ, continues to guide and test the church's practices. Both proclamation and sacraments are occasions in which the living Christ as Word of the Father and Sacrament of the Spirit is heard and received. The gospel is received through both. And both are mutually defining. The gospel proclaimed comes to us through sacraments too, preventing them from being viewed "magically" or "mechanically" as dispensers of grace. On the other hand, the sacraments help us to view the gospel proclaimed as more than a mere idea to be intellectually grasped. The proclamation of the word is like a physical event that confronts us with the divine presence, the very call of Christ.

Baptism confirms and deepens our participation in the baptism in the Spirit, which is anchored in our initial acceptance of the gospel of Christ by faith, for it is by faith alone we are united to Christ and incorporated into his body. Yet, though not essential to salvation, baptism is still a spiritual experience of confirmation; it is indeed a bridge-crossing experience. Baptism signifies the burying of our condemned and sinful selves and the rising of our new selves centered on Christ. Implied is the impartation of a spiritual gift and the acceptance of our vocation in Christ. We are to live out this new life in the power of the Spirit. Since baptism points to our union with the *risen* Christ, its ultimate point of reference is to our resurrection from the dead. The Spirit baptism signified in water baptism refers ultimately to the swallowing up of mortal life into the immortal existence of the risen Christ (2 Cor. 5:4). The Lord's Supper follows as signifying our ongoing communion with Christ in a way that occasions actual communion. Lord's Supper thus shows us what the Spirit-baptized life substantively looks like. It invites us to remember (gaze upon) Christ's total self-giving for us in love and invites us all to united communion with and in him. It calls us to repentance and new commitment to follow in Christ's path and it looks ahead in hope to the messianic banquet in the kingdom of God. Footwashing recalls our cleansing in him and calls for the humility of service that comes from gratitude.

All members of the church participate in proclamation and sacrament. And the Spirit overflows these means to involve a diversity of gifted ministries by which we are all built up in Christ while mediating his love to one another. Ministry is not solely a description of those who exercise leadership or oversight in the church. It belongs to all. We are a prophethood and a priesthood of believers. Moreover, mission is not something we merely do. It is something we are. Though the destiny of the world is earmarked for the *koinonia* of the church, the church is elect and called to be there for the world. The horizon of the church's life and mission is the kingdom of God. God will come to reign; the new heavens and new earth will be God's dwelling place. Then church and the world will no longer know a distinction.

# Author Index

Albrecht, Daniel   121 n.34, 161 n.2
Alter, Robert   16
Althaus, Paul   118–19
Althouse, Peter   205
Arminius, Jacob   60
Athanasius   41
Augustine   87, 114, 166
Augustine, Daniela   35, 52, 127, 208
Aulen, Gustaf   121

Barth, Karl   30, 38–9, 50, 65, 71, 96–104, 106, 122, 174–5, 176–7, 181
Basil, St.   124 n.38
Bauckham, Richard   166 n.15
Berkouwer, G. C.   122, 128, 131, 143, 194 n.78, 196
Blumhardt, Johann   122
Bonhoeffer, Dietrich   3, 51, 53, 55, 114, 142–3
Brown, Colin   26 n.34
Brown, Raymond   34
Brueggemann, Walter   16–17 n.10–13
Buber, Martin   51

Calvin, John   54, 60, 191
Cavanaugh, William T.   208
Chan, Simon   11, 35, 42, 108, 120 n.32, 163, 205
Childs, Brevard   180 n.37
Clement of Rome   151
Congdon, David   107 n.11
Coulter, Dale   8, 152
Cox, Harvey   105
Craig, William Lane   102 n.59
Cullmann, Oscar   137
Cyril of Jerusalem   145

Dabney, D. Lyle   29 n.37
Dayton, Donald   8
Driver, Tom   189, 191
Dulles, Avery   159
Dunn, James D. G.   22–3, 33 n.42, 34

Ebeling, Gerhard   177, 185

Faupel, David William   6
Fitzmyer, Joseph A.   27 n.36
Flower, Joseph   140
Fuchs, Lorelie   35, 132
Fuller, R. H.   18 n.15

Ganzel, Tova   19 n.17
Gee, Donald   150
Gelpi, Donald   12
George, Timothy   119 n.31, 131, 144
Green, Chris   107, 131, 175
Grindheim, Sigurd   62, 98

Hafemann, Scott   77 n.20
Hagner, Donald   24 n.27
Harris, Tanya   180
Hayes, Richard   109 n.16
Hegel, G. W. F.   101
Hiers, Richard H.   148 n.123
Hollenweger, Walter J.   161, 207, 208–9
Horton, Michael   114–15
Hütter, Reinhard   163

Ignatius of Antioch   151
Irenaeus   144, 180

Jay, Eric G.   49
Jenson, Robert W.   171 n.24
John Paul II   157
Jung, Carl   51–2

Kärkkäinen, Veli-Matti   146, 150–1, 205
Käsemann, Ernst   112 n.17, 138, 141 n.93, 142 n.97
Kasper, Walter   156
Klotz, Jerome   100
Koch, Kurt   62 n.2
Kruger, Michael J.   180
Küng, Hans   106, 113, 132, 148 n.122, 149, 152, 157, 192 n.73, 74, 194 n.77

Ladd, G. E.   106 n.4
Land, Steven J.   143
Lim, David   118
Lindbeck, George   152 n.137
Lochman, Jan Milíč   3, 18 n.14
Lohfink, Gerhard   89
Lohmeyer, Ernst   24 n.36
Lord, Andrew   205
Luther, Martin   107, 195, 197

Ma, Julie and Wansuk   205
McBride, Jennifer M.   114 n.22
McDonald, Suzanne   98
McDonnell, Kilian   6, 25 n.31, 156
McKenna, John H.   198 n.89
Marcion   180
Marcus, Joel   25 n.30
Moltmann, Jürgen   13, 24, 30, 38–40, 47–8, 108, 158, 204 n.95
Montague, George   20 n.21
Morris, Thomas V.   27 n.35

Neve, Lloyd R.   16
Nolland, John   23 n.25
Nyssa, Gregory of   44, 106

Origen   60

Page, Sydney   93
Pannenberg, Wolfhart   40–2, 44, 100–1
Paulson Steven D.   100
Pelikan, Jaroslav   152, 182, 195–6, 197 n.85
Pinnock, Clark   25, 30, 44, 47, 161, 162, 163, 166, 201

Rad, Gerhard von   20, 65–6
Rahner, Karl   48, 188–9
Reiche, Bo   74 n.18
Richardson, Alan   74, 114 n.21, 146 n.118, 47–8 n.119, 120, 121
Ritschl, Albrecht   100
Robeck, Cecil M.   1, 5, 138

Schillebeeckx, Edward   187
Schleiermacher, Friedrich   38, 54, 100
Schmemann, Alexander   186
Schmidt, K. L.   69 n.12
Schweizer, Eduard   20 n.22, 23, 172 n.25
Seymour, William   130
Sheppard, Gerald T.   180 n.37
Sloan, Robert   74 n.18
Small, Joseph D.   135 n.73
Smith, James K. A.   3, 179, 191
Soelle, Dorothea   42
Solivan, Samuel   209
Stephenson, Lisa   115 n.27, 203
Storr, Anthony   51
Stronstad, Roger   149 n.124
Synan, Vinson   140

Terrien, Samuel   18 n.16
Tillich, Paul   198
Torrance, Thomas   97
Tyra, Gary   205

Vischer, Lukas   126, 130
Volf, Miroslav   9, 45, 48, 50, 52, 54, 107, 114–15, 138, 145–6, 154, 182, 207
Vriezen, Th. C.   19 n.18

Wainwright, Geoffrey   37, 120 n.33, 144, 162, 191
Webber, Robert   8
Weber, Otto   65, 96, 100
Webster, John   129, 164–5, 174 n.29, 180–1
Weinandy, Thomas   46
Wesley, John   60, 143, 155
West, Cornel   50
Wink, Walter   123
Wright, N. T.   19

Yong, Amos   127 n.41, 129, 138, 209
Yun, Koo Dong   12 n.3

Zizioulas, John   140

# Subject Index

anthropology  38–46
apostolicity  146–58
apostolic succession  151–3
army of God  121–5
athletic model  124–5

baptism  31–2, 142, 170–1, 191–8
Baptism, Eucharist, Ministry
    (WCC)  150, 155, 196
body of Christ  111–17
bride of Christ  115–17

Canon, Biblical  148
catholicity  144–6
Christology
    anointing  23–6
    atonement  29–33, 46, 142
    election  96, 99
    fire baptism  26–30
    incarnation  27 n.23, 24, 25, 35
    messianic expectation  19–20
clergy/laity  118–19, 145, 151–5
costly grace  51, 53, 55, 114, 142–3

dialogues
    Anglican-Lutheran  105, 151,
        153, 168
    Anglican-Reformed  128 n.45
    Anglican-Roman Catholic  133 n.67,
        135
    Evangelical-Roman Catholic  134
    Lutheran-Roman Catholic  130–1,
        132, 134, 136–8, 141–2,
        154–5, 157 n.157, 167 n.18,
        172–3, 186
    Methodist-Roman
        Catholic  157 n.160
    Old Catholic-Orthodox  129 n.50,
        131 n.60
    Pentecostal-Roman Catholic  140–1,
        151, 154, 157, 173–4, 194, 196

Reformed-Roman Catholic  117,
    151, 173
WCC-Roman Catholic  129, 135,
    157 n.156
donatism  114

ecumenical movement  126, 130–2,
    139
election  60–104
    Christocentric  96–9
    communal  99–101
    Ephesians  67–72
    eternal/temporal  101–3
    Gospel of John  90–2
    individual/corporate  76–8
    love  60
    Luke-Acts  75–90
    messianic  66–7
    Old Testament  60–6
    1 & 2 Peter  93–5
    potter/clay  81–4
    Revelation (Book of)  92–3
    revocable/irrevocable  77–8, 80
    Romans  73–85
    universalism  103–4
eucharist  32

field of God  108–11
foreknowledge  61, 74–5, 102–4
full communion  135–9

hardening  78–84
hierarchy of truth  136
holiness  120, 139–43
Holy Spirit
    creation  16–17
    judgment  17–18
    new creation  18–19

individualism  54–5, 118–19
inspiration of scripture  181–2

invisible/visible church   129, 131, 133
Israel and the nations   60–6, 76–85,
    86–9, 111, 190–2

Joint Declaration on the Doctrine of
    Justification   141
justification by faith   141–2

*koinonia* (communion)   35–7, 132–6

Lord's Supper   189–91, 198–200

mediation, ecclesial
    Christological basis   119–20
    definition   164–6
    instrumental practices   161–8, 171–2
mission   204–7
Montanism   152

perseverance   75–6
Petrine Office   155–8
predestination   68–9, 74–5
priesthood of all believers   118, 149
Prophethood of All Believers   149

sacraments   185–200
salvation
    faith and repentance   55

pneumatological   17–19
    salvation machines   2–5
sanctification   142
scripture   174–82
Second Vatican Council
    Decree on Ecumenism   145
    Lumen Gentium   106–7, 118, 133–5,
        156–7
social justice   207–8
Spirit baptism
    definition   11–16, 163–4, 200
    eschatological   23–5, 164
    New Testament Development   20–34
    Old Testament background   17–20
    Pentecostal views   5–9
spiritual ecumenism   130–1
spiritual gifts   112, 144–5, 179, 200–5
spiritual warfare   123–4, 148

temple of the Spirit   117–21
totus Christus   114–15
Trinity   35–47

*Unitatis Redintegratio*   134
unity   125–39
*Ut Unum Sint*   157

worship   117, 120–1

# Scripture Index

**OLD TESTAMENT**

**Genesis**
| | |
|---|---|
| 1:1 | 16 |
| 1:1-2 | 16 |
| 1:1-3 | 173 |
| 1:27 | 49, 87 |
| 1:28 | 87 |
| 2:7 | 16, 49 |
| 2:18 | 49 |
| 3:15 | 17 |
| 3:19 | 17 |
| 3:21 | 17 |
| 3:22 | 17 |
| 4:7 | 122 |
| 11 | 127 |
| 11:4 | 127 |
| 15:4-6 | 61 |
| 22:16-17 | 61 |
| 22:17 | 61 |
| 22:18 | 100 |
| 25:23 | 78 |
| 50:20 | 61 |

**Exodus**
| | |
|---|---|
| 6:5 | 61 |
| 9:34 | 79 |
| 14:18 | 81 |
| 19:5 | 68, 94 |
| 20:1-3 | 18 |
| 24:4-8 | 93 |
| 32:32 | 93 |
| 33 | 18 |

**Numbers**
| | |
|---|---|
| 11 | 44 |

**Deuteronomy**
| | |
|---|---|
| 4:37 | 62 |
| 6:4 | 18 |
| 7:6-7 | 62 |
| 7:7 | 62 |
| 7:7-9 | 62 |
| 7:9 | 62, 82 |
| 8 | 18 |
| 10:15 | 62 |
| 10:16 | 196 |

**Joshua**
| | |
|---|---|
| 3 | 189 |

**Nehemiah**
| | |
|---|---|
| 9:7 | 62 |

**Job**
| | |
|---|---|
| 19:26 | 17 |
| 33:4 | 17 |

**Psalms**
| | |
|---|---|
| 2:7-8 | 64 |
| 2:8 | 14, 16, 19, 21, 32, 67, 86, 89, 98, 146, 205 |
| 69 | 80 |
| 81:12 | 79 |
| 90:2 | 101 |
| 102:13 | 88 |
| 105:6 | 62 |
| 119 | 18 |
| 135:4 | 62 |
| 139:9 | 17 |

**Isaiah**
| | |
|---|---|
| 1:5 | 80 |
| 1:18 | 80 |
| 6:6-7 | 20 |
| 6:9-10 | 80 |
| 6:11 | 80 |
| 11:1-3 | 19 |
| 11:2 | 65 |
| 26:19 | 17 |
| 29:16 | 82, 83 |
| 30:28 | 17 |
| 32:15 | 16 |
| 38:18 | 18 |
| 40:22 | 17 |
| 41:8 | 62 |
| 42:1 | 64, 66 |
| 44:1-3 | 70 |
| 44:2-3 | 63 |
| 51:1-3 | 62 |
| 53:4-5 | 31 |
| 53:5 | 31 |
| 53:6 | 31 |
| 53:11 | 20 |
| 59:19 | 63 |
| 59:20 | 66 |
| 59:20-21 | 63 |
| 59:21 | 24 |
| 61:1-2 | 65 |
| 61:1-3 | 19 |
| 63:8-10 | 65 |
| 63:9 | 63 |
| 63:9-14 | 69 |
| 63:10 | 63, 69 |
| 63:11-12 | 63, 73 |

**Jeremiah**
| | |
|---|---|
| 2:21 | 110 |
| 18:5-10 | 83 |

**Ezekiel**
| | |
|---|---|
| 20:5 | 62 |
| 36 | 19 |
| 36:22-23 | 64 |
| 36:22-27 | 19, 29 |
| 36:23-27 | 21 |
| 36:26-27 | 64 |
| 37:3 | 19 |
| 37:3-4 | 77 |
| 37:6 | 19, 64, 173 |
| 37:11 | 18 |
| 37:14 | 19 |
| 39:7 | 19 |
| 39:29 | 64 |

## Daniel
| | |
|---|---|
| 7:13 | 21 |
| 7:13-14 | 19 |
| 12:2 | 17 |

## Hosea
| | |
|---|---|
| 2:1-16 | 116 |
| 2:16 | 62 |
| 11:1 | 32, 61, 62, 66 |
| 11:1-2 | 18, 65 |
| 11:2 | 62, 66 |
| 13:4 | 167 |
| 13:4-5 | 62 |

## Joel
| | |
|---|---|
| 2 | 1, 14 |
| 2:18-32 | 65 |
| 2:28 | 19 |
| 2:32 | 19 |

## Jonah
| | |
|---|---|
| 2:3-6 | 17–18, 27 |
| 4:1-3 | 28 |

## Malachi
| | |
|---|---|
| 1:2-3 | 78 |

## NEW TESTAMENT
## Matthew
| | |
|---|---|
| 1:1-5 | 14 |
| 1:21 | 167 |
| 1:23 | 191 |
| 3:2 | 14, 23, 164 |
| 3:11 | 13 |
| 3:13-17 | 23 |
| 3:15 | 28, 190 |
| 3:17 | 66 |
| 4:17 | 55 |
| 5:17 | 180 |
| 5:17-18 | 175 |
| 5:20 | 176 |
| 6:9 | 29, 209 |
| 6:10 | 52, 126 |
| 6:12 | 105 |
| 11:27 | 29 |
| 12:18 | 66 |
| 12:28 | 20, 23, 106, 126, 202 |
| 12:28-29 | 123 |
| 12:38-41 | 28 |
| 13:24-30 | 111 |
| 15:24 | 20 |
| 16 | 155 |
| 16:13-20 | 155 |
| 16:16 | 148 |
| 16:18 | 20 |
| 16:19 | 148 |
| 18:17 | 20 |
| 18:18-19 | 148 |
| 18:20 | 146 |
| 19:14 | 196–7 |
| 24:2 | 29 |
| 24:14 | 205 |
| 24:35 | 176 |
| 28:18 | 33 |
| 28:19 | 21, 167, 192 |
| 28:20 | 100, 155, 175 |

## Mark
| | |
|---|---|
| 1:4-11 | 23 |
| 1:8 | 13, 192 |
| 1:12 | 29 |
| 1:34 | 123 |
| 2:10-12 | 29 |
| 4:1-8 | 110 |
| 5:37 | 155 |
| 9:2 | 155 |
| 10:43 | 147 |
| 10:45 | 122 |
| 11:12-14 | 111 |
| 11:15-18 | 111 |
| 13:3 | 155 |
| 13:20 | 98 |
| 13:27 | 67, 98 |
| 14:33 | 155 |
| 14:34 | 29 |
| 14:36 | 29 |
| 14:38 | 29 |
| 16:7 | 155 |
| 16:9 | 190 |

## Luke
| | |
|---|---|
| 1:1-2 | 179 |
| 1:6 | 14 |
| 1:15 | 21 |
| 1:22 | 23 |
| 1:35 | 21, 67, 85 |
| 1:44 | 197 |
| 1:50 | 21 |
| 2:38 | 85 |
| 3 | 85 |
| 3:16 | 13, 85 |
| 3:16-17 | 22 |
| 3:17 | 13 |
| 3:21-22 | 23, 86 |
| 3:22 | 13, 23, 66, 85 |
| 3:38 | 20, 24, 66 |
| 4:4 | 50 |
| 4:16-20 | 86 |
| 4:18 | 208 |
| 4:18-19 | 29 |
| 4:24-27 | 20 |
| 9:35 | 66, 85 |
| 10:16 | 148 |
| 11:2 | 21 |
| 12:49-50 | 14, 27, 67 |
| 13:6-9 | 111 |
| 14:27 | 204 |
| 15 | 207 |
| 15:1 | 29 |
| 22:15 | 190 |
| 22:32 | 157 |
| 23:34 | 86 |
| 23:47 | 20, 85 |
| 24:13-35 | 190 |

## John
| | |
|---|---|
| 1:1 | 21 |
| 1:1-5 | 22, 90, 173 |
| 1:1-18 | 26 |
| 1:4-5 | 173 |
| 1:6-8 | 23 |
| 1:10-12 | 91 |
| 1:11 | 76, 91 |
| 1:12 | 23, 28, 174 |
| 1:14-16 | 90 |
| 1:18 | 21, 92, 94, 173 |
| 1:32-34 | 66 |
| 1:33 | 13, 24 |
| 1:33-34 | 23, 59, 90, 92, 100, 192 |

# Scripture Index

| | | | | | | |
|---|---|---|---|---|---|---|
| 2:10 | 199 | 15:16 | 67 | 2:11 | 170 | |
| 2:19 | 29 | 15:26 | 34, 126 | 2:14-41 | 86, 155 | |
| 2:19-21 | 119 | 16:7 | 34 | 2:17 | 117, 144 | |
| 3:16 | 60, 91, 92 | 17:2 | 22, 26 | 2:17-18 | 14, 127, 146, 149, 164, 169, 170 | |
| 3:19 | 91 | 17:5 | 25, 91, 92 | | | |
| 3:21 | 91 | 17:15 | 204 | | | |
| 3:33-34 | 14 | 17:19 | 24, 31, 91, 142 | | | |
| 3:34 | 25 | | | 2:17-21 | 1 | |
| 3:36 | 91 | 17:21 | 8, 36, 39, 45, 46–7, 50, 132, 201 | 2:23 | 85, 102 | |
| 4:13 | 163–4 | | | 2:24-36 | 85 | |
| 4:13-14 | 22 | | | 2:32-36 | 4, 24 | |
| 4:14 | 7, 91, 167, 190, 194, 200 | | | 2:33 | 169 | |
| | | 17:23 | 36, 91, 128 | 2:33-35 | 144, 169 | |
| | | 17:24 | 92 | 2:33-36 | 21, 25, 31, 37, 121 | |
| 5:24 | 91 | 20:21 | 92, 147, 204 | | | |
| 5:26 | 22, 25, 92 | | | 2:36 | 126 | |
| 6:35 | 91 | 20:22 | 167 | 2:38 | 6, 170, 192 | |
| 6:37-39 | 91 | 20:23 | 148 | 2:38-42 | 37 | |
| 6:44 | 91, 92 | 21:15-19 | 155 | 2:42 | 37, 122, 149 | |
| 6:51 | 91 | | | | | |
| 6:70 | 90 | **Acts** | | 2:42-47 | 170 | |
| 7:38 | 6, 25, 91, 188, 190, 200 | 1:1 | 149, 201 | 2:47 | 86, 89 | |
| | | 1:1-5 | 204 | 4:12 | 29, 204 | |
| | | 1:1-8 | 164 | 4:31 | 89, 200 | |
| 7:39 | 187 | 1:5 | 13, 14, 86, 149 | 4:33 | 89 | |
| 8:12 | 92 | | | 5:17-21 | 89 | |
| 8:51 | 92 | 1:5-8 | 169 | 5:39 | 89 | |
| 10:1-39 | 156 | 1:6 | 170, 205 | 6:7 | 89 | |
| 10:9 | 92 | 1:6-8 | 100 | 7:51-52 | 85 | |
| 10:10 | 22, 25, 31, 43, 174 | 1:7 | 86, 87, 88, 99, 205 | 7:54-8:8 | 89 | |
| | | | | 7:60 | 86 | |
| 11:26 | 92 | 1:8 | 14, 16, 37, 56, 67, 86, 89, 142, 144, 146, 149, 169, 170, 172, 198, 205 | 8 | 170 | |
| 12:32 | 144 | | | 9 | 89 | |
| 14:6 | 29, 174 | | | 9:1-19 | 89 | |
| 14:16 | 34, 167 | | | 9:5 | 114 | |
| 14:26 | 34 | | | 9:15-16 | 89 | |
| 15:1 | 92 | | | 9:31 | 89 | |
| 15:1-2 | 67 | | | 10 | 89, 155, 169, 170, 171, 192 | |
| 15:1-4 | 92, 109 | 2 | 3, 4, 34, 127, 169, 170, 203 | | | |
| 15:1-6 | 111 | | | | | |
| 15:1-8 | 21 | | | 10:15 | 169 | |
| 15:1-17 | 22, 110 | 2:1-4 | 86 | 10:34-35 | 209 | |
| 15:4 | 111 | 2:1-12 | 117 | 10:44 | 169 | |
| 15:4-5 | 92 | 2:1-36 | 86 | 10:44-48 | 117 | |
| 15:5 | 111 | 2:3-12 | 169 | 10:45-46 | 200 | |
| 15:6 | 21, 92 | 2:4 | 7, 126, 171, 200 | 10:46 | 170 | |
| 15:7 | 111 | | | 10:47 | 171, 192, 193 | |
| 15:8 | 111 | 2:4-12 | 87 | | | |
| 15:10-11 | 111 | 2:5 | 87, 99 | 11:1-18 | 172 | |

| | | | | | | |
|---|---|---|---|---|---|---|
| 11:18 | 79, 117 | 6:6 | 142 | 9:21 | | 82 |
| 13:48 | 90 | 7:14 | 18 | 9:22-23 | | 84 |
| 15 | 156, 172 | 8 | 73, 76 | 10:17 | | 77, 197 |
| 15:9 | 142, 169, 171, 172, 192 | 8:4 | 74 | 11 | | 77, 80, 81, 82 |
| | | 8:9 | 200 | | | |
| | | 8:13 | 81 | 11:2 | | 74 |
| 15:15 | 128 | 8:14-17 | 73 | 11:7 | | 77 |
| 15:28 | 128, 172 | 8:15 | 32, 55 | 11:10 | | 80 |
| 17 | 87, 88, 127 | 8:15-16 | 7, 31, 32, 37 | 11:11 | | 77, 79, 80, 84, 100, 111 |
| 17:23 | 88 | 8:15-23 | 25 | | | |
| 17:24 | 127 | 8:18 | 73 | | | |
| 17:24-25 | 87 | 8:19 | 25 | 11:11-12 | | 80 |
| 17:25 | 48–9, 87 | 8:19-20 | 76 | 11:12 | | 21, 81 |
| 17:25-26 | 127 | 8:21 | 73 | 11:17-24 | | 82 |
| 17:26 | 88, 99, 205 | 8:22 | 106 | 11:19-23 | | 82 |
| 17:27 | 88, 90, 127 | 8:22-23 | 144 | 11:22 | | 76–7 |
| 17:28 | 72, 89, 126, 127, 208 | 8:23 | 7, 32, 73, 75, 106, 194 | 11:22-24 | | 21 |
| | | | | 11:28 | | 77 |
| 17:30 | 88 | | | 11:28-29 | | 80 |
| 17:32-34 | 90 | 8:24 | 75 | 11:29 | | 77 |
| 19:6 | 200 | 8:25 | 75 | 11:32 | | 77, 78, 79, 81, 82, 111 |
| | | 8:26 | 55, 75, 112, 201 | 11:33-36 | | 85 |
| **Romans** | | 8:28 | 103 | 12:1 | | 56, 117, 120, 199 |
| 1:1-2 | 120 | 8:28-30 | 73 | | | |
| 1:4 | 24, 25, 31, 32, 141 | 8:29 | 102 | 12:1-2 | | 143 |
| | | 8:30 | 74, 75 | 12:2-3 | | 207 |
| 1:16 | 141 | 8:31-39 | 75 | 12:3 | | 202 |
| 1:20 | 81 | 8:32 | 81 | 13:14 | | 194 |
| 1:24 | 79 | 8:37 | 122 | 14:17 | | 106 |
| 1:28 | 79, 81 | 8:38-39 | 76 | 14:8-9 | | 133 |
| 2:4 | 81, 83–4, 84 | 9 | 76, 78, 79, 81 | | | |
| 2:28 | 196 | | | **1 Corinthians** | | |
| 3:8 | 81 | 9–11 | 21, 76, 77, 78, 79, 81, 84 | 1 | | 109 |
| 3:23 | 74, 79, 81, 121 | | | 1:7 | | 144 |
| | | | | 1:13 | | 109, 126 |
| 3:23-24 | 111 | 9:1-4 | 60, 77, 79, 80 | 2:3 | | 148, 184 |
| 4:11 | 196 | | | 2:13 | | 147 |
| 4:25 | 31, 81, 168 | 9:1-5 | 82 | 2:16 | | 184 |
| 5:5 | 12, 37, 198 | 9:2 | 80 | 3:4 | | 140 |
| 6 | 192 | 9:3 | 80 | 3:5 | | 147 |
| 6:1 | 81 | 9:3-4 | 77 | 3:5-9 | | 110 |
| 6:1-2 | 81, 142 | 9:6 | 76, 77, 78 | 3:9 | | 109 |
| 6:1-5 | 73 | 9:13 | 78 | 3:11 | | 117, 147 |
| 6:1-6 | 32 | 9:16 | 78, 82 | 3:12 | | 117 |
| 6:3-5 | 36 | 9:17 | 79 | 3:13 | | 117 |
| 6:4 | 142 | 9:19 | 83 | 3:15 | | 118 |
| 6:5 | 7, 14, 31, 74, 164, 190, 193 | 9:19-21 | 60 | 3:16 | | 120 |
| | | 9:20 | 82 | 3:17 | | 117 |

| | | | | | | | |
|---|---|---|---|---|---|---|---|
| 4:7 | 166 | 14:18 | 112 | 1:1 | 148 | | |
| 4:9 | 202 | 14:23 | 204 | 1:12 | 147 | | |
| 5:1 | 141 | 14:23-24 | 112 | 2:2 | 34, 128, 147, 155 | | |
| 6:11 | 141 | 14:26 | 179, 201, 203 | 2:6 | 147, 155 | | |
| 6:15 | 114, 116 | 14:31-32 | 179 | 2:7 | 156 | | |
| 6:19 | 116 | 14:32 | 148 | 2:20 | 24, 37, 50, 56, 142, 143, 195 | | |
| 8:1 | 112 | 14:37 | 148 | | | | |
| 8:12 | 114 | 14:38 | 148 | | | | |
| 9:16 | 185 | 15:3-6 | 147 | 3:16 | 100 | | |
| 9:24-27 | 124 | 15:5 | 155 | 3:27 | 194, 208 | | |
| 9:27 | 124 | 15:24-28 | 41 | 3:27-28 | 116, 208 | | |
| 10:3-4 | 116, 199 | 15:26 | 121 | 3:28 | 116, 146, 170 | | |
| 10:4 | 126 | 15:42-45 | 24 | | | | |
| 10:16 | 36, 126, 142, 199 | 15:44 | 5 | 5:5 | 142 | | |
| 10:16-17 | 113 | 15:44-45 | 7 | 5:6 | 93 | | |
| 10:17 | 200 | 15:45 | 21, 26, 31 | 5:16 | 143 | | |
| 10:21 | 116 | | | 6:2 | 56 | | |
| 11:16 | 199 | **2 Corinthians** | | | | | |
| 11:23-28 | 56 | 1:1 | 147 | **Ephesians** | | | |
| 11:25 | 32 | 1:3-7 | 112 | 1 | 67, 69 | | |
| 11:26 | 199, 200 | 1:6 | 56 | 1:3 | 68, 69, 70, 72, 101 | | |
| 11:27-32 | 189 | 1:20 | 203 | 1:3-4 | 68, 72, 94 | | |
| 12–14 | 52 | 3 | 179 | 1:4 | 69, 70, 71, 100 | | |
| 12:1-3 | 202 | 3:3 | 120, 142, 178, 201 | | | | |
| 12:3 | 144 | | | 1:5 | 69, 71 | | |
| 12:4 | 151 | 3:5 | 185 | 1:9-10 | 69 | | |
| 12:4-6 | 141, 202 | 3:15-16 | 178 | 1:10 | 68, 69, 70, 71, 72, 76, 97, 103, 113, 128, 139 | | |
| 12:11 | 112, 202 | 3:18 | 2, 188 | | | | |
| 12:13 | 7, 14, 25, 32, 111, 112, 116, 126, 127, 163, 198, 199 | 4:6-7 | 107 | | | | |
| | | 4:7 | 2, 107, 178 | | | | |
| | | 5:4 | 4, 5, 7, 12, 14, 16, 31, 33, 56, 108, 144, 146, 193, 194, 199, 210 | 1:11 | 68 | | |
| | | | | 1:11-12 | 68, 71 | | |
| 12:17 | 202 | | | 1:12 | 68 | | |
| 12:24 | 112 | | | 1:13 | 68–9 | | |
| 12:26 | 45, 113, 201 | 5:4-5 | 163–4 | 1:13-14 | 68, 72, 101 | | |
| | | 5:14 | 185 | 1:14 | 69, 194 | | |
| 12:27 | 111 | 5:17 | 106 | 1:22-23 | 71 | | |
| 12:28 | 198 | 6:1 | 92 | 1:23 | 113 | | |
| 13:1-3 | 203 | 8:23 | 148 | 2 | 172 | | |
| 13:8-13 | 112 | 12:1-10 | 112 | 2:9 | 142, 143 | | |
| 13:12 | 175 | 12:9 | 124, 185 | 2:14 | 141 | | |
| 13:13 | 203 | 13:13 | 36 | 2:20 | 118, 147 | | |
| 13:14 | 112 | | | 2:22-23 | 118 | | |
| 14:2 | 112, 203 | **Galatians** | | 3 | 132 | | |
| 14:4 | 52 | 1 | 147 | 3:14-15 | 133 | | |
| 14:14-15 | 112 | 1–2 | 34 | 3:16-19 | 138–9 | | |

| | | | | | |
|---|---|---|---|---|---|
| 3:17 | 120 | 1:15-20 | 72 | 4:14-16 | 133 |
| 3:17-19 | 120 | 1:16 | 91, 97 | 5:8 | 188 |
| 3:18 | 113, 133, 164 | 1:19-20 | 25 | 5:8-9 | 31 |
| | | 1:27 | 107, 120 | 5:9 | 174 |
| 3:18-19 | 37, 128, 144 | 2:11-12 | 196 | 6:5 | 178, 202 |
| | | 2:15 | 121 | 9:14 | 30, 42, 190 |
| 3:19 | 12 | | | 9:24 | 190 |
| 3:20-21 | 139 | **1 Thessalonians** | | 9:26 | 119 |
| 4:3 | 69, 128 | 3:2 | 147 | 10:4 | 120 |
| 4:4-6 | 167 | 4:17 | 133, 175 | 10:5 | 119, 165 |
| 4:5 | 191 | | | 10:7 | 165 |
| 4:6 | 38, 126 | **2 Thessalonians** | | 10:9 | 119 |
| 4:7-8 | 113, 153 | 2:13 | 142 | 10:10 | 119 |
| 4:7-10 | 34 | | | 11:16 | 124, 189 |
| 4:8 | 121 | **1 Timothy** | | 11:40 | 124, 133, 175 |
| 4:11-13 | 113 | 1:2 | 147 | | |
| 4:13 | 128 | 2:5 | 165 | 12:1 | 133, 175 |
| 4:15 | 55, 56, 111, 113, 118, 170, 178, 185 | 3:15 | 24, 141, 168 | 12:2 | 166, 209 |
| | | | | 12:1-2 | 124 |
| | | 4–5 | 149 | 12:1-3 | 175 |
| | | 4:12-15 | 184 | 12:28 | 120 |
| 4:15-16 | 201 | | | 13:15-16 | 117 |
| 4:16 | 202, 203 | **2 Timothy** | | 13:17 | 118, 149 |
| 4:30 | 69 | 1 | 184 | | |
| 5 | 113 | 1:2 | 147 | **James** | |
| 5:18 | 69, 117 | 1:4 | 184 | 1:14 | 123 |
| 5:18-19 | 200 | 1:6 | 200, 202 | 1:17 | 126 |
| 5:21 | 112, 116, 203 | 3:15-16 | 181 | | |
| | | 3:15-17 | 184 | **1 Peter** | |
| 5:28-30 | 113 | 3:16 | 178 | 1:1 | 93 |
| 6:10 | 122 | 3:16-17 | 178 | 1:2 | 93, 94, 120 |
| 6:10-11 | 121 | 3:17 | 184 | 1:4 | 94 |
| 6:12 | 123 | 4:7-8 | 125 | 1:5 | 94 |
| 6:13-14 | 122 | | | 1:19-21 | 94 |
| 6:17 | 184 | **Titus** | | 1:20 | 100, 102 |
| 6:20 | 148 | 1:4 | 147 | 1:20-21 | 94 |
| | | | | 1:21-22 | 94 |
| **Philippians** | | **Philemon** | | 1:23 | 173 |
| 1:1 | 147 | 1 | 147 | 2:4 | 94, 117 |
| 2 | 144 | | | 2:5 | 94, 118, 148 |
| 2:6 | 26 | **Hebrews** | | | |
| 2:6-11 | 26–7 | 1 | 178 | 2:24 | 31 |
| 2:7 | 122 | 1:1-2 | 178 | 5:8 | 122 |
| 2:9-11 | 121 | 1:3 | 22, 26, 173, 178, 187 | | |
| 3:10 | 24 | | | **2 Peter** | |
| | | 2:12-15 | 26 | 1:3 | 95 |
| **Colossians** | | 2:14 | 28, 121 | 1:5-11 | 94–5 |
| 1:1 | 147 | 2:14-15 | 31 | 1:9 | 95 |
| 1:15 | 173 | 3:1 | 146 | 1:10 | 95 |

| | | | | | | | |
|---|---|---|---|---|---|---|---|
| 1:11 | 95 | 2:5 | 116 | 17:9 | 116 | | |
| 1:19 | 178 | 2:7 | 168 | 17:18 | 100 | | |
| 2:20 | 95 | 2:11 | 149 | 19 | 122 | | |
| 2:22 | 95 | 2:13 | 93 | 19:6-9 | 115 | | |
| 3:9 | 60 | 3:5 | 93 | 19:7-9 | 199 | | |
| 3:15-16 | 148, 179 | 3:8 | 93 | 19:8 | 115, 143 | | |
| 3:16 | 179 | 3:12 | 92 | 19:9 | 115 | | |
| | | 5 | 133 | 19:10 | 149 | | |
| **1 John** | | 5:6 | 116 | 19:11-21 | 122 | | |
| 1:3 | 36 | 5:6-14 | 121 | 19:13 | 93 | | |
| 4:9 | 36 | 5:8 | 133 | 19:15 | 122 | | |
| 4:12 | 36 | 5:13 | 119 | 19:16 | 93, 122 | | |
| 4:13 | 36 | 10:1-11 | 168 | 21 | 104, 166 | | |
| | | 10:10-11 | 168 | 21:1-3 | 209 | | |
| **Jude** | | 11:1-12 | 168 | 21:3 | 93 | | |
| 3 | 148, 177, 182 | 11:13 | 168 | 21:5 | 92 | | |
| | | 11:18 | 93 | 21:22 | 119 | | |
| | | 12:11 | 122, 168 | 21:22-27 | 210 | | |
| **Revelation** | | 13:8 | 93, 100 | 21:25 | 104 | | |
| 1:7 | 81 | 13:17 | 93 | 21:27 | 93 | | |
| 1:17 | 168 | 15:4 | 93 | 22:14 | 104, 210 | | |
| 2:3 | 93 | 16:13 | 116 | 22:17 | 116, 210 | | |

www.ingramcontent.com/pod-product-compliance
Lightning Source LLC
Chambersburg PA
CBHW052038300426
44117CB00012B/1869